Coffee Nation

EARLY AMERICAN STUDIES

Series editors: Kathleen M. Brown, Roquinaldo
Ferreira, Emma Hart, and Daniel K. Richter

Exploring neglected aspects of our colonial,
revolutionary, and early national history and culture,
Early American Studies reinterprets familiar themes
and events in fresh ways. Interdisciplinary in
character, and with a special emphasis on the period
from about 1600 to 1850, the series is published in
partnership with the McNeil Center for Early
American Studies.

A complete list of books in the series is available from
the publisher.

COFFEE NATION

How One Commodity Transformed
the Early United States

Michelle Craig McDonald

PENN

UNIVERSITY OF PENNSYLVANIA PRESS

PHILADELPHIA

Published by
University of Pennsylvania Press
Philadelphia, Pennsylvania 19104–4112
www.pennpress.org

Printed in the United States of America on acid-free paper
10   9   8   7   6   5   4   3   2   1

A Cataloging-in-Publication record for this book is
available from the Library of Congress.
Hardback ISBN 978-1-5128-2755-2
Ebook ISBN 978-1-5128-2754-5

Research in this volume was funded by the Society of
Colonial Wars Fellowship in Memory of Kenneth R. LaVoy Jr.

*For my husband, Roderick McDonald, my partner
in this as in all things.*

*And for my late mother, Susan Bierly Craig, who never
stopped asking, "Is the book done yet?" Yes, mom,
the book is done.*

CONTENTS

INTRODUCTION

Women began to gather in front of a warehouse in Boston early on the morning of July 24, 1777, a little over a year after the Declaration of Independence and two years after the start of the Revolutionary War. At first they came alone or in pairs, milling around in small groups as the sun rose and the sky lightened. By mid-morning they numbered in the dozens, and as the temperature climbed so did the tension among those assembled. When the building's owner, local merchant Thomas Boylston, finally arrived on the scene, more than one hundred women clamored to be let in. For years the city's residents had grumbled about the cost of their weekly groceries. It was not a new complaint and was not without good cause. Since Boston passed its nonimportation agreement in 1768 to protest the Townshend Duties, which levied taxes on imported British goods, storekeepers' stocks had steadily dwindled. The situation only got worse after the outbreak of war, hampered by both the end of trade with the West Indies and the increasing requisitions of livestock and food by colonial and British troops. Imported commodities like sugar and molasses disappeared from the shop shelves first, but eventually even local staples like flour, potatoes, and butter became scarce, and what could be found was dear. Those colonists supporting the military effort recognized that a certain amount of belt tightening was necessary for the cause, of course, but they were less sanguine when they thought their mercantile neighbors might be benefiting from the situation. Patriotism was one thing, but profiteering was something else.

Abigail Adams lived in Boston during these years while her husband, John, was in Philadelphia, and she frequently noted the challenges of living in a city under siege, as well as the growing animosity against importers and retailers who some thought contributed to the problem of paucity. "There is a general cry against the Merchants," she wrote to him in April of that year, "who tis said have created a partial Scarcity" for "every article not only of Luxury, but even the necessaries of life."[1] Indeed, what transpired that July morning was one of at least thirty food riots that took place in New England between 1776 and 1779. But the women confronting Boylston in the summer of 1777 came with one specific life necessity in mind—coffee.[2]

By the time of this standoff, coffee was thought so important to the public welfare that colonial legislators had fixed its price to avoid precisely the kind of fiscal gouging Boylston was accused of practicing. Just eight months before his troubles began, delegates from Massachusetts met with representatives from New Hampshire, Rhode Island, and Connecticut to see what they could do to alleviate the burden of "extravagant prices" resulting from the "unbounded Avarice of many Persons."[3] Coffee was among the twenty-six goods they singled out for special consideration, and it sat in very good company. Sugar and rum also made the list, as did wheat, rye, pork, salt, beef, cotton, beans, and potatoes. Coffee, in other words, was deemed "a necessary and convenient article of life" by colonial delegates in language that was strikingly like that of Abigail Adams. So many people drank coffee, and so often, that it had become a staple to be protected rather than a discretionary expense.[4]

The legislators' hard work produced an "Act to Prevent Monopolies and Oppression by excessive and unreasonable Prices," which passed on the last day of 1776 and set the cost of "good coffee" at one shilling and four pence per pound. Local newspapers began circulating lists of the affected groceries in January, or two weeks before the regulations would go into effect on February 1, 1777.[5] The same legislation spelled out the means of enforcement by empowering selectmen, locally elected officials, to search the stores and warehouses of suspected violators, confiscate overpriced goods, and sell them to the public at regulated rates. Those convicted of price gouging frequently also suffered the additional indignity of public shaming when their names and business addresses appeared in the local paper for all to see.[6]

But selectmen could only be in so many places at once, and potential profits often tempted less scrupulous merchants and shopkeepers to run the risk. It was in these cases that the public sometimes stepped in to mete out their own form of justice. Several Boston stores suspected of hoarding coffee had been ransacked in the months before women targeted Boylston, and there had been a "scramble" for coffee in April at nearby Salem wharf.[7] Taken together, these efforts to protect the price of coffee, regulate the behavior of its vendors, and stage protests to confiscate caches when all else failed, demonstrate how widespread its consumption had become in British North America by the 1770s. Consuming coffee was not the practice of a privileged few, but the daily habit of many.

At first glance the coffee riot that Adams recounted seems to resemble a far better-known colonial escapade with tea, which became one of the most famous stories of the American Revolution. The Boston Tea Party took place a few years earlier and championed the efforts of a handful of underdog patriots in their quest for self-determination against the vast machinery of empire. This story has all the elements of a classic intrigue: disguises, covert action, local heroes, and a clearly defined enemy—in this case, imported tea. Political rallying cries need to be catchy to succeed, however, and "no taxation without representation" is no different. Like most slogans, however, it tends to reduce complex historical events into an easily digestible sound bite that masks a far more nuanced reality. For on the very same day that Parliament passed its fateful vote to continue taxing tea, it also agreed to radically reduce taxes on colonial coffee.[8] How did one caffeinated beverage become reviled as an emblem of expanding imperial interference at precisely the same time that another was embraced as a fragile economy in need of protection?

Tea was a powerful symbol, both for British authorities who sought to break colonial defiance and for colonists who sought to control their ports and customs houses. But as Adams' letter illustrates, more than one commodity caused colonists consternation. Moreover, while the Boston Tea Party was about efforts to limit consumption of a commodity, Boston's coffee rioters sought the opposite—access to more. So, how does the story about the material impact of the American Revolution change if we consider the larger network of commodities that crossed the Atlantic Ocean during the long eighteenth century and transformed the experiences of those living around its shores? And how do our perceptions about the struggles for independence change when colonial shop and kitchen shelves are fully stocked?

What coffee and tea did have in common in late eighteenth-century colonial North America was the need for importation. Neither plant grew successfully on the continent, and so it was not—despite some botanists' best efforts—until the United States annexed Puerto Rico, Hawaii, and the Philippines at the end of the nineteenth century that the nation had a domestic supply for either beverage. And yet both goods also had a long and loyal following. Tea drinking did not end after the American Revolution (indeed, scholars have demonstrated how successfully tea drinking quietly persisted even during the war).[9] Coffee not only kept pace with tea, however, but also far outstripped its caffeine cousin, skyrocketing to unprecedented levels of demand after 1800. Indeed, U.S. citizens' widespread embrace of this beverage in their kitchens, dining rooms, parlors, and public meeting houses, as well as their willingness literally to drink it morning, noon, and night, is why coffee is one of the best examples of how reliant the new nation remained on economies outside of its continent. This was no sideline pastime. Coffee became indelibly linked with U.S. culture and, by extension, with the nation's commerce. This is not a unique argument, of course; while there had been some important industrial growth in North America before 1776, most people's furniture, cloth, metalware, ceramics, and several kinds of food and drink still came from overseas. But coffee illustrates in a way that few commodities can how much the colonies of British North America, and then the United States, relied on the production systems of the larger Atlantic world and invested in industries that only ensured such patterns would widen and deepen. Whether consumed at the family breakfast table, while visiting with friends in the afternoon, at the local coffeehouse, or following an evening's repast, this broadly popular commodity had to be imported. America's dependence, in other words, persisted long after any political rift with Britain ended.

The women who stood armed with hand trucks and carts to confiscate and sell Boylston's secreted coffee that summer morning could not have known how important their morning repast would become to their children and grandchildren. These women were neither traders nor investors, and likely did not know the origins and destinations of the profusion of goods arriving and leaving Boston's wharves. Even the more economically savvy Boylston would probably not have guessed how important coffee would be to the future U.S. economy. What he knew is that he had a stash of beans when few people did, and the women who faced him knew it too. They also knew how they and their families preferred to start their day, and that the comfort of a warm cup of coffee should not have been beyond their means, although tea—with its much higher price tag—usually was. Perhaps these actions weighed especially heavy on Abigail Adam's mind because Boylston was her husband's cousin and the man after whom they had named their third child. His hoarding was, she complained, the actions of "an eminent, wealthy, stingy merchant." Clearly, her neighbors agreed. They demanded his keys and, when he complied, entered the property and "hoisted out the coffee themselves, put it into the truck and drove off." Adams concluded her remarkable account by describing how "a large concourse of men stood amazed," having remained "silent spectators of the whole transaction," leaving their wives to confiscate the coffee that was subsequently brewed and served in their respective homes.[10]

* * *

U.S. citizens have long seen themselves as an independent and industrious people. Indeed, references to independence shape the traditional national narrative about nearly all aspects of North America's development after 1776—the establishment of new forms of government, rise of domestic economies, exploration west across the continent, creation of urban manufacturing centers, and construction of large-scale transportation networks that connected all these developments together and made possible the waves of migration that linked the Pacific and Atlantic Oceans. More recently such celebratory narratives have been tempered by historians who try to calculate the cost of such "progress" on the environment, as well as by studies that highlight those who were routinely, systemically, and deliberately left out of the independence project, especially women, enslaved and free African Americans, and indigenous peoples.[11] Such challenges, however, often face resistance, and efforts to shift deeply held ideas about the nation's origins move slowly.

Working hand in hand with notions of independence in crafting Americans' image of themselves and their heritage are those of self-reliance, another U.S. cultural touchstone. The image of a strong, autonomous new nation has ebbed and flowed over the last two centuries but never disappeared. Indeed, there has been a powerful and, at times, troubling resurgence of ideas about national autonomy and greatness in recent years. Tea plays nicely in this sandbox, so much so that, since 2009, it has once again been adopted by members of a modern "Tea Party" purportedly championing limited government and individual responsibility by undermining governmental support programs, such as those for housing and health-care subsidies.[12]

Coffee, by contrast, disrupts this story. The trajectory of how and when coffee became popular, the prequel to its omnipresence on U.S. breakfast tables, could not be more different than its East Indian counterpart. While tea was controlled through a single monopoly charter, the commercial interference that colonists so resented, coffee had a global network of suppliers by the third quarter of the eighteenth century. All European empires—the

British, French, Portuguese, Spanish, and Dutch—had Atlantic colonies to supply them, and West African nations and East Indian sources expanded the global coffee market further still. By 1773, when tea was floating in Boston's harbor, the question was not where coffee was grown, but where it was not.[13] This many options meant coffee importers had choices, albeit some more legal than others. But regardless of where North American merchants chose to do business, importation was the key, because what coffee did have in common with tea was that it could not be grown in North America. Every cup of coffee enjoyed by any British colonist—and later U.S. citizen—had been brewed from beans that came from somewhere else. There was no home-grown option.

In this sense, coffee's spectacular profitability in U.S. markets and popularity on its tables by the mid-nineteenth century is the antithesis of autonomy. Each step of the industry's development relied on outside support and external influences. Coffee was first transplanted to the Caribbean in the 1720s, in large part because European governments sought to circumvent their reliance on Middle Eastern and North African brokers, and hoped that coffee farms would encourage the migration of aspiring, smaller-scale farmers to the West Indies. After all, coffee planting was an easier and cheaper market to enter than the sugarcane plantation system that had radically transformed the region in the century before. But progress was slow. Indeed, so few would-be British planters initially risked investing in coffee that Parliament drastically cut duties in 1732, and kept domestic taxes low and foreign taxes high for the next hundred years to encourage production.[14]

Dependence shaped coffee's development in even more fundamental ways than tax rebates, however. It relied on coerced labor both in early experiments off the west coast of Africa and, on a much larger scale, in the Americas. It was the backbreaking work of enslaved women and men that cut farms into steep mountainsides by clearing dense forests, and then planting, harvesting, and preparing coffee for export. Enslaved laborers also, of course, built their homes as well as those of their owners, the coffee-works required to process the crop, and the roads necessary to connect these often-remote and inaccessible locations to urban ports. In the process, these laborers systematically refashioned West Indian, and later Central and South American, landscapes into productive and profitable estates.

The small-scale farmers more typical in coffee cultivation in turn relied on establishing and maintaining successful connections with export merchants, and not always from the same nation. The profitability of their industry depended on ensuring steady access to markets, which inextricably linked those same enslaved laborers and their enslavers to traders and mariners, dockworkers, warehouse owners, wholesalers, retailers, and ultimately the consumers that the coffee cultivators relied on to eke out the often-meager living that was typical for most of them and those that they held in bondage.

North Americans' dependence on coffee continued well after the point of importation. From its early stages as an experimental colonial commodity in the mid-eighteenth century, coffee's popularity grew by leaps and bounds until it became a leading global economy by the 1830s. The United States was central to this growth as the young republic imported ever-increasing amounts of the commodity for drinkers at home, as well as for more buyers overseas through a growing reexport trade in foreign goods. But while income generated from coffee sales made up an important portion of U.S. trade revenue overall, it is important to remember that this growing investment always depended on steady access to a commodity that the United States could not grow for itself.

As coffee consumption increased, social practices surrounding how to prepare and present the beverage properly added different pressures. The proliferation of coffee-related brewing and serving implements, recipes, and advice manuals created dependence in both cultural terms and material expense, since such accoutrements cost time and money. A failure to understand the etiquette of consumption divided those who understood the niceties of social engagement from those who could not afford to do so. Increasing dependence on coffee, in sum, transformed biogeographies, created cycles of profit and debt, and ultimately changed dietary habits so fundamentally that the effects are readily evident to this day.

But if people living in the eighteenth century considered coffee's fate alongside that of tea, this connection has all but disappeared in modern scholarship, a circumstance that represents more than a lost opportunity to compare the two caffeinated beverages. Tea was an Eastern import that traveled by sanction of government-approved charters and was enjoyed primarily by the wealthy few. Coffee, by contrast, grew around the world but especially in the Caribbean during the eighteenth century, where it formed an important part of the balance of trade between Britain's colonies in North America and those of the West Indies. Moreover, because it was so much cheaper than tea, many more people from all walks of life drank coffee than tea. And yet despite the coffee's growing availability and popularity, most studies of the commodity allocate, at best, a few pages to this early chapter in its history before moving on to its admittedly spectacular rise in Central and South America in the later nineteenth century.[15] The importance of tea to the political rhetoric of revolution and independence is palpable, but the comparable silence about the early history of coffee is troubling as it masks an equally powerful example of growing dependence at the same moment in time.

*   *   *

British North Americans' interest in coffee stretches back to the early years of the continent's colonization and is associated with other touchstones as hallowed as the Boston Tea Party. John Smith, best known for his role in founding Jamestown, described "coffaa" or "coava" in his travel accounts from Turkey more than two decades before he landed in Virginia, and the *May-flower* is credited with carrying the first recorded coffee grinder to North America, listed in the ship's manifest as a wooden mortar and pestle used by the parents of Peregrine White to grind beans for brewing.[16] In fact, several pilgrims migrating from Amsterdam, Europe's main coffee entrepôt by the mid-seventeenth century, brought the beverage with them to New England, and coffeehouses were operating in most major North American port cities within a generation of their landing.[17]

By the mid-eighteenth century, colonists' coffee habit was well entrenched. Coffee is listed on the menus of coffeehouses and taverns throughout colonial Pennsylvania. Coffee and the equipment needed to prepare it appear in wills and probate inventories in rural South Carolina, and in shopkeepers' records in central Virginia. Indeed, by the time of Boston's tea antics, the thirteen North American colonies imported almost half of all coffee produced within the British Empire, and demand continued to grow after 1776. So common were coffee pots and cups on U.S. tables within years of independence that some European visitors considered the commodity a quintessential part of the new nation's identity. "Our supper was rather scanty," wrote François Jean Chastellux, a major general in the French expeditionary forces sent to North America during the American Revolution, "but our breakfast the next morning better." "We are perfectly reconciled," he concluded, "to this American custom of drinking coffee."[18]

Coffee's early drinkers were no less diverse than its purveyors. Colonial Virginia elites, such as Landon Carter or George and Martha Washington, describe the beverage in their letters and diaries, as do the politically powerful New Englanders John and Abigail Adams. But the commodity's popularity was not limited to those with means. Coffee appealed to members of the working class, like John Ashmead, a mariner, and Norton Pryor, a biscuit maker, whose purchases appear repeatedly in the account books of Philadelphia-based West Indian importers Mifflin & Massey. Coffee also shows up in the accounts of Phill Easton and Sol Fleming, enslaved men laboring at an iron manufactory located nine miles from Lexington, Virginia, who used credit for working extra hours to buy coffee beans along with sugar and calico from the company store for their enslaved families. Even Philadelphia Quaker Elizabeth Drinker, whose merchant husband, Henry Drinker, ran afoul of the city's Committee of Compliance for selling tea after 1773, regularly entertained with coffee. On October 5, 1775, Mrs. Drinker recorded that "Nathanial Yarnel and wife, Hannah Williams, and G. Churchman" stopped by for coffee after dinner. Just weeks later, guests arriving with news of the British victory at "Mud Battery Fort," or Fort Mifflin, sat and "drank coffee" with the Drinkers.[19] Such examples from the many references scattered throughout the archives of the late colonial and early national periods reflect the beverage's widespread appeal. Poor and rich, women and men, enslaved and free, all drank coffee. How, when, and where they drank it varied in important respects, of course, and such differences form one major theme of this book, but what these disparate consumers shared was an absence of controversy about their habit. Indeed, this may be one reason that coffee's history has received so little attention.

For a few months in 1773 and early 1774, coffee served as a kind of patriotic proxy. One English visitor to Alexandria, Virginia, on July 14, 1774, witnessed the election of town burgesses and later recorded in his diary: "In the evening the returned Member [George Washington] gave a Ball to the Freeholders and Gentlemen of the town. This was conducted with great harmony. Coffee and Chocolate, but no Tea. This Herb is in disgrace amongst them at present."[20] Even the Boston Tea Party had its coffee moment when William Russell, a schoolteacher who participated in the uprising, reputedly emptied his family's tea canister into the fire and wrote "Coffee" on one side of the canister and "No Tea" on the other.[21]

But in 1774, North Americans added Caribbean commodities to their embargo of British goods, effectively ending coffee's utility as an icon of insurgence. Some colonial representatives understood the depth of mainland merchants' dependence on such goods and pleaded that a ban on trade to the British West Indies would "produce a national Bankruptcy," but their arguments received short shrift from those who considered tropical goods to be

habit-forming and "intoxicating poisons and needless luxuries" that exacerbated economic imbalances and should be sunk at sea "rather than [brought]
ashore."[22] When Edmund Pendleton, a Virginia delegate, questioned whether
the Continental Congress had the right to impose such sanctions, none other
than John Adams responded. "How is the Purchaser to know," Adams
argued, "whether the Molasses, Sugar, or Coffee has paid the Duty or not? It
can't be known. Shan't We by this hang out to all the World our Intentions
to smuggle?"[23] By 1777, Adams had made up his mind. Writing to his wife,
Abigail, following her account of Boylston's coffee debacle he expressed his
"hope the females will leave off their attachment to coffee" as it created, he
argued, an untenable economic dependence on foreign trade. "I assure you,"
he concluded, that "the best families in this place have left off in a great
measure the use of West India goods. We must bring ourselves to live upon
the produce of our own country."[24]

Then as now, however, immediate gratification often eclipsed more
ephemeral ideas about financial dependency, and colonists continued to drink
their coffee in ever-increasing amounts. Their habit was enabled by the fact
that coffee, unlike tea, whose trade was tightly controlled through monopoly,
flourished throughout the Caribbean when the American Revolution began,
so that a ban on British goods only encouraged North American traders and
retailers to seek new suppliers in other empires. Most turned first to the
French West Indies and then, by 1780, to the neutral, free ports of the Dutch
and Danish Caribbean; other less scrupulous vendors smuggled coffee out
of Spanish ports in Puerto Rico or Cuba. Both kinds of enterprise—legal and
less so—could yield a handsome profit in the coffee trading business. Prerevolutionary embargoes might have disrupted access to British coffee, in other
words, but as North Americans still could not grow their own and the habit
was still very much in vogue, new sources, and thus new lines of dependence,
necessarily developed to take Britain's place.

And yet despite the growing amount of coffee shipped in cargo holds, displayed on store shelves, and gracing dining room tables, the commodity's
story remains difficult to tell. While the association of tea to taxes and trade
restrictions can be readily tracked in newspapers of the day, North Americans warmed to coffee far more quietly and certainly less controversially. It
appears in diary entries from early adopters, and later in colonists' letters to
each other as they compared prices and scarcities during the turbulent 1760s
and 1770s, as well as in bills of lading for merchant vessels and the auction
notices of privateers trying to appease an ever-increasing demand. Coffee is

Introduction11

also recorded in merchants' ledgers that tracked its travel through trade networks from cities to towns and backcountry parishes as sacks of it took their place among bolts of cloth, ribbons and buttons, local wares, and other imported West Indian commodities in the long litanies of goods advertised for sale in rural shops. Newspaper advertisements hawked the equipment needed to prepare and present coffee on the tables of the urban middle class, poured from tin or earthenware vessels or perhaps silver plate if they were fortunate, and from sterling silver in the after-dinner parlors of the well-to-do, who invented ever-more elaborate rituals and tools for its consumption.

Indeed, North Americans drank so much coffee by the end of the revolutionary era that when U.S. politicians sought to identify which goods to tax themselves, "in aid of the Public Revenue," coffee topped the list.[25] South Carolina's House of Representatives began taxing coffee in August 1783, and Connecticut, Massachusetts, and Pennsylvania all proposed similar legislation between 1785 and 1789. While this legislation may seem ironic given the role that taxation played in creating the conflict that resulted in a new nation's political independence, state governments needed to balance their budgets and relied on the continuation of coffee's widespread popularity to generate a steady income.

Coffee thus can be found nearly everywhere in the late colonial period and the years of the early republic. But this very commonness, while clear evidence of social and cultural acceptance, also complicates its study. Boston's coffee rioters were an exception; most references are brief—a record that someone "drank coffee" on a particular Sunday or went "to the Coffee-house" on a Tuesday evening to hear the latest political or commercial gossip. Elsewhere, it is a newspaper notice that some number of hogsheads or bags of coffee arrived at or left port, or a price listing that coffee sold for a penny or two more than the week before. Rarely is this evidence more than fleeting, but cumulatively these details carry weight. They offer clues about the fiscal and diplomatic systems upon which North American trade relied, as well as about the social and cultural customs that created new kinds of dependence as the fledgling United States sought to find its footing in the world after 1783. Most importantly, coffee's story raises questions about just how much independence the new nation actually enjoyed.

Coffee's steady integration into North America's domestic and export economies established it as one of the largest and most lucrative markets of the early United States. From just over 4 million pounds in 1789, coffee imports had grown to almost 53 million pounds five years later. By 1802 the amount of British colonial coffee coming into the United States was valued at approximately $1.5 million, while over $8 million worth of beans had arrived that year from other parts of the world.[26] North Americans drank roughly a quarter of this coffee, and the balance went back abroad to make up 10 percent of the United States' total income from exports and roughly 25 percent of its income from reexported goods, in particular.[27] Comparatively, by the end of the first quarter of the nineteenth century, North Americans made more money trading coffee than they did from sugar, tea, and wine combined—astonishingly high figures for a commodity they did not—could not—produce.[28] By any measure, the coffee industry was a financial success story, but it is one that runs counter to a national narrative of autonomy. Distribution, not production, lay at the heart of North America's coffee business, and its profitability and expansion relied on securing and maintaining strong ties, first with the Caribbean and then with Latin America. If North Americans' rejection of tea symbolized freedom, then their embrace of coffee dictated dependence.

*   *   *

Historians of early America have spent much time and energy trying to define independence. At the beginning of the twentieth century, scholars tended to emphasize political developments and documents such as the Declaration of Independence, the U.S. Constitution, and the Bill of Rights as evidence of a new vision of governance and social order. By the 1960s practitioners of the new social history, less interested in constitutional debates, looked instead for evidence of distinctive national characteristics further down the socioeconomic scale. They studied grassroots movements, mob action, and men's and women's associations for evidence of a new broad-based political awareness that emerged in the young nation. Other historians examined architectural styles and compared the number of locally manufactured bedsteads to imported ceramics to determine how, even as colonists, people in mainland British North America had begun to see themselves materially as a breed apart—not yet citizens but no longer subjects. Legal and education historians have weighed in as well, persuasively arguing that the creation of local colleges and universities, court systems, and legislative bodies undermined imperial authority by boosting a spirit of autonomy, while literary scholars have mined revolutionary rhetoric for linguistic evidence of a language of liberty and the origins of a separate national identity.[29]

Economic historians also contributed to the definition of independence. Many of these studies argue that mainland North America's abundant natural resources lessened reliance on the metropole in ways that the rest of Britain's empire could not hope to emulate. Although these circumstances did not make revolution inevitable, this historiography suggests that growing populations and North American industrialization increased the chances of an imperial rift. Unfortunately, these same studies also tend to promote ideas about the new nation's self-sufficiency as well as an early history that looks inward more than outward, a perspective all too often reinforced by the textbooks that shape how high school and college students learn about the sweep of North American history before the Civil War.[30] Thomas Jefferson and Alexander Hamilton occasionally stand in for the series of pamphlets and congressional sessions that debated whether the United States' future lay overseas or overland, but for the most part the impact of regions and entities outside the U.S. receives scant attention after 1783. Textbook sections that touch on international affairs most often focus on discussions of immigration or war, interspersed with a series of "revolutions"—the market revolution, industrial revolution, transportation revolution, and communications revolution—that each in its own way somehow made possible a sovereign nation from sea to shining sea. The overarching narrative of early U.S. history, in other words, is still—at its foundation—about autonomy. It emphasizes the role of nation over empire, internal rather than external developments, independence over regional entanglements. What is important to North American history, such a framework suggests, occurred at home rather than abroad and on land rather than at sea.

The history of coffee demonstrates otherwise while also contributing to a burgeoning literature about the importance of studying things people make, sell, and consume day to day. Commodities have received significant scholarly and popular attention in the last two decades, as books about wine, cotton, rice, and chocolate sit side by side in bookstores and college libraries with those on tea, bananas, salt, and mahogany. Some of this scholarship is geared toward academic readers while other books are written for a broader, general audience. The best of this new research blends the concerns of history, material culture, and consumer studies to ask not only where goods traveled and how they moved, but also who wanted them and—most elusive of all—why they were desirable.[31]

The results have been several strong analyses, some tracking "commodity lifecycles" through production, distribution, and consumption, and others contributing to the understanding of "consumer revolutions" in both western Europe and the Americas.[32] But less often have such works explored the legal, political, and diplomatic systems that made the movement of such goods possible in the first place. The world of goods, in any time and place, is dictated by the constraints of supply, price, competition, social acceptance, and adaptation as much as it is by demand. Even seemingly free choices are not free of their context. In seeking to reunite these concerns, this book is thus less a traditional commodity study, or a study of the history of coffee, than it is a history that uses coffee to explore how the early United States relied on the production economies beyond its borders into the nineteenth century, as well as how this reliance shaped other arenas of dependence—economic, social, and cultural.

Finally, *Coffee Nation* expands the boundaries of Atlantic history, which—despite several important advances—still tilts toward the seventeenth and eighteenth centuries and to studies that privilege the perspective of individual European nations and their empires.[33] Even the handful of studies that tackle the natural permeability of the region, in which some neighbors were separated by oceans and others by mere nautical miles, less often extend far past the American Revolution, thus making it difficult to assess how the United States, rather than the British North American colonies, fits into this dynamic system. The result has been not only a tendency to continue to see the world through imperial eyes, or what historian Alison Games refers to as "old wine in new bottles, or in this case the old colonial history repackaged as Atlantic history," but also the creation of an artificial historiographical divide that assumes North America's separation from its pre-independence markets after the American Revolution.[34]

The United States' financial health remained deeply intertwined with that of neighboring colonies and nations throughout the nineteenth century. Internal developments and industrial innovation helped move cotton from the southern states and wheat from the Midwest, as well as push migration and settlement south and west. But these same systems also ferried coffee, sugar, and other trade goods from the eastern seaboard farther and farther inland until these "foreign" commodities became intrinsically linked to the "domestic" world of the expanding frontier.

This book also demonstrates the centrality of Atlantic trade to North America well beyond Britain, to explore relationships to the coffee-producing and trading colonies of France, Holland, and Denmark as well as that of Haiti and Brazil. The consequence of these commercial connections was a complex, growing business network best understood as "a creole economy," a financial system that blended elements of different cultures when expedient and whose reach was defined, not by national borders, but by a very differently demarcated world of exchange. In sum, this history of coffee advances three interwoven arguments. It challenges the notion of the American Revolution as a watershed event in the new nation's economy, arguing instead that the United States remained deeply invested in interimperial trade. It does so by tracking the increasing acceptance and incorporation of coffee—a foreign import—into mainstream American life. And it uses both arguments to dispute the validity of postrevolutionary ideas about American freedom and independence as measured by the material and economic state of the nation.

While this book is ultimately about how a foreign good is remade into an American habit, it is necessary to start far away from North America to understand when and where coffee first became popular. Chapter 1 charts the transition from Africa and Middle East coffee suppliers to plantations of the Caribbean, and the enslaved people forced to produce the ever-increasing amounts of coffee on which European and North American markets depended. Holland and France were early pioneers in the West Indies, but the British Caribbean became more important for North America's buyers, particularly after acquisition of the Ceded Islands following the Seven Years' War. Because coffee planters often lacked both the social and economic capital of their sugar counterparts, this chapter does not feature prominent individuals or large estates. Instead it weaves together fragmentary plantation records and account ledgers, comparing them with official reports, customs tabulations, and trade laws to determine when and where coffee became important in the Atlantic world, and to whom.

Chapter 2 moves from production to distribution, turning attention to the North American importers, retailers, and advertisers who built the market around caffeine dependency. This development relied on fluid, multidirectional relationships of exchange in which buyers were not passive nor sellers autocratic. British Caribbean coffee planters had the advantage of tax rebates favoring a closed system through the support of Parliament. But North Americans also exerted leverage because their proximity to producers from several nations allowed them to test the boundaries of British mercantilism, and they did so frequently. As early as the 1730s, advertisers and retailers touted the merits of coffee from Java, Mocha, or the French West Indies over that from British colonies, drawing distinctions in quality and taste that

would be refined and amplified over the ensuing decades. Chapter 2 also explores the range of coffee purveyors, from import warehouses to auction
blocks, urban retailers, and backcountry storekeepers, each of which played
an important role in promoting the commodity's widespread availability and
popularity, and deepening North Americans' habit.

As coffee drinking expanded, whole industries emerged to shape and refine the experience, fueled in no small part by social arbiters concerned with
policing boundaries between social classes. While coffee was broadly popular,
consumers—like those in other cultural rituals—developed ways of distinguishing the haves from the have-nots. Chapter 3 explores the creation of
coffee-related equipment, including brewing implements, serving pots, cups,
spoons, and the like, that was fabricated in a variety of materials to suit a
range of tastes and price points. Some coffee drinkers purchased elaborately
wrought sterling silver and Chinese export porcelain, expensive and largely
imported objects that created new lines of dependence on foreign manufacturers and obsequious adherence to European notions about etiquette. Other
consumers used silver plate or creamware and delftware, certainly cheaper
but still produced abroad, to enact the habits they aspired to emulate but could
not afford. And yet others made do with painted tin or locally produced clay-
ware, and used the same drinking vessels for coffee, beer, cider, or rum-based
grog, depending on the time of day and the occasion.

Chapter 4 moves from the home to the coffeehouse, as coffee drinking
was both a public and a domestic pursuit. Coffeehouses were established early
and often in North American port cities before appearing further inland,
and they adapted themselves to performing important social functions in
particular locales, just as they had done in Europe the century before. This
chapter explores how these institutions developed as places of public exchange, where a mostly male community of affairs and money assembled
for matters of business, politics, and commerce, and where patrons shared
information gleaned from published newspapers while swapping the gossip
of travelers and captains who arrived from overseas.

Because coffeehouses were so intrinsically tied to commercial affairs, they
also often served as a natural forum for the increasingly vitriolic political and
commercial discourses of the 1760s and 1770s, emerging as vital sites of protest about colonial dependence. The second half of this chapter explores the
resultant politicization of coffee and the attempts to curb consumption of this
"foreign" good, efforts that proved largely unsuccessful. Privateering, which
had already been a conduit for bringing non-British coffee to North America

before tensions erupted, flourished during these decades, replenishing dwindling stocks of the much sought-after commodity after the outbreak of the American Revolution. Such extralegal incursions, however, could not satisfy the demands previously met by legal trade, so coffee became embroiled in debates over scarcities, hoarding, and price controls, evidence of just how entrenched Americans' coffee-drinking habits had become before 1776. Frustrations with these circumstances were expressed in private letters and public notices, and ultimately led to violence in public arenas. Far from a luxury, coffee had become a necessity, one that people were willing to go to great lengths to procure during the war years and into the post-Revolutionary era.

Chapter 5 returns to questions of interdependent, or creole, economies. Sugar production in the French and British West Indies plateaued in the 1780s and 1790s, decades when coffee cultivation dramatically expanded. Meanwhile, the most lucrative years in the American empires of Spain and Portugal would only emerge after the Haitian Revolution had transformed Saint Domingue, France's richest colony, into the second independent nation in the Western Hemisphere but at the expense of its coffee and sugar trade dominance. This trajectory demonstrates not only the ongoing vitality of West Indian agriculture after the American Revolution, but also the increasingly international focus of U.S. coffee interests. Discussions of the commodity peppered debates over taxes and tariffs in Congress; encouraged diplomatic overtures to France, Spain, Portugal, Holland, and Denmark; and contributed to North America's repeated efforts to define and defend neutral shipping rights through the wars of the late eighteenth and early nineteenth centuries.

Coffee's availability would have meant little if consumers had not come to rely on it, so Chapter 6 considers how the beverage became embedded in U.S. daily life by the mid-nineteenth century. Cookbooks and prescriptive literature document how widespread the beverage became in North Americans' diets, and offer insights into the individual choices of how and when to indulge in one of the world's fastest-growing commodity industries. Politicians and newspaper editorialists debated the wisdom of encouraging U.S. reliance on "foreign produce," while other commentators voiced health concerns about coffee, denigrated it as a symbol of overseas dependence, or, by contrast, considered it essential to every well-stocked kitchen. By the early nineteenth century, coffee purchasers could exert even more control over nuances of taste through home coffee roasters, grinders, and specialized percolators,

many of which were backed by federal patents as part of an emerging manufacturing sector devoted to housewares.

The ability to manipulate the taste, strength, and color of coffee in U.S.
homes, stores, and restaurants is part of what made it possible to downplay
coffee's foreign provenance. The book's Epilogue concludes this study by arguing that U.S. purveyors de-emphasized the commodity's tropical origins
by the mid-nineteenth century and worked hard to recast it as part of a dis-
tinctly North American way of life. In their hands, coffee became blended
with clear overtones of domestic economy and a national ingenuity. What
had been one of the most important articles of foreign trade was remade as
American, effectively erasing the many forms of dependence that made the
industry possible in the first place.

CHAPTER 1

Coffee Comes to the Caribbean

As he gathered up his papers and personal belongings, Sir Nicholas Lawes (ca. 1652–1731) surveyed his office one last time. For four years, from 1718 to 1722, he had led Jamaica's government during a challenging and tumultuous period. He was tired and more than ready to leave public service. He then boarded the carriage that would take him from Spanish Town, Jamaica's seat of government, to Townwell, his estate just north of Kingston. The route wended its way through the city center and then out past the cane fields that lined both sides of the road. The journey would take several hours, and he probably spent some of that time reflecting on his term as governor.

Lawes had come to Jamaica as a child when his father's political leanings had run afoul of Oliver Cromwell's protectorate government. The family had prospered on the island, invested in sugar planting, and steadily worked its way up Jamaica's social ladder, aided in part because Lawes's marriages to no fewer than four wealthy widows over the course of twenty years had aligned him with several leading local families.[1] In 1703, Lawes returned to England, married for a fifth time, and established himself at Isleworth, just outside of London, in the luxury that befitted his status as a prominent absentee planter. He likely had anticipated spending the rest of life dabbling in local politics and pursuing the botanical experiments he had begun in the West Indies, distant from—but financially supported by—the proceeds of his five plantations worked by enslaved labor abroad.[2] Disquieting news from "gentlemen and merchants," however, about the island's state of affairs encouraged him, at the advanced age of sixty-five, "to quit the retreat I had given myself up to" and seek an appointment as Jamaica's governor.[3]

When Lawes got back to Jamaica, he found the situation even worse than he had imagined. Weak politicians and mismanagement of funds had left the colony deep in debt, the local assembly profoundly divided, and the customs house rife with graft. A drama-filled four years ensued. Lawes began by addressing Spanish incursions on British shipping and British collusion with Spanish smuggling. During his first two years in office, he wrote, collected, and forwarded more than forty letters, affidavits, shipping reports, and depositions to Parliament that documented widespread maritime malfeasance.[4] He also wrote to authorities in Cuba, threatening them with reprisals if they failed to return detained Englishmen and property. When Spanish authorities alleged that the captured men were guilty of smuggling, Lawes responded by hanging as pirates forty-three members of a Spanish vessel that had been detained in Jamaica.[5]

Lawes then turned his attention to internal threats and negotiated a 1720 treaty with Jeremy, King of the Mosquito Indians, to hire fifty men from Central America to come to Jamaica to track and capture enslaved people who had escaped into the island's mountainous interior.[6] Two years later, Lawes helped bring the colony back from near economic collapse after one of the most devastating hurricanes of the early eighteenth century. "We were left destitute of any other coverings than the Heavens," he wrote to the Council of Trade and Plantations in London, after reputedly selling some of his own property to help defray the cost of government.[7] And during his last year as governor, Lawes presided over the trials of Captain John Rackham—the celebrated "Calico Jack"—and ten others accused of piracy. Included in this indictment were two prominent female pirates, Anne Bonny and Mary Read, both of whom fled to Providence Island after learning of Lawes's charges against them.[8]

It is little wonder that at age sixty-nine, all Lawes wanted to do was return to his plantations. He died nine years later, but in his last years he left Jamaica a legacy that proved more enduring than his efforts to staunch smuggling, capture enslaved people who had escaped their bondage, provide hurricane relief, or prosecute pirates.[9] That is because in 1728, Lawes planted Jamaica's first coffee trees, irrevocably changing the island's economy as well as the lives of thousands of enslaved African and African Jamaican workers coerced within this new commodity system over the next century. Although Lawes only lived long enough to see the first harvests, the crop showed enough promise that more than twenty of his fellow planters petitioned Parliament to support the fledgling enterprise.[10] Their goal, a reduced tariff for coffee traded within the British colonies as well as steep taxes on coffee imported from elsewhere, ensured that from the outset North America's interest in the commodity necessarily relied on the British islands.

The planters' petition went before the House of Commons on March 2, 1731, and could not have been better timed or found a more receptive audience. The Commons immediately formed an exploratory committee whose membership included Martin Bladen, an outspoken advocate of West Indian interests. Micajah Perry and John Baynard also served on the committee, and both seized the opportunity to undermine the East India Company's monopoly on coffee from the East Indies, something the two men had already tried to overturn just a year before.[11] Under the guise of promoting economic growth, the committee's recommendations effectively broke the trade and pricing control that British importers working in the Middle East had been enjoying, while making any large-scale importation of coffee grown by other nations prohibitively expensive.

British coffee importers had been looking for ways to end their reliance on East Indian suppliers, but the petition, with its emphasis on encouraging more colonists to migrate from the metropole, addressed another concern of British investors and regulators—the overreliance of Caribbean planters on the labor of enslaved Africans. Coffee planting, petitioners argued, had a lower threshold for entry than sugar cultivation and so might entice "the poorer sort of people, whose stocks and plantations are small." James Laws, one of the signers of the Jamaican petition, accompanied the document to London, where he elaborated in his presentation to Parliament on what he saw as the "poorer sort" and why he thought they would make a desirable addition to Jamaica's planter community. Uppermost in Laws's estimation was the need to strengthen the white population in Jamaica, an island that "at present," he noted, was "very thinly inhabited by white people."[12] Nearly 44,000 whites lived in the British Caribbean in 1650, making up more than three-quarters of the colonies' population. But by 1700 the brutal requirements of sugar cultivation had resulted in a dramatically escalating demand for enslaved Africans, and the white proportion of the British West Indian population dropped to 20 percent. By the time Jamaica's planters pled their case to Parliament in the early 1730s, white colonists made up only 14 percent of the region's inhabitants.[13]

The changing face of the empire's Caribbean communities alarmed British legislators, who resorted to land grants, free passage, and gifts of start-up capital to entice potential white migrants, as the legislators sought to stem, and ideally reverse, the demographic trend. When such incentives made little headway in Jamaica, the island's House of Assembly tried other means of exerting pressure to encourage white European migration. The legislators passed a "deficiency law," for example, requiring plantation owners to employ at least one white worker for every thirty enslaved people they owned or risk being fined, but it proved ineffective. Planters often found it easier to pay the fine than hire white employees, so that by the eighteenth century, funds raised from these penalties had become a steady source of revenue. According to planter historian Bryan Edwards, "the bill is now considered one of the annual supply bills" in Jamaica, as more money was generated from "deficiency" fines than from the taxes on the importation of enslaved Africans imports and the sale of rum combined.[14]

British and colonial officials hoped that coffee would offer an alternative strategy to attractive gifts or punitive laws for reducing West Indian reliance on slavery and lure larger numbers of white migrants to the islands. Coffee cultivation's more modest demands in terms of land, labor, and equipment, proponents claimed, would appeal to a different cohort of settlers, especially those lacking the considerable means required to engage in sugar planting. James Laws arrived in the House of Commons armed with a slew of details to support his case. He knew that it took a coffee tree four to five years to mature and that once it bore fruit, it remained productive for roughly the same length of time. He even brought a sample of roasted beans from Jamaica to be passed around for parliamentary members to touch and smell, and which he claimed had already been tested by several "Druggists in London," who "all agreed that it was very good."[15]

The arguments of Laws and others proposed a solution to the empire's population problems while also capitalizing on coffee's growing popularity and potential profitability. Laws also took pains to point out that coffee would complement rather than compete with sugar because it thrived on the island's steep inclines and high elevations unsuitable for cane cultivation. Coffee farms might even provide a stepping stone for upwardly mobile colonists who, as they "get money by the produce of coffee," he speculated, "will be encouraged to erect sugar-works."[16] In reality, such transitions rarely occurred. A handful of coffee planters did manage to move into the upper echelons of plantocracy, but more remained among the ranks of small and middling farmers, and many failed altogether. Start-up and maintenance costs for sugar planting were simply too high for any but the very wealthy, and the individual profits from small coffee estates rarely made such capital accumulation possible.

The largest expense, either for sugar or coffee production, came from the need for the labor of enslaved Africans and African Jamaicans, about whom

Laws revealingly said nothing in his 1731 presentation on the Commons floor. His silence on the institution and the people it held in thrall speaks volumes, however, for by the time Laws addressed Parliament the connection between slavery and coffee production in the Caribbean was well established. The French and Dutch West Indies already relied on enslaved labor to produce coffee, and it was also, of course, how the crop had been planted, harvested, and roasted on Nicholas Lawes's Townwell estate in Jamaica. That there is almost no mention of the potential impact of coffee farming on enslaved people, except in the oblique and unsubstantiated assertions that the industry would promote use of free labor, is telling. The story being sold to Parliament was that coffee held out the prospect of self-sufficiency and upward mobility for those white farmers of lesser means who took their chance on the crop. Electing to be silent about slavery in Parliament that spring was more than an omission, it was a conscious decision that would be repeated during other efforts to entice new investors. Whitehall responded with 1732's "An Act for Encouraging the Growth of Coffee in his Majesty's Plantations in America," the first of several laws that paved the way for cultivation to thrive in the British West Indies.[17] But understanding the British Parliament's enthusiastic support for Caribbean-based coffee also requires understanding the restrictive supply chains it hoped to break.

Coffee Crosses the Atlantic

Coffee has always been a carefully controlled commodity. It originated in Ethiopia west of the Great Rift Valley, where local inhabitants had been gathering it for sale as early as the mid-1400s. By the fifteenth century, coffee was being shipped through the port of Zeila to countries along the coast of the Red Sea.[18] Only after it became affiliated with Islamic religious practice, however, did coffee drinking spread more broadly. Hajj pilgrims from the Horn of Africa brought coffee with them to Mecca, and from there it traveled a vast Islamic diaspora across Java, India, Persia, Turkey, and Morocco before crossing the Sahara to western Africa.[19] By the end of the fifteenth century, coffee consumption was well established in Cairo, where it first found favor with religious orders and university students before becoming a common practice among the city's population. The earliest records of coffee trading date to around the same time, when it appears in the 1497 letters of an Egyptian merchant who sold it with pepper and indigo.[20]

The expansion of coffee trading in the sixteenth century represented an important industry innovation, but traders still sought to control access by western Europeans through exclusive trade agreements and export taxes. Such arrangements benefited several cities associated with the early trade. Mocha, for example, located on Africa's northeast coast at the intersection of the Arabian and Red Seas, thrived under Turkish rule, especially after the empire passed legislation requiring all ships entering the Red Sea to put into port and pay duty on their cargoes.[21] The trade's impact on the coastal city was profound, as was the wealth it generated, transforming Mocha into an international business center by 1600. Letters from early Dutch East India Company employees describe "high towers" and mosques "all white wash'd on the Outside," and "a great many Palm-Trees which seem'd to us to run along the Shore as far as the Town," affording "a very agreeable Prospect."[22] Caravans sent coffee from Mocha's marketplaces overland to Egypt, Syria, and Turkey, while its cargo ships linked the harbor to numerous ports along the coasts of the Indian Ocean and the Arabian Sea. These in turn supplied the city's merchants and bazaars with a broad range of goods, including spices, textiles, sugar, and tobacco. Although frankincense, myrrh, and precious metals made up part of the outbound cargoes, coffee took the lion's share of the trade, becoming Mocha's largest and most profitable export, and so tied to local interests that the name of the commodity and that of the city would for a while become synonymous.[23]

Coffee drinking grew alongside the popularity of coffee trading, and a range of establishments emerged to serve these early clienteles. Jean de Thévenot, a French linguist, natural scientist, and botanist who traveled extensively throughout the Middle East during the 1650s and 1660s, described these as places catering to those who wanted to see and be seen. "There is even without doors stone seats, covered with mats," he wrote, "where those that would see those that pass by, and take the air, sit" (Figure 1).[24]

By early in the seventeenth century, coffeehouses operated in most Red Sea ports. John Ellis, the island agent for Jamaica in the last quarter of the eighteenth century, collected many of the earliest descriptions about the commodity and published them as *An Historical Account of Coffee* in 1774, estimating that by the seventeenth century there was "no house or family, rich or poor, Turk or Jew, Greek or Armenian," where coffee was not "drunk at least twice a day, and many people drink it oftener." The beverage had become so identified with hospitality throughout the Middle East, South

Figure 1. Philippe Sylvestre Dufour, *Traitez nouveaux & curieux du café, du thé et du chocolate* (Lyon: I. Girin & B. Riviere, 1685), face plate, American Philosophical Society.

Asia, and beyond that it was routinely offered to every visitor, so much so that "it was reckoned an incivility to refuse it."[25]

While coffee found early enthusiasts in the Ottoman Empire, it conquered the west more slowly. The London-based Levant Company imported small cargoes of coffee from Turkey by the 1590s but only experimentally and for a few select clients. Less than a generation later, however, the creation of the English East India Company (EIC) in 1600, followed two years later by the Dutch East India Company (VOC), changed the coffee trading landscape irrevocably. Initially these newcomers saw coffee as a way to expand trade networks within the Middle East rather than develop new markets for Europe.[26] John Jourdain, for example, who headed the EIC factory in Mocha, included several descriptions of local merchants, coffeehouses, and coffee farm terraces in his journal but never suggested that coffee would be a suitable British import. "The seeds [are] a great merchandize, for it is carried to the Grand Cairo and all other places of Turkey, and to the Indias," he wrote.[27]

Almost another half century would pass before western European interest in eastern commodities was high enough to encourage any real investment in

coffee. But then it did so steadily and sometimes spectacularly. In 1681 the
Levant Company, frustrated by its dependence on Ottoman suppliers shipping through Mediterranean ports, tried to circumvent the EIC and establish its own direct trade to Mocha. While the British Court of Admiralty
ultimately denied the Levant claim, seizing its cargo and condemning its
vessel, the *Arcana Merchant*, when it reached London, the incident highlighted the growing importance of coffee and Mediterranean trade to Britain.[28] The creation of the New East India Company (NEIC) by Parliament in
1689 briefly escalated competition further still. In 1708, EIC directors noted
that "coffee continues to be greatly in demand," and that year the two companies merged. The volume of coffee imports continued to rise in the early
years of the eighteenth century, from just under 6,000 pounds between 1699
and 1701 to 11,000 pounds by 1724.[29]

The incursions of pirates and smugglers threatened Ottoman control over
coffee even more directly while at the same time escalating inter-European
rivalries. France, for example, made a dramatic entry into the Mediterranean
trade in 1647 when a French pirate ship seized a British coffee cargo in the
Persian Gulf en route to the port of Basra. Although the EIC advised its agents
to use "what ever means you can as we did formerly to ruinate their voyages,"
it proved difficult to stop all interlopers, and smuggling incidents pepper the
records of the late seventeenth century. In December 1692, for example, a ship
named the *Mary*, financed by Irish backers, brought Mocha coffee to Kins-
dale in County Cork, and the following year the *Success* surreptitiously carried 252 bales of coffee to Newcastle, England.[30]

Smuggling coffee could generate tidy profits, but those involved might
face fines and retribution too. The threat of violence also loomed, as Henry
Watson found to his dismay when he set sail on August 14, 1698, aboard the
British ship *Ruparrel* "bound to Bombay, having freighted on her thirty-five
bales of coffee." Just one day into its voyage, the *Ruparrel* was boarded by what
Watson described as "babs. Pirates," who had most likely shipped out of Bab
al Mandab at the mouth of the Red Sea. The bandits proposed ransoming the
vessel for 35,000 pieces of eight and steered for the port of Aden. When the
Ruparrel docked, however, its owners refused to pay, whereupon the pirates
"fell again to plundering," which, Watson added sardonically, he "thought
had been effectually done before." The ship was then set ablaze "with the
English ensign flying."[31]

The EIC responded to such threats and depredations by standardizing
and regulating its investments, and authorizing an annual voyage direct to

Mocha that gave England the largest and most regular access to that port of any western European nation. Such initiatives reflect the growing revenue produced by the trade as well as the desire to safeguard it. Coffee, which had represented less than 2 percent of the EIC's income between 1664 and 1688, had grown to 15 percent in 1720 and over 20 percent of the company's profits just four years later.[32] What began as a curiosity, and then developed into a lucrative but still regional market, had become a popular British import by the beginning of the eighteenth century and an industry well worth the investment to grow and protect. Indeed, as the seventeenth century drew to a close, Europeans increasingly chafed at the degree to which they relied on foreign imports for this increasingly popular commodity, which encouraged the first western experiments in coffee cultivation.

With England established in Mocha, other European nations began looking elsewhere for their coffee supplies. In the 1720s the Dutch turned first to Ceylon (today known as Sri Lanka) and then moved further south and east to Java and Ambon.[33] Within a decade these efforts had paid off and the first Dutch-produced colonial coffee was being sold at auction in Amsterdam. This so-called India coffee or Java coffee became as closely identified with the commodity as Mocha had previously been. Growing numbers of Dutch consumers drank coffee raised on Dutch East Indian plantations, which accounted for nearly 25 percent of the company's total income at the end of the 1730s. "Maids and seamstresses," one Amsterdam resident wrote, "now had to have their coffee in the morning or they could not put their thread through the eye of their needle."[34]

France likewise sought to mitigate its dependence on foreign produce as well as on British or Dutch imports, and concentrated its production efforts on Bourbon, a small island off the African coast near Madagascar.[35] François Cauche first raised the French flag there in 1638, but the island remained unsettled until a dozen French mutineers were transported there from Madagascar in 1642. Most of the convicts had died or returned to France, however, by the time the French East India Company (FEIC) sent its first twenty colonists to the island. Wild coffee, known as Mauritiana coffee or "café marron," grew on Bourbon, and its early proponents argued that the beverage it produced rivaled that of Yemen. But while Bourbon coffee was well received in France, most other European nations thought it to be "longer, smaller, and greener than that of *Arabia*, and when burnt has a bitterer Taste."[36]

In 1715 the FEIC began importing coffee trees to Bourbon from Mocha. These transplanted seedlings thrived, and coffee quickly became the island's dominant crop; 7,000 Mocha trees grew on Bourbon by 1720, rising to nearly 100,000 trees within three years. Coffee production on the island developed under a system of "concessionaires," where each worker was tasked with cultivating a minimum of ten trees. Unlike the VOC's experience in Java, however, Bourbon had no native population to compel into service, so French planters turned to enslaved Africans, marking the first time the crop was associated with this form of coerced labor.[37]

By the beginning of the eighteenth century, European demand for coffee had grown too high to depend reliably on the produce of either Middle Eastern suppliers or Indian Ocean plantations, and traders once again sought options to increase supply. Ethiopian coffee remained an important niche market among elite buyers prepared to pay a higher price for what they deemed a better-quality product, but most consumers were by now drinking East Indian coffee, which, while less expensive, essentially meant they had exchanged Britain's near monopoly in the Red Sea to Holland's dominance in the Indian Ocean. Imperial expansion across the Atlantic, however, brought new territories into play—places whose climates and topographies might be conducive to agricultural experimentation. Richard Beresford, for example, who had been elected to the South Carolina House of Commons in 1702, proposed coffee as one of a number of possible crops suitable for the fledgling colony, while a 1721 Barbadian pamphlet listed coffee among the "great Number of Plants in a fruit bearing state."[38] Coffee did not ultimately thrive in either South Carolina or Barbados, of course, because their topographies were much too flat, but such initiatives reflect the growing British interest in the commodity's future.

Holland also looked to the Americas in its efforts to expand coffee production. As early as 1700, Samuel Beekman, governor of the South American colony of Essequibo, lobbied the Dutch West India Company (WIC) to invest in coffee, noting "we have already spared no efforts in the attempt to grow coffee . . . but hitherto without succeeding." If, however, "we were provided with a proper plantation" and "we further apply ourselves to this matter," he anticipated a successful transplantation of the industry.[39] Beekman became embroiled in charges of illicit trade to Britain, however, so the WIC declined his request. Instead, it chose neighboring Suriname for the company's first large-scale trans-Atlantic coffee venture, using transplanted cuttings from a Batavian Mocha tree sent there via the Botanical Gardens in Amsterdam in 1718.[40]

If Dutch planters were the first to experiment with growing coffee in the Americas, British planters did not lag far behind. In 1720 the governor of Barbados imported trees from Suriname and subsequently shipped some cuttings back to England. These saplings went to the gardens of some of the country's most powerful people, including the future King George II, then Prince of Wales, a sure sign that coffee had caught the interest of the nation's elite.[41] But as noted previously, Barbados's near total commitment to sugar, and even more its flat topography, doomed the effort from the start. Instead, the mountains of Jamaica, bolstered by parliamentary protections based on the early successes of Lawes's experimentation and his fellow planters' pleas for assistance, became the proving ground for coffee cultivation in Britain's empire in the Americas.

Imagining the Coffee Industry

Coffee's expansion relied on more than tax relief and tariff protection. To capture the imaginations of would-be planters, it also depended on prescriptive literature like published travelers' accounts and planters' manuals. Both were popular genres of the day, and much more than literature for vicarious vacationers or practical instruction books. They were each, in their own way, a form of advertising intended to persuade potential farmers that coffee was a lucrative opportunity that aligned their individual fortunes with those of the empire. Both publications also perpetuated the image of self-sufficient coffee farms, which previously targeted British politicians, to build the industry's reputation and desirability. Most of these volumes at least alluded to the enslaved people who were necessary for any hope of success, so they were one step above the report Jamaican planters had argued before the House of Commons committee in 1731, but they did so most often in the margins and in passing, never as a primary focus. Instead, volumes invariably opened with a basic botanical description of arabica coffee, the variant of the plant most suited to West Indies cultivation, as if production was principally a matter of botany.

Descriptions of coffee trees were fairly standard and included height, component parts, and an overview of the growing cycle. Readers would learn that arabica trees stood from eight to twelve feet high, for example, and once a year blossomed with small white flowers that eventually wilted and dropped

Figure 2. "Coffea Arabica," John Ellis, *An Historical Account of Coffee: with an engraving and botanical description of the tree* (London: Edward and Charles Dilly, 1774), plate V, American Philosophical Society.

from their branches, leaving round, hard coffee pods (Figure 2). These pods earned their name of berries or cherries because, although initially green, they would darken over several weeks to a deep, rich red hue that signaled maturation. The coffee cherry itself had several segments. Most of them contained two green coffee beans, although about a fifth of all cherries, referred to as a peaberries, held only one bean. Two coatings protected the beans inside their casing—a white gum that separated them from the red outer skin, and a second sticky membrane attached to the beans themselves. These were known respectively as pulp and parchment, and both had to be removed—laborious processes—once beans were extracted from their cherries to prevent fermentation.[42]

Planters' manuals did more than lay out the basic rules of cultivation and production, however. Like other colonial recruitment strategies, they sought to fuel aspirations by appealing to the dreams of hopeful stakeholders, particularly in linking agricultural and financial success to idealized notions of order and control. John Lowndes, in his tract entitled *The Coffee Planter*, for example, held that "neatness in Plantership is, as in everything else, a very desirable object" and that "symmetry and regularity contribute to increase of revenue."[43] Similarly, Henry Bolingbroke's description of a Demerara coffee estate recalled the planter's "dwelling house—an elegant brick mansion [that] stood in the midst of a garden, which the occupier took the greatest delight in" (Figure 3). The reality looked very different. Most coffee planters' homes were basic affairs, particularly at the outset, and Bolingbroke was even more disingenuous when he claimed that "even the Negro cottages . . . were built on brick foundations, neatly boarded and covered with shingles," an image that stands in stark contrast to the mean structures that typically offered the most rudimentary of shelter for enslaved people.[44]

Captain John Stedman's account of Suriname took the idealization of coffee enterprises a step further in emphasizing what he saw as the essential connections between organization, simplicity, and profitability. He advised that a coffee farm should be "elegant, as well as perfectly regular," and thus "convenient, as having everything at hand and under the planter's own inspection."[45] The sketch accompanying Stedman's text tries to capture this orderly ideal, with the plantation house at bottom center flanked by buildings that accommodated all functions and requirements of this enterprise, such as living quarters for enslaved and free laborers as well as a coffee-works, barns, stables, and other miscellaneous outbuildings (Figure 4). The kitchen gardens, too, are neatly laid out, as are the pasture lands for horses and sheep,

Figure 3. John Lowndes, *The Coffee Planter, or an Essay on the Cultivation and Manufacturing of That Article of West India Produce* (London: C. Lowndes, 1807), frontispiece. The main house of this estate faces the viewer, with four windows on the second floor and a porch beneath. To the left stands a warehouse to store processed beans, and in the foreground is a wheel-driven mill. The level area between buildings is the drying bed, or barbecue.

and beyond those both the "Negro gardens" and the platforms used to dry coffee beans before they were packed for shipment overseas.[46] The coffee trees themselves appear almost as an afterthought, sketched along three sides of the image to symbolize the groves of such plantings that would have reached far beyond the page's borders.

The reality of coffee farming was not only far less orderly and autonomous than Stedman's image, but also much more precarious. Prospective planters risked their investment on unpredictable weather, market demand, and other such vagaries that accompanied this new agricultural venture. They also, of course, were enslavers who relied on the coerced labor of African captives transported across the Atlantic, as well as their American-born descendants. Slavery drove the industry's expansion in the West Indies, notwithstanding the vague and disingenuous pronouncements of coffee's early lobbyists to the contrary. It was, at its core, an economy based on dependence.

The documentary record for the earliest coffee plantations is sparse. Coffee farmers were typically not absentee owners, living back in the metropole and regularly corresponding with resident overseers and attorneys, an

evidentiary source that has helped historians understand sugar cultivation. Fewer still held positions of local authority, again unlike island-based
sugar planters like Sir Nicholas Lawes, and so their opinions and political
preferences appear infrequently in the minutes and votes of local assemblies
and councils. They were also, for the most part, less affluent than their sugar
plantation counterparts, so their personal and professional papers were not
donated to colonial and metropolitan archives, private and public, to the
same extent. Surviving documentation does, however, suggest that at least
some of Parliament's early hopes for coffee came to fruition. Coffee production did, for example, encourage the migration of more middling whites to
the Caribbean and the establishment of more small farms where absentee-
ism rates were low—not because coffee planters had any special attachment to either their industry or their colony, but because their income
rarely supported the option of living abroad.

Not surprisingly, the scant information that does survive about coffee
farms reveals considerable divergence from the fanciful plantation descriptions of commentators like Bolingbroke and Stedman. Coffee holdings tended
to be modest in both size and expense. Edward Long, a wealthy planter and
judge in Jamaica's Vice Admiralty Court, drew on his experience to suggest
that one hundred acres in coffee, "which require not more than the same
number of Negroes, would yield equal profit annually."[47] Historian B. W. Higman, in his analysis of early Jamaican plantation maps, offers similar figures
and provides some sense of the scale of the island's coffee-works. Higman
estimates that eighteenth-century coffee farms averaged no more than seven
hundred acres in total, of which less than a hundred acres might be planted
in coffee, and only two-thirds of the acreage—given the rugged terrain—
cleared at all.[48] Many farms that grew coffee were smaller still, such as the
holding advertised for sale in the Kingston Journal in 1760, which contained
only twenty-four acres total with planting divided among "four acres in Ginger, three in Coffee, and Twelve in Provisions."[49] Sugar plantations, by contrast, often comprised over a thousand acres of cleared land.

Nor did most coffee planters' homes remotely resemble the great mansions often found on sugar plantations. Instead, their one- or two-story
wooden structures were probably closer to the house described a Kingston
Journal advertisement, which had two rooms, a hall, and a piazza, where one
room and the hall were "floored" with wooden planking while the remaining rooms had only hard-packed earth underfoot.[50] Typically, coffee planters' residences were small, cramped, and crowded together with the property's

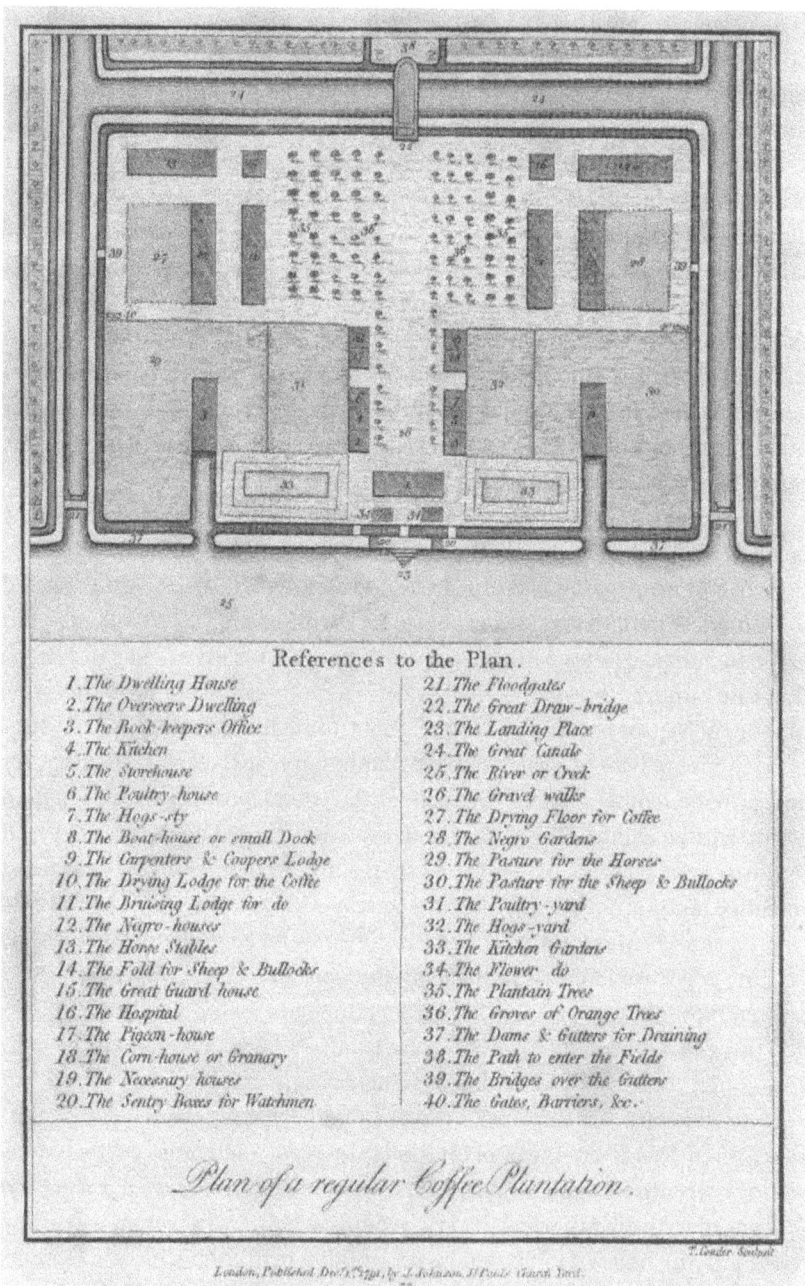

References to the Plan.

1. The Dwelling House
2. The Overseers Dwelling
3. The Book-keepers Office
4. The Kitchen
5. The Storehouse
6. The Poultry-house
7. The Hogs-sty
8. The Boat-house or small Dock
9. The Carpenters & Coopers Lodge
10. The Drying Lodge for the Coffee
11. The Bruising Lodge for do
12. The Negro-houses
13. The Horse Stables
14. The Fold for Sheep & Bullocks
15. The Great Guard house
16. The Hospital
17. The Pigeon-house
18. The Corn-house or Granary
19. The Necessary houses
20. The Sentry-Boxes for Watchmen

21. The Floodgates
22. The Great Draw-bridge
23. The Landing Place
24. The Great Canals
25. The River or Creek
26. The Gravel walks
27. The Drying Floor for Coffee
28. The Negro Gardens
29. The Pasture for the Horses
30. The Pasture for the Sheep & Bullocks
31. The Poultry-yard
32. The Hogs-yard
33. The Kitchen Gardens
34. The Flower do
35. The Plantain Trees
36. The Groves of Orange Trees
37. The Dams & Gutters for Draining
38. The Path to enter the Fields
39. The Bridges over the Gutters
40. The Gates, Barriers, &c.

Plan of a regular Coffee Plantation.

London, Published Dec.r 1.st 1791, by J. Johnson, St Pauls Church Yard.

Figure 4. Capt. John Gabriel Stedman's *Narrative, of a five years' expedition, against the revolted Negroes of Surinam, in Guiana, on the wild coast of South America; from the year 1772 to 1777* (London: Printed for J. Johnson, St. Paul's Church Yard, & J. Edwards, Pall Mall, 1796), 2:354, American Philosophical Society.

other buildings on plots of land that enslaved workers labored to carve out of heavily forested and mountainous regions. Higman estimated that coffee proprietors' homes stood, on average, only 650 feet from the property's coffee-works and less than 575 feet from the habitations of the people they held in bondage.[51]

This physical proximity of the enslaved and their enslavers is an important distinction between coffee estates and sugar plantations, as it underscores that coffee farmers were necessarily aware of their reliance on others to survive. Lady Maria Nugent, wife of Jamaica's lieutenant governor, noted some of the implications for such spatial organization in a diary entry describing her visit to "Mr. Sheriff's coffee estate." Nugent initially nods to the aspirations common in prescriptive literature: "The house is a good one, quite new, and every thing neat about it," she reported, and "it is situated in the midst of mountains, out of which issue abundant streams of water." But when darkness fell, her opinion changed: "In the evening," she complained of discomfort since "the house is very damp and cold, owing to the numerous streams." It was not just the temperature, however, that upset her. She grumbled about the "number of Negroes, men, women, and children," whom she saw "running and lying about . . . in all parts" of the place. "Never in my life did I smell so many," she complained.[52] Such comments highlight insidious aspects of white racism, of course, but also suggest that the tighter quarters and resultant immediacy and intimacy between a coffee farm's enslavers and those they enslaved created a very different dynamic than that which occurred on the larger estates, often the property of absentee owners living in Europe. Coffee planters worked and lived alongside the people over whom they held socially prescribed and legally enforced positions of authority, in other words, but upon whom they depended daily for their livelihoods. Regardless of the images of self-sufficiency that enticed planters to try their luck in the West Indies, there was no escaping the dependence on others upon which even minimal success relied.

Even with legislative encouragement, Britain's coffee economy got off to a slow start, its West Indian initiatives lagging behind those of Holland and France through the mid-eighteenth century. For an empire seeking fiscal independence from East Indian suppliers, it was, ironically, only after acquisition of the formerly French territories in Dominica, St. Vincent, and Grenada at the end of the Seven Years' War (1756–1763) that the situation began to change. Although these were among Britain's smaller islands—the largest, Dominica, is less than three hundred square miles—they all came into

the empire with extensive coffee cultivations intact. Collectively these eastern Antillean farms exported a combined 3.3 million pounds of coffee to London over the next decade, or over nine-tenths of all British West Indian
coffee produced between 1763 and 1774.[53]

British investors soon realized the potential of the Ceded Islands and
rushed to stake their claims.[54] Among these were the Senior family, Jewish
merchants and planters who operated out of their home base in London. The
Seniors, who had invested in Barbadian sugar plantations since the seventeenth century, had already earned enough from their colonial speculations
to relocate the administration of their West Indian affairs back to England,
where they continued to expand their interests on the other side of the
Atlantic. When France lost most of its Lesser Antilles colonies in 1763, the
Seniors mobilized quickly and bought land in Dominica. Their correspondence about these investments with agents operating on the island provide a
rare glimpse into decision-making processes in these newly acquired territories. The Senior family hired Robert G. (R.G.) Bruce, a Dominican factor
or agent, to work as their estate manager, and in 1771 he wrote to William
Senior describing efforts to purchase land on the latter's behalf. Competition was fierce, Bruce informed Senior, and "I took a great deal of pains and
made some efforts to get an estate for you adjoining the sea." The acquisition
was not without difficulty, he reported, since "the value of lands have risen
so surprisingly that it was impossible without giving an exorbitant price."
Bruce struck gold, however, at a commissioner's sale, a special event organized
to sell land in foreclosure, where he bought 387 acres of land for Senior "on
the banks of a large river called St. Mary's." Bruce even bought a plantation
for himself "in the neighborhood of yours," he told Senior, and "adjoining
an excellent shipping bay," a move, he suggested, that would "enable me to
give great assistance in the infancy of development."[55]

William Senior initially hoped to replicate his family's Barbadian success
by focusing on sugar cultivation, but Bruce was skeptical since "the Leeward
part of the island is rough and mountainous" and so not good terrain for
growing cane. But this same land, he responded confidently, could produce
a "great abundance of excellent coffee, for which," he thought, it "seems pe-
culiarly calculated."[56] Senior clearly pushed back, as in a second letter Bruce
felt it necessary to reiterate to his London-based investor that "after having
very fully considered the subject on the spot, and consulted the best planters, I have determined to plant your Estate in Coffee in preference to Sugar."
Bruce offered several reasons for his decision. First, he noted, coffee farms

required less capital to start, pointing out bluntly that Senior had committed "not equal to half the Expence of settling a good sugar estate." Second, coffee would yield a better rate of return when the cost of land, buildings, and labor were calculated against profits. Bruce estimated that sugar estates required a start-up investment of between £15,000 and £20,000, with "the profits arising from them inadequate as yet to the advance." Coffee farms, he continued, "have cost much less" in initial funding, so that, he claimed, "all the Coffee Planters are getting rich."[57] Bruce may have been exaggerating coffee's profitability to justify his own choices and preferences, but he certainly pushed Senior to involve himself in a new market whose potential was attracting significant interest.

Other British planters, most of more modest means than the absentee Seniors, also experimented with coffee growing on the Ceded Islands, and the cumulative efforts definitively shifted the balance of Britain's coffee trade. East Indian imports had accounted for almost all of Britain's coffee imports between 1749 and 1751, but that share had dropped to 5 percent by 1774 while West Indian coffee rose correspondingly from 3 percent to 94 percent over the same period.[58]

Coffee's Annual Cycle

If coffee farming became more profitable for some, it did so on the backs of others, as the industry was the very model of dependence, starting with the labor required to reshape mountainous topography. The dense timber groves that so fascinated seventeenth-century visitors to the British colony had been eliminated from coastal areas a century later to make way for sugar but still covered the cooler elevations of island interiors. Such highland locations were not as swelteringly hot; "rain is more frequent [and] in general the declivity is less," wrote one planter, who also noted that "the time of crop is longer, and more convenient; the [coffee] trees, in short, are more lasting."[59]

Planters tasked their enslaved workers with various strategies to clear the land. Some used slash-and-burn tactics, which involved felling larger trees— and, if possible, recouping some expenses by selling the timber—then igniting controlled burns to clear remaining stumps and brush. A less drastic strategy skipped the fire and left some natural ground cover between trees to create a natural fertilizer of the felled and decaying foliage, twigs, branches, and stumps. "Though ashes are a kind of manure," planter-agronomist John

Lowndes argued, "burning could be dispensed with because it destroys more of the salts contained in the soil than the ashes provide."[60]

Clearing options often depended on the size of an estate. Large-scale burning was more common on bigger estates but less practical for small farms with only a few acres of cultivable land and a handful of enslaved workers, "where every spot must be converted into use"—and speedily. Instead, modest farms were likely cleared by hand, and coffee trees were brought into production more quickly while the space in and around them could be used to fill more immediate needs, including "a speedy and ample supply of ground provisions, and vegetables of all sorts."[61] Regardless of the size of the estate or the means of establishing it, however, the one constant in this preparatory work was the planters' reliance on people they had purchased and whose labor they coerced.

Despite Henry Bolingbroke's fanciful descriptions of "Negro cottages" with brick foundations, extant plantation maps and archeological evidence indicate far more basic structures made of wattle and daub. During the first few weeks of establishing Radnor Plantation, for example, a journal recorded three or four people "making huts," with another assigned to cut thatch.[62] Enslaved people, of course, would also have been charged with building their enslavers' better accommodations, as well as the construction of coffee-works, including a mill to wash coffee and remove its outer casings, a second mill with a grinding wheel to remove the sticky inner parchment coating, and a platform—also referred to as a barbecue—where processed beans dried in the sun. If money was unavailable to invest in these structures, as could be the case in these fledgling, cash-poor enterprises, buckets and water could suffice for pulping, and, in the absence of a mill wheel, beans could be cleaned and processed—albeit painstakingly—by hand to remove their skins and parchments. One planter estimated that when resources were scarce, each enslaved laborer could get by with only a "hoe, a scraper, an axe" as well as "two suits of clothes" and "a store of provisions" at the outset of operations.[63] Of course, these necessities were defined by someone not forced to endure the situation, but this vignette at least offers a glimpse into the material circumstances of those that coffee enslaved.

Surviving survey maps suggest that planting strategies likely responded to a range of considerations and imperatives. A plan for Orange Vale Plantation in St. George's Parish, Jamaica, one of the earliest surviving maps of a coffee estate, includes three discrete acreages planted and identified as "old coffee," "newer coffee," and "young coffee." The oldest coffee occupied just over seven acres and stood at five hundred feet above sea level, while the twenty acres of "newer" coffee had been located at a far higher elevation— some fifteen hundred feet above sea level. Meanwhile, the latest groves of coffee trees on the estate were the ten acres of "young coffee" that had been planted back down on the same five-hundred-foot elevation as the "old coffee."[64] These spatial arrangements suggest that proprietors were weighing and adjusting their plantings to balance the better quality of coffee grown at higher eleva- tions against the ease and convenience, and thus increased productivity and perhaps profitability, of beans produced farther down the hillsides.[65]

Most work assignments on coffee estates were dictated by the plant's an- nual growth cycle. July through December were spent weeding and pruning, while harvesting—including pulping, drying, peeling, winnowing, and the "picking," or sorting beans for sale—lasted through most of the rest of the year. Any remaining time was devoted to sundry tasks related to the upkeep of the property and plants. Young trees required constant weeding as roots often ran close to the surface where they could absorb soil impurities, in- cluding acids produced by decaying weeds and other vegetation, which could affect taste.[66] Weeding was a tedious task, done primarily by hand to protect a fragile topsoil that was already thin on steep slopes, a condition exacerbated by frequent heavy rains. To make the crop easier to access, enslaved workers pruned coffee trees through a process called "stopping," which involved trim- ming the tallest branches to reroute nourishment to the rest of the plant. Pruning also reduced the possibility of wind damage and, by bringing more coffee cherries within arm's reach, limited the potential damage caused by pulling down or bending boughs when coffee cherries were harvested.[67] Even if tended carefully, however, coffee fields had a limited lifespan since the plants drew so many nutrients from the soil. After only a few years, fields were "abandoned and are altogether unfit," noted one Jamaican House of Assem- bly report, the soils having been so depleted that they were unable even "to yield a grass fit for rearing cattle."[68]

The length of the harvest period depended primarily on how many acres of coffee had been planted, when the beans matured, and the number of la- borers available. On some farms this process lasted only six to eight weeks, while on others it extended over several months, with the work measured by the number of acres or pounds of coffee each enslaved person had to pick per day. Such yields varied by time of year.[69] On Radnor Plantation, for example, workers picked just over two pounds of coffee cherries per day in early Janu- ary but harvested between twelve and sixteen pounds daily in March and

April. By late July, the totals had dropped back down to around three pounds a day.[70] Most of this picking work was done by bondswomen whom their enslavers considered more dexterous than men and thus less likely to damage trees during mind-numbingly repetitive work that nevertheless required considerable attention to detail.

Planters with more workers than they needed frequently leased out surplus labor to short-handed estates through a system called "jobbing." Jobbing thus supplemented the income of some planters while giving others temporary access to hired labor. This system, of course, resulted in the dislocation of enslaved people from their families and communities, at least temporarily, and there was also no guarantee that leased workers would be either available or needed at the right time or place. John Wemyss, the attorney of Hermitage Plantation, found himself short of labor one harvest, for example, but wrote to his employer complaining that "no jobbing gang could be hired to assist, even at offering so high a price."[71] Those who could afford to purchase large enough gangs of enslaved people did so, while those who could not, or would not, risked the vagaries of the rental market for labor.

Once coffee cherries had been picked and washed, they were run through a series of hoppers and rollers that separated the outer hull from the two coffee beans inside. These machines, known as pulpers or grater-mills, were either turned by hand or powered by animals or water. The beans then soaked in water at least twenty-four hours before being tossed with a hoe to loosen the white gum coating and then drained through sieves, a process called "wailing," to remove any remaining residue from coffee seeds before they were moved outdoors. From this point on, it was essential that the crop remain completely dry, and enslaved workers were tasked with stirring and moving the beans to ensure even evaporation and to prevent mildew or rot. If rain or dew threatened, these workers either moved the beans into drying huts—small structures erected on the sides of drying platforms—or quickly combed them into piles or into holes dug into the middle of the platforms, protecting these stashes against moisture with a covering of plantain leaves or tarpaulins.[72]

On smaller farms, where the construction of mills was too expensive or impractical, coffee underwent a more rudimentary process described by contemporaries as the "in cherries" method, whereby the coffee cherries were left to dry intact before the casings were removed.[73] While certainly cheaper, this technique had risks since coffee beans took up to three times longer to dry with their outer skins still attached and consequently were more likely to ferment. Some smaller planters avoided this problem by shipping their coffee to larger estates nearby for milling, figuring that avoiding potential losses of processing their harvest by hand outweighed the additional cost.[74]

Even after coffee beans had been milled and dried, a thin membrane called parchment still covered them. This was detached by a separate milling process known as peeling or grinding, which involved placing beans in a grinder and lightly rolling over them with a wooden wheel. The parchment waste was sifted away by "winnowing," which required workers to waft air over the beans with sturdy woven fans, and then pass them through hand sieves to ensure the elimination of all remaining detritus. The final stage of the harvest involved picking, or sorting the cleaned kernels into various gradations. Like harvesting, this too was primarily done by bondswomen. Any broken or discolored beans were considered "triage coffee" and set aside for local sale or consumption on the estate, while the rest was weighed and bagged for shipment overseas. Picking and bagging, however, were less time sensitive, since after winnowing, coffee beans could be stored for years if kept dry.[75]

Bound to Coffee

As coffee estates multiplied, so too did the number of enslaved people forced into production. In Dominica, for example, the number of enslaved men and women who harvested coffee surpassed those cultivating sugar by the mid-eighteenth century and made up a quarter of the enslaved people in the French colony of Guadeloupe. In Martinique and other French territories, coffee production occupied as many laborers as all other secondary crops combined, while in Saint Domingue, the economic driver of the French Empire in the Caribbean, more than a third of the enslaved population worked in the colony's coffee economy. In Jamaica, Britain's largest coffee colony, the number of enslaved people on coffee farms more than doubled as the eighteenth century drew to a close. In short, from the 1750s on, hundreds of planters in numerous islands tied their fate to this crop and exploited the labor of thousands of enslaved men, women, and children to make it profitable.[76]

As noted above, most coffee estates were modest undertakings, and the size of their labor forces reflected this reality. Instead of hundreds of people, as might be employed on sugar plantations, most of coffee's enslaved lived and worked in communities of fifty people or fewer.[77] For the most part, the work was not dictated by the gang system that their sugar plantation counterparts faced, although all enslaved people—old and young, women, men, and children—were pressed into service. And although working units were called "gangs," coffee cultivation was structured around tasks. The strongest adults worked in the first gang and were responsible for cleaning land, burning brush, and lining and planting trees. Six days out of seven, their work began just before daylight, when they received either hoes for weeding or bags for collecting coffee cherries, depending on the time of year. Pregnant women, those who had recently given birth, children, and the elderly still deemed fit to work made up the second gang, and did different tasks such as weeding, raking the drying coffee, and picking and sorting dried beans. Late-term pregnant women might be pressed into field work if enough coffee trees had ripened at the same time, but planters usually redeployed those in advanced stages of pregnancy to "picking or turning coffee on the platforms, or in sewing for the negroes," which they hoped would prevent miscarriages (a strategy that, incidentally, was not motivated by humanitarianism but rather the profits from reproducing an enslaved labor force).[78] Coffee farms with larger populations of enslaved workers organized children from six to twelve years of age into "children's gangs" whose chores included weeding, grass cutting, and livestock and poultry tending. On Sundays the enslaved worked the provision grounds allotted to them to provide food for themselves that would supplement the meager rations they received at their enslavers' expense.

Planters' manuals offered additional advice on the organization of labor. Pierre Joseph Laborie, for example, thought that "a gang ought to be, as much as possible, composed of the same nation," to ease communication and to produce a more efficient work effort and a less recalcitrant labor force that he hoped would be less likely to rebel or resist. He even preferred men and women from specific regions of Africa, noting that "to form a gang of young Guinea Negroes is the best choice."[79] With less money to spend and a smaller share of enslaved laborers available to them, however, coffee farmers often found themselves purchasing those people that remained after sugar planters had had first pick, which of course limited their options. Absentee Dominican coffee planter William Senior learned from his estate manager R. G. Bruce, for example, that the latter had purchased some enslaved workers for his estate but complained that they were "new" rather than "seasoned," although he had "employed agents both in Barbados and Antigua to endeavor to procure some Creol Slaves if possible." The distinction, Bruce concluded, was critical, as "New Negroes sent into a New Estate in the Woods without being mixt with old ones answer very ill and occasion great losses."[80]

At least one contemporary source also indicated a preference for female workers. While coffee proprietors favored men for the initial hard labor involved in clearing land and planting trees, the situation changed once the crop began producing. "Women," Laborie noted, "are more handy at delicate work than men" and so were preferred for both harvesting ripe cherries and sorting dried beans (Figure 5).[81] Three extant journals from Jamaican coffee plantations back up his assertions. Women made up most full-time field laborers on Radnor Plantation, which had seventy-seven women compared to fifty men. At Balcarres nearly two-thirds of the labor force was female, or sixty-six women to thirty-eight men, while on Martin's Hill—the largest of the three properties—167 women labored alongside 104 men. These patterns confirm observations by historians B. W. Higman and Marietta Morrissey that certain plantation economies, including coffee production, relied increasingly on women's labor as the eighteenth century progressed.[82]

Those enslaved men who did work on coffee estates had greater access to a variety of skilled positions. Carpenters and tillers oversaw building maintenance and roofing, while masons ensured that basins and drying platforms remained in good working order. Mule handlers packed bags of cleaned and dried coffee for transport to market and were among the few enslaved workers to regularly travel any distance from the property. Almost all estates used at least one or two drivers to oversee field production, unless the enterprise was so small that the owner assumed this role himself. "It is commonly and justly said," Laborie wrote, "that Drivers or Commanders are the soul of a plantation," and he outlined at length just what qualities he deemed essential:

> They should know how to preserve distance and authority, make themselves acquainted with all that the negroes do or intend to do, chiefly during the night, keep an eye upon the nocturnal visits and excursions; observe, while at work, if any are indisposed, give attention to every thing, and render account of everything to the master. . . . A double share is given to the drivers, if they behaved properly.[83]

Some estates installed white managers to direct, or even replace, enslaved drivers, while smaller farms might share a driver to save expenses. Bruce made such an arrangement with the Senior family after he purchased land and bondspeople in Dominica. He was, of course, resident on his own estate, and so he conformed to the standard model of a coffee planter, but he also worked on commission as an attorney for both Senior and a Dr. Walker.

PLANTATION SCENE—COFFEE

Figure 5. William Blake, *The History of Slavery and the Slave Trade, Ancient and Modern* (Columbus, OH: H. Miller, 1858), 288, Library Company of Philadelphia. "Plantation Scene—Coffee" depicts female slaves picking coffee cherries from trees little higher than head height while male slaves turn drying cherries to ensure equal evaporation.

When Bruce set up these coffee works, he recommended cutting costs by sharing not only a manager but also a gang of enslaved workers. "The person I have engaged as Manager is one that came from England with me, and in whom I have the greatest confidence," Bruce wrote to William Senior in July 1771, "and as the Estate I purchased for Dr. Walker is separated from yours by only a river, and is to be settled at the same time, I propose to give him the care of both while they are in their infancy." Bruce likewise divided expenses between the two properties. "The agreement I have made with him [the Manager] is to allow him one hundred Pounds Sterling a year" as well as "his provisions, for Both Estates."[84] Eight months later, Bruce reported on his progress: the "Manager answers my utmost expectations in his care and activity. He has 40 Negroes under his management, of which 25 are yours, and 15 Dr. Walker's, and as the settlements are opposite to each other," he concluded, "I have made the whole gang work hitherto under one driver and divide their time on each side of the river in proportion to the above numbers."[85]

The only other position among the enslaved workers that rivaled the importance of the driver was that of the coffee man, who oversaw the millworks and platforms, and prepared the goods for sale. In many ways the responsibilities of the coffee man began where those of the driver ended, at the transition from harvesting to processing. He would oversee the processes of coffee washing, pulping, wailing, drying, winnowing, and packing that created the finished product ready to ship to market. Skilled tasks did not necessarily take up all of a worker's labor year-round, even on large farms, but serving as coffee man did allow the enslaved thus occupied to avoid some of the drudgery and tediousness of the coffee fields and works. Few women managed that. The only skilled positions that women regularly occupied were as healers, child or poultry tenders, domestics, or seamstresses, and then only if older or injured. The remaining women made up the bulk of coffee's labor.[86]

The very location of coffee estates, of course, also indelibly and materially shaped the lives of the laborers compelled to work there. Some eighteenth-century writers thought that the cooler, wetter conditions of the higher-altitude sites were healthier than what prevailed in the valley and coastline locales of sugar estates, and historians have demonstrated significantly different work regimens and associated mortality rates between these two plantation economies. Other evidence suggests that coffee estates may have escaped the worst ravages of smallpox and malaria epidemics that were a consequence of the more crowded conditions on sugar plantations.[87]

But if enslaved coffee workers suffered fewer diseases than their counterparts in sugar plantations, they faced other challenges. Few coffee farms, for example, were connected to major thoroughfares or public roads because they were so remote. Some had access to the coast via gullies and river courses, and thus could float their produce to market, but the clustering of estates in interior highlands meant that overland transport by mule was far more common.[88] These journeys could take days or even weeks through formidable terrain and on narrow roads that abutted sheer precipices and created dangerous conditions for enslaved workers. Matthew Smith, who lived near the Jamaican port of Savannah la Mar, could not even afford mules and so used his bondsmen as porters to move his produce. Smith was a minor planter who appeared in the archival record because of a complaint registered by British port officials in 1770 that his coffee bags were underweight. Colonial law dictated that coffee be shipped in bags of 112 pounds, while Smith's all weighed between 72 and 79 pounds each because, as he argued, 79 pounds was "as much as a Negro can carry upon his head."[89] Such work placed brutal demands on coffee workers, as Thomas Ewbank attested to when he visited

Brazilian coffee plantations a century later. "The average life of a coffee-carrier does not exceed ten years," he averred. "In that time the work ruptures and kills them."[90]

Coffee's Planters

Images of eighteenth-century plantation owners often portray sugar barons and their wealthy estates replete with porticoed mansions, vast fields, imported furnishings, expensive habits, and of course, usually on the periphery, the enslaved labor that made this lifestyle possible. Coffee holdings also depended on slavery but on a markedly different scale because, as already noted, venturing into coffee cultivation required a much more modest investment. Edgar Corrie, a British merchant, thought that as few as ten to twenty enslaved workers and two hundred acres of land could turn a profit, while James Knight, a Jamaican planter writing in 1742, thought even fewer resources would suffice: "a Poor man with five or six Negroes and a small tract of Land, may, with Industry," he estimated, "be able to support himself and his family."[91] Such small-scale enterprises, however, often lacked the reserves to see them through hard times.

Some coffee farmers hedged their bets, relying on other employment to get by. Jamaica plantation records include the papers of three coffee estates owned by working carpenters and another by a man employed as a coppersmith, and all of their farms were relatively small operations worked by between twenty and fifty enslaved people. Two additional properties, more modest still, belonged to men employed as overseers on other plantations who had purchased small coffee operations for themselves, and owned five and thirteen enslaved people respectively. But as William Williams, a carpenter in Jamaica's capital of Spanish Town, discovered, the hopes of small coffee holders could be quickly dashed. After only two years as a part-time planter, he went back to his woodworking trade full-time and put up for sale the remaining thirteen-year lease on a mountain property in St. John Parish, which contained "a large Plantain Walk, some young coffee, and a quantity of pasturage in good order."[92]

Other planters took different steps to spread their risk, like investing in crops beyond coffee or in livestock management. When Joseph Newall died, for example, the executors of his estate advertised the sale of his Amity Hall property in St. Ann, Jamaica. In addition to the eight acres dedicated to coffee groves, it had a "Penn of 300 acres" and 150 acres of guinea grass to feed livestock, as well as five acres planted in plantain.[93] Similarly, when Jacob Hill advertised his plantation for sale, he listed thirty acres of plantains, eight of coffee, and "a great deal of Scots and Guinea grass." His property's amenities included its proximity to several streams and orchards of fruit trees. Better still, what he termed his "mountain plantation" lay only sixteen miles from Kingston and nineteen to Spanish Town, "sixteen of which is a carriage road and the rest good horse road," and contained a "genteel dwelling house and out-offices fit for a family."[94]

While advertisements for the Newall and Hill properties did not specify why their owners were selling, Charles Elliot, whose Dominica estate was confiscated because of tax debt, had his failure broadcast publicly. In 1768, when the island's local authorities announced the auction, Elliot's property included "sixty-four acres of cleared land, planted with Coffee, Cotton, Cocoa, and Negro Provisions; and thirty-seven acres of Woodlands," as well as his one remaining bondsman, a man named Chance. The terms of sale for Elliot's property, human and otherwise, were "ready gold or silver money" in hand, while those with mortgages against either the enslaved man or the plantation had ten days to file their claim.[95]

Elliot was not alone in facing financial woes, nor was Chance the only bondsperson to confront its consequences. Coffee properties as well as everyone and everything on them, including those belonging to Jean Baptiste Bunel and Sorhaindo Jaison, also planters in Dominica, could find themselves on the auction block for unpaid debts, with buyers hard to find. Notices for Bunel's and Jaison's estates reappeared in the *Dominica Chronicle* for several weeks and were joined by others, such as the coffee farms of Ulysses Fitzmaurice and Louis Chauveteau.[96] The notice for Fitzmaurice's Bowood Estate was particularly detailed, as he died deeply in debt and his executors hoped the property's sale would settle his accounts. Bowood included twenty-five acres of coffee, three and a half of plantains, two of pasture, and another twelve of provisions. It also included thirty-one enslaved people, listed in the newspaper notice by both name and occupation:

Peter a carpenter, Tom a Mason, James a driver, Othello, Kingston, Ross, Cyrus, Edwards, Ned, Caesar, Cassus, George, Anthony, Pompey, Wilkes, Dominica, Harry, Cato, Dublin, being men, Chloe and her child Nanny, Peggy and her child Peter, Betsey, Lucy, Suky, Phillis, Charlotte, Fanny, Silvia, Juliet, Nanny, and Nelly, being women.[97]

A set of twenty-eight probate inventories included in the Jamaican Accounts Produce, or Crop Accounts, provides more details about the scale and range of coffee cultivation in the second half of the eighteenth century, as well as the planters' reliance on diverse options of making ends meet, and the marginal existence of both the free and enslaved people living and working in the enterprise.[98] Drawing precise conclusions from this number of inventories is challenging, since outputs ranged from 200 to 53,000 pounds of coffee a year and labor forces numbered from a few to fifty enslaved people, but such information at least allows some generalizations about the nature of coffee growing as well as profitability and the patterns of estate owner residency.

Like the Dominica examples above, almost all of the Jamaican Accounts Produce properties included significant income from sources other than coffee. These most often included livestock and pasturage, pimento (allspice) cultivation, jobbing (leased-out enslaved labor), woodcutting, or property rental. In only two instances, and despite the prognostications of early coffee lobbyists and the dreams of investors, did coffee planters engage in any production of sugar or rum.[99] The records also confirm the resident status of coffee planters, since no proprietors from the sample lived abroad. By comparison, absentee rates for sugar planters had reached 80 percent by 1790.[100]

Just over half of these Jamaican Accounts Produce inventories came from estates of recently deceased owners, so matching these documents with wills or other probate records provides an even more comprehensive picture of how coffee planters divided their capital between labor, housewares, livestock, and loans or debts.[101] The largest estate was worth more than £10,000, although average values ran closer to £5,000. This latter sum, while undoubtedly a significant amount of money in eighteenth-century terms, came nowhere near the £40,000 or more that contemporaries estimated was needed to establish a sugar plantation.[102]

Probate inventories also reinforce the industry's unwavering dependence on slavery. While other expenses fluctuated, enslaved people invariably made up at least half—and frequently much more—of these estates' total value.[103] When Captain John Strachem died in 1775, for example, his coffee farm was worth roughly £4,200, more than 80 percent of which was tied to the forty-nine people he owned. Most of these were coffee field hands, although a few were assigned to tend goats and hogs, while one, Jack, was a driver and five men—London, Aura, Depflora, Quaco, and Ned—worked as sawyers. The inventory also includes three old whipsaws and a crosscut saw, the tools of the conscripted woodworkers' trade.[104] Strachem was no great planter, and he did not get rich. He died in debt, in a meager home furnished with a bedstead, bedding, and "a few broken tables and chairs."[105] Even smaller coffee holdings listed in the Accounts Produce exhibit similar tendencies. On the five smallest probate inventories available—all valued at under £500—enslaved labor still averaged half or more of the property's value.[106] Whether coffee planters focused only on that crop, spread their risk by investing in other agricultural activities, or worked as skilled tradesmen, they always invested heavily in the labor of the enslaved.[107]

While coffee, like all plantation economies, was predicated primarily on white men's exploitation of enslaved labor, the same low threshold for entry into the industry also attracted others with more modest means, such as white women and people of both sexes who were classified as free colored. Indeed, Susanna Lowe, the daughter of Henry Lowe, a physician to Kingston's military personnel, was among the original Jamaican petitioners to Parliament in favor of "An Act for Encouraging the Growth of Coffee" in 1731, and other women appear as coffee planters throughout the eighteenth-century records. Many were either the widows or children of men already involved in coffee enterprises, such as Martha Cole, who inherited her deceased husband's coffee plantation and twenty-seven enslaved laborers in St. Ann's Parish, Jamaica, and "gentlewoman" Eleanor Smith, who, after the death of her husband, took over the management of a coffee farm in the island's southern parish of Vere and depended on the labor of over thirty-nine enslaved.[108]

Women confronted the same array of problems and pitfalls that all planters encountered, of course, but they also faced additional hurdles. Deficiency laws, outlined at the outset of this chapter and designed to increase the presence of white people on estates and plantations by regulating ratios of white to non-white inhabitants, were particularly "oppressive to white females possessing small properties," according to one member of Jamaica's House of Assembly.[109] Male plantation owners and white overseers might share accommodations on a coffee estate, or the owner could choose to save money by running the operation himself, since the cost of hired help was considerably higher than the fine he would pay for not meeting the deficiency law quota of white workers. But such alternatives were not available to women. Female coffee planters invariably had to hire and pay a white overseer and, according to historian Edward Kamau Brathwaite, "maintain a separate establishment on their properties, as it could not reasonably be expected that a female would introduce a single man to reside in the same dwelling with her."[110] Women proprietors thus faced the additional costs of housing their white employees separately or risk their reputations in island societies where, as Edward Long averred, "scandal and gossiping are in vogue."[111]

Obstacles facing non-white Jamaican planters were more daunting still. Deficiency laws did not bar free people of color from owning property, but their free status could not be counted when calculating the proportions of enslaved or non-white workers on an estate. As a result, free colored planters were legally obligated to engage white employees in proportion to the number of enslaved people they owned, since neither they nor their families automatically counted toward racial compliance. The difficulties in doing so, particularly on small coffee holdings, meant that, more often than not, they would pay the fines instead.[112]

The ability of non-whites to own property caused even greater challenges, at least in Jamaica, after the island's assembly passed legislation in 1761 that restricted the size of bequests whites could leave to free people of color to a maximum of £1,200 sterling, or £2,000 local currency.[113] Legislation could be manipulated, however, by those who had money or family connections, so a few free people of color did manage to accumulate properties well in excess of legal restrictions. Some applied successfully to the Jamaican assembly for "the same Rights and Privileges as English subjects, born of white parents," a recourse usually referred to in period documents as a request for "special privileges." But this was a narrow window of opportunity, most often reserved for common-law wives and mistresses, or the sons and daughters of wealthy whites. If successful, however, the benefits could be substantial since the recipients were then legally considered white and could count themselves, and in some cases their immediate relatives, toward the deficiency law requirements for their coffee estates.[114] An increasing number of such applications came before Jamaica's House of Assembly from the mid-eighteenth century on and in some cases offered free people of color access to considerable holdings in the growing coffee industry.

One such estate had belonged to John Rome, a white man and one of Jamaica's leading land surveyors, who had started growing coffee in Clarendon Parish by the early 1790s. When he died in 1797, his coffee farm, including the forty-one workers held there in bondage, was valued at £4,112—an average-sized enterprise at the time. What was less usual about Rome's will and testament, however, was his decision to appoint Dorothy Manning, a 47-year-old mulatto woman, as his sole executrix.[115] While Manning did not inherit Rome's property outright, her legal standing as executrix gave her significant control over its administration. It also granted her a portion of the estate as compensation for her services, specifically a lease in trust for two enslaved men and three women worth £370 which likely ran until her death. The precise nature of Manning's relationship to Rome is unknown, but their economic entanglements continued long after the latter's death.

When Manning herself died thirteen years later, her probate inventory included several produce notes and bills that were still being drawn on Rome's estate. Moreover, she had used the proceeds she had garnered from Rome's will to invest in coffee herself and steadily enhance her financial portfolio. By the time she died, she owned twenty-six steers, thirty-five head of cattle, and "sundry sheep and horses," and had several minor debts owed to her estate, indicating that she had expanded into both pen-keeping and the extension of credit for small loans. It is hard to know whether the estate she owned was connected to the one she administered as executrix, but whether she built Rome's enterprise or founded one of her own, her holdings were worth more than £6,143—or over £2,000 more than Rome's original property—by the end of her life. She willed her coffee farm to her sons, being empowered to do so since the Jamaican House of Assembly had granted her petition for special privileges in 1783 on behalf of herself and her children, Thomas and George, ensuring that her family would continue to circumvent Jamaica's inheritance limitations into the next generation.[116]

Johan Casper Weise also successfully petitioned for special privileges, in Port Royal Parish. He was the Kingston-born, mixed-race son of John Weise and Elizabeth Hyne, and brother of Elizabeth Weise, who in 1800 married John Mais, another free colored Jamaican. When Johan Casper Weise died in 1809, his brother-in-law served as the executor of his estate that included a coffee farm valued at £6,978.[117] Like Manning, Weise had established a successful enterprise; his property was worth almost £1,000 more than hers, and he enslaved nearly three times as many people—ninety-three men, women, and children to her thirty-five. And while Manning expanded into livestock and money lending, Weise became an exception among free colored coffee farmers by moving into sugar cultivation. By the time he died, his sugar plantation, including sugar-works and enslaved people, was valued at £10,099. Weise would still have been firmly situated among Jamaica's middling class, but with combined properties totaling £17,077 he was far from the bottom rungs.[118] Notwithstanding these individual success stories, the control of coffee production remained for the most part in the hands of white men, whose cohort expanded year after year through the late eighteenth century.

*   *   *

Most British West Indian port cities exported some coffee to British North America by the mid-eighteenth century, but Kingston, Jamaica, dominated the empire's trade. The port's export merchants assembled cargoes made up of small quantities from many farms across the island, so they rarely developed the kinds of long-standing relationships that linked traders with the island's sugar plantation elite. But if the business was less personal, it required the same attention to administrative detail. Consigning coffee for sale initiated an extensive paper trail first outlined in the 1732 law rebating taxes and designed to curtail smuggling—a move that Nicholas Lawes' fellow planters had successfully persuaded Parliament was essential for their success. Planters had to take an "oath or affirmation" in writing before two justices of the peace "in or near the place where said coffee grew," attesting that the produce they sold had come solely from their estates located within British colonies. A second oath, this time sworn before the collector, comptroller, or naval officer in the port from which the beans were being exported, also certified that all the coffee had been grown and processed in territories within the British Empire. Shipmasters retained copies of all oaths or affirmations for the coffee on board their vessels, to which they added one of their own attesting that they held all the appropriate documentation for transporting the coffee they were carrying. If a cargo lacked any of the requisite papers, it could be deemed contraband and subject to forfeiture, while the captain would face a fine and up to twelve months in prison.

When ships bearing coffee arrived at their destinations, what had become a sizable collection of oaths would be turned over to the local collectors or comptrollers who, in exchange for a fee, affixed the proper marks to the coffee barrels and lodged the cargoes at designated bonded warehouses. This process, which was complicated to the point of redundancy, attests to the coffee economy's importance to British trade officials and their efforts to ensure the commodity's colonial provenance while safeguarding against contraband. This same paperwork, of course, also helps document how coffee wended its way across the Atlantic and up to the ports and harbors of the North America seaboard, where mainland merchants eagerly awaited its arrival.[119]

CHAPTER 2

Coffee's Many Shops

On April 16, 1765, the ship *Polly* set sail for Philadelphia from Kingston, Jamaica, carrying casks of coffee and sugar, bags of limes, and barrels of rum in its hold. Nothing about this journey was particularly remarkable. The goods onboard were common island exports that had become increasingly popular with North American buyers, and the route the ship traveled was likewise familiar, one sailed by hundreds of ships in and out of Philadelphia's busy harbor that year. William West Jr. was one among dozens of the city's wholesale merchants awaiting the ship's arrival that spring afternoon. West held a stake in the *Polly*'s coffee, which he would ultimately send on to Charleston, South Carolina. Other casks belonged to William Redmond, another Philadelphia merchant, and would travel as far north as Newport, Rhode Island. But most of the *Polly*'s coffee had been bought by the local firm of Craig, Fuller & Ash to be sold to nearby traders who would carry it to local towns in Pennsylvania and the neighboring colonies of Delaware and New Jersey.[1] The arrival of coffee into Philadelphia was, in this sense, only one step in a chain of transactions that linked plantation owners in British Caribbean islands to traders and mariners plying the waters between the West Indies and North America, and importers in urban coastal cities to backcountry traders and shopkeepers. Each one of these economic actors relied on the others, and the breadth and depth of their relationships resulted in a network of interconnectedness and interdependence as the eighteenth-century coffee economy expanded.

Scanning docks to his left and right, West would have seen flour, pork, and wooden barrel staves being loaded for shipment abroad. Thanks to the Delaware Valley's flourishing grain and timber industries, Philadelphia enjoyed a lucrative export economy that reached east to southern Europe, south to the Caribbean, and up and down the North American seaboard from Nova

Scotia to Florida, as well as into the western interior. To sustain these branches of trade, ships from around the world arrived daily, creating a bustling and cosmopolitan scene that filled the city's warehouses with a profusion of goods and products, from the exotic to the mundane, drawn from places far and near. The mid-eighteenth century was a time of tremendous material expansion in colonial British North America, when the proliferation of goods for sale and who could buy them grew at unprecedented rates. Rather than being restricted to the wealthy few, coffee and other goods that had been luxuries just years before now found their way to the kitchens and tables of the middle and lower classes. And as demand expanded, so too did the opportunities to capitalize on coffee's popularity and profitability.

Customs agents would have examined West's casks as dockworkers unloaded them, comparing them to the bills of lading that listed each by number and marking to confirm they contained only coffee grown within the British Empire as per legislation, first passed in 1732, that sought to bolster production by offering buyers a rebate on all import duties and taxes if they bought their coffee from British suppliers. Once cleared, West would have confirmed that his coffee was safely lodged in a nearby warehouse, after which he likely proceeded to the Old London Coffee House on Front and Market Streets to meet his fellow investors and report on the day's activities.[2] This favorite gathering place of the city's merchants stood just three blocks west from where the *Polly* had docked on the Delaware River.

On that spring day, eleven casks of coffee moved the short distance from a ship's deck to a warehouse, but this brief journey was part of a more elaborate series of commercial transactions that the coffee trade depended on, that had developed over the last half century, and that reveal the extent to which North America's investment in this evolving industry relied on the larger Atlantic world. The casks aboard the *Polly* had been made in Jamaica, most likely from barrel staves exported from North America's mid-Atlantic seaboard. They contained coffee grown on a British-controlled island that used techniques adapted from French cultivators to grow plants descended from progenitors brought to the West Indies by the Dutch in the early eighteenth century. After the *Polly* arrived in Philadelphia, its cargo would have been distributed to consumers throughout the city and region, as well as up and down the North American coastline, and miles into its hinterlands. West's coffee investment, in other words, and the economic, legal, and social structures of exchange that surrounded its production and trade, tapped into the larger colonial and imperial economic system that North American merchants needed to understand and navigate to succeed.

Philadelphia was not the only British North American city to import coffee, of course, but it brought in the most. Colonial Pennsylvania's principal port had entered the West Indian market later than either New York or Boston, both cities with tight connections to the sugar and rum markets since early in the eighteenth century. Instead of competing with these rivals, Philadelphia's traders looked for other opportunities and began testing consumer interest in several goods that collectively became known as the "secondary commodities." This route to financial success paid off, so much so that by the 1760s, Philadelphia led North American importation of ginger, pimento, and pepper, but especially coffee. In return for these foodstuffs, mid-Atlantic provisions merchants traded pork and wheat—the latter sent as both flour and bread—which helped supply the Caribbean's growing enslaved populations, along with wooden planks, boards, shingles, and staves used to construct the hogsheads, barrels, and casks carrying the islands' outbound cargos that this same enslaved labor force had produced. While coffee rarely made up the bulk of any one shipment, it appeared in some quantity on almost every schooner, ship, and brigantine arriving from the West Indies. At least a third—and often more than half—of the coffee imported into Britain's mainland colonies each year came through Philadelphia by the early 1770s.[3] Consequently, this city is necessarily the focus of any study of colonial North America's coffee trade.

In addition to the amount of coffee recorded in official trade registers, coffee was common among the range of illicit goods either evading or intercepted by Philadelphia's customs officials by the 1760s.[4] The commodity even arrived masked as privateer bounty to be sold at auction. Some smuggled coffee, like almost all legally imported coffee, came from the British Caribbean, but other clandestine cargoes originated in different parts of the world. Oftentimes these foreign beans were more highly esteemed by coffee connoisseurs within an increasingly globalizing market that had already, by the mid-eighteenth century, become sophisticated and diverse. Such activities attest to Philadelphia merchants' willingness from the outset to trade beyond imperial boundaries, practices their counterparts in other colonial ports along the Atlantic seaboard, of course, would also embrace, and which foreshadow the multinational arena of trade that U.S. coffee merchants developed after their new nation's independence from Britain.

How Coffee Was Traded

All forms of commerce—dry goods, provisions, and local trade—dealt in coffee, albeit in different ways. Dry goods merchants rarely bought and sold the commodity itself, since they focused primarily on importing durable objects, such as furniture, textiles, and household items from British suppliers eager to satisfy colonial demand for European fashions. But joining the handcrafted chairs, block-printed calicoes, and sundry other manufactures transported to North American ports came an increasing number of ceramics and metalwares connected to coffee's preparation and consumption. While seventeenth-century drinkers might have contented themselves simply with pan-roasted beans ground by a mortar and pestle, colonial consumers from the mid-eighteenth century on found themselves with more disposable income that they were willing to spend on specialized tools for making and drinking their daily brew. Hence there was a proliferation of coffee grinders, pots, cups, saucers, spoons, and other tools to refine the experience as coffee drinking became more popular (such enhancements to the coffee-drinking experience are the topic of the next chapter in this book).

Coffee was much more central to the business of provisions merchants, who trafficked—as their name implies—primarily in consumable goods. A few of these traders did business with Ireland, the Canary and Madeira Islands, and elsewhere on the other side of the Atlantic, but many more focused on the West Indies, which would become the most important provisions sector in terms of both scale and profitability as the eighteenth century progressed. Some of these importers transported goods aboard their own vessels, occasionally leasing some leftover freight space to other cargoes. Others, either because they could not afford to or because they sought to spread their risk, placed their cargoes in the ship holds of others for an agreed-upon rate, a strategy known as "adventuring." Although traders could meet their financial obligations in these transactions through bills of exchange or extensions of credit, just as often they were willing to accept coffee, sugar, rum, or other island produce in exchange for the wheat, wood, cloth, and other staples they sent to West Indian plantation economies.

A ledger kept by the Philadelphia firm belonging to Benjamin Mifflin and Samuel Massey shows the operation and profitability of this trading process. Between April and June 1761, Mifflin & Massey assembled a cargo of flour, Indian corn, lumber, and shipping supplies aboard its ship *Live Oak*, which, under the command of Master John Ashmead, then set sail for

Kingston, Jamaica. The cost of these goods, as well as the local labor to weigh and load them onto the ship, amounted to just over £1,189. The following year Mifflin & Massey paid a bit more, £1,857, to outfit a second Jamaican voyage that, this time, they paid £129 to insure with another Philadelphia merchant, Thomas Wharton. These two shipments were substantial investments, but they yielded handsome returns in West Indian produce. Gross receipts would total over £8,500, so that after expenses Massey & Mifflin realized a net profit of just over £5,323, an almost 60 percent return on the two voyages combined. Coffee, which had made up roughly a fifth of these ventures, formed a proportionately important part of the firm's overall business as the years progressed. Between 1760 and 1763, Mifflin & Massey's coffee imports rose 25 percent, from 15,470 pounds to 20,540 pounds of beans, and sales revenue grew even faster still—approximately a 65 percent increase, from £787 a year to nearly £1,200 a year.[5]

Coastal and inland traders made up the third type of commercial operator in Philadelphia and redistributed coffee further still, connecting urban centers to smaller coastal towns and backcountry communities. Unlike the dry goods trade, which required significant capital investment and long-distance cosmopolitan connections, or even the provisions trade, conducted in vessels that could cost thousands of pounds to build and outfit, coastal traders operated smaller sloops or schooners that could be purchased for much more modest sums and stocked cheaply.[6] Inland traders relied on even smaller craft, such as shallow, flat-bottomed skiffs, to bring their wares to rural consumers, and reached more remote locations by horse and wagon across overland roads. Wherever they journeyed, along sparsely populated coastlines and isolated hinterlands, these traders found their coffee consignments increasingly in demand.[7] Matthias Slough, for example, who operated a mill and store in Lancaster, a heavily German community in southern Pennsylvania, sent local carters an average of three times a year to Philadelphia to trade his grain for coffee, sugar, rum, and imported textiles, which he in turn retailed to his local customers.[8] Slough, and merchants like him throughout Britain's North American possessions, helped feed a growing caffeine habit among colonists through trade networks that were drawn farther west as populations moved, facilitated by better road systems that tied what had been marginal communities more tightly to the sphere of coastal commerce and culture.[9] Backcountry consumers depended on local traders and coastal importers for their daily brew. Those traders in turn needed ships' crews and harbor personnel and, ultimately, the coffee planters and their enslaved laborers in the forbidding terrain of West Indian mountains, on whose toil this chain of exchange relied. Taken together, these were economic actors who produced North America's caffeine dependence.

From Coffee to Coffees: Differentiating Taste

Before the American Revolution, most North Americans' coffee—whether imported through Philadelphia or some other maritime port, consumed in an urban coffeehouse, or bought from a backcountry store to drink at home—had come from the same place, the British West Indian colony of Jamaica. Philadelphia port records for 1773 document almost two hundred ships, comprising more than half of the city's voyages to the Caribbean, sailing to this one colony and returning with ever-growing amounts of coffee beans. In 1768, 115,350 pounds of Jamaican coffee had landed on the wharves along the Delaware River; five years later importations had more than doubled, to 288,632 pounds.[10] Such increases were the results of British trade restrictions in action. In the five decades leading up to the war for North American independence, tariff legislation had done precisely what West Indian planters hoped it would do, by protecting the British Caribbean coffee market and restricting consumer choice. In return, planters responded as those in Parliament had intended in 1732, by expanding their farms and exploiting the forced labor of more and more people to support production. An increasing number of coffee ventures, coercing an increasing number of enslaved people, harvested larger and larger crops for a global market, with the lion's share of Jamaica's produce going to North America.

Such increases in production, however, were not without some growing pains, and misjudgments and errors on the part of planters sometimes caused a raft of problems that adversely affected product quality. Too little rain dried up coffee berries on the plant, resulting in smaller beans that tasted bitter. Too much rain produced blander tasting beans. Decisions to stretch old fields by replanting trees in tired, nutrition-depleted soil meant mediocre harvests, while paying insufficient attention to cleaning the beans of chaff, dried cherry pods, and other detritus marred what was packed and shipped for sale. Even worse, if planters failed to ensure that harvested coffee had been thoroughly dried before being packed into bags or barrels ready for shipment, the beans would rot. Upon the arrival of one particularly bad shipment in October 1756, Henry Drinker wrote to his business partner that their investment was practically unsellable. It arrived "very bad Colour'd and Musty," he wrote, and he was "obliged to open and hand pick some of the casks."[11]

What was a coffee connoisseur to do? Fortunately there were options for those with means. Benjamin Smith Barton, a prominent Philadelphia botanist, for example, advised one friend that coffee from the port of Mocha or Java was best, followed by that produced from French islands. Coffee from Jamaica, he thought, should be avoided "as it was rumored that their coffee diffused a most unpleasant odor."[12] But decisions about what coffee to drink often involved more than taste. Beans from Java or Ceylon were expensive to ship and hard to acquire, since most of them passed through Amsterdam and London and were destined for western European markets. And while the French West Indies were much closer to North America, the combined effect of taxes on foreign produce and tax breaks that protected the British coffee market meant that this coffee could be two or three times more expensive in stores. Circumstances such as these, which Jamaican planters counted on to protect their market, restricted the availability of foreign coffee and gave North America's importers, retailers, and consumers far less choice than coffee's increasingly widespread production base might suggest.

Colonial shopkeepers in larger cities might stock some non-British coffee for special customers but relied primarily on British colonial plantations as most consumers could not afford to be so choosy. Ironically, the dominance of British coffee in the retail sector is easy to track by what is *not* there—namely, any special attention to coffee in period advertising.[13] Abraham Usher and Joseph Wharton, for example, opened a store on Philadelphia's Walnut Street Wharf in April 1754, and for the next three years they advertised an almost identical inventory of dry goods and foodstuffs. When provenance made a difference, Usher and Wharton were sure to note it, including "Florence oil," "Madeira and Lisbon wine," and "English cables and anchors." British colonial coffee, however, garnered no special distinction, appearing simply as "coffee," the ninety-fifth item in their list of over one hundred goods for sale.[14]

Usher and Wharton were not alone, so some of the best evidence for the ubiquity of British coffee on the North American market comes not from what sellers chose to say, but from when they remained silent. Not a single North American shopkeeper's advertisement between 1755 and 1770 promoted or mentioned the Jamaican or British West Indian provenance of the coffee the shop was selling. The absence of such descriptors is noteworthy, particularly since, by the eighteenth century, advertising was producing what some historians consider "a strikingly new commercial language of allurement" used to "spark curiosity and desire" that would, merchants hoped, "entice potential customers into their shops."[15] Clearly this new language worked better for some goods than others. An understanding of weight, weave, color, design, and price might sway a customer's choice between ging-ham or muslin. Likewise, reassurances from respected Thomas Anderton might persuade buyers that Dr. Storck's "tincture for the tooth ache" did in-deed "infallibly cure in a few minutes," while Prussian Ladies Patent Balsam banished unwanted and unsightly blemishes, leaving "the skin delicately white, soft, and smooth."[16] Sellers of foodstuffs, however, were rarely so cre-ative. Most advertisements for food were simple, bulk listings. Some consum-ables, like wine, merited descriptors such as Lisbon, Madeira, Teneriffe, or Fayal, designating ports of origin. Coffee, however, was almost always just "coffee," most often sold as whole beans since "ground" coffee did receive spe-cial mention when it was available.[17] Vendors rarely wasted valuable page space or money with a qualifying adjective when none was necessary.

The exception to this rule occurred when sellers were lucky enough to have landed a shipment of East Indian or French colonial coffee. Then the rare origins of this stock invariably received pride of place in advertisements proclaiming its availability.[18] In early 1764, for example, Philip Livingston boasted of "a parcel of Jamaica sugar in hogsheads, ten hogsheads of French powdered sugar, and a parcel of choice French coffee, seven years old."[19] Later that same year, Samuel Hart publicized availability of "the Country Rum, by the hogshead, single refined loaf sugar, by the quantity; French coffee, the best sort, a small Bean and Green colour."[20] Even privateers singled out the non-British provenance of their wares when they had it, such as the cargo being auctioned by New York merchant Isaac Adolphus that included a "parcel of the choice Prize Coffee, by the hogshead, tierce or barrel," which sold in De-cember 1763. In this case it mattered less where the coffee had come from and more that it was not British. Adolphus apparently had secured a partic-ularly large cache of coffee, since his advertisement reappeared with the same phrasing and same price for three months in a row, and what was likely some of the same consignment remained on offer through most of 1764, although as the year progressed, his seven-year coffee turned "eight years old." Adol-phus also included a price that, at fourteen pence a pound, was on par with the cost of British coffee in Philadelphia and even four pence less than prices in Virginia. More importantly, it was at least ten pence below the price of the nonprize French coffee that had been imported through customs and had paid the requisite taxes.[21] Prize coffee was clearly a benefit for sellers and a bargain for buyers.

As coffee became more widely available—and differences in grades of product more commonly understood—a range of practices developed to meet the needs of those who considered themselves connoisseurs. Public auctions, particularly from marine salvage or privateers (as in the case of Adolphus above), offered one option for those seeking better coffee at bargain prices. In these settings, emphasizing provenance was routine. In September 1755, for example, the *Boston Evening-Post* reported that three French vessels sailing to Nantes had sought safety in the port of Plymouth, having been chased there by "the wind blowing very hard." Although the crews had made it safely ashore, they wrecked their boats the following morning when they tried to set sail. Some of the cargo was salvaged, and an auction notice appeared the following week, the authors of which took pains to note that the rescued coffee had come from the French colony Saint Domingue. Auctioneers in Philadelphia used a similar strategy later that year when advertising goods from the captured French prize ship *Snow*. Naval action rather than bad weather had brought the *Snow* to port, as it was captured by a North American privateer just two days after leaving Martinique "laden with sugar, coffee, and cotton." The loss suffered by the *Snow*'s owners was a boon for Philadelphians, who leaped at the chance to buy "French coffee" at significantly under market prices.[22]

Local retailers were at times more successful at these auctions than West Indian importers would have liked. When the Philadelphia-based firm of James & Drinker, owned by Henry Drinker and his partner, Abel James, brought its coffee to market in September 1756, Drinker noted, "We are selling thy coffee at 9 d. and 9½ d. [pence], but it is still very dull sale as the Prize Coffee is so much better and that is sold so low." Over the next several months, the situation only worsened as more cargoes of captured privateers' prize goods arrived in port, so that by October prices had fallen nearly 30 percent. "Coffee has become a prodigious glutt both at New York and here," Drinker complained, "having been sold at 6 d. per lb., good French Coffee . . . has stagnated the Sale . . . not having the least prospect of its rising whilst we have so many privateers to send in prizes."[23] One 1756 notice from Boston even tried to estimate how much coffee British and British colonial privateers had taken from France since the Seven Years' War began, calculating "3,600,000 lbs. of coffee from Martinique, Grenada, Guadeloupe, Saint Lucia, and Saint Vincent; 22,000 lbs. of coffee from Saint Domingue; and in the eastern Atlantic, 680,000 lbs. of coffee from Mauritius (Bourbon)." Unfortunately, the source does not specify how it arrived at these figures but does suggest that the presence of French beans transformed consumption by "a prodigious degree . . . when compared with their former imports from these places."[24]

These accounts are only a few among hundreds of prize and privateer notices that appeared in North American newspapers between 1755 and 1775 whose seizures included coffee. Indeed, privateering had become so lucrative that Philadelphia's officials came to suspect merchants of using it as a ruse to dispose of not just prize goods but also illegal, smuggled wares. Consequently, harbor authorities reasoned that if they could not catch such smuggling at sea, it might be possible to do so at the coffeehouse, where most public auctions took place. The city council drew up detailed instructions for those managing and overseeing public sales, who were often called vendue masters, requiring them to take an oath (or affirmation if they were Quakers) not to "receive or take into possession or dispose of by public sale, or otherwise, any goods, wares, or merchandize, that [they] may have reason to believe have been imported contrary to the rules governing foreign trade." Eleven men oversaw enforcement of these regulations and were empowered to conduct surprise inspections of any invoices and goods they deemed suspicious, and to halt any sales that lacked appropriate documentation. Nevertheless, efforts to circumvent the law continued, and even those sworn to uphold it were not immune from accusation. "The Officers of the Revenue in North America, the Naval Officers particularly are very blameable," wrote the authors of one petition decrying North American collusion with non-British colonies. "All our Colonies," they continued, "would trade independent of the Mother country if they could."[25]

Coffee also frequently featured in sales that offloaded overstocked, out-of-date, or damaged merchandise, or those intended to raise quick cash to pay off debts. In these circumstances, consignments of beans shared the auction block with just about everything from stem to stern of the vessels that had transported them. In 1774, for example, the owners of the ship *Medusa* and brigantine *Seven Brothers* sold the vessels' sails, anchors, and cables "by public Vendue at Mr. Hamilton's Wharf" while their cargoes of "sugars, coffee, and other effects" could be "seen at James's Coffee House" at three o'clock that same afternoon.[26] Likewise, Samuel Howell offered "a few casks and bags of old Coffee" at auction in December 1765.[27] Sometimes coffee even appeared

London Coffee House.

Figure 6. Edward Mumford, "London Coffee House," Library Company of Philadelphia.

for sale alongside the enslaved people who might have contributed to its planting and harvesting, and who were transshipped from the Caribbean along with the products of their forced labor, as evidenced by one image of the Old London Coffee House (Figure 6) and the myriad advertisements that appeared in various sites announcing the availability of people and goods for sale.[28]

Philadelphia's prize auctions became so lucrative that they soon outgrew the Old London Coffee House, resulting in the creation of yet another retailing amalgamation—the vendue store. In some respects, these stores operated like auctions, with licensed vendue masters facilitating the rapid turnover of stock through public sales to the highest bidders. They differed from prize auctions, however, in that they were not restricted to particular days or times stipulated by public notices, and could instead conduct their business depending on the availability of goods. Coffee sold at vendue stores shared advertising and shelf space with all manner of other goods, just as it did in more standard retail operations. Richard Footman, for example, who had run a shop near the wharf district since the 1760s, shifted his business by 1775 to managing a vendue store that sold British manufactures and West

Indian goods. "At Nine O'Clock" on March 15, 1775, he offered "the SALE of 100 pieces Irish linens" as well as other cloth and ribbons, and then five hours later, at "two o'clock precisely," he was accepting bids on "12 quarter casks Lisbon wine, 600 weight of pepper, 20 barrels coffee," and a parcel of iron pots and furniture.[29]

Vendue stores soon broadened their appeal by breaking up lots and offering, for example, coffee in "barrels or smaller quantities," while accepting payments of cash or providing "short-term credit." As peacetime channels of imports and exports declined during periods of interimperial conflict, the increasing quantities of goods arriving through privateering and salvage auctions filled a crucial gap, and brought merchants and vendue masters into ever-closer alignment. Even the Continental Navy opened its own vendue store in Philadelphia in the 1780s, "northward of Willing and Morris' Wharf," to sell "muscovado sugar and coffee . . . by the single barrel" from the increasing number of prize cargoes its ships had seized and brought into port.[30]

A Smuggler's Harvest

The provenance of coffee entering North America was, with good reason, a constant source of concern for port authorities. But by the mid-eighteenth century, the British islands could not produce enough coffee to satisfy both its European and American markets, creating what one merchant called, in a letter to the British Board of Trade, a "Smuggler's Harvest" that merchants considered "worth the risque."[31] While it might be tempting to see smuggling as an example of colonial chafing against commercial restrictions, it was as much about forming reliable partnerships and making money as it was about economic autonomy. North Americans had come to depend on foreign produce so much that one contemporary author suggested "they are no longer British colonies, but Colonies of the Countries with which they trade."[32]

The movement of illicit coffee, of course, is far harder to track than legal trade, but correspondence between colonial agents, governors, excise officers, and British colonial Treasury officials offers some tantalizing glimpses into this clandestine world. In many cases, extralegal traffic was the consequence of three related features of Atlantic colonization: the pressure to fill growing demand, the proximity of colonies of different empires to each other, and their distance from their respective metropoles. British, French, and Dutch possessions were often hostile toward each other to be sure, but their physical closeness—on islands often within sight distance of each other—also pro-duced a kind of regional reliance that at times favored local needs and aspirations above European law.

William Shirley, governor of the Bahamas, provided an example of such cooperation across imperial lines when describing how the Bay of Monte Cristi became a flourishing coffee-smuggling haven during the Seven Years' War. Monte Cristi lay just east of the border between the colo-nies of Spanish Santo Domingo and French Saint Domingue, which shared the large Caribbean island of Hispaniola. Britain, of course, had banned any commerce between its dominions and those of French colonies, among which Saint Domingue was the most prosperous. Spain, however, remained neutral at the outset of the war and so could still legally trade with both na-tions. This created a tempting loophole that merchants could exploit, and Shirley had it on oath that, despite hostilities, "the French of Hispaniola are supplied from the English colonies through the Bay of Monte Cristi" with "provisions, warlike stores, dry goods, and money." Many hands contributed to these covert transactions. To bypass the legal ban on trading with the enemy, ships from North America arranged for their cargoes to be "purchased" by Spanish colonists in Monte Cristi on credit. Spanish colonists then "carried [the cargoes] to the French settlements on their own account" and sold them for French sugar, coffee, and other produce, which they then sold back to North American merchants. These maneuvers created a booming busi-ness, with Shirley estimating that "between 400 to 500 vessels from British colonies have been loaded in Monte Cristi within the last year." The motiva-tions, he thought, were as transparent as the transgressions were brazen. Pro-visions from North America cost less than Saint Domingue merchants would have paid for the same goods from France, while the tropical produce they exchanged would find a ready market in the North American main-land. Spain benefited by being literally and economically in the middle.[33]

Coffee was even more central to interimperial trading in Guadeloupe, where geographic immediacy and the desire to avoid taxes resulted in similar strategies to circumvent the law. British merchants had done a brisk business in Guadeloupean coffee during the British occupation of the island from 1759 to 1763, and some wanted the partnerships established under duress to continue, even if clandestinely, after the island returned to French control. In-deed, a few British West Indian planters even suggested that, while Britain controlled the island, sugar production there should be discouraged, "there being too much competition already" with the English colonies. Instead, they promoted the expansion of the colony's coffee and cocoa farms, "both valuable branches of Trade" and already the principal industries of Guadeloupe's satellite islands, particularly Marie Galant. Metropolitan authorities and merchants, however, soon found out that, while Guadeloupe's farmers were happy to smuggle coffee outside the French Empire, they preferred the markets of Amsterdam and North America to those of London. "Some time after we had been in possession of Guadeloupe," one trader reported, "it was discovered that the coffee produced on the island was chiefly sent to the Island of St. Eustatius," a Dutch West Indian territory, "to be thence shipped to Holland or the mainland instead of England," the mainland referring to North America. Similar patterns appeared in the French West Indian colonies taken over by Britain after the Seven Years' War, with customs officials reporting to Parliament that "the planters of the Ceded Islands, in some of which coffee makes the principal part of their produce," particularly Dominica and Saint Vincent, were continuing to "smuggle to and from the French islands and St. Eustatius."[34]

The physical realities of the Caribbean region—small islands set among broad seas—reinforced the propensity to see the borders between empires as more fungible than what authorities had defined on paper and in law. Although European states claimed various islands as their colonies, planters from different nations could be found setting up their operations on all of them. The rapid development by mid-eighteenth century of the British islands in the Lesser Antilles and Jamaica, for example, had left fewer opportunities there for latecomers from the metropole, who instead established plantations in Dutch Guiana, Danish Saint Croix, and Spanish Puerto Rico to gain their toehold in tropical agriculture.

The same held true in the maritime world; although Parliamentary trade law very specifically defined British produce in terms of its place of production and mandated the use of vessels registered in British colonies to qualify for the significant financial tax credits on goods that remained with the empire, the reality was far less clear-cut. British planters operated in non-British territories, ships' polyglot crews came from many nations, and even the consumers in Britain's colonies had migrated there from many places, not necessarily from Britain or other parts of the British Empire. As a result, colonists often saw imperial lines as permeable, questioning what was and was not British, in other words, and operating accordingly, despite Europe's best efforts to impose metropolitan laws and policies.[35]

It did not help that British merchants and ship captains frequently looked the other way or even colluded with planters to manipulate or circumvent trade restrictions, as they themselves sought to exploit commercial loopholes for their own financial gain. In January 1773, for example, Captain John Ash wrote to his financial backers, the Liverpool firm of Brown & Birch, of the safe arrival of his ship, the *Mary*, in the Caribbean. He also informed the company of a change in plans. Contracted to secure a cargo of wood and mules, Ash had gone first to British Tortola and then to Danish Saint Thomas without success. He sailed next to the Spanish colony of Puerto Rico, where "we loaded what of the wood we could get," he reported, "and sent express to the out bay near us, who returned for answer, that there was very little and so situated that we could not get at it either with ship or boats." At this point, Ash altered his ship's manifest, because while he had been unable to find wood or mules in the quantities his employers sought, he had found "a good deal of coffee." Ash saw advantages in this alternative cargo but also advised Brown & Birch about potential pitfalls. Coffee was among Puerto Rico's principal exports, and Ash was facing significant competition in securing a deal. He described a coast "full of vessels that can supply them [Puerto Rican exporters] on better terms than we," so he suggested offering at least one-third to one-fourth of the purchase price in cash, supplemented by "an assortment of very fine goods." Puerto Rican coffee sellers had demanded full payment in cash or trade, Ash told his employers, refusing to conduct business by accepting samples, or examples of produce from next year's harvests as evidence of the potential for future payment, which was how Ash often operated.[36]

Ash eventually managed to secure a cargo of five thousand pounds of coffee, hiring local labor to ferry it to the *Mary*. He wanted to avoid paying the Spanish export duties, however, because they would have cut into his profits, a maneuver that his Puerto Rican sellers had no qualms about aiding and abetting. Indeed, it was they who had recommended that he transport the goods to his boat while it was anchored offshore rather than in port and under the eye of harbor agents. Ash and his Puerto Rican partners were clearly willing to plot what was, to all intents and purposes, a smuggling operation designed to circumvent the mercantilist trade policies imposed by distant imperial authorities. Ash concluded the transaction within a matter of days, a speed that suggests this was not his first time with such an undertaking, and set sail for Kingston. While Jamaican merchants there were unlikely to buy the coffee, since they produced enough of their own, Ash thought he might be able to resell it at a profit to a ship bound for North America.

All might have gone well, and the *Mary* might have sailed on with its contraband unknown to history, but for some reason Ash changed his plan, opting instead to off-load his cargo in Kingston, where he announced it would be sold publicly and at prices considerably less than the going rate. A local coffee planter did not appreciate Ash's entrepreneurialism and went to the local harbor authorities to report the arrival of unlicensed foreign produce. Within hours, his ship had been seized and its cargo condemned, an event recorded by a minor customs official who clearly had a flair for the dramatic. Under "cover of dark" and aided only by "lantern light," he reported, customs officials had approached the moored vessel. Initially, they found only four casks of coffee, but a more thorough examination revealed that the crew's bunks were full of beans, and notations of this concealment strategy appeared in both the captain's log and first mate's journal. Unfortunately for Ash, these records cast more than a shadow of reasonable doubt on his protestations of innocence. Ultimately, Brown & Birch chose to pay the fine for importing foreign produce rather than forfeit their vessel and in doing so managed to keep Ash out of prison, although their terse communications seemed to exhibit less concern about his welfare than that of their ship.[37]

Only failed smugglers become part of the evidentiary record, of course, but cases like Ash's are an indication of broader, more widespread, and more deeply entrenched pathways of colonial noncompliance through which coffee traveled. Ash and his crew were keenly aware of the coastline configurations of non-British colonies and knew which remote bays offered staging grounds for trade with complicit local partners. Ash recognized that Puerto Rico and Cuba did little to police their shores, although Spanish "ships from the main" sailed by on a regular basis and could intercept foreign vessels like the *Mary*, "so that a ship," he warned, "should at all times be prepared to defend herself." Similarly, Jamaica-based British customs officials were irked, but not surprised, at Ash's efforts. Contraband trade had become commonplace, with Kingston's port authorities noting that "it was publicly known that great quantities of French coffee had been about that time smuggling into this place." In fact, Ash was initially accused of being "employed in this illicit trade" rather than his actual infraction, which was smuggling Spanish goods.

The most convincing evidence that smuggling was widespread and contributing to a growing interisland coffee trade can, however, be seen in the ingenious redesign of the *Mary's* crew quarters that was intended to hide contraband cargo almost in plain sight. Such an undertaking required significant investments of time and materials to execute. It also relied on sufficient carpentry skills to create sophisticated false panels and walls designed to trick the eye of most observers. Surely such effort would not have been undertaken for a single voyage. The *Mary* was a contraband vessel by design, and those who used her were interested in more than the occasional shadow venture. They sought to build and sustain a regular pattern of commerce outside the law.[38] In many ways, this activity portended colonial efforts to trade with multiple partners throughout the western Atlantic that only grew in scale and strength after the American Revolution ended. After 1783, in other words, when North America was no longer under an imperial umbrella, what appears to be rapid inroads into trade with other nations was in fact the continuation of interimperial economies that Ash and his fellow mariners put in motion well before some colonists began agitating for independence.

By the Books: Coffee's Distributors and Redistributors

Regardless of whether it arrived in port legally or otherwise, coffee still had to pass through several sets of hands before it was served as a warm beverage in a consumer's cup. Following the conclusion of the importation process, the beans' next destination would have been one of a variety of retail outlets, which, in the eighteenth century, ranged from public markets and specialty stores to informal shops operating out of homes or other businesses. The number and nature of such enterprises varied by the size of the town and its inhabitants as well as by the amount of money customers had to spend. Coffee's increasing availability throughout these outlets reveals just how quickly buyers incorporated this imported commodity into their daily routine.

While colonial communities did not have coffee shops in the modern sense of the term, beans could be found in a broad array of retail spaces. Public markets, which dealt principally with meats and fresh produce, sold small amounts of coffee from businesses abutting market stalls. Samuel Garrigues, for example, opened a "grocery warehouse" next to Philadelphia's Front Street Market in 1770 for the service of "masters of vessels," where he sold powder, shot, iron castings, and cargo boxes alongside coffee, rum, spirits, and spices. Patrick Wright, meanwhile, opened a confectionary shop near Front Street, where he invited shoppers to refresh themselves with candies, jams, and jellies as well as coffee, tea, and chocolate, either consumed on the premises or purchased to take home. And when Ann Royall visited an outdoor market in Annapolis, Maryland, she saw an "old woman sitting with a table spread with nice bread and butter, veal cutlet, sausages and coffee." Even vendors and storekeepers not selling coffee themselves would sometimes offer a free cup of the beverage to lure customers into their place of business. Peter Anspach, a shopkeeper in Reading, Pennsylvania, was convinced that "sugar Tea Coffee & some other Trifling thing is only the one thing that Brings a Store Customers." One Boston newspaper, describing the joys of continental travel, reprinted a letter that depicted an even more remarkable combination of coffee and service. Within an hour, the author raved, patrons could have their shirt washed, enjoy a "dish of coffee, two slices of bread and butter," and read the session papers, all for the price of one shilling. The article concluded "that many people in these days would be glad of" what the author called this "conveniency," that he envisioned as a model for North American businesses.[39]

Larger amounts of coffee were bought and sold in Philadelphia's wharf and warehouse district, where one visitor noted that "the voice of industry perpetually resounds" and piers boasted "groves of masts" and ships "heaped with commodities of every kind."[40] Dockside merchants sold coffee and sugar by the hogshead, rum and molasses by the barrel, and cotton by the bale. Robert Eliot advertised coffee by the "hundredweight from his warehouse on Market Street," while William Forbes of Walnut Street Wharf sold his "coffee by the bag."[41] Both of these amounts, at 112 and 190 pounds respectively, were well above the means, or needs, of individual households. Instead, shopkeepers and public house operators patronized these sites, and in turn sold coffee in smaller quantities or brewed the beverage for consumption in their establishments. Distinctions between public and private purchasers became blurred, however, in the wholesale/retail operations that gained popularity by the third quarter of the eighteenth century. Like conventional wholesale merchants, these businesses stocked a limited range of goods, but unlike bulk vendors, they offered price and payment options that depended on purchase size, thus attracting customers with more modest needs.[42]

Levi Hollingsworth, a merchant specializing in the sale of wheat, whiskey, and flour, opened just such a wholesale/retail warehouse in Philadelphia beginning in the 1770s, where he sold the tropical imports that Caribbean planters had traded for his grain.[43] His newspaper advertisements retained some of the same language used by wholesalers, with "COCOA in Barrels, Coffee in Hogsheads, and Barrels, and Sugar in ditto," but his store, he claimed, was a place "where merchants or others may be supplied," indicating his willingness to deal in smaller quantities.[44] By 1775, more than half of Hollingsworth's coffee customers were buying less than a barrel at a time, and some purchased as little as a pound or two every few weeks. They paid a premium, however, for their ability to do so, about 12 percent above the bulk rate.[45]

Almost a third of Philadelphia's imported coffee left the city almost as soon as it arrived, traveling overland, by river, and along the coast, to reach backcountry traders in neighboring counties and vendors in smaller coastal towns.[46] John Baynton, for example, resold coffee to small retailers up and down the Delaware River during the 1750s, while Samuel Neave's network included over a hundred retail shopkeepers in Philadelphia and surrounding counties. Most of Neave's sales were on his own account, but some were commission sales on behalf of larger provision merchants, including his cousin and supplier Richard Neave.[47] Philadelphia-based Mifflin & Massey's reexport business extended further still. The two trading partners had entered the coffee business early, and unlike Baynton or Neave, they imported most of their goods directly from the West Indies rather than through wholesale merchants.[48]

Mifflin & Massey dealt with shopkeepers scattered throughout locations in Pennsylvania and Delaware counties, including Kent County, Delaware County, Moyamensing, Germantown, and Newcastle. On average, at least a fifth of its coffee imports were immediately reexported outside of Philadelphia, with 10 percent going to Kent County alone in the three years (1760–1763) covered in their accounts. Like most of its contemporaries, Mifflin & Massey listed both customers' names and their occupations in the records of their transactions, thus providing some sense of its client base. Comparisons with tax records, business directories, and, in the case of other shopkeepers, newspaper advertisements, provide additional details about Mifflin & Massey's coffee business.

Just over a third of the firm's coffee purchases went to other merchants, many of whom operated reexport businesses or stores of their own. Retail shopkeepers bought about 40 percent of the coffee, and the balance of the transactions went in smaller amounts to an array of individual purchasers variously identified by their trades or status. These included sugar boilers, brewers, yeomen, and widows, some of the best evidence of how extensive caffeine dependence was becoming. Transactions varied widely in their size and frequency, with large merchants buying several hundreds or even thousands of pounds of beans at one time. Smaller retail operators were more likely to purchase limited batches on schedules spread out over many months. John Clowes, for example, who managed a store in Port Lewes, Delaware, bought 165 pounds of coffee from Mifflin & Massey in March 1761 followed by another 197 pounds the next month and 358 pounds later that year, in October. Clowes followed a similar pattern of three to four transactions over the following two years.

Mifflin & Massey's records also demonstrated coffee's utility beyond consumption, as both its popularity as a consumer good and its durability encouraged its use as a form of quasi-currency at times. Coffee was used to pay a variety of men in the maritime trades for services rendered to the firm, including shallop pilots employed to ferry coffee and other goods through interior waterways, as well as sea captains who oversaw the reshipment of goods along the Atlantic's western shores. Alexander Miller, a shallop pilot from Newport, Delaware, for example, was paid 56 pounds of coffee in September 1760, while Joseph Oliver of Kent County received 50 pounds the next month for his transportation work. John Ashmead, the captain responsible for outfitting Mifflin & Massey's ships to Jamaica in 1761 and 1762, received 62 pounds of coffee in April 1761 and another 805 pounds two weeks later as partial payment for his services, with similar payments to him from the firm in April, May, and July of the following year.[49]

The frequency and regularity of these exchanges suggest that coffee was commonly used as a salary in kind for those employed in its traffic. Beans were a durable and valuable commodity that could recirculate easily in places where ready money was in short supply. Some of Mifflin & Massey's other clients, including a shoemaker and a goldsmith, may well have been patronizing the firm to fuel their personal drinking habits, but the quantities of coffee they received, as well as the debts such transfers subsequently discharged, suggest that here too the beans functioned as payment for goods or services. The firm's clients may not have been paid for goods with bags of coffee regularly, but advertisements and account books do suggest that importing merchants "spent" some of their stock as if it were money. Those receiving coffee in lieu of cash, meanwhile, would have understood its popularity and value, and been confident of a ready market for their stash of beans.

Newspaper advertisements further confirm coffee's utility as currency. In July 1780, for example, Richard Footman and William Delap posted a small notice in Philadelphia's *Daily Advertiser* promoting the sale of a lot of land on Vine Street, "containing in breadth east and west twenty-two feet, and in depth ninety-six feet, with the privilege of Holme's Alley," for which they would accept payment "in cash or West India produce."[50] Likewise, Mrs. Campbell advertised "several tracts of good land, in Cumberland and Westmoreland counties," in exchange for loan certificates, continental or state money, or "West India goods, or tobacco."[51] Even the canny and parsimonious Benjamin Franklin on one occasion accepted 290 pounds coffee from the Jamaican merchant firm of Minot & Reed for almanacs worth just over £16 and later sold another batch of almanacs, along with eight hundred books with gilt edges and over a thousand sheets of paper, for 590 pounds of coffee.[52]

Bartering, of course, had a long and respected tradition in colonial North America, but several of coffee's characteristics made it ideal for such transactions. Beans could be stored for months, or even years in the right conditions, until a buyer was found, and the commodity remained remarkably stable in price throughout the eighteenth century—much more so, in fact, than either colonial or congressional printed currencies. Coffee's recirculation as a means of exchange throughout the market helps explain why it appears in so many colonial advertisements that focused principally on something else. Such was the case in an advertisement by Joseph Drinker, merchant Henry Drinker's brother, offering an English "SERVANT LAD'S TIME, who has six Years to serve," along with stocks of "sugar, tea, coffee, and dry goods."[53] Meanwhile, when Richard Waln wanted to "lett a PLANTATION, in Germantown, three miles from the city" of Philadelphia, he also noted that he had available "a few hogsheads of Barbados Rum, and sugar, cotton, coffee, Congo and Souchong Teas" at his store on Water Street. Waln offered coffee for sale again the following month in what reads as an addendum to his notice of a reward of ten shillings for information on the whereabouts of his "light brindle Cow [who] went astray."[54] While coffee seems something of an afterthought to these sellers, a casual retail transaction tagged onto a notice posted for a very different reasons, its ubiquity is nonetheless striking.

For Sale by the Pound

Public markets, wholesale warehouses, auctions, and vendue stores were all crucial intermediate stages in coffee's dissemination to colonial consumers, but retail sales—the final step in its journey from port to pot—offer the best evidence for how widely and rapidly North Americans came to depend on the beverage as part of their day-to-day lives. Retail spaces multiplied in both number and kind during these years across all colonies, and they also grew increasingly specialized. Again, Philadelphia, with its especially strong connections to the trade, provides the best example. Along with the wholesale and retail outlets of the city's large merchants, scores of middlemen and middlewomen began to infiltrate the coffee business as grocers, store owners, and shopkeepers. Although their inventories may have overlapped on occasion, distinctions between types of coffee vendors emerged that make it possible to identify to whom they sold the product and what other goods they offered alongside it.

Grocers like Philadelphia's Isaac Gray specialized in the sale of nonperishable foodstuffs. Advertisements for his shop, which stood on Chestnut Street near Strawberry Alley, varied little from the mid-1770s through the early 1780s and featured "coffee, pepper, chocolate, loaf and muscovado sugars, indigo, [and] spices," as well as "Old Madeira, Lisbon, Mountain and Teneriffe wines," and "claret, red port, and sack wine." Occasionally he included "old Jamaica spirit" and brandy as well as imported English beer and locally produced "Philadelphia bottled beer and cidar" in his inventory, and less often he offered small selections of cheese and pickles.[55] The scale and scope of Gray's inventory resembled those of the seventeen other grocers who, according to the city tax lists, operated within the Philadelphia city limits in 1775. Most of these storekeepers were men, but not all. Rebecca Robinson advertised an almost identical stock of coffee and other imported goods in her grocery just two blocks south of Gray's business and "about mid-way between Front and Second Streets."[56] Inventories such as these matched most closely those offered by wholesale merchants, and so these grocers were the branch of the retail sector most directly affected by the rising number of wholesale/retail warehouses and vendue stores, like that of Levi Hollingsworth, and they made their resentment of the wholesalers' encroachment on their clientele known. "Every Merchant is a shopkeeper & every Shopkeeper is a Merchant," read one grocer's lament appearing in print in 1775.[57] But their concerns probably meant little to cost-conscious customers, who were happy to walk a few extra yards or forgo the fancy displays on grocer's shelves for the chance to save money by buying direct from the importer.

Forty-two Philadelphians listed their occupation as store owner or storekeeper in the 1775 tax lists, distinguishing themselves from grocers by their

Figure 7. James Thackara, "A View of the New Market from Second and Shippen Streets, Philadelphia, 1787," Library of Congress. The store to the right advertised wine, tea, brandy, and coffee.

sale of durable goods alongside consumables. George Habacker, for example, stocked coffee, sugars, teas, and spirits along with lumber ("good oak scantling") and "sundry other" dry goods in his store.[58] John Mitchell advertised his coffee stock beside an extensive variety of textiles, including "wide Irish linens" as well as "sheetings, a general assortment of Damasks, diaper and huckback table linen," which he had "determined to keep a constant supply" for sale at "the most reasonable terms."[59] In addition to establishments like those of Habacker and Mitchell, which can perhaps best be described as general stores, some shopkeepers concentrated on a particular commodity or range of goods, such as wine and spirits, books, or dry goods. Yet coffee could be found even in these specialty stores (Figure 7). Beans were sold alongside hair powder, linseed oil, hooks, thimbles, and "a great variety of Queen's ware, of the newest Fashion," as well as silk stockings, worsted breeches, split bone knives and forks, and "an elegant assortment of blue, white and enameled china bowls," in the dry goods stores of Robert Caldwell and William Sitgreaves. And coffee, along with Jamaican spirits, West Indian rum, and Spanish sugars, as well as an assortment of "dry goods, imported in the last vessels from France and St. Eustatia, and among which are a great variety of coarse and fine linens," comprised the stock of Miller & Taylor's store. Even Thomas Anderton, owner of the Philadelphia-based London Book

Store, who dealt principally in primers, prints, gentlemen's desks, and traveling cases, sold coffee from the back of his shop, "by the barrel or smaller quantity."[60]

Coffee's increasing availability at a range of retail outlets is hardly surprising given how much of it was imported into North America from the middle of the eighteenth century onward, but the escalating number of those involved in supporting the spread of this habit is still striking. The number of advertisers selling coffee in various newspapers increased by 25 percent between 1765 and 1770 and by an additional 60 percent by 1775. Even between 1775 and 1780, while a war was being waged, the number of vendors continued to grow apace, particularly notable since nonimportation agreements followed by the cessation of trade with the British West Indies had eliminated the city's chief prerevolutionary sources of coffee supply.

Tracking coffee's sellers on a map of colonial Philadelphia gives even more credence to the commodity's omnipresence. Between 1765 and 1780, scores of grocers and storekeepers advertised coffee for sale in Philadelphia's leading and most popular weekly newspapers, the *Pennsylvania Gazette* and the *Pennsylvania Packet*.[61] Table 1 maps these vendors in five-year intervals between 1765 and 1780. It is based on the notices of ninety-three different shopkeepers, operating in all the city's nine wards, who collectively posted more than a thousand notices of coffee for sale, and similar patterns appear in other ports up and down the North American seaboard.[62]

That the number of advertisements for coffee was rising quickly is one finding, but just as important is what these notices reveal about where it was sold and, by extension, to whom. In 1765 a third of these sellers were based in the High Street, Chestnut, and Walnut Wards, the districts closest to the city's ports and the sites of its largest public markets, which is to be expected. Roughly another third came from the adjacent North, Middle, and South Wards, which contained not only businesses but also some of the city's most affluent residential neighborhoods, which is also not surprising. But coffee consumption was not confined to the commercial arena and the homes of elite citizenry, since the Upper and Lower Delaware Wards, which accounted for a quarter of all coffee retailing venues, were working-class neighborhoods. Among these were sailors, longshoremen, and other occupations affiliated with shipping and maritime trade, who may have developed their taste for coffee abroad. But even Mulberry and Dock Wards, which contained some of the smallest and poorest homes in the city, and housed a significant number of single or widowed women as well as most of Philadelphia's free Black

Table 1. Philadelphia Coffee Vendors by City Ward, 1765–1780

	1765		1770		1775		1780	
Ward	Coffee Vendors	As % of Total Vendors	Coffee Vendors	As % of Total Vendors	Coffee Vendors	As % of Total Vendors	Coffee Vendors	As % of Total Vendors
High Street	3	19%	1	5%	2	6%	5	12%
Chestnut	2	12.5%	2	10%	4	12%	6	14%
Walnut	—	—	1	5%	5	18%	4	10%
North	3	19%	3	15%	3	9%	4	10%
Middle	2	12.5%	1	5%	5	16%	4	10%
South	1	6%	1	5%	2	6%	2	5%
Upper Delaware	1	6%	3	15%	2	6%	2	5%
Mulberry	4	25%	5	25%	3	9%	3	7%
Lower Delaware	—	—	—	—	—	—	3	7%
Dock	—	—	2	10%	2	6%	6	14%
Not Listed/ Unable to tell	—	—	1	5%	4	12%	3	7%
TOTAL	16		20		32		42	

Sources: *Pennsylvania Gazette*, 1765, 1770, 1775, 1780 and *Dunlap's Pennsylvania Packet and General Advertiser*, partial 1770, 1775, 1780.

residents, had at least four stores that sold coffee.[63] So while the principal retail districts and more well-heeled residential neighborhoods dominated the retail market numerically, coffee vendors, and by extension coffee's drinkers, ranged far more broadly throughout the city.[64] In other words, what Table 1 indicates is that anyone who lived in any part of Philadelphia and who wanted to buy coffee could find it within easy walking distance, and that even the city's most marginal citizens did so in large enough numbers to sustain retail operations in their locales. Moreover, these findings are, at best, conservative estimates of coffee's ubiquity and availability, since not all coffee vendors would have advertised in the newspapers. Smaller grocers or store owners, unable or unwilling to spend money on marketing, as well as transient and petty vendors of all sorts, would have been responsible for an even broader distribution and consumption of the beverage.

The creation of this prospering market in coffee had been the work of many hands. William West and his colleagues managed larger and larger

quantities of beans as they arrived from the Caribbean. Mifflin & Massey redistributed these imports to an ever-widening network of retailers within
the city limits and beyond into adjacent towns and boroughs. At the same
time, auctioneers flourished and people like Levi Hollingworth pioneered
new retail models to capitalize on the influx of West Indian goods brought
in by the privateers, who were profiting from the near-constant state of interimperial warfare during the long eighteenth century. Hollingsworth's initiatives enabled coffee, in large and small quantities, to reach a rising number
of coffeehouse and tavern owners, as well as a proliferating range of private
consumers, poor, middling, and rich. All these men and women, in other
words, participated in the creation of a new commodity market in North
America, one that tied the mainland inhabitants inextricably to their West
Indian counterparts. Coffee's customers also wielded increasing influence.
Just as the strategies of coffee purveyors encouraged people to buy, consumer
demand and preferences contributed to developments in ancillary industries, such as those involved in ceramics and metalwares, and resulted in the
refinement and policing of proper behaviors through advice literature and
cookbooks, upon which coffee drinkers relied to learn how best to perform
their habit in accordance with social custom.

CHAPTER 3

Building a Culture of Coffee Consumption

In 1772, Mary Shippen wrote at length to her husband, Joseph, about her stay with family friends in Lancaster, Pennsylvania. Overall the visit was going well, Shippen reported. She thought the home was lovely and the company delightful, if a little provincial, but she took pains to alert her husband to what she considered a serious social gaffe. Her hosts, it seemed, would routinely put out fewer coffee cups than there were guests and remedied the situation by substituting teacups. While Shippen did not point out this faux pas at her friends' gathering, which would have been its own breach of etiquette, it reminded her that half of her own coffee set was cracked or chipped, and she implored Joseph to order replacements in her absence so that she would not have to face the same dilemma. These etiquette rules, of course, were social constructions and circumscribed by a variety of factors, from place and time to class and clique. Shippen may have thought coffee cups and teacups to be mutually exclusive in table settings, but her Lancaster hostess apparently did not. Some families could afford to display "complete" coffee sets, such as those advertised in one London 1769 auction catalogue with no less than forty-three matching pieces. Others were apparently less scrupulous in adhering to the conventions of the parlor and the table, and so they mixed and matched pieces to just make do.[1]

Scholars have suggested many implications for the transition of goods from the exclusive to the everyday. Several studies over the last two decades have argued that the proliferation of formerly expensive objects in late eighteenth-century households produced a common consumer language based on rising living standards that made "'necessaries' of goods that were their fathers' 'decencies' and their grandfathers' 'luxuries.'"[2] Some even suggest that British imports helped unify North American colonists by creating an increasingly standardized way of life that helped bridge other kinds of regional differences.[3] While most of this work on material self-fashioning focuses on durable goods, such as furniture, fabrics, and ceramics, consumables, like coffee, also created common everyday experiences in North America. But while more people had disposable income and used it to express their identities, this was not necessarily a liberating act. Most of coffee's equipment needed to be imported from England, and consequently strengthened connections between the colonies and the metropole both financially and materially.[4]

The range of people drinking coffee grew steadily during the colonial period, especially the rising merchant and artisan classes who saw the drink as a tangible marker of their success as well as a testimony to their cosmopolitan sensibilities. Moreover, the distinctions between coffee types and flavors that accompanied the market's expansion allowed consumers to discriminate by taste. So too did the proliferation of coffee-related wares, which varied greatly in terms of material, size, decoration, and expense, and could thus accommodate customers with different aesthetics and budgets.

Underlying this emerging consumer trend, however, was a persistent reliance on the imperial marketplace. Just as British North American colonists imported their coffee beans, they also imported most of their coffee pots, sugar bowls, cream pitchers, and spoons, whether fashioned of silver, porcelain, or ceramic. British North American colonists, in sum, depended on others to grow, process, and ship their coffee, as well as to produce nearly everything needed to properly prepare and serve it. It was an extensive, and could be an expensive, habit.

Consumers High and Low

Most of North America's coffee poured in through Philadelphia during the eighteenth century, but consumption quickly spread to neighboring colonies, where its adoption can be traced in early journals and letters. One early enthusiast was the wealthy Virginia planter Landon Carter Sr., a prominent member of his state House of Burgesses, and son of the equally notable Robert "King" Carter. Landon Carter maintained an active social life at Sabine Hall, his plantation in Richmond County, about sixty miles north of Williamsburg, where he experimented with the latest trends and styles from both the colonies and abroad. Carter was also a frequent correspondent and an inveterate diarist who recorded, in voluminous detail, everything from his thoughts on government and plantation management to issues about diet, etiquette, entertainment, and other social and domestic affairs. His diaries, which began in 1752 and lasted until he died in 1778 at the age of 68, provide a rare, sustained look into evolving ideas of taste among the colonial upper classes in the second half of the eighteenth century.[5]

Carter first mentioned coffee in November 1763, when he described interactions with a shopkeeper over a transaction that had not gone well. Casks of molasses had arrived at Sabine Hall underweight, Carter complained, while the almonds he received were overpriced: "There is some mistery in this," he recorded. More perplexing still, the store owner had provided him with samples of coffee, chocolate, and ginger, but no prices accompanied them, which led Carter to conclude, "I won't deal with this man any more," because he did not like operating "in such an uncertainty."[6] These problems did not discourage Carter's interest in coffee in general, however, since the following month found him experimenting with his new "spit roaster."[7] This machine would most likely have been some variation of the cylindrical coffee roaster first perfected by the Dutch in the 1670s. A simple device, it included a long, closed body made of tin, about six to eight inches long and five inches in diameter, attached to which was a three- to four-foot iron rod with a wooden handle. Green coffee would have been inserted into the cylinder through a sliding door, and the whole device balanced over a low fire, with one end of the iron rod inserted through the hearth's cooking crane.

Carter offered a typically detailed account of the process to prepare a pound of beans: "Yesterday I had the West India Coffee roasted," he noted, "it was gently turned. Took near 4 hours to roast it well and wasted just 2 ounces which is equal to 1/8 loss."[8] The following month, on New Year's Day 1764, one of Carter's sons asked him for "a supply of coffee by my Overseer as you live where its plenty," whereupon Carter sent him ten pounds of beans.[9] While he again described the ease of coffee roasting, the process doubtless looked very different from the standpoint of those domestics, likely enslaved, who did the work. If the first pound took four hours to roast, the gift to Carter's son might well have taken ten times as long, all the while requiring the watchful attention of those turning the handle until beans reached their desired color and flavor.

Diary entries over the next several years confirm the Virginia plantation owner's enduring interest in coffee and his range of experiences with the beverage. Just two weeks after fulfilling his son's request, for example, Carter suffered a bout of vertigo, a condition that plagued him throughout his lifetime. He complained of nausea and hand tremors, and went on to self-diagnose the problem. "Perhaps my Coffee that I used for breakfast," he mused, "may have contributed a little to it," and for a while he reverted to drinking ginseng tea instead. But at other times Carter embraced what he thought were coffee's medicinal qualities. On one occasion he even prescribed "a decoction of Coffee berries," which he "boiled in a quart of water till it looks green with a little lime water," when Jack, one of the older enslaved men on his estate, felt unwell.[10]

Carter's notions of coffee's impact on the body varied depending on who was drinking it, when, and why, but he nonetheless continued to buy and consume the beverage regularly, serving it to family, friends, and visitors to his plantation. Indeed, the amount of money he spent on coffee was a recurring source of irritation in his diary. Despite being a wealthy man, Carter was notoriously frugal and routinely scrutinized the cost of everything he purchased. His family complained repeatedly about his penny-wise ways, and Carter recorded their grumblings just as assiduously, providing historians with a rich trove of minutely detailed information about coffee consumption among elite Chesapeake Bay colonists, as well as evidence of how much they spent on what had become an everyday part of their diet.

In January 1770, for example, Carter bought sixty pounds of coffee for nineteen pence a pound from Tappahannock merchant John Corrie, an Essex County justice of the peace. Despite Corrie's legal standing, Carter had misgivings about his business practices as a merchant. He thought some of Corrie's products were poor quality or adulterated, while he considered others, like coffee beans, overpriced. Consequently, Carter vowed to limit his caffeine consumption. "I suppose he thought my necessities will compel me to submit to his extravagance," he complained of Corrie, "but he is mistaken. I will go without at any time rather than indulge the least villainous imposition."[11] But Carter's actions tell another story. He first tried unsuccessfully to buy coffee from the British navy before negotiating with his neighbor John Tayloe to borrow twenty pounds of beans from him. Carter then sent Talbot, one of the men he held in bondage at Sabine Hall, "over the River to H[obbes] Hole" to buy molasses and coffee from Archibald McCall, a Scottish storekeeper with whom Carter had done business in the past. Carter's instructions specified that Talbot should purchase up to twenty pounds of coffee if it was available for eighteen pence a pound, but "if cheaper," Talbot should buy up to one hundred pounds of beans.[12]

Virginia newspapers of the time did not yet include coffee among their current price listings, so it is hard to know if Carter was driving a hard bargain or just looking for a fair price. But in port cities like Philadelphia, the conduits coffee came through before reaching places like Hobbes Hole and Sabine Hall, published prices were regularly advertised by mid-century. These records reveal that by 1770, when Carter hoped to find coffee for no more than eighteen pence per pound in the Virginia countryside, he still faced markups resulting from the transportation of coffee from the coast, as Philadelphians at the same time would have been paying between 20 and 25 percent less.[13]

In addition to documenting how colonists bought their coffee and how much they paid, personal papers reveal when colonists drank the beverage and with whom. Coffee had become an expected part of some North Americans' breakfasts by the mid-eighteenth century. William Byrd II, a contemporary of Carter, recorded in 1739 that when he "rose about 6" one December morning, only God took precedence over his morning cup. "I prayed," he noted, "and had coffee."[14] And when Olney Windsor stayed at a boarding house in Alexandria, Virginia, on business, he recalled having coffee for breakfast. But a morning repast offered just the first opportunity for coffee drinking—others would present themselves throughout the day. Colonists frequently imbibed coffee after lunch, during what Landon Carter usually referred to simply as "coffee time."[15] And Claude Blanchard, who traveled as a commissary of the French auxiliary army during the American Revolution, commented on North Americans' penchant for coffee in the late afternoon. "They do not take coffee immediately after dinner," Blanchard noted, "but it is served three or four hours afterwards with tea." The Frenchman also noted that the preparation techniques, and even the taste of the brew, differed from back home. "This coffee is weak and four or five cups of it are not equal to one of ours," he concluded, perhaps betraying a modicum of national pride, "and so they take many of them."[16] Meanwhile, despite a growing awareness from published literature about coffee's tendency to disrupt sleep, colonists often drank it after supper and late into the evening. Returning home very late from a Twelfth Night celebration and drenched from a sudden rain, Carter indulged himself: "[I warmed] my inside well with some Coffee," he recalled, "and a small dose of my domestic elixir," the effects of which he likely found salutary when he rose the following morning and noted "I have slept well."[17]

Wealthy households not only drank and entertained with coffee but also often offered a cup to people beyond their social set of family and friends, including those they employed. John Harrower, for example, a tutor for another

Chesapeake family, described coffee as a regular part of his morning meal in letters he wrote home to his wife.[18] Likewise, Philip Fithian, a tutor at Nomini Hall, a Virginia plantation belonging to Landon's nephew Robert Carter, regularly took coffee with his employers and their children.[19] He drank the beverage in the morning, as part of lunch, for an afternoon refreshment, and before retiring for bed, and his drinking companions would vary based on time and occasion. Robert Carter's wife, for example, arranged for coffee to be served to herself and Fithian one early July evening in 1774, and despite the sweltering heat, they drank it together as they watched the progress of a violent thunderstorm.[20] Fithian also mentioned coffee as part of his breakfast a few weeks later, when he was roused from his bed still suffering the aftereffects of dancing until two in the morning the night before. "We were call'd up to Breakfast at half after eight," he complained, and "We all look'd drugged, pale, & haggard!"[21] His subsequent observation that "here we must drink hot Coffee on our parching stomachs!" may have been in reaction to the queasiness he felt after this raucous evening, but it might also be an acknowledgement of the restorative powers for which coffee was earning a reputation, especially among those recuperating from overindulgence or overexertion.[22] When cooler autumn weather arrived, however, and "a pure, cold northerly wind" blew, he was unreservedly grateful for the "Milk and Hominy at Breakfast" that accompanied his "Coffee & Sage Tea."[23]

During his two years at Nomini Hall, Fithian described drinking coffee no fewer than thirty times in his diary, sure testimony of the beverage's pervasiveness in his daily life. He drank coffee with a local doctor while they compared notes about the health of one of Carter's sons, again with Mr. Carter while discussing philosophy and eclipses, and on another occasion with his employer's family as they all sat around listening to a harmonica recital after dinner.[24] Most of Fithian's accounts of coffee drinking are inconsequential, unremarkable parts of the everyday routines for certain classes. Indeed, it was almost impossible to find a time when coffee was not on offer in Nomini Hall, even well after dark. "We have now entered on the Winter plan," noted Fithian one January evening, "have Coffee just at evening & supper between eight and nine o-Clock."[25] More than once his journal entries recorded that he ended his day just as his employer had begun his—with a cup of coffee and a conversation with his Maker: "[I] drank my Coffee, soon went to my Room, and gave thanks to my divine restorer & laid me down to rest."[26]

Although most eighteenth-century diaries and correspondence come from the affluent and literate classes, other records demonstrate that coffee was limited neither to well-to-do homes nor to elite functions. John Hook's small retail store in Bedford County, Virginia, was about as far as a traveler could get from the grand plantation homes of the Chesapeake. In this hard-scrabble town in the shadow of the Blue Ridge Mountains, enslaved laborers excavated iron ore, mountaineers trapped and skinned animals for the hat trade, and small-time farmers tilled the patchwork of tobacco fields that dot-ted the countryside. Low population densities and far-flung communities meant that Hook's clientele often had to travel miles over rivers and moun-tains to buy what his store had to offer. They arrived with wagons full of pro-duce and hogsheads of tobacco to sell or barter, and returned with the imported goods that provided vicarious links to coastal cities and overseas colonies that most of these backcountry residents would never see in person, but which nonetheless influenced what they ate and drank.

In most respects the daily circumstances of Hook's customers were worlds apart from the likes of Landon Carter or William Byrd, but already by the eighteenth century they shared some tastes. Only sugar and salt, both of which were preservatives as well as seasonings, proved more popular with the store's customers than coffee beans. Hook did not always record the size of each transaction, which makes it difficult to determine what he charged per pound or the amounts bought. Nevertheless, beans invariably showed up among the purchases of these rural customers for whom other foreign tastes, like cinnamon or ginger, often exceeded their means. In fact, it was one of Hook's most reliable sources of revenue from imported goods. While twenty-six of his customers bought coffee in 1771, only ten purchased tea and just six sought chocolate.[27]

Probate records, valuable accounts that documented household furnish-ings when an owner died, provide additional evidence of coffee's increasing popularity and geographic reach by the mid-eighteenth century. The 1764 probate inventory for Joseph Bradford, a small Virginia planter, recorded a coffee pot among his possessions, which also included a table, four chairs, and an iron pot, while the inventory of Samuel Golden Parsons' estate in Binghamton, New York, listed four china coffee cups and saucers and a blue-and-white coffee pot, along with two teapots, three small china bowls, and a miscellany of other service items and crockery.[28] Even as far inland as Detroit, Michigan, specialty dining wares, such as coffee and tea sets, had become commonplace by the 1780s.[29]

Some of the best evidence of the broad diffusion of coffee drinking in co-lonial North America comes from an exhaustive study of more than three hundred probate inventories dating between 1744 and 1810 conducted in the 1990s to aid in the ongoing restoration of Gunston Hall, the home of George Mason. It remains one of the most extensive analyses of mid-eighteenth-century interiors and domestic life ever completed. Mason was a prominent Virginian who served as one of his state's representatives to the Constitutional Convention. He came, of course, from the upper strata of Virginia society, and consequently the inventories that researchers chose to try to reconstruct a faithful representation of Gunston Hall drew more heavily on the estates of Mason's social and economic peers. But the overall sample set includes some examples of households further down the social scale, as is evidenced by the range of materials—and price points—included in the analysis. Nine out of ten inventories mentioned at least one coffee pot, and more than 60 percent of the inventories included either coffee cups or saucers. The range of materials used to construct these pots confirms that coffee appealed to people from varied walks of life. Half were made of copper and a quarter of tin, both less expensive metals, with the balance made either of silver, from wealthier families, or a variety of ceramic types common in households lower down the economic scale.[30]

Although these objects differed in appearance, reflecting changes in style over time, personal preferences, and the decorative possibilities and limitations of the material used, the pervasiveness of pots in so many households offers important insights into the broad-based adoption of coffee drinking. Rare and expensive just a few decades earlier, coffee—while still an imported indulgence—was no longer an exclusive taste limited to the wealthy few. More middling Americans also sought out this commodity to add a touch of refinement to their diets and dining tables. The result was an ever-escalating array of equipment to fuel their habits and deplete their pocketbooks.

The Presentation of Pouring

A host of accessories, from roasters and grinders to sugar bowls, creamers, cups, and saucers, played important supporting roles in the ritual of coffee consumption, but the coffee pot always stood front and center in the service. Most North Americans would have used imported coffee pots through the mid-eighteenth century, and these would have been fashioned from a variety of materials and come in different sizes and price points to meet the needs of coffee consumers, from the unpretentious to the grand. John Hook sold only two coffee pots from his rural Virginia store in 1771, the year his records were most complete, and both were utilitarian pieces that cost their respective buyers less than a few shillings each.[31] But those with more means used much more elaborate and costly coffee services, accompanied by social pressures and attendant costs, which Mary Shippen's urgent letters to her husband at the beginning of this chapter demonstrate, as coffee drinking became associated with increasingly complex culinary rituals.

Coffee pots are easy to distinguish from teapots. The latter were smaller, with seventeenth-century versions often brewing only enough for a single serving.[32] These "bachelor" pots, as they were called, could still be found well into the early nineteenth century, although by the 1750s, teapots in most colonial homes would have held between four and six small servings. By comparison, a standard-sized coffee pot ranged in capacity from twenty-five to forty ounces by the 1760s, or nearly twice the capacity of teapots.[33]

The shape of coffee pots and teapots differed as well to accommodate the preparation techniques required for each beverage. Coffee was usually brewed in a kettle before being transferred to a pot just before serving. The serving vessel was both tall and slender, modeled initially after Turkish ewers, with a spout sufficiently high to avoid accidentally pouring out any sediment. Teapots, by contrast, would have commonly been used to both brew and serve the beverage, and were shorter and rounder to compress the space where the tea leaves steeped in boiling water.[34]

North Americans with elite aspirations and sufficient funds poured their coffee from silver. Philadelphia's Joseph Richardson Sr. is remembered as one of colonial America's leading silversmiths. He had inherited the business when his father died in 1729 and, over the next several decades and later joined by his sons Joseph Jr. and Nathaniel, worked hard to make it one of the most successful such enterprises operating in the city.[35] Their storefront faced Front Street, just opposite the busy docks of Carpenter's Wharf, from which they had a perfect vantage point to watch the steady flow of ships entering and leaving port as the Quaker city grew into a leading mid-Atlantic financial center by the middle decades of the eighteenth century. Philadelphia's developing export trade resulted in rising imports, of course, and that meant more money to spend and, eventually, a broader range of goods to spend it on.

Most of the earliest entries for coffee pots in the Richardson family account books were not for pieces they made or sold. Instead, they were for objects, likely passed down through families, in need of new handles or lids, or brought in so that initials and engraving could be reworked to suit the tastes of a second or third generation of owners. By the 1740s, however, Richardson was also fashioning coffee pots himself. His first silver commission came from James Poolgreen, who provided his own raw materials, bringing Richardson just under sixty ounces of silver in 1747 "to be made into a Coffe Pott tea Pott Creem Pott & weighter to hold six Scarcers [saucers]."[36] Crafting new objects from recycled precious metals was a common practice in both the British colonies and Europe, and one that Richardson performed several times. Few would have been more elaborate, however, than the coffee service that he made—using, in part, reworked family silver—for the 1754 wedding of Sarah Shoemaker to Edward Pennington. The groom was a Quaker merchant and member of the Pennsylvania Provincial Assembly, and his coffee pot befit a man of his social stature. The result (Figure 8) was a classic example of rococo styling, with an acanthus floral finial as well as matching repose-work on the upper half of the body, a cast-shell applique on the lower half of the spout and base, and an exquisitely carved wooden handle.[37]

While Richardson himself handmade many of the coffee pots he sold, he put his apprentices to work on some less complicated pieces. David Harper, who worked under Richardson in the mid-1740s, started with small items like cups, whistles, bells, and casters but soon progressed to larger items, including coffee pots, tea sets bowls, and sugar dishes. In 1747, Harper completed a coffee pot that weighed some thirty ounces. Unfortunately, no detailed description of the object survives, but records show that Harper's services were much less expensive, at only fifteen pence an ounce, than Richardson's charge of two shillings (or twenty-four pence) for each ounce of silver he worked.[38]

Within twenty years of taking over the business, however, demand for such wares had grown sufficiently high that Richardson was regularly importing coffee pots to supplement what he could produce. A 1759 order, for example, included four silver-plated coffee pots, two "Neatly Chasted [chased]" and two "Plain Coffe Pots with stands," and thereafter he sent for both decorated and plain coffee pots every two or three years from his London-based supplier, How & Masterman.[39] The increasing number of coffee wares readily available in his store, and conspicuously present in his clients' homes, reveals just how quickly this once novel practice had become commonplace among and beyond the well-to-do.

If the number of silver coffee pots imported and commissioned in Boston is any indication, coffee's popularity there matched that in Philadelphia.

Figure 8. Joseph Richardson coffee pot made for the Shoemaker-Pennington wedding, 1754, Philadelphia History Museum at the Atwater Kent/Courtesy of Historical Society of Pennsylvania Collection.

According to his ledgers, silversmith Paul Revere worked on only two coffee pots between 1761 and 1767, but he made six more in 1769 and another four in the three years before the American Revolution. By contrast, this well-known revolutionary-era figure crafted two teapots on average by the early 1760s, before relations between the colony and Britain began deteriorating.[40]

This shift from tea to coffee equipment indicated more than a change in dietary habits or political leanings, although both undoubtedly influenced the goods Revere sold and what his customers bought. Investing in high-end coffee equipment was a serious and expensive commitment. In 1773, for example, Revere began working on the silver service that William Paine ordered for his marriage to the silversmith's distant relative, Lois Orne. Paine, who was a doctor in Worcester, gifted his fiancée the full forty-five-piece silver service appropriate to his social and professional standing. Revere's ledger detailed the sumptuousness and elegance of the set, which included a teapot, coffee pot, cream pot, matching tankard, a pair of canns (or smaller mugs), a pair of butter boats, a pair of porringers, a pair of tea tongs, twelve large spoons, eighteen teaspoons, four salt spoons, and a wooden case to hold them all. Each piece bore the Orne arms, crest, or initials, with some larger pieces having all three emblems worked into the silver (Figure 9).[41]

Orne's service was as much, or perhaps more, about presentation than about preparation. The service took £74 of silver to manufacture and needed another £34 to pay for the labor. Admittedly, the set's teapot is stunning, with elaborately engraved sides, a chased spout and lid, and a pineapple finial, but the coffee pot is the service's centerpiece. Revere charged £7.9.4 for "making and engraving" the coffee pot, which was nearly twice the £4.12.0 cost of fabricating its teapot companion, and there was an even more marked distinction in the silver content of the two pieces. The coffee pot took over forty-five ounces of sterling silver to create and, indeed, was the heaviest such piece Revere ever crafted. Orne's teapot, by contrast, used only eighteen ounces of silver, so accordingly it was worth much less.[42]

Most coffee pots were, of course, far less ostentatious than the one that graced the Orne sideboard, although as the eighteenth century progressed and the price of coffee declined while its popularity increased, customers began opting for ever-larger vessels. The coffee pot Richardson made in 1739 for Samuel Blunston held only twenty-five and a half ounces of brewed coffee, but a pot made a decade later by Richardson's apprentice, John Hutton, held over thirty ounces of the beverage. The size of vessels imported from England increased as well.[43] In his earlier orders for silver-plated coffee pots,

Figure 9. Selections from the Paul Revere Paine Wedding Service, 1773, Worcester Museum of Art.

Richardson usually requested thirty-ounce vessels, but by 1760 he routinely wanted pots that could "hold about 3 wine Pints" (or roughly forty fluid ounces), an increase in average capacity by a third in just a few years.[44] Coffee had become a cheaper and more ubiquitous product that could be brewed in larger amounts and served in greater quantities, and the size of coffee pots that Americans sought reflected this change.

Revere and Richardson, along with other leading colonial silversmiths, produced goods that inspired awe and even envy among the guests who were served from them. But these were expensive objects that also at times attracted the attention of thieves, whose felonies were reported in the press. Admittedly a less conventional evidentiary source, advertisements for stolen coffee pots testify not only to the allure of these valuable items to those willing to risk acquiring them illicitly, but also to developments in their styles and fabrication. They confirm, for example, that coffee pots were getting bigger. In January 1760, Jack Tabor Kempe advertised in the *New York Gazette* for "a large silver coffee pot, holding about a quart," or thirty-two ounces, which he believed had been stolen and which bore no identifying marks except a dent on the back part of the lid "where the same had fallen back on the handle in opening." In 1762, Judah Hayes of Providence, Rhode Island, noted in the local press that his one-quart coffee pot had gone missing, while Jonathan Evans of Philadelphia reported in 1765 that parties unknown had made off with his "plain Silver Three Pint [forty-eight fluid ounce] Coffee Pot, made in London, marked with JEH in a cypher and weighing forty ounces." Evans was willing to pay a reward of eight dollars "and no questions asked" for the coffee pot's safe return, but he probably had little likelihood of success since the purloined item's association with coffee would quickly disappear, melted down and refashioned into silver bars or other small objects before reentering the precious metals market under a different guise.[45]

The amount of silver required to fashion the coffee pots and services that earned Richardson and Revere their reputations was pricey, of course, but not all aspirational coffee drinkers were a Paine or Pennington. Silver plating offered one acceptable and more accessible alternative, and from the 1760s on such wares increasingly became the bread-and-butter business of craftsmen like Richardson. Early forms of plating, sometimes referred to as French plating because the process had originated there, involved coating pure silver over a less expensive base metal, such as copper or tin. The progressive application of up to fifty or sixty leaves, or coating, determined both the thickness of the silver and the durability of the veneer. Although French plating was still expensive in terms of time and labor, the savings in materials were considerable and allowed buyers to purchase the appearance of luxury at roughly a third of the expense.[46] In addition to his sterling silver items, Richardson also routinely ordered silver-plated wares from London that appealed to a clientele wanting to capture elegance and sophistication in their coffee consumption but unable to afford pure metal. Richardson bought four silver-plated coffee pots in 1759, for example, four more in 1760, and another nine the year after that. All told, he imported twenty-four silver-plated coffee pots between 1759 and 1774.[47]

The market expanded further still, and dramatically so, after the introduction of Sheffield plate in 1743. This process, which bonded silver to copper alloyed with a small amount of zinc and lead, differed from French plate in that the metals were fused before the objects were fashioned. The resulting laminate could thus be worked in much the same way as solid silver, which had important implications for both form and function. French plate only covered an object's exterior, but Sheffield-style plating coated the insides of coffee wares, particularly pots and other serving items. As a result, it was increasingly difficult to tell solid silver from what just looked like it, something advertisers quickly exploited.[48] Charles Dutens, a London jeweler who had relocated to Philadelphia, promised buyers that his silver plate wares had been "just imported from London" and were "choice, and gilded within," while Benjamin Booth of New York promised that all of his wares had been "made in a new and elegant taste."[49] These phrases conveyed critical information to potential buyers. A gilded interior meant that the pretense of silver went beyond what could be seen by a casual observer. People at table or in the drawing room could hold an item, turn it over, look inside it, and even drink its contents and still not know whether it was silver or not. Likewise, assurances of adherence to the latest fashions appealed to those who worried that their choices would expose them as either cheap or déclassé.

Choices about embellishment likewise figured into a coffee pot's bottom-line cost. Chased pots were more expensive than those left plain, as were pots ordered with matching stands or decorative details such as scalloped edges or pearl-work beading.[50] And just as coffee pots grew larger during the eighteenth century, so too did they become more sophisticated and ornate. The one Joseph Richardson made for his wife Mary in 1748 was an elongated pear shape, known as a single-bellied pot, with a low-domed lid and a circular base. Modest ornamentation decorated the lower half and top of the spout, and counterbalanced its carved wooden handle, while a swirled finial topped the pot's lid.[51] Some six years later, the coffee pot he manufactured for the Shoemaker-Pennington wedding featured far more dramatic embellishments. The body of the pot had a more pronounced bell, and its top half, base, and spout were covered in repoussé decoration, including an elaborate floral finial, as well as cast and chased leaves around both the neck and foot. Even the silver plate orders Richardson filled became more elaborate and detailed over time, such as the "silver Single Belleyed Coffee Pot to hold 3 wine Pints" that he ordered from London in 1770. This item boasted a "Gadround Border Round the lid & foot," referring to its gadroon decorative edgings formed by inverted flutings, such as those visible on the coffee and milk pots of the Revere silver set in Figure 9.[52] So, while customers were apparently willing to economize on materials by choosing plate over sterling, they still wanted to impress their guests by their service's presentation.

Exporters eagerly accommodated such requests, and garnered praise and encouragement from Richardson for their efforts. He commonly encouraged his manufacturers to "Let them be Good work & of the Newest fashion" and, of course, wanted to purchase the items "on the Lowest Terms." Not all of his transactions went smoothly, however, such as in December 1760 when he informed his London connections that a recent order of silver-plated wares was "Not Altogether Agreable to My Mind." He complained that the consignment had been "So ill Packt that Several of the Coffe Potts were Brused," indicating that they had arrived dented and scraped.[53] Following up on the incident a few months later, Richardson reiterated his request for only "the Best work & well finished" and noted that two of the chased coffee pots sent as replacements had sprung leaks near the upper socket, a problem that he suggested diplomatically had "I Suppose Escaped your Notice."[54] All of these examples provide glimpses, if admittedly small ones, into the homes and habits of British colonists as they worked to keep up with their European counterparts and worried that a wrong design, a gauche table setting, or an ill-chosen menu might expose them as socially inferior. Distinctions quickly appeared in the colonial market as well, evident in the increasing range of wares available at different budgets. As the price of coffee was falling through the eighteenth century, making it accessible to more buyers, what constituted drinking "properly" became more expansive and expensive.

A Bevy of Options

Coffee drinkers from the middling and poorer classes certainly enjoyed their brew but likely could afford neither the silver nor the silver-plate services described above. Fortunately for them, coffee pots also came in a range of baser metals and ceramic forms, again predominantly imported, which better suited their needs. Eighteenth-century advertisements document the broad range of materials priced to accommodate these cohorts of colonial coffee consumers, targeting both middle-class customers and those further down the social scale. John Neide's "copper and tin coffee pots," for example, appealed to those on tighter budgets, ranging in price from one pound to one pound ten shillings for the former and less than four shillings for the latter.[55]

Coffee pots could also be fashioned in Chinese export porcelain, ceramic, or stoneware, and examples of each of these also appear in period newspapers.

Wallace, Davidson & Johnson stocked stoneware alongside their copper pots, for example, advertising "1 Doz. Setts Yellow Coffee Potts" in 1771. A few months later they imported a dozen ceramic coffee pots wrought in ivory "Queens Ware."[56] While only a small percentage of colonists could aspire to a silver-laden sideboard like the Orne family, these earthenwares, salt-glazed stonewares, and soft- and hard-paste porcelains—many richly decorated—ensured that options for displaying personal taste and a sense of style were available to all ranks of coffee consumers.[57]

The least expensive coffee pots, and the only ones that were routinely produced in the colonies, were made of a fired clay pottery known as redware. It used locally available clay that, with little refinement, could be shaped and baked into a characteristic buff or red-brown color, then decorated with a syrupy coating of clay and water, known as slip, in a contrasting color—hence redware was also known as slipware. This coating was applied in simple trailed designs, crudely executed flowers and leaves, to which occasionally the owner's initials appeared as an additional embellishment. To keep costs low, potters often used just enough lead glaze to make the vessels impermeable to liquid, so flat dishes often received glazing only on their upper surfaces, while hollow wares, such as coffee pots, were coated on their interior but only partially on the exterior. No glaze, for example, appears on the underside of the foot or the lid in Figure 10. Redware, which was cheap, utilitarian, and easy to fashion from the abundance of brick clay found along the Atlantic coast, was one of the few ceramics never governed by British trade legislation. Such serving pieces were common in the kitchens of private homes, and in shops and public venues throughout rural and urban North America. William Grant, for example, sold coffee pots and "earthen wares" from his store on Water Street in Philadelphia, while Benjamin Harbeson advertised his "general assortment" of earthenware, including "white, brown, and red ware," for sale by the crate just a few blocks away.[58]

Except for slipware, however, few ceramics were produced in North America before the nineteenth century. It was not for lack of trying. Philadelphia was an important center for earthenware production in the eighteenth century, and some craftsmen tried expanding into stoneware and porcelain, most notably the American China Factory, which opened in 1770. The joint venture of Gousse Bonnin, born in Britain, and George Anthony Morris, of Philadelphia, the American China Factory succeeded in perfecting a technique to produce porcelain domestically, a real challenge to Chinese exports.[59] It was ultimately unable to compete in volume and price, however, particularly

Figure 10. Redware slip-decorated coffee pot, 1740–1800, Winterthur Museum and Library.

after the repeal of the Townshend Duties during the same year the factory opened resulted in a glut of pent-up English wares flooding the colonial market at record low prices. The factory closed its doors just two years after it launched, and for the remainder of the eighteenth century colonists, and subsequently citizens of the fledgling United States, continued to rely heavily on imported wares for their ceramic needs.[60]

In large part, this was because British imports were so inexpensive, particularly after two major advances in the 1740s transformed ceramic production.

The first of these was the technique of salt-glazing stoneware that made it both less porous and more durable than earthenware. These stoneware vessels most often had a pale grey cast and, like redware, could be decorated with simple abstract or naturalistic designs etched into the clay that would later be filled with cobalt blue pigmenting or, in rarer cases, deep purple or brown hues. By the 1750s some manufacturers favored elaborate molds that, when pressed into the sides of uncured vessels, created intricately decorated panels. These wares were fired at very high temperatures to vitrify the surface, which gave it a glassy sheen. When the kiln reached its maximum heat, salt was added, and it vaporized to create a thin clear glaze that coated but did not obscure the underlying decoration.[61]

A second innovation was the introduction of the cream-colored earthenware that would become the most common kind of coffee service in North America. Initially known simply as creamware, it was more popularly advertised as queensware after Josiah Wedgwood successfully completed his first commission for Queen Charlotte in the summer of 1765. Creamware employed a lead-based glaze rather than the earlier tin glazes, and this improved a pot's ability to withstand significant fluctuations in temperature, making it ideal for serving coffee and other hot beverages.[62] Despite Wedgwood's associations with royalty, basic creamware was cheap enough for importers to advertise it for sale by the hogshead or crate, which made it popular with tavern and coffeehouse keepers who found it sturdy enough for everyday use, and cheap and easy to replace when chipped or broken.[63] Several dozen "Queens China coffee cups," as well as saucers, milk pots, and teapots, for example, appeared in the 1771 inventory of Anthony Hay, who kept the Raleigh Tavern in Williamsburg, Virginia.[64] Other establishments, meanwhile, employed a variety of service wares, perhaps catering to the range of different classes among their patrons. When James Shields died in 1751, for example, the inventory of his English Coffee House in York County, Virginia, included some creamware cups and saucers, but also listed "China saucers and cups" and "earthen bowls and coffee pots."[65]

Creamware, meanwhile, was also not just cream colored. Several variations, including tortoiseshell ware and agateware, sported bright colors and bold designs. For tortoiseshell ware, colored metallic oxides would be sponged onto unglazed ceramics before firing, to create mottled blues, greens, and browns; for agateware, unfired vessels were dipped into the same sorts of colors to cause a swirled effect. Both styles became immensely popular in colonial North America. When Nicolas Flood, an apothecary from Richmond

County, died in 1776, his inventory listed coffee cups in "Aget," while Philadelphia shopkeeper Joseph Stansbury's lengthy list of stock included "tea pots, sugar dishes, cream pots, coffee pots, sauce boats," and "tea and coffee pots, handled and plain" among his "extensive assortment of all kinds of earthen wares, and plain and enameled Queens ware, and blue and white stone ware; tortoise-shell, black and colli-flowered Dutch stone and Bristol Stone Wares."[66]

"Colli-flowered" Dutch stoneware was another popular form of coffee pot design, where images of fruits and vegetables, including corn, cabbages, pineapples, and cauliflowers, decorated the outer surfaces of the vessels (Figure 11). While such whimsical coffee and tea wares were popular in colonial America through the third quarter of the eighteenth century, a 1767 letter from Josiah Wedgwood to his partner Thomas Bentley indicates that such "green and gold" items were already out of fashion in England. Wedgwood told his fellow English potter that he was glad to see these outdated goods shipped to America, since he was gaining both income and much-needed space in his warehouses.[67] This was, for ceramic exporters, a winning combination. Colonists so relied on imports to support their growing caffeine habits that they were at times less choosy about what options were available.

Porcelain, particularly Chinese export porcelain, was the most desirable ceramic coffee pot of all. It was formed from a hard-paste clay that had to be fired to extremely high temperatures, making it almost glass-like. It ranked as the finest of the eighteenth-century ceramics and, like silver, could only be afforded by the wealthiest buyers. The composition of porcelain's raw materials and the manufacturing process remained carefully guarded secrets in China until the third quarter of the eighteenth century, so consequently all hard-paste ceramics found in North America before the American Revolution would have been imported, and at no little expense, from the Jingdezhen region of China.[68] Soft-paste porcelain, also known as bone china, was England's answer to Chinese export, but this product was fired at lower temperatures than hard paste, so it did not achieve the latter's much-sought-after translucence. On the other hand, bone china was much more available and affordable, produced by several British ceramics manufacturers in Worcester, Derby, and Liverpool by the 1740s.[69] It took almost a generation for this ceramic form to make its way into North American homes, but it appeared with increasing frequency in import records and shopkeepers' notices by the 1780s. Bone china cost less than hard-paste porcelain, and was more desirable than creamware or salt-glazed ware, but it was still a British

Figure 11. Cauliflower coffee pot from Staffordshire, England, 1762–1780, Winterthur Museum and Library. Museum purchase with funds provided by the Henry Francis du Pont Collectors Circle, Mr. Charles O. Wood, III, Mrs. W. L. Lyons Brown, and the Special Fund for Collections Objects.

export. These ceramics, all of them imported, thus maintained the tradition of culinary dependence that defined the performance of colonial and early American coffee-drinking rituals.

Setting a Proper Table

If coffee pots were the centerpieces of consumer performance, several other objects played important supporting roles. Today's concept of a coffee service as a carefully matched pattern on a full range of vessel and dish shapes would have been a rare sight in North America and even in Europe until well into the eighteenth century. Instead, most coffee drinkers built their sets over time and combined items made from a variety of materials. In the 1710s an elegant set might include a coffee pot of unglazed red stoneware combined with a European-style milk jug and sugar bowl, as well as mismatched bowls, cups, or saucers. As ceramic prices fell and disposable incomes grew, however, matched sets of coffee wares became more common. New York shopkeeper James Rivington advertised "coffee sets of blue and white china," which he assured buyers had "landed this day from Canton," while Baltimore merchant William Matthews offered "a quantity of China Ware for sale" consisting primarily of "breakfast, tea, and coffee sets" just two years later.[70] European visitors remarked on North Americans' interest in proper deportment. "They are very choice in cups and vases for holding tea and coffee," Claude Blanchard noted, and "breakfast is an important affair with them." These concerns for proper etiquette, he suggested, extended beyond urban centers and well into the backcountry.[71] Historian Lorena Walsh, in her study of Chesapeake Bay merchants and shopkeepers, estimated that up to a third of urban residents and at least a quarter of rural residents regularly drank coffee, for which they would have accumulated the appropriate accoutrements, a habit that Blanchard implied was widespread. "This use of tea and coffee is universal in America," he concluded, and "the people who live in the country tilling the ground and driving their oxen take it as well as the inhabitants of the city."[72]

Just as coffee pots, milk jugs, and sugar bowls appeared at table in a range of shapes, sizes, and materials, coffee cups were far from uniform. These items usually had handles, whereas teacups were more often handleless Chinese-style bowls, but this was not a hard and fast rule, and as the century wore on, distinctions between the two kinds of cups became even more blurred. Merchants and manufacturers preferred ordering handleless cups since they packed more easily and broke less often during shipment, although they usually had both styles available to their customers. Philadelphia store owner William Simmonds, for example, advertised his stock of "large breakfast and coffee cups and saucers, with and without handles."[73] And as coffee consumption increased, etiquette protocols developed around how the drink should be served at different times of day and in various settings, as well as the requisite equipage. Large mugs, often called "breakfast cups," would have been appropriate for morning coffee drinking, such as the "12 Breakfast Cups 12 Saucer B & W China" that were part of an order that George Washington purchased for Mount Vernon in 1762.[74] Smaller cups, known as "afternoon size," were thought more appropriate both for later meals and for the repasts between lunch and dinner. Rawleigh Downman of Virginia, for example, stipulated that the "Sett" of crockery he ordered include two dozen china teacups and saucers, and another two dozen coffee cups "of the afternoon size."[75]

Ceramic cups and saucers, especially chinaware, were by their very nature fragile. Accidents happened, saucers chipped, and cups smashed to the floor. The slender ceramic sides of fragile creamware and chinaware were also susceptible to cracking if hot coffee was poured into them when they were cold. Such wear and tear, for example, had reduced Downman's service of two dozen teacups and coffee cups each to a mere four teacups, four coffee cups and eight saucers in less than ten years.[76] Not surprisingly then, merchants had to keep restocking their shelves with new shipments of imported cups and saucers as their customers went back for replacements time and time again.[77] Shipments from family and friends abroad could also fill gaps in family cupboards. Writing from London in 1758, the year he first published *The Way to Wealth*, Benjamin Franklin wrote a letter to his wife Deborah to detail some purchases he was sending her way. His gifts included carpets, blankets, and printed cotton, as well as a beer jug, which Franklin described as "like a fat lady Dame, clean & tidy, with a neat blue & white calico gown on, good natured and lovely" which put him in mind of "somebody."[78] Packed within the jar, nestled in "the best crystal salt" for added protection, were coffee cups decorated with figures, which Franklin urged Deborah to examine "with your spectacles on; they will bear examining."[79] Some buyers, like Franklin, may have found perfect matches, but many more likely found wares that were close enough.

Conventions about the etiquette of consumption varied, of course, for diverse constituencies who were motivated by factors that ranged from frugality to expediency and beyond. Charles Lanman's description of the southern hospitality he received traveling through the Allegheny Mountains, for example, might have surprised Mary Shippen, whose letters opened this chapter, given her stance against the interchangeability of coffee cups and tea-cups. Richard Bushman included descriptions of Lanman's travels in his book *Refinement of America*. Lanman spent the night with strangers on a rural estate of over one thousand acres, where "it was evident the family was well enough off to live in some comfort." He thought their furnishings rudi-mentary, however, and their behavior coarse, where "wooden benches," he noted, "were used in the place of chairs [and] one iron spoon answered for the whole family." Service at table was a far cry from what had become the standards for refinement and propriety expected by people like the Ship-pens, and even Lanman himself. The latter was taken aback when the host family's "mother added the sugar ... to the coffee with her fingers, and tasted each cup before sending it round to ascertain if it was right."[80] While the visitor expressed his gratitude to his hosts at the end of his stay, he apparently thought their lifestyle and manners uncultured. They knew what to serve a guest but, from his perspective, not how to do so properly. Strip away the cultural biases that separated the expectations of an upper-middle-class northern traveler from the realities of the domestic arrange-ments in a rural, southern family's home, however, and both hosts and guests drank the same hot beverage that would have been served in whatever private residence, tavern, or inn Lanman visited across the length and breadth of North America.

Vignettes such as these also challenge one of the most tenacious assump-tions about the eighteenth-century consumption of caffeinated beverages—that men drank coffee while women preferred tea. The historian David Shields, for example, has posited what he terms the "homosociality of cof-fee," and James Walvin proposes that coffee consumption was limited by the "male exclusivity of the coffee-house," which "seemed to exclude women" while "attracting men of all social classes."[81] Along the same lines, T. H. Breen has suggested that "polite women" used tea drinking as a civilizing ritual they "devised to lure gentlemen away from tavern society," but he omits any men-tion of female coffee drinking.[82] This mischaracterization lies in part with the erroneous conflation of coffeehouses and coffee drinking. Admittedly, few women patronized colonial coffeehouses, but as the accounts above suggest, coffeehouses were neither the only nor even the principal places where people drank coffee.

Coffee featured prominently in the menus of various venues as they vied for the patronage of both men and women. For those looking to leave the hustle and bustle of city life behind, for example, Robert Mullan operated a private tavern "at that beautiful situated house lately occupied by his good father Thomas Mullan" just west of Philadelphia, in nearby Manayunk, where he intended to keep "the best genuine liquors" and provide "dinners, suppers, coffees &c. at the shortest notice" to those who wanted to enjoy eating out during the summer season in this bucolic setting on the banks of the Schuylkill River. Robert boasted of the location's "great number of very elegant views, consisting of the grandest palaces, gardens, cities, public and private buildings," where "Ladies and Gentlemen . . . may agreeably amuse themselves while their coffee is preparing."[83] Daniel Grant opened a similar establishment in 1769 to the south of Philadelphia, in Moyamensing. His advertisements described gardens and summer houses "with the most pleasant situations" in which, he boasted, his patrons "may depend on his keeping the best tea, chocolate, and coffee" available "for breakfast or for afternoon."[84] In 1773 Grant sold his business to Thomas Mushett, who continued to offer "tea and coffee, morning and evening," for "ladies and gentlemen that ride for the benefit of air."[85]

Some public house advertisements not only implied that women drank coffee, but also hinted that coffee, as well as tea, offered women an alternative to the consumption of alcohol. In 1773, for example, when Mullen moved his business from his father's former home to "a house called Vaux Hall, on the agreeable banks of the Passyunk" south of Philadelphia, he reassured his clients that "they may depend on finding good Eating, and the best of Liquors, with Coffee, Tea &c. for the Ladies."[86] Daniel Ducheman offered a similar option during the year's colder months. He proposed "keeping coffee, tea of the best," and "oysters, beef-a-la-mode, beef-stakes" for consumption by "such ladies and gentlemen as please to favor us with their custom for the winter season." Located further from the city, in Lebanon, Pennsylvania, Ducheman offered complimentary transportation "with two good chaises, and a sleigh with horses" to his establishment "when the weather permits of snow."[87] The sleigh rides were offered at no extra charge, although Ducheman had no doubt factored the costs into his other catering services. Such pleasure gardens offer ample evidence of the public consumption of coffee by both women and men, as well as the increasingly elaborate array of customs that had developed around the beverage and could be enjoyed by that segment of the population who could afford such leisure repasts.

* * *

Poor and rich, women and men, urban residents and backcountry farmers—
they all drank coffee, with their letters, diaries, and ledgers reflecting the
variety of material circumstances in which they did so. Men of means or connections, like Carter or Fithian, enjoyed their coffee made from freshly
roasted and newly ground beans, served to them in imported Chinese porcelain cups as they relaxed on columned porticos or in elegant drawing
rooms. But shopkeepers' notices for "blue and white Tea and Coffee cups . . .
very low" or "coffee pots and sauce pans tinned" attest to coffee's popularity
well beyond the parlors of the well-heeled.[88] Small-town farmers, tradesmen,
and store owners would more often have drunk their coffee from miscellaneous ceramic or earthenware mugs. A few of these middling men and women
might have owned matched sets of dishes, but their cupboards were just as
likely to contain a hodgepodge of different styles and designs, most of which
were imported, that they either inherited from others or bought up in bits
and pieces over years when cash was available.

Travelers to inns, taverns, and coffeehouses also used ceramic creamware,
some of it likely chipped and cracked from frequent use, and they enjoyed a
brew that had been prepared with the establishments' equipment and kept
warm on their front hearths in tall, undecorated copper or tin vessels. Some
drinkers flavored their coffee with milk, sugar, or honey, while others preferred more exotic additives, such as cinnamon, cloves, or anise, or even clarifying agents ranging from butter or oil to fish skins. Coffee drinking, in
other words, was not a monolithic experience in the eighteenth century any
more than it is today. It had become a multifaceted convention whose popularity sparked a proliferation of refinements in equipment, and modifications
in preparation and presentation that catered to personal tastes, employed different materials, and accommodated purses large and small. Coffee drinking also reinforced colonials' dependence on Europe, however, to shape both
the tools of this trade and the etiquette that surrounded it. Taken together
these developments created a performance of consumption that would
come to characterize coffee drinking, a habit that colonists would find hard
to break, even as tensions with Britain escalated.

CHAPTER 4

Coffee and Conflict During
the American Revolution

In September 1765, several Philadelphia merchants and store owners met at the Old London Coffee House to discuss their response to the Stamp Act (1765), the latest in a series of parliamentary laws intended to tighten control over colonial commerce. Residents had been uneasy since the legislation passed in March but had grown more agitated over the ensuing months. Their discontent reached a crescendo when details about John Hughes's appointment as royal stamp collector for the city became public. What began as political discourse quickly escalated into threats against Hughes's person and property, leaving him so terrified that he would later recall how he had fortified himself "with Fire-Arms" and resolved "to stand a Siege," aided by several of his friends who patrolled the neighborhood "between my house and the Coffee House."[1]

It was no coincidence that coffeehouses became the staging grounds for those protesting British trade legislation in the 1760s and 1770s. The Sugar Act (1764), while named for the most profitable West Indian export, also taxed foreign coffee imported into any British colony as well as any British coffee sold outside the empire.[2] The Currency Act, passed a few months later, required that colonists pay these duties in hard currency. The impact of the Stamp Act went further still, taxing everything from the bills of lading and invoices used to conduct daily business to the newspapers that were essential instruments of commerce. Additionally, the Townshend Duties (1767) and Tea Act (1773) were levied to increase imperial revenue. Such legislation, in other words, sought to impose more thorough, systematic regulations and concomitant tariffs on what colonists could buy or sell, as well as how they paid for their purchases, and even how they conducted the formalities of their business dealings. Clearly these tactics were designed not only to raise revenue but also to strengthen the empire's grip over its territories and ensure colonial dependence.

The central role of the Old London Coffee House in this vignette offers a powerful example of how such establishments functioned in revolutionary North America. They had become the hubs of political and commercial affairs in the colonies, as they had earlier in England's port cities, earning their place as some of the most important social and financial institutions of the British Atlantic world. Often located near docks and wharves, along interior waterways, or at the intersection of principal roads, coffeehouses would become transformed in the years leading up to the American Revolution into the epicenters of agitation and action over issues about empire and independence. The men and women who patronized these spaces sought to assert their own ideas about how commerce should be conducted, including what goods could come ashore and under what terms.

Both coffeehouses and coffee figured prominently in these debates. Merchants and local leaders used coffeehouses, for example, to stage ritual destruction of hated pieces of legislation, as well as to post the nonimportation agreements that they drafted and circulated. Coffeehouses also became the meeting places of the Committees of Correspondence, which sought to ensure intercolonial alliances against Great Britain, and the Committees of Compliance, which enforced the embargoes that colonists hoped would compel Parliament to reconsider its approach to colonial governance. Coffeehouses, in other words, were places where theories of colonial politics found their expression in the daily lives and material conditions of the citizenry. The "deliberations of Congress are impenetrable secrets," John Adams mused from Philadelphia in 1775, "but the conversations of the city, and the chat of the coffee house, are free, and open."[3]

Coffee itself also became politically charged. Once British West Indian commodities were added to colonial embargoes, scarcities became commonplace and North Americans found themselves without ready access to what had become a daily ritual. Some communities tried to control escalating costs by regulating prices. When this proved ineffective, colonists took matters into their own hands, targeting stores and warehouses to demand lower prices for coffee and, in the most extreme cases, even confiscate and redistribute coffee sold at what they felt were usurious rates. Tea has been held up as an emblem of colonial abstention, but this chapter demonstrates that coffee remained both desired and demanded—and also played a pivotal role in colonial protests.

Coffeehouse Proprietors

The proliferation of coffeehouses in colonial North America gives some indication of both their potential profitability and their attractiveness as business ventures. Nonetheless, many coffeehouse proprietors, like the coffee planters on whose produce their enterprises depended, hedged their bets by supplementing their incomes through second occupations, especially when they were just getting started. Some stayed in related fields and operated taverns or inns, while others worked in the print trade, as book or newspaper publishers or sellers. Both were complementary professions. The former offered experience in catering to a diverse clientele, which frequently sought much more than a cup of coffee, while the latter would have been well acquainted with governmental and economic affairs of the day as they pertained to patrons' local communities, their colonies, and beyond to the empire and the wider world.[4] This experience became all the more relevant when coffeehouses began to host the political discussions and committee actions that accompanied increasing tensions with Britain.

William Bradford's well-documented career offers important insights into the life of a colonial coffeehouse proprietor by the mid-eighteenth century, as well as into how business blended with politics. Bradford had published a newspaper and run a bookstore on Blackhorse Alley, less than two blocks from Philadelphia's central wharves, for just over a decade when, in 1754, he moved even closer to the waterfront and established the Old London Coffee House at the corner of Front and Market Streets. Almost immediately, Bradford sought a liquor license, and his application not only discloses the clientele he hoped to attract, but also what he considered the place of coffee drinking in his coffeehouse. He had been "advised to keep a Coffee House for the benefit of merchants and traders," he told the licensing authorities, but as "some people may at times be desirous to be furnished with other liquors besides coffee," he intimated that "your petitioner apprehends it is necessary to have the Governor's license" to serve alcohol.[5] Bradford expanded the remit of his establishment further still a few years later when he set up a maritime insurance company.

Bradford also encouraged his patrons to use the Old London as a post office. While a fair number of those who did so were ship captains, maritime
travelers, shopkeepers, or merchants, others also availed themselves of a facility that was in essence functioning as a community center. A 1776 notice
in the *Pennsylvania Journal* included a list of the "Letters now in the Coffeehouse, which the owners are desired to call for," among which were letters to
carpenters, ministers, painters, blacksmiths, weavers, widows, and others
who comprised a veritable cross section of the city's professional and working-
class communities.[6]

In some ways coffeehouses operated like taverns and inns. They offered
comparable menus that featured a range of food and beverages, including coffee of course, but also, almost invariably, beer, wine, and spirits. Only one
Philadelphia coffeehouse tried to operate without a stocked bar during the
eighteenth century, and it failed in less than a year.[7] Such licenses added to
the cost of doing business, but those who thought to skirt these regulations
could face stiff penalties, as Sarah James, proprietor of James's Coffee House,
learned when she was fined £5 for selling wine without a license.[8]

Coffeehouses also functioned, like other hostelries, as places of refreshment and relaxation. The account book that John Shuebart kept during his
tenure at Carpenter's Coffeehouse in Philadelphia in the late 1730s described
the typical fare. Some customers, like Samuel Griffin and John Hyatt, ordered
coffee at three or four pence a cup, but glasses of beer were available for one
shilling and Madeira wine for two shillings for those who preferred something stronger. Carpenter's also offered an extensive food menu, with a range
of choices to satisfy a customer's appetite. Robert Spice bought his modest dinner, which included coffee, for two shillings and seven pence, while the sump-
tuous supper that John Van Horn enjoyed included punch and wine, and cost
him nine shillings and eleven pence, nearly four times what Spice had paid.[9]

But if public houses shared some business practices, they differed in
others. Taverns and inns offered entertainment and nourishment for their
own communities, to be sure, but a sizeable number of their clientele were
travelers. They rented rooms to visitors by the day or week, and provided pasturage and stabling for horses and other livestock. Taverns and inns also
usually offered greater flexibility for dining and refreshments, including coffee served "for breakfast, or afternoon" and indeed, "all hours of the day," to
be enjoyed by "Ladies and Gentlemen." Through the eighteenth century,
the range of services available at taverns and inns grew ever more complex.
Establishments located near key byways or river stops, for example, became

involved in the fast-developing transportation business, arranging ticketing and serving as stops for ferries and stagecoaches.[10]

Coffeehouses, by contrast, catered to those who lived, and especially worked, locally. They were, of course, the venues patronized by those involved in maritime affairs and transoceanic travel, but coffeehouses integrated these operatives from outside the community with the local businesses with whom they dealt. Inside coffeehouses could be found informal banks, international currency exchanges, and commercial insurance providers, while their buildings hosted meetings and, as already noted, held extensive newspaper libraries and served as community post offices. Edward Shippen, a lawyer and later judge, commented on the distinction between taverns and coffeehouses in a letter he wrote to his son shortly after the latter moved to Philadelphia in 1754. Only "crowned heads and other great men who have their incomes sleeping and waking," Shippen warned, wasted time at taverns "in pursuit of pleasure," games, or gambling. Serious businessmen, on the other hand, met at the local coffeehouse.[11] Information, people, and goods from around the world passed daily through the doors of North America's coffeehouses, and such establishments were firmly situated at the heart of their communities' social and commercial spheres rather than oriented toward those on their way elsewhere.

In this sense, coffeehouses thus became conduits of trade, nodes of business activity, and sites of debate and discussion, where interactions between individuals and parties were made more conducive by the amiable surroundings, and more palatable by the omnipresent liquid refreshments that lubricated exchanges and sealed deals. A key ingredient in all of this, of course, was the font of information amassed in the coffeehouses and trafficked there. People seeking family and friends asked that word be left at the coffeehouses. Others looking to find stolen property or reclaim wandering livestock did the same. Ship captains regularly contracted with coffeehouses to help find parties seeking freight, passage, or a berth, while being warned against harboring fugitives via notices displayed on the establishments' walls by those who sought the apprehension of servants fleeing indenture or enslaved people seeking freedom.

Coffeehouses even functioned as de facto employment brokers by facilitating connections between people in need of work and those looking to hire help. A prospective employer whose 1769 advertisement sought "a servant man, either white or black, who can wait on a gentleman's family" requested that prospective applicants leave word at the local coffeehouse. Likewise, the owner of the ship *Myrtilla* advised those seeking employment to "present themselves at Bradford's coffeehouse" for consideration. Coffeehouses could, at times, be proving grounds for those advertising their skills. When James Bryon offered his services "to any gentleman" seeking a chef "who understands cookery in all its branches," he could assure prospective employers of his qualifications for such work by noting that he "lately attended at Robert's Coffee-house to the satisfaction of all the gentlemen that frequented it."[12] Even military authorities capitalized on coffeehouses' reputations as wellsprings of information and used their facilities for their own purposes. For example, when Lieutenant Edward Trelawney sought the whereabouts of "James Renolds and Archibald Weathers, soldiers in his majesty's regiment" who had absconded from their posts, he asked anyone with information to leave word at Roberts' Coffee-house, promising a forty-shilling reward and "reasonable expenses" if the two were apprehended.[13]

Setting the Stage for Protest

By the 1760s, Bradford's Old London was Philadelphia's undisputed leading coffeehouse. Centrally located in the business district and adjacent to the waterfront, it was a landmark well known and often frequented by local residents and travelers alike. In most years it hosted more public gatherings and auctions than any other institution in the city, and in some years almost as many such events as all the others combined.[14] It was thus the ideal location for merchants and storekeepers to meet when they began formulating their responses to new, and largely resented, commercial legislation.

No doubt some demonstrators would have been drawn to Bradford's establishment because he himself so openly challenged the expansion of British financial policies, using both his newspaper and his coffeehouse as vehicles to decry laws that he thought undermined local autonomy. The Stamp Act, passed in March 1765, had raised the cost of printing by taxing every pamphlet and periodical, as well as "every advertisement to be contained in any gazette, newspaper, or other paper."[15] In response, that October, Bradford issued a four-page edition of his *Pennsylvania Journal* to try to galvanize public opposition and force Parliament to reconsider its actions. The paper's articles were bordered in black, to signify mourning, while a death's head skull and crossbones and Masonic symbols adorned the masthead. The language accompanying this arresting visual imagery was just as inflammatory and spoke directly to fears about colonial dependence. Bradford announced the immediate suspension of his newspaper because he found himself "unable to bear the Burthen" of the new taxes and "thought it expedient to stop a while, in order to deliberate, whether any Methods can be found to elude the Chains forged for us and escape the unsupportable Slavery." He also incorporated a running commentary at the right margin of the front page, bidding "Adieu, Adieu to the Liberty of the Press," and on the back page, next to a woodcut image of a coffin, he included an epitaph that mourned "the last Remains of The Pennsylvania Journal, Which departed this Life, the 31st of October, 1765, Of a Stamp in her Vitals."[16]

Bradford's support of the colonial cause was as conspicuous at his coffeehouse as it was in print. Two months after he announced the "death" of his newspaper, another city paper, the *Pennsylvania Gazette*, reported that "a piece of Parchment with a Stamp on it" had been "purified by Fire at the [Old London] Coffee House, in the presence of a full Company who all expressed their satisfaction therewith."[17] Bradford also oversaw the burning of "effigies of Alexander Wedderburn, Esq. [Britain's Lord High Chancellor] and of Thomas Hutchinson, Governor of Massachusetts Bay" that December, which, one Philadelphia resident noted in his diary, had been "exposed for several hours in a cart" before being "hung on a gallows erected near the Coffee House," set alight "by electric fire and consumed to ashe about six o'clock in the evening."[18]

In addition to encouraging local anti-British activism, Bradford took care to keep up with developments in neighboring colonies and pass on any such information to the residents of Philadelphia that he thought were sympathetic to the patriot cause. When a "company of armed men" in January 1766 boarded a vessel docked in New York's harbor, for example, seized its stamped paper, and "with some tar barrels and other combustibles" made "a bonfire of them," Bradford secured a remnant from the conflagration (Figure 12) and promptly posted it on his coffeehouse walls for all his patrons to see.[19]

Several like-minded groups and individuals followed Bradford's lead. Merchants and other businessmen routinely met at the coffeehouse to decide on the imposition of trade embargoes as a strategy for reversing parliamentary policies, and Bradford posted each of the nonimportation agreements they devised on the Old London's walls. Residents would consequently know not only what goods might be politically suspect, but also which local merchants and businessmen had backed this effort by signing their names to the documents, and by extension, of course, the identities of those who had chosen to refrain.[20]

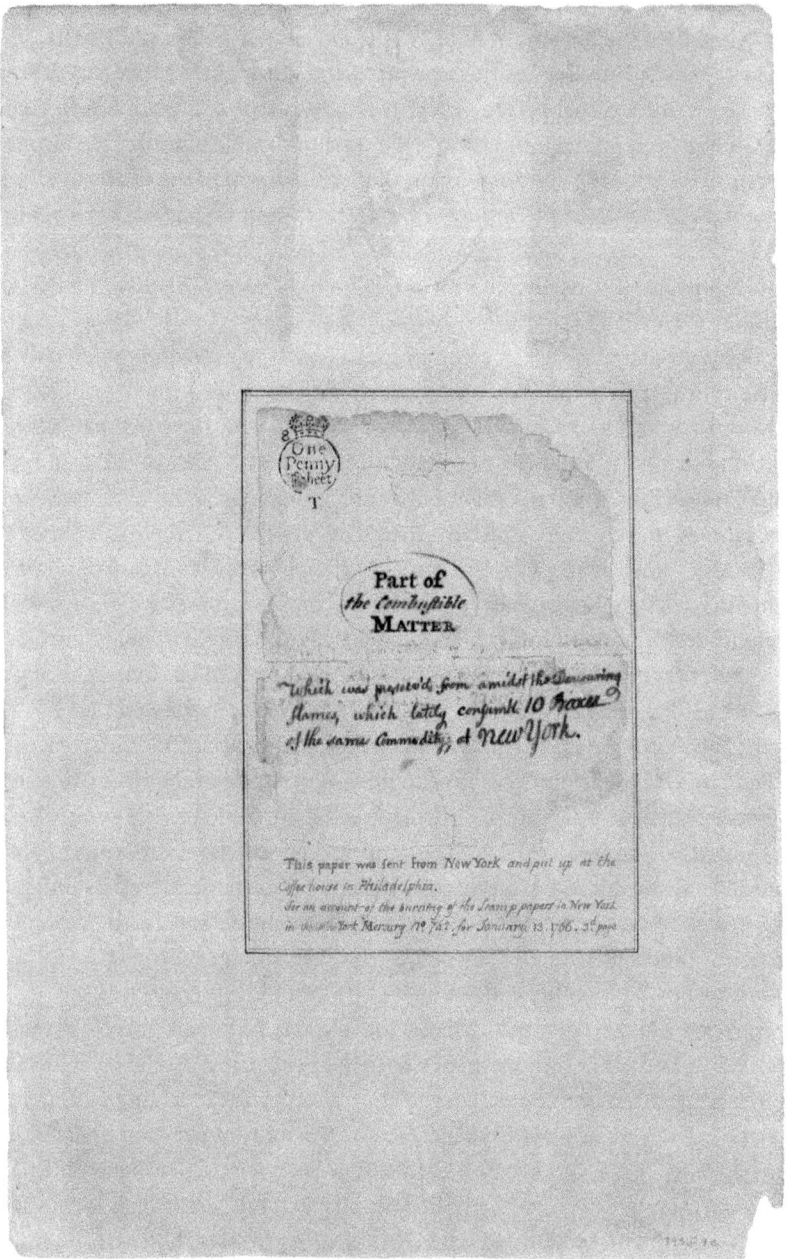

One Penny Sheet
T

Part of
the Combustible
MATTER

which was preserv'd from amidst the devouring flames, which lately consum'd 10 Boxes of the same Commodity, at New York.

This paper was sent from New York and put up at the Coffee house in Philadelphia.
See an account of the burning of the Stamp'd papers in New York in the New York Mercury N° 742 for January 13, 1766, 3d page.

Figure 12. Paper remnant from New York Stamp Act Protest, Library Company of Philadelphia. The caption reads, "This paper was sent from New York and put up at the Coffee house in Philadelphia."

The Stamp Act was repealed less than three months after Bradford published his special issue of the *Pennsylvania Journal*, but the role of coffeehouses in colonial protest would continue for the next several years. When
Philadelphia imposed a second embargo in March 1769 in reaction to the Townshend Duties, the city organized a Committee of Compliance to ensure that
importers and storeowners observed the terms of embargo once it went into
effect, and the Old London hosted the committee's meetings to review
possible infractions. That June, for example, the ship *Sharp* arrived from
Glasgow, and for two weeks its captain negotiated with the committee to
sell its cargo. When he failed to acquire the necessary permissions, the master sought to circumvent the committee's authority rather than leave port
without the profits he expected from the voyage. Nearly all the city's traders had signed the embargo that had been forwarded to London and was
now preventing the *Sharp*'s master from doing business. But the prospect of
financial gain proved sufficiently enticing for some to put profit ahead of
patriotism, and the ship's captain "succeeded in discharging some of the
goods by night." Within weeks, however, those merchants who had bought
goods from the *Sharp* had been identified and forced to sign a public apology that was posted in the coffeehouse as a warning against other would-be
dissenters.[21]

In 1774 the coffeehouse would again serve the purpose of community
policing when it became the regular meeting place of Philadelphia's Committee of Observation and Inspection. This local body had been formed to
enforce the dictates of the "Continental Association," a ban passed by the
Continental Congress in response to the Coercive Acts, punitive laws intended to punish the citizens of Boston after its notorious tea party.[22] The
parameters of the Continental Association were broad. It was the first embargo to embrace all thirteen colonies, and it called for an immediate ban
on British tea as well as a ban, beginning on December 1, 1774, on importing
or consuming any goods from Britain, Ireland, and the British West Indies.
This was the action that made coffee as undesirable as tea. The agreement
also threatened an export ban on any products from the thirteen North
American colonies to Britain, Ireland, or the West Indies if the Coercive
Acts were not repealed.

To ensure compliance, boards were to be formed in every "county, city, and
town," and given the authority to examine all imports that arrived after the
ban went into effect, as well as every export, consignment, reshipment, or sale
of goods completed after September 10 of the following year. In addition to

challenging parliamentary authority, the goal was to demonstrate how much the empire had come to rely on its North American colonies, rather than the other way around. To apply pressure effectively, however, the ban needed to be complete, and to underscore this point, the authors of the Continental Association went on to vilify any merchants who failed to adhere to the embargo. They deemed the noncompliers "enemies of American liberty," and encouraged their communities to withhold all social and commercial contact until such time as the offenders admitted their culpability and undertook to honor the ban on trade.[23]

Philadelphia's merchant community had established their Committee of Inspection and Observation by November 1774. It began as a large assembly of over sixty members but, to monitor affairs more efficiently, soon divided up into subcommittees responsible for the oversight of importers and retailers in Philadelphia's various districts and neighborhoods. Ten men were assigned to District 4, the most densely populated section of the city's waterfront, reaching "from the North side of Chestnut Street to the North side of Spruce Street," and the surviving minutes from their meetings at Bradford's coffeehouse reveal the frequency of the meetings, the kinds of goods they examined, and the penalties imposed on those who defied the committee's mandates.

The committee was a busy group, meeting at least once a week for the first six months after its formation, and hearing dozens of cases ranging from ship captains arguing that the cargo they sought to sell was essential or had originated somewhere other than Britain, to store- and shopkeepers offering assurances that they had purchased their stock of English goods before the embargo took effect. The entry for each hearing included the date it occurred and name of the petitioner, as well as a description of the commodities involved and the case's ultimate resolution. When noncompliance could be established, the goods that had thus been deemed contraband were immediately scheduled for sale "at the Coffee house by Vendue."[24]

The terms of the Continental Association ensured that coffee would become embroiled in public debates about commerce and consumption. Early embargoes focused on trade goods from England, Ireland, and Scotland, but when terms expanded to include the British West Indies, coffee came under fire.[25] Before this development, coffee had enjoyed a few brief months as a suitable patriotic replacement for tea. In May 1774, for example, just after Lord Dunmore dissolved Virginia's House of Assembly for speaking out against British policies, Robert Carter and his wife attended a dinner at the home of

Colonel John Turburville along with their children and their tutor, Philip Fithian. "Politiks were the topic" at the gathering, Fithian recalled, "and indeed the Gentlemen seemed warm." After covering local matters, there followed a spirited discussion of the Coercive Acts and subsequent closure of Boston's harbor. But ending the evening on a less contentious note, they "had a Grand and Agreeable Walk through the Garden" as well as light refreshment, although even this stage of the proceedings became colored with revolutionary fervor. "[We] drank Coffee at 4," Fithian recounted, with the guests opting for this beverage because "they are now too patriotic to use tea."[26] John Adams likewise recalled arriving at an inn after a grueling horseback ride across the Massachusetts backcountry and asking the proprietress "is it lawfull for a weary Traveller to refresh himself with a Dish of Tea, providing it has been honestly smuggled, or paid no Duties?" But the lady of the house, Mrs. Huston, replied, "No sir . . . we have renounced all Tea in this Place . . . but [I can] make you Coffee." Thereafter Adams claimed to "have drank Coffee every Afternoon since," which he seemed to have considered something of a sacrifice, since he concluded by noting that he had "borne it very well."[27]

But by 1775, coffee had become a political liability in its own right. In a letter that October to James Warren, a paymaster in the Continental Army, Adams warned about the dangers of imported goods and wondered whether North America could dispense entirely with foreign trade. He thought that basic foodstuffs, such as meat, cheese, butter, and grain, were produced in sufficient amounts locally, as were wood and iron. Clothing, Adams conceded, was more difficult, but he speculated that hands currently employed in making goods for export might profitably be turned to flax and wool. It was the less essential foods that Adams recognized would prove the trickiest. "We must at first indeed Sacrifice Some of our Appetites for Coffee, Wine, Punch, sugar, Molasses," he averred, "and our Dress would not be So elegant—Silks and Velvets and Lace must be dispensed with," and he concluded, in the ringing tones of a patriot, "But these are Trifles in a Contest for Liberty."[28] By 1777, Adams became even more emphatic, singling out coffee for special attention. Writing to his wife, he expressed his "hope the Females will leave off their Attachment to Coffee. I assure you, the best Families in this Place have left off in a great Measure the Use of West India Goods. We must bring ourselves to live upon the Produce of our own Country. What would I give for some of your Cyder? Milk has become the Breakfast of many of the wealthiest and genteelest Families here."[29] This raised a real concern for Abigail

Adams, who frequently purchased coffee for her own use and when entertaining guests. After Henry Lee and another acquaintance visited Abigail in July 1775, she wrote to her husband that "I persuaded them to stay and take coffee with me, and he was as unreserved and social as if we had been old acquaintances."[30] She also drank the beverage when calling on friends and on people of both sexes whom she had just met. When she visited "Mrs. Morgan, who keeps at Major Mifflins" in December 1775, for example, she "had the pleasure of drinking coffee with the Dr. and his Lady, the Major and his Lady and a Mr. and Mrs. Smith from New York" as well as "many others who were strangers to me," and she concluded, "I was very politely entertaind."[31] It was not that Abigail Adams did not recognize the economic pressure that embargoes could bring to bear, but that coffee had become so ingrained in her daily experience that it was difficult to consider life without it. She was not the only one to worry. As trade disruptions narrowed supply chains, more and more colonists had to forgo their caffeine habits, and the extent that some went to find their fix indicates just how much coffee had become part of people's routines.

Pent-up demand led some less scrupulous retailers to try their luck, and coffee regularly appeared before the Committee of Compliance for authentication. Two of the first cases considered in Philadelphia were that of Aenias Urquhart, whose seventeen barrels of coffee, along with eleven hogsheads of molasses and four bags of pimento, were deemed suspect, and the merchant firm of Meredith & Clymer, which tried to sell two parcels of coffee totaling nine tierces, a cask size between a barrel and a hogshead, and thirty-one barrels of beans. The committee quickly deemed both contraband and earmarked them for auction in mid-December of 1774.[32] The largest quantity of coffee to go before the committee came from shopkeeper Thomas Harper, who had over 25,000 pounds of beans, between what he owned in his own name and what he was holding on consignment. Initially the committee voted to store Harper's goods, as they did when unable to ascertain unequivocally the dates of importation. But by January 1775, more documentation had come to light and Harper's entire lot was reclassified for sale at auction.[33] Like the Continental Congress before it, the Committee of Inspection and Observation punished offenders not only by imposing economic sanctions but also by publishing the identities of the offenders in local newspapers along with an assessment of the harmful impact of their selfish and unpatriotic actions. Mordecai Levy was labeled disrespectful to the "General Congress and all Military men who defend our liberties," for example, while

John Bergum's trafficking in British goods was condemned as "derogatory to the liberties of this country."[34]

The Impact of War

By late 1775, the question was not whether coffee should be consumed, but whether it could be found at all, and if so, at what price. In 1772, Jamaica had sent nearly as much coffee to North America as to England, but after the intercolonial embargo of 1774 went into effect, trade dropped precipitously. The following year, Abigail Adams was lamenting that the scarcities of imports meant that "we shall very soon have no coffee nor pepper here," which obviously would have had implications not only for availability but also for cost.[35]

As in past periods of scarcity, privateering stepped into the breach. In June 1776, for example, the *Connecticut Gazette* reported that the brigantine *Cabot* had captured the British ship *True Blue* en route from Jamaica to Lancaster, England. Its cargo included twenty tierces of coffee containing roughly 6,000 pounds of beans. A few months later, Connecticut's *Norwich Packet* advertised the arrival of "a Prize Brig, having a large Quantity of Coffee on Board taken by the privateer sloop *Trumball*."[36] Whereas privateer notices had served to buttress public opinion of British naval capability during the Seven Years' War, they acted as rallying cries for revolution by the early 1770s, and were quickly reprinted from city to city to boost local support of colonial military efforts. News of the *True Blue's* capture, which had first been reported in Norwich, was reprinted in the New York, Salem (Massachusetts), and Philadelphia papers within a matter of days.[37]

Occasionally such privateering engagements even hinted at the possibility of political alliance. In August 1776, for example, the *Swan*, a North American sloop, captured the *Amiable Reine* as it left Martinique and subsequently brought the vessel before the Admiralty Court in New York. The *Amiable Reine* was captained by a French colonial, Paul Berthelot, but since it was sailing under a British registration, the court condemned its cargo of coffee, sugar, tobacco, and indigo, and consigned it to auction. Berthelot claimed to have filed for restitution, but Andrew Frazer, Britain's ambassador to Paris, suspected something untoward since, he reported, many French colonists secretly sympathized with North American interests and "surrendered" their ships voluntarily.[38]

Almost all privateer notices followed a specific formula, noting the names of both the privateer vessel and the captured vessel as well as those of their masters. In most cases they included ports of embarkation and disembarkation, and some announcements even estimated the number of days since the vessel had set sail, this last bit of information no doubt to reassure readers that the engagement had occurred in international waters as required by admiralty law. Reports about privateering engagements also frequently featured itemized lists of cargo, including not only the types of goods on board, but also their specific quantities down to the hogshead, bag, or tierce. In April 1776, for example, Adams wrote to her husband that she had traveled to Cohasset, Massachusetts, thirty miles from Boston, to see "a Snow from the Grenades, laiden with 354 puncheons of W.I. Rum, 43 Barrels of Sugar, 12,500 weight coffee, a valuable prize." The detail of such information smacks as much of the practical as the patriotic. It blends seamlessly the language of martial prowess and economic opportunity, providing detailed information about the availability of increasingly scarce commodities within a context of naval triumph over an adversary. Abigail Adams's letters to her husband indicate that she actively tracked reports about privateer engagements and that she cultivated a network of sources who were likewise keeping abreast of the movement of goods. "We have a Rumour of Admiral Hopkings being engaged with a Number of Ships and tenders off Road island," Adams wrote in April 1776, and "are anxious to know the event. Be so good as to send me a List of the vessels which sail with Hopkings, their Names, Weight of Mettal and Number of Men," she concluded, as well as "all the News you know &c."[39]

Privateering, however, could not hope to make up for all the losses from legal trade regardless of how successful it was, and the ramifications of coffee's declining availability necessarily affected cost. During the decade before the American Revolution, the price of beans had been remarkably stable throughout the colonies, retailing for between fourteen and eighteen pence a pound, whether sold in Philadelphia, New London (Connecticut), Providence (Rhode Island), or Savannah (Georgia). Even after 1767, when prices of domestic products like flour and wheat fluctuated wildly, those for West Indian staples remained relatively constant. Indeed, in Providence, the price of coffee had dropped by 12 percent between 1770 and 1771.[40]

But by March 1776, as British troops were evacuating Boston, the cost of both coffee and sugar rose precipitously, followed soon after by other West Indian commodities, both in real prices and in cost relative to the value of domestic products. Locally produced flour, for example, sold at 23 percent more in the mid-1770s than before the war began, but West Indian goods skyrocketed an astronomical 1,300 percent. This increase was in large part due to wild fluctuations in the value of colonial paper currency, but even when the costs are converted to currency, goods like coffee still reached some 380 percent above their prewar levels as the result of what economic historian Thomas Doerflinger has termed "the shock of war."[41]

Such dramatic price spikes resulted from scarcities, both real and manufactured, as colonists increasingly turned to commodities as a place to invest their money in lieu of paper money. Some merchants bought up nonperishable commodities, while others withheld existing stock, either to protect their savings or inflate prices. One prominent Philadelphia merchant, for example, sent $2,000 in continental currency to a trading partner with directions to purchase "any article, except flour, and those goods which are liable to perish in a short time by laying by."[42] Perishability was a critical consideration in these transactions, and merchants understood that coffee, as well as sugar and rum, could be stored for long periods if warehoused properly. The same durability that encouraged the use of coffee as a kind of currency in the decades before revolution, in other words, made it equally attractive as an investment in the 1770s, allowing merchants some flexibility to withhold or release goods for sale when increasing demand and decreasing supply ensured greater profits.

Customers, however, experienced the same deprivation whether shortages were genuine or created, and some were quick to broadcast allegations of pecuniary self-interest in the local press. In March 1776, for example, a long letter to the editor in the *Pennsylvania Evening Post* included the following sardonic couplet targeting hoarders: "But patriots differ, some may shed their blood, We STORE our COFFEE for the public good."[43] Those who hoarded goods for private profit, the author contended, were practicing a fiscal duplicity, the effects of which were as egregious as Parliament's efforts to restrict open commerce, and he singled out "those who have lately purchased up all the coffee and other articles now in use among us" as particularly grievous offenders. Importers and retailers who "hid" their stock to create a false illusion of scarcity were "monsters and monopolizers" whom the author condemned as "enemies of the country."[44] A correspondent to the *Connecticut Courant* drew the comparison more starkly still, asserting that price gouging was "the very thing we are fighting against" on the battlefield.[45] To give up coffee because doing so furthered a larger political aim was one thing. To

be unable to buy it at reasonable prices because greedy vendors sought to capitalize on colonists' caffeine dependence was something else entirely.

Historian T. H. Breen and others have suggested that one measure of patriotism was the willingness of colonists to pay—or not pay—higher prices
for certain goods during the boycotts of 1765 to 1774. Coffee price-fixing
would also emerge during the Revolutionary War as a tool of local control as
early as 1776, when colonies initiated their first efforts aimed at combatting
hoarding. That March, for example, the New York Committee of Correspondence published a list of recommended prices for certain goods in several
local newspapers and threatened to "expose such person or persons, by Name,
to Public View, where they will no doubt Experience the just Punishment of
mercenary Demerit" if they failed to comply. Soon thereafter, the *Pennsylvania Ledger* reported that "several persons whose names are returned to this
committee (but from tenderness to their families are not published [in the
newspaper])" had, "by collecting great quantities of and exacting exorbitant
prices for" tropical goods, produced a "public calamity most barbarous and
oppressive." To combat the situation, Philadelphia's Committee of Correspondence, like its New York counterpart, instituted a plan to publish a list of
recommended prices, promising swift and public retribution for those who
charged more. Coffee featured prominently on both lists.[46]

The mandate of New England's intercolonial committee was even more
detailed than those of New York and Philadelphia. In December 1776, representatives from Connecticut, New Hampshire, and Rhode Island met to discuss "the now most intollerable exorbitant Price of every necessary and
Convenient Article of Life."[47] The committee proposed price caps for a range
of goods, both agricultural and manufactured, that included coffee. Although
the restrictions covered both domestic and foreign goods, it was the latter imports that posed particular problems according to the committee, since they
were routinely marked up 500 or 600 percent above their former market value,
in what committee members characterized as nothing other than shameless
opportunism.[48]

The goods that city councils chose to monitor reveal as much about colonial desires and dietary habits as they do about greed, however. Wheat and
pork were obvious essentials, but the inclusion of coffee among the "necessary and convenient articles of life," particularly for what one city council
characterized as the "poor and middling ranks of life," provides clear evidence
that, at the brink of this war for independence, a previous generation's luxuries had become their sons' and daughters' staples. A consensus emerged over

the committees' recommended price for coffee in the three regions, which they set quite close to the prewar price, averaging about fourteen pence per pound. Some places established even lower benchmarks, with Connecticut limiting the price of coffee to ten pence per pound, while Rhode Island and Boston mandated that the cost of even "good coffee" could not "exceed 1s. 4d. [or sixteen pence] by the single lb. in any part of the state."[49]

Setting a value, however, was not the same as enforcing it, and when Boston's price legislation took effect that March, Abigail Adams lamented that "the late act will annihilate every article we have, unless they will punish the Breaches of it," before describing how "this person has nothing and the other has nothing, no Coffee, no Sugar, no flax, no wool." Rather than sell at mandated prices, in other words, merchants and shopkeepers simply withheld their goods from the market entirely. Two weeks later, Adams again complained that "many articles are not to be had tho at ever so great a price" and went on to blame the actions of greedy men for manufactured scarcities. "Sugar, Molasses, Rum, cotton wool, Coffee, chocolate," she concluded, "cannot all be consumed. Yet there are none, or next to none to be sold, perhaps you may procure a pound at a time, but no more." Three days later she managed to find some of the goods she desired, although not at the prices she wanted. Instead of the recommended price of thirteen pence per pound, coffee was selling in Boston for more than twice that amount, while other goods were still not available for any amount of money. "There is a general cry against the Merchants, against monopilizers &c. who tis said have created a partial Scarcity," Adams reported. "That a Scarcity prevails of every article not only of Luxery, but even the necessaries of life is a certain fact. Every thing bears an exorbitant price."[50]

Not all vendors acted like the Boston merchants that Abigail Adams accused of hoarding and overcharging, of course. The account books of storekeepers elsewhere indicate some effectiveness of policing and self-policing. John Drinker of Philadelphia, for example, was selling coffee to William Redmond in 1776 at below the city's recommended price, while Redmond's retail and wholesale transactions consistently conformed to colonial mandates.[51] But those who did flout price limits could face civic reprisal when local authorities carried out their threats of public shaming. In April 1776, Peter Ozeas's apology to the Philadelphia Committee of Inspection and Observation appeared in the *Pennsylvania Evening Post*. Ozeas admitted to "having bought and sold two barrels of coffee at a higher price than that limited by you," a decision that he claimed "has given me great pain" since it ran counter to the "regard I have for public welfare, and the interest I have taken in the present struggle for liberty."[52]

Other vendors, however, even when caught, were not so ready to admit their culpability. In these cases, citizens had few qualms about taking direct action against the perpetrators. Historian Barbara Clark Smith has analyzed more than thirty instances of public violence in reaction to food rationing and price inflation during the first three years of the American Revolution in New York, Pennsylvania, Massachusetts, Rhode Island, and Connecticut. Some towns had few, if any, cases of food rioting—East Hartford, Connecticut, and Beverly, Massachusetts, for example, each experienced only one event. But in other cities, most notably Boston and Philadelphia, they were much more common. Eleven cases, or about a third of Smith's sample, do not specify the goods that sparked customers' activism, but of the remaining twenty-six, over half involved tropical or West Indian goods, some of which undoubtedly included coffee, and four events focused on coffee specifically.[53] In most instances, the crowds behaved in an orderly and focused way as they targeted specific businesses and commodities, and sought ways of selling what they confiscated at agreed-upon prices, rather than engage in wanton destruction of property or theft. In Longmeadow, Massachusetts, for example, protestors calmly presented Jonathan and Hezekiah Hale with a written list of grievances including "the very wrong behavior in selling at extravagant prices, particularly West Indian goods." The Hales defused the situation by immediately complying with the demands and lowering costs for their wares. When Samuel Colton, also of Longmeadow, was less accommodating, however, the crowd took action, and while Colton claimed that they had ransacked his store and stolen his property, in fact his goods were delivered directly to the town clerk, who sold them at "reasonable prices."[54]

The goals of such public mobilization went beyond simple punishment of specific merchants and shopkeepers or immediate personal gratification from seized goods. These were clearly measured approaches to collective action aimed at seeing that goods the community wanted were made available at rates agreed upon by the town's leaders rather than the inflated costs imposed by self-interested merchants. Patriots to the cause for independence were willing to pay for their merchandise, just not at what they considered to be usurious prices that resulted from greedy neighbors exploiting the disruptions of war.

Moreover, the prominent place of women in many of these crowds, as well as the language they used to articulate their discontent, complicates gendered assumptions about the politics of consumption and coffee's place therein. Their circumscribed political and legal position left women with fewer formal avenues for expressing their discontent, and so they at times turned to extralegal means. Women initiated nearly one-third of the riots of the mid-1770s and were the primary actors in all altercations over coffee. Abigail Adams wrote only as an observer, never a participant, but in these demonstrations of the public will, her tone implies that she thought such actions were justified: "There is a great Scarcity of Sugar and Coffee," she noted, adjudging them "articles which the Female part of the State are very loth to give up, especially whilst they consider the Scarcity occasiond by the merchants having secreted a large Quantity."[55]

Class and place also shaped both the frequency of this form of political participation and the kinds of goods at its center. While women's role in tea embargoes has been well documented, that commodity largely remained the habit of the upper classes, along with those who scrimped and saved to emulate them. Moreover, despite its negative political connotations, some people never gave up their tea drinking, even using the interchangeability of hot beverage services to mask their actions. Peter Oliver, an associate justice of the Massachusetts Superior Court, mused about how "it was really diverting, to see a Circle of Ladies about a Tea Table, and a Chocolate or Coffee Pot in the midst of it filled with Tea, one chusing a dish of Chocolate, & another a Cup of Coffee."[56]

A broader swath of the popular and political spectrum, however, protested in favor of coffee drinking, and their demonstrations decrying its scarcity and cost underscore how popular the habit had become. Most coffee protests occurred in city centers but drew participants from up and down the socioeconomic scale, some of whom traveled considerable distances to voice their support for the cause. Protestors came to Boston from as far afield as Enfield, Connecticut, and Palmer, Massachusetts, while those "from different parts of the country" converged on riots concerning the price and availability of West Indian goods in Kingston, New York.[57] These were not isolated events. Taken together, these actions and their associated fervor over coffee demonstrate that access to it had become integral to the daily lives of most North Americans, who considered their purchases neither extraordinary nor extravagant. For women from all stations, regular access to coffee at a reasonable cost had become an expectation, almost a right.

Not all contemporary accounts viewed women's activism kindly. William Pynchon, a Salem attorney, recorded several instances of public activism in the diary he kept from 1776 to 1789, and was more critical of women's role in the action, but in so doing, of course, he confirmed their prominent place in the politics of the streets. Pynchon, a political conservative who favored reconciliation with Britain, frequently drank coffee for breakfast. He even self-prescribed it when feeling ill, such as on July 28, 1776, when he had bread and egg pudding called "a whitpot for breakfast" as well as "a cup of coffee and cake," after which he noted "my fever is much abated." But Pynchon also worried about coffee's increasing politicization. "The Marblehead and Salem people quarrel for bread at the bakers," he recorded on April 28, 1777, before reporting on "a scramble at the wharf in weighing out Capt. Derby's coffee." A couple of months later, when he noted that "the ladies rise and mob for coffee," his reaction suggests that he preferred restraint over such public remonstrations. "Is it not become a duty," he asked, "to take care of tomorrow," concerned that what he considered to be rash, impulsive actions would adversely affect the course of future events. Coffee and its consumption, it seemed, was playing an important part in the increasingly heated contest around material need, speculation, and want.[58]

Critics of this transformation in taste and consumption also made their voices heard in print. A fictitious conversation between a "citizen" and a "farmer" in reaction to Philadelphia's price-fixing ran on the front page of the *Pennsylvania Packet* in June 1777. In lamenting the high cost of West Indian commodities, the farmer noted that the poorer classes "cannot live without them," to which the citizen derisively replied, "Tea and coffee, with the not inconsiderable quantity of sugar used with them afford no nourishment to the body." When the farmer then suggested that the fight for freedom and independence might fail if access to Caribbean commodities continued to be stymied, the citizen's reply was sterner still and came couched in the language of nascent nationalism. "I am sorry to hear such a sentiment from the lips of an American," he admonished, "What! Set Liberty in competition with a dish of tea or coffee! Unworthy practice!"[59]

And yet consume colonists did. So scarce had some goods become by 1778, that Pennsylvania passed an act to encourage fair dealing. Rather than target sellers, however, this legislation took coffee consumers to task. The broadside posted for all to see began by acknowledging "the present interruption of commerce, and the great demand for many necessary articles occasioned by war," which were unfortunately exacerbated by "the practices and combinations of evil and designing men, to the great injury of the poor." Rather than focus on these nefarious characters, however, legislators thought the remedy was to regulate access and declared that "no person or persons within this Commonwealth shall purchase (except in small quantities for their own use and the consumption of their families)."[60] It even became a crime, punishable by up to three months in jail, to transport coffee—and other goods defined as "necessary articles"—across state lines.

In a war premised on principles of unfettered trade, however, price-fixing and purchase quotas posed obvious problems that extended far beyond the minority who felt West Indian goods unworthy of such protection. As early as February 1777, a Pennsylvania representative to the Continental Congress, Benjamin Rush, was arguing that commodity prices had little to do with social ethics. "We estimate our Virtue by a false barometer," he argued, "when we measure it by the price of goods." Meanwhile that fall, both New Hampshire and Massachusetts had shifted their stance and repealed price equity legislation.[61] Consensus on the issue proved evasive, however, and it took longer for most others in the Continental Congress to agree with Rush's assertions. In November 1777, the Congress entertained a resolution to hold three summits on price control, two of which were scheduled for January 15, 1778, with New Haven selected as the site for deliberations concerning New Hampshire, Massachusetts, Rhode Island, Connecticut, New York, New Jersey, Pennsylvania, and Delaware, while a meeting in Fredericksburg would hear the cases of Virginia, Maryland, and North Carolina. A third meeting took place a month later in Charleston to consider the circumstances facing South Carolina and Georgia. All three events aimed to provide redress for the general population against extortion, as well as to regulate the prices levied on goods sold to Continental armies and militias.[62] The immediate war effort took precedence, with priority given to what was perceived as rampant overcharging of the military. Even George Washington commented on the difficulties of provisioning his troops. "There is such a thirst for gain," he complained in 1778, "and such infamous advantages taken to forestall and engross those Articles which the army cannot do without." But he was also aware of the broader burden imposed on the American people by such speculation since price gouging of goods had a subsidiary effect of "enhancing the cost of them to the public fifty or a hundred percent." He concluded angrily "that it is enough to make one curst their own Species for possessing so little virtue and patriotism."[63]

Most delegates addressed the price inflation issue, or at least its military aspects, by recommending that individual states issue temporary regulations on supplies deemed essential to the war effort. Difficulties arose, however,

with the definition of "essential," which, like the general public's "necessary," was very much in the eye of the beholder. In a 1780 letter to military
headquarters, Philip Schuyler, Jonathon Matthews, and Nathaniel Peabody lamented the impoverished circumstances of the colonial army, "their
starving condition, Their want of pay, & the variety of hardships they have
ben drivin to sustain" that they claimed "has soured their tempers, & produced a spirit of discontent." Material scarcities resulted in low morale. Thus
"the Medical department," the three men claimed, "are destitute of those necessaries, which are indispensable for the sick. They have neither wine, Tea,
sugar, Coffee, Chocolate, or spirits," before concluding their communication
with a plea that "orders may be given for an immediate supply, as the army
grow more sickly every hour."[64] In their eyes, coffee was an essential medical
supply for the ailing and infirm troops of the Continental Army, one that the
circumstances of war had made prohibitively expensive. This was a striking
and notable change in coffee's reputation, since as recently as 1766, doctors
at Pennsylvania Hospital had responded to nurses' complaints about patient
excitability and restiveness from coffee drinking by reducing daily allotments
of the brew and posting notices to attendants to monitor its intake carefully.
Less than two decades later, coffee was now associated with military pre-
paredness and regaining health.

Efforts to redirect coffee from personal to military use were easier to pre-
scribe than to enforce, however, and soldiers moaned about shortages and
usurious prices as often as private citizens. John Chaloner, for example,
who worked with the Pennsylvania army quartermaster, complained that
he had been "trying day after day" to acquire an adequate supply of coffee
for his contingent. "It may be bought," he grumbled, "but at about 25s per
pound," which was roughly twenty times the recommended rate. For a time,
coffee had become so dear that Philadelphia city leaders tried to limit the
amount private citizens could purchase for their personal use; those who
bought more could face accusations of smuggling. "It is very dangerous to
get [coffee] out of town," Chaloner noted, "for the least trifle you must produce your bill and swear that you have given no more and made no pre-
sents."[65] But even members of the Continental Congress did not always
comply. In 1779, Pennsylvania delegate John Armstrong Sr. wrote to his
wife, Rebecca, in Carlisle, and after inquiring after the family farm, recommending a harvesting schedule, and gently chastising his sons for failing to
write regularly, he concluded, "I have purchased some Coffee and Sugar &
may possibly get it up soon."[66]

By 1779 the scarcity of provisions motivated Gouverneur Morris, a New York delegate to the Continental Congress, to try to impose price controls on goods sold to military officers, because "the subsistence money allowed to the Officers of the United States," he proposed, "hath become insufficient for their support." His motion, which was seconded by Thomas Burke, a North Carolina delegate, recommended pricing West Indian rum at no more than two-thirds of a dollar per gallon; coffee, Muscovado sugar, and chocolate at half a dollar per pound; and tea at one dollar and two-thirds per pound. And although it failed to pass the resolution, Congress did designate the itemized goods, including coffee, as "the necessaries of life."[67]

At times the military alleviated shortages of provisions by accepting donations from private citizens. Elizabeth Drinker, whose diaries chronicle the life of an upper-middle-class woman in revolutionary-era Philadelphia, sent her servants Jenny and Harry with coffee to wounded Continental soldiers billeted at the local playhouse one day in early October 1777, and a few days later the pair set out again, this time with coffee for wounded soldiers at the State House. By October, troops of both British and Continental soldiers were encamped just two to three miles away, near Germantown, further inhibiting what little trade had still been coming into Philadelphia. "Provisions are so scarce with us now," Drinker recorded, and "ye people round ye country dare not come near us with anything." But her donations to the patriot cause continued. "Jenny and Billy," she recorded, "went this afternoon with coffee and whey for the soldiers."[68]

By 1780 both the Second Continental Congress and most states had soured on the viability of price controls. Some credited this reversal to either difficulties in enforcement or incompatibility with revolutionary rhetoric touting unfettered commerce. The reality was probably far less idealistic: there were profits to be made. "Open your ports to foreigners," advised one congressional delegate, and "Your Trade will become of so much consequence, that Foreigners will protect you."[69] Although the Congress had signed the Treaty of Amity and Commerce with France in 1778, British occupation of Boston, New York, and Philadelphia had effectively made the commercial elements of the agreement moot. When British forces moved south to Virginia and South Carolina after the Battle of Saratoga and the evacuation of Philadelphia, however, the war's landscape and seascape changed. What had been largely diplomatic overtures about open trade now went into practice. The number of ships sailing between mid-Atlantic and New England ports and French colonies in the West Indies increased appreciably between 1780 and

1781, and by 1782 nearly equaled the peacetime levels that had prevailed before 1776. The value of goods coming from the French Caribbean to North America increased more dramatically still, from a value of just over 5,000 livres in 1775 to almost 12,000 livres by 1783. Merchants celebrated rising profits. "All our ships have been and continue to be employed in carrying flour to the French and Spanish Islands," reported Philadelphia merchant Robert Morris, and "our port is filled in return with West India produce."[70]

The implications of this widening of suppliers were profound for the coffee trade and set the stage for North America's increasingly complicated engagement with the broader Caribbean. Coffee from the British Caribbean had been the colonies' mainstay for decades, but by 1781 less than 1 percent of the commodity legally imported into Philadelphia originated from British islands. Instead, over 90 percent came from the ports of Cap-François and Port-au-Prince in the French colony of Saint Domingue. Additional shipments from Martinique and Guadeloupe brought the French Caribbean contribution to over 93 percent, with the balance coming from Spanish Santo Domingo supplemented by small shipments from the British Windward Islands of Dominica and Grenada.[71] The resolution of debates over pricing policies and rates, in other words, came about neither because local legislators had a change of heart, nor in reaction to public protest, but rather because the vagaries of war had brought an end to scarcity itself.

These new legal arrangements revitalized and legitimized some prewar Atlantic commercial networks, such as those examined earlier through Monte Cristi or Guadeloupe, which British colonial authorities had considered illicit before 1776, but they also built stronger and more profitable ties directly with principal French West Indian ports, especially those of Saint Domingue. No longer confined to remote bays or smuggling operations, North American merchants set about systematically expanding their trade with France's richest colony and the eighteenth-century world's leading coffee producer. The impact on North American consumers within their local context was immediate. Coffee prices quickly returned to their prerevolutionary levels, where they largely remained until the end of the war. By mid-1779, newspapers in Philadelphia, one of the last cities to abolish recommended pricing, now reported that the wholesale price of coffee had plummeted to seventeen pence per pound, and within a month had dropped even further to fifteen or even fourteen pence. By 1780, New York's current prices listed coffee beans at twelve pence per pound for the six months between January and July. The military too managed to secure better access to their popular brew. Unlike during the earlier privations experienced in Philadelphia, a circular published by the *Pennsylvania Gazette* about the impact of British occupation in Charleston reassured readers that "there is plenty of rice, rum, sugar, and coffee" still to be had, and that "a portion of each of these articles is regularly served out to the men."[72]

Retailing beans once again became more predictable when subject to neither shortages nor price fluctuations. After nearly a four-year gap that began in 1774, Philadelphia merchant Levi Hollingsworth resumed advertising coffee for sale from his store on "the third Wharf below the Drawbridge," at first occasionally in the late 1770s and with increasing regularity after 1782. Meanwhile, two of Hollingsworth's brothers, Samuel and Thomas, had moved to Baltimore and established their partnership there in the West India trade, arranging consignments both on their own behalf and for their family up in Philadelphia, in an intercity arrangement that persisted into the second decade of the nineteenth century.[73] George Habacker was also back in business by 1780, advertising coffee along with sugar, teas, spices, and spirits at his "new store in Second Street, between Race and Vine."[74]

William West Jr., the prominent prerevolutionary Philadelphia merchant, had continued his business through much of the war, and when he died a year before the American Revolution ended, his nephews Francis and John took over the family business as its prospects were picking up; a third nephew, James, moved to Baltimore, where he became a partner in the firm of West & Haxall. Although dry goods remained the bulk of the cousins' businesses, all three invested in the Caribbean provisions trade, and their choice of suppliers from the region reflected the new political and economic realities of their postcolonial world. Rather than deal with ships and their cargoes outbound from British Jamaica as their uncle had, the succeeding (and successful) generation met vessels outbound from the colonies of French Saint Domingue and Guadeloupe or Spanish Cuba.[75] Moreover, the trade in coffee, a reliable but certainly ancillary enterprise for their colonial-era mercantile ancestors, became increasingly important to the Wests' businesses in the first few years of the new republic, so much so that by the early 1790s coffee beans would come to represent almost one-fifth of their import revenue in some years.

Investments and initiatives such as these are what helped coffee emerge as one of the fastest-growing industries of the immediate postrevolutionary period, both in its scale of production and in its significance to North American interests. They also epitomize U.S. traders' ability, once free from

British authority, to capitalize on local opportunities, exploit competition, and circumvent legal restrictions. Rather than a flowering of commercial independence, however, the regional trade networks they developed would ensure that the new nation remained deeply and inextricably tied to the economic networks of the widening Atlantic world.

CHAPTER 5

Coffee's Creole Economy

In 1787, a customs officer in the British Caribbean colony of Dominica alerted the island's House of Assembly to a serious error in bookkeeping. He had been comparing the harvest yields of certain goods in that year's Crop Accounts, documents sent annually to the London Board of Trade, when he realized that far less coffee was being exported than "what ought to have been expected." Since the discrepancy between what coffee planters said they were growing and what merchants recorded as shipping abroad was much too high to be accounted for by local consumption, the House demanded that all internal records be monitored, hoping that an explanation for "not only the deficiency would appear, but the several delinquents" responsible for it would be identified as well.[1] Part of the answer ultimately emerged from the dockets of the Court of the Vice Admiralty, which recorded several instances of coffee moving between Dominica and neighboring non-British territories in the years immediately following the American Revolution.

For most of the long eighteenth century, Britain, France, and Spain had been at war with each other, and several West Indian colonies shifted between these empires like pieces in a hemispheric game of chess; some islands, like Dominica, had changed hands more than once. But just because a new polity governed a colony, it did not necessarily follow that those living there altered their allegiances as readily or their business practices either.[2] Commercial partnerships often took years, in some cases generations, to form. Consequently, they were unlikely to be jettisoned quickly. The addition of a newly independent United States would reconfigure the power dynamics of Atlantic commerce yet again, as France, Spain, and Holland all experimented with free trade to the new nation in the 1780s and 1790s, while the colonial governors of these European powers expansively interpreted mercantile law, and smuggling flourished among traders and seamen willing to chance their hands and risk their fortunes. These activities may have differed in some respects, not least of which was their place on the spectrum from the technically legal to the clearly illicit, but all in their own ways ensured that U.S. economic affairs would remain intimately interwoven with the crops and markets of the Caribbean well beyond the young republic's political independence. This was especially the case for coffee, a commodity that only grew in regional importance after 1790.

The livelihood of Joseph Vidal, one of the coffee planters whose activities appear in Dominica's Vice Admiralty Court records, depended on this tenacity of commercial relationships regardless of his island's current metropolitan affiliations. According to the testimony of Pierre Rondeyon, Vidal's overseer during the late 1780s and early 1790s, Vidal had long done business with Lawrence Stoddart, agent for the merchant firm of Brayshay & Stuart, which routinely sent shipments to nearby Guadeloupe and further north to Saint Eustatius, the former a neighboring French colony and the latter a Dutch entrepôt renowned for its connections in rerouting British and French goods to North American markets.[3] Rondeyon's deposition offered crucial proof to prosecutors as they tried to mount a case against a suspected smuggler. It also outlined not only how interisland trade worked within a local context, but also just how porous imperial boundaries could be.

In early spring 1792, Rondeyon had set sail with two canoes carrying sixteen bags of coffee from Roseau, Dominica's capital town and chief port. As he approached Woodbridge Bay, he was hailed by another vessel just north of the harbor and asked to identify himself. Although Rondeyon, a free colored man, initially ignored the request, he testified that "a musket or some kind of gun was twice fired," and he subsequently stopped for fear that either he or Vidal's enslaved workers with whom he was traveling "might be killed or in some way injured."[4]

The ship that had approached the canoes was a British naval frigate, the 28-gun H.M.S *Prosperine* captained by James Alms, who ordered Rondeyon to board so that he could question him about the nature of his business. Through a translator, because like many Dominican residents Rondeyon spoke French, Alms learned that the overseer was ferrying coffee from Vidal's plantation, "where it was produced," to "Messrs. Brayshay and Stuart, Merchants of Roseau they having purchased it to resell in Basse-Terre," the capital of neighboring Guadeloupe. When pressed for more information about the ultimate destination of his cargo, Rondeyon speculated that it would then be sent to the United States, as it was his understanding that North American ships visited the French colony on a regular basis. Selling British coffee outside the empire without first paying the requisite export taxes was illegal, of course, and Alms asked to see the cargo's customs papers. Rondeyon responded in disbelief that "he had not" any such documents and, moreover, "he had been long accustomed to carrying coffee in like manner and never before had heard of such a thing as a permit being requisite."[5]

Roseau merchants moved quickly to handle the situation, ultimately persuading the courts that Vidal's overseer had "misunderstood" his instructions, whereupon the coffee was released into their custody with a strong admonition that they be sure to secure appropriate documentation in the future. By his own admission, however, and that of the merchants who availed themselves of his services, Rondeyon had been coordinating the movement of coffee around Dominica's coasts for many years. The case's testimony supports this conclusion, with its richly detailed description of the labor needed to transport coffee to various ports in both islands, as well as the length of time and types of vessels the routes required. Given the length of his employment as well as his obvious understanding of the intricacies of the coffee business, claims of Rondeyon's confusion about the destination of this particular shipment defy belief. Instead, the *Prosperine* had no doubt encountered the very tip of a metaphorical iceberg in these warm Caribbean waters, seizing two canoes out of an untold but sizeable number of vessels and cargoes that Rondeyon and others had successfully piloted beyond British imperial borders to supply the coffee needs of a thirsty U.S. populace.[6]

Rondeyon and Vidal, along with the merchants in Dominica and Guadeloupe with whom they did business, and the U.S. consumers they ultimately hoped to supply, were all component pieces of a complex, fluctuating but integrated regional coffee economy. From under 2 million pounds just before the American Revolution began, the amount of coffee imported into the United States rose to 4.5 million pounds in 1791, and to more than 40 million pounds a year just under a decade later.[7] Some of this coffee continued to come via traditional pre-1776 sources, like Jamaica and Dominica, albeit extralegally. Indeed, some of the prerevolutionary beans might even have come from Joseph Vidal's Dominica coffee farm, which first appears in a property survey taken when the island was ceded to the British after the 1763 Peace of Paris. Of course, had Vidal exported coffee between 1763 and 1775, these shipments would have been lawfully traded between members of Britain's 26-colony American empire, and so they would not have needed to be rerouted through Guadeloupe.[8]

After 1783, however, coffee was coming into the United States from the colonies of Holland, Spain, and especially France in ever-increasing quantities. This broadening supply chain not only fed the new nation's increasing appetite for the beverage, but also made possible the commodity's rapid ascent and prominent place among the goods it reexported to other nations. The U.S. coffee industry thus offers an excellent case study for understanding how the young republic's investment in regional enterprises grew after it left the British Empire, as well as how ably and quickly North American merchants were able to navigate a volatile economy where success depended on their ability to act decisively and reallocate resources quickly. Analysis of coffee and the boom economy that developed around it in the United States by the turn of the nineteenth century, however, does suggest something of a "new brew in old pots" scenario. These later successes, rather than blazing new commercial pathways, relied on the revitalization and continuation of tactics that had been working since the colonial era, like, for example, Vidal's decision to route his beans through an international network of associates. The new republic's coffee economy, in other words, was built on tried-and-true practices. Planters, diplomats, and traders engaged in a hemispheric market that used international connections, both competitive and collaborative, as well as legal finessing that was too systemic and entrenched to be defined by either the strictures of imperial boundaries or the particular legalities of various metropoles. It was, instead, the product of decades of collaboration that can better be characterized as a creole economy.

Few areas of historical scholarship have expanded so dramatically in such a short time as the study of creolization. Early studies most often applied the term to the impact of the transatlantic slave trade on cultural developments in the Americas, and more specifically to the multiracial and multiethnic constructions of identity in the Atlantic world that were necessarily fashioned by their particular places and times.[9] Edward Kamau Brathwaite was one of the first scholars to consider the creolization of institutions such as political systems, social structures, and economies.[10] Ironically, he did so while arguing that the American Revolution had removed North America from the Caribbean's commercial orbit, a position that runs counter to this book. Brathwaite was particularly interested in the implications of U.S. independence for West Indians and suggested that growing tensions within the empire had caused some contemporaries to emphasize colonial self-sufficiency over trade. He pointed, for example, to Edward Long, a planter and judge in Jamaica's

Vice Admiralty Court, who was promoting investment in particular island industries "for our own growth" and to ensure a steady supply of goods "far cheaper than we can buy them." Long had singled out coffee for special attention because of its ability both to promote white settlement in Jamaica's mountainous interior and to contribute to "agricultural diversification and self-reliance," thus echoing ideas espoused by proponents of the industry since the early eighteenth century.[11] Brathwaite's ideas, while innovative, nevertheless remained tethered to one locale, Jamaica, and drew extensively on the interpretation of traditional imperial sources, such as laws, patents, and petitions.

Other historians have applied the concept of creolization to less formal economies. B. W. Higman, for example, pointed out that scholars' emphases on Jamaica's export trade has overshadowed the island's internal economy, where the circulation of coffee, sugar, livestock, and enslaved people formed a kind of currency in places where formal money was scarce, creating a "creole economy" of local goods.[12] Roderick McDonald, in turn, explored the economic dynamics within plantations to determine how enslaved laborers earned and spent money in early nineteenth-century Jamaica and Louisiana. Transactions between planters, urban residents, and the enslaved, he argues, whether tacit or formalized by custom or legal recognition, operated within a specific creolized system that allowed enslaved communities in both locales a degree of economic agency even within a larger context of overwhelming oppression.[13] More recently, Tessa Murphy explored the cultural hybridity of "an interconnected maritime world that became a center of broader imperial experimentation and contestation" and "did not align with the borders imposed by distant crowns," in her study of efforts by indigenous peoples and free and enslaved Africans to shape their lives in the Lesser Antilles during the 1780s and 1790s, a time when both the notion of empire and specific imperial boundaries in the eastern Caribbean were very much in flux.[14]

Whereas the concept of a creole economy has thus been fruitfully applied in studying the actions of indigenous and Afro-Caribbean peoples, plantations, and even individual colonies, an analysis of U.S. investment in the late eighteenth- and early nineteenth-century coffee industry deploys the term on a different scale, one that transcends colonies, nations, and empires to encompass the larger Atlantic world. North America's coffee economy exhibited fundamental continuities before and after the American Revolution, but the imperial rupture brought them into stark relief. North American independence did not create a new commercial model. Instead, the exit of these thirteen former North Atlantic seaboard colonies from the British Empire made more visible preexisting avenues of interimperial exchange, whose importance now were heightened and openly acknowledged.[15]

A creole economy that had been emerging through the eighteenth century was more than a sum of its transactions, whether legal, questionable, or illegitimate; it was a business ethos that privileged local needs and exigencies against national or imperial prescriptions. Those who participated within it did so for profit, but they also made choices about where and with whom commerce should be conducted, creating patterns that shaped the region's livelihood in ways as powerful as any legislation enacted by European governments. North American merchants had relied on a range of producers as they navigated their way through complex systems of mercantilism in their search for coffee for more than a century by the time of the American Revolution, and through a variety of familiar avenues and tried-and-true strategies, they would continue to do so profitably thereafter.[16]

Coffee by Fair Means and Foul

Writing from The Hague in July 1783, John Adams marveled at the volume of West Indian commodities arriving in the city and destined to be reshipped throughout Europe. Thousands of bags of coffee, hogsheads of sugar, and barrels of molasses, he wrote, "are annually brought in this Republic and exported at a great profit to Germany, Denmark, Sweden, Russia, Poland, and Italy."[17] Initially Adams thought that North American produce would fare equally well with European consumers and suggested that merchants would benefit from "a large trade in Italy, every part of which had a constant demand for our tobacco and salt fish, at least."[18] But by the early nineteenth century he realized that European demand for tropical commodities, rather than U.S. goods, "secured to all these [foreign] cargoes a ready sale" with the best profits, so he recommended that U.S. trade focus on access to the West Indies.[19]

The prospect of a robust legal trade between North America and the British West Indies, in coffee or anything else, seemed unlikely immediately after the American Revolution. On July 2, 1783, Parliament issued an order in council that declared the United States subject to the same duties and taxes as any other foreign nation, a move that officially ended the commercial protections that were available to colonies within the British Empire. North

American lumber, grain, and livestock could be sent to Caribbean ports "as if they were cleared out for a British colony," and coffee was among the goods that could be traded in return, but Britain reduced its excise taxes on coffee sent to the metropole in its effort to entice West Indian planters away from shipping to the U.S. market. More detrimental still to U.S.-Caribbean relations were the edicts that all goods, whether arriving into or out of British Caribbean colonial ports, had to be carried on British vessels. Thomas Jefferson reported that several members of Congress believed "our commerce is got and getting into vital agonies by our exclusion from the West Indies," and James Madison concluded in 1785 that "we have lost by the Revolution our trade with the West Indies, the only one which yielded us a favorable balance without having gained new channels to compensate it." Although initially the July 1783 order was a temporary measure, Parliament would extend it for the next five years until, in 1788, a new act was passed that permanently excluded U.S. ships from British home or colonial ports.[20]

In response, the U.S. Congress created a commission, composed of John Jay, John Adams, and Benjamin Franklin, charged with overseeing negotiations and authorizing trade treaties with several European nations as well as with the Barbary Coast of North Africa. Its strategy was to take a multinational approach that would ensure U.S. economic autonomy from Britain, while exploring new trade partnerships in Europe and a reopening of commercial relations in the Caribbean.[21] Initially, U.S. merchants sought West Indian business connections to meet the demands of a growing domestic market for, and consumer interest in, tropical goods, especially coffee. By the end of the eighteenth century, however, just as Adams had predicted, North American commercial interests had expanded in important respects, aided by the near constant military hostilities between Britain and France, and ultimately Spain, which would come to a head during the Napoleonic Wars and severely diminish the ability of these European nations to furnish their home markets, much less other western European countries, with Caribbean commodities.[22] The ability of U.S. traders to avail themselves of the opportunities these circumstances brought about became a driving force behind U.S. claims to neutrality in the carrying trade, and although coffee had not been central to the reexport business during the colonial era, or even during the 1780s, it would become a crucial trade commodity in the next few decades. Coffee, in other words, may not have been high on the commissioners' list of priorities at the outset, although they often returned to it in their negotiations with different nations, but ultimately it secured a place of prominence as one of the fastest-growing industries of the new nation on an expanding stage of international commerce.

The commission had ambitious goals, especially for a fledgling nation whose small army and even smaller navy meant that it could not promote or secure its objectives militarily.[23] Instead, Congress equipped its European emissaries with its strongest weapon, the purchasing power of the United States, and threatened discriminatory tariffs and market restrictions for nations that refused to deal freely with the new republic. Over the next several years, the commissioners negotiated with several potential trade partners, to whom they offered a range of commercial options. The United States' three savvy statesmen quickly realized, as had many planters and merchants before them, that the most viable and reliable paths between ports were often the indirect ones. Time and again their correspondence tracks the circuitous routes that ships, coffee, and captains would travel to circumvent what contemporary maps showed as neatly segmented empires and circumscribed imperial divisions.[24]

Given the postcolonial commercial and military rivalry between the United States and Britain, members of the commission quite reasonably expected a warm welcome from the Netherlands. "The Dutch," John Adams mused, "will avail themselves of every error that may be committed by England."[25] After all, in 1776, colonial officials in Saint Eustatius had been the first governmental body to recognize the legitimacy of North American claims to independence.[26] But competition in the carrying trade strained U.S.-Dutch trade relations in the Caribbean in the postrevolutionary era. Holland did allow North American ships to land in Saint Eustatius, Curacao, Sint Maarten, and Dutch "colonies upon the continent," including Surinam, Berbice, Demerara, and Essequibo, but limited what they could bring or take in return.[27] Dutch West Indian coffee could be imported duty-free, but Dutch East Indian coffee remained subject to foreign produce taxes, and all tropical commodities except molasses had to be carried on Dutch vessels. In practice this arrangement was little better than what Britain had offered, and although Adams speculated that even these modest gains might open the door to opportunity, since "some quantities of sugar and coffee are always smuggled, as they say," the search for more reliable coffee suppliers continued.[28]

Denmark imposed fewer restrictions on trade to the United States, in large part because its colonies of Saint Thomas, Saint Croix, and Saint John did not actually produce the goods North American traders sought.[29] At best the Danish islands served as transshipment or reexport centers of tropical foodstuffs, and several of Philadelphia's importers took advantage of the ability to import coffee freely from the Danish Caribbean, especially in the early 1780s. But the islands' reliance on other locations for their inventory meant supplies varied greatly at any given time and prices fluctuated unpredictably. Moreover, while coffee could be imported duty-free into the United States, Denmark insisted on the same prohibitions on North American shipping to Europe as Amsterdam had done. Consequently, relations with the Danish West Indies were valuable enough, but constraints on coffee's availability and on U.S. shipping abroad meant that the commodity's trade through these islands did not meet North American needs. The islands were too small, and their trade too tied to external factors, for U.S. importers to rely on them, especially those engaged primarily in the reexport business.[30]

The U.S. commission also approached Portugal. In July 1783, Benjamin Franklin wrote to the Portuguese ambassador in Paris about getting access to Brazilian coffee plantations, but he was rebuffed and told that "Portugal admitted no nation to the Brazils." Undaunted, Franklin went on to suggest that U.S. ships could use Portugal's "Western Islands" of Madeira or the Azores as a "depot" for importing Brazilian "sugars, coffee, cotton, and cocoa," which he calculated "could furnish us [the United States] with these articles at Lisbon fifteen per cent cheaper than the English could from their West India islands."[31] The ambassador this time seemed more amenable to Franklin's overtures, but unfortunately the Portuguese court was less enthusiastic and rejected the proposal.[32]

The commission also appealed to Spain through its minister to Paris, the Count de Sanafee. "What objections there could be to admitting North American vessels to the Spanish islands of Cuba and Hispaniola, to carry their produce," John Adams asked Sanafee, just as they did with the ports of the "French and Dutch colonies?" Sanafee demurred, suggesting that Spanish authorities "would be afraid of the measure" since "free ports were nests of smugglers" that "afforded many facilities of illicit trade." Adams then tried a proposal that echoed Franklin's offer to Portugal. If U.S. ships could not directly import Spanish colonial coffee, he ventured, could goods "be carried to the free ports of France, Holland, and Denmark, in the West Indies," perhaps even, he suggested, "in Spanish vessels, that they might be there purchased by Americans?" Sanafee responded cautiously, indicating that "he could not pretend to give any opinion upon any of these points, but that we must negotiate them at Madrid."[33]

Trade with Spain's colonies offered real potential for the United States. During the final years of the American Revolution, North Americans had established a thriving commerce with Spanish possessions, especially Cuba, its principal Caribbean holding. Philadelphia, for example, recorded over forty vessels arriving from Havana in 1781, which accounted for the largest annual number of Spanish vessels docking in any North American port city, with an additional twenty ships arrived the following year.[34] But in 1784, with the conclusion of the Revolutionary War's hostilities, Spain moved to tighten its imperial control by banning all trade to Cuba, whereupon the island's governor issued orders for U.S. ships to leave Havana immediately. Spain briefly reopened both Havana and Trinidad, its southern Caribbean possession, to U.S. shipping in 1785 when Count Galvez, who was considered "a confirmed friend of the United States," became Cuba's new governor. True to his reputation, Galvez "proceeded to shew every favor to the Americans," but his appointment was brief, and when he was transferred to Mexico in less than two years, his successor proved far less receptive to U.S. interests.[35]

In addition to these more obvious options for developing U.S. trade in tropical goods like coffee, the commissioners' quest for viable partners saw them considering some very unusual options in the early years of their negotiations. In 1784, for example, the *Pennsylvania Gazette* reported the possibility of a commercial treaty between the United States and Russia.[36] Russia did not then possess any West Indian colonies but, according to some Dutch sources, was presently involved in negotiating the purchase of "an island in the West-Indies (believed to be St. Martin's)."[37] Saint Martin was the smallest shared colony in the Caribbean, controlled by Holland in the south and France to the north, but Adams included the tiny, divided, and rather infertile island in a list of possible West Indian partners, although he noted that with few established towns and limited agriculture, "it does not flourish."[38] Even if Russia had succeeded, of course, Saint Martin would not have been able to grow any of the coffee that U.S. traders sought, so at best it could have served as a neutral clearing station, similar to Dutch Saint Eustatius or Swedish Saint Bart's, offering merchants and ship captains an opportunity to circumvent the restrictions imposed by mercantilist policies.[39] The *Pennsylvania Gazette* made no mention of the Dutch response to these overtures, but shortly thereafter Holland joined Prussia in declaring war on Austria and Russia, so any prospects of the island's sale disappeared in the smoke of battle.

If U.S. diplomats made little headway with their European counterparts in securing international trade policies that benefited North American merchants, however, local officials, traders, and planters, particularly those based in Europe's West Indian colonies, were often more sympathetic. Indeed it was through these less formal channels that coffee trading between North America and the British Caribbean reemerged by the end of 1780s. From the vantage point of London, the 1783 order excluding U.S. vessels from British colonial ports was an effort to bolster its own commerce at the expense of U.S. shipping. But colonists in the Caribbean realized just how badly Parliament had underestimated their reliance on ships built and registered in the former North American colonies that had now been transformed into an independent republic. Although Britain had promised the thirteen West Indian colonies remaining loyal to their mother country that ships from the metropole would fill the void left by North American vessels, contemporary accounts reveal such efforts falling woefully short. Traffic bound west from British ports arrived sporadically and with cargoes insufficient to meet the colonies' needs. Jamaican planters warned Britain's leaders that excluding U.S. ships would have disastrous effects, and begged the island's governor, Archibald Campbell, to petition Whitehall for an elimination—or at the very least, a reduction—of foreign taxes on coffee and sugar. Planters made special pleas for these commodities because, of course, they were the goods that North Americans most wanted, and the ability to sell them at competitive prices would help ensure the reestablishment of the regular supplies of food, lumber, and other necessities from the North American mainland, on which their plantation economy relied.[40] Campbell refused to do so, however, with calamitous results for the island's economy. Coffee shipments from Jamaica to North America, which had already dropped more than 40 percent from prerevolutionary levels by 1777, reached nearly zero by 1783.[41]

Other colonial governors were more responsive than that of Jamaica, however, employing a variety of tactics to ameliorate the declining fortunes of their merchants and planters. While not necessarily ignoring metropolitan policies, these leaders recognized the need for flexible interpretations of Parliamentary law and, in so doing, facilitated coffee trading, albeit at levels that remained far lower than before the war. One common practice was the gubernatorial prerogative to use special concessions that temporarily relaxed trade restrictions and redefined shipping laws in favor of their island's export commerce. Such concessions were nearly as old as the Navigation Acts themselves, which dated back to the seventeenth century, and gave local administrators the authority to open their ports to foreign vessels in times of great need, such as in the aftermath of an earthquake or hurricane, or to counter privations caused by war. Some governors, however, interpreted special concessions far more liberally than metropolitan authorities thought necessary. Indeed, Admiral Horatio Nelson complained that collusion between the United States and colonial officials was so pervasive that it allowed local leaders to remake British law at their whim. "To see the American ships and vessels with their colours flying in defiance of the law," he wrote to the British admiralty from Nevis in 1785, "and by permission of the officer of customs landing and unloading in our ports was too much for a British Officer to submit to."[42] Nonetheless, the practice continued and by 1786 had become so widespread that Parliament passed an act of general indemnification that exempted governors from prosecution for Navigation Act violations.[43]

The legality of such actions varied, of course, by the eye of the beholder. What Dominican and Grenadian officials sanctioned as legal coffee trading, Jamaican planters characterized as thinly disguised efforts by these Lesser Antillean British colonies, with whom Jamaica was in competition, to whitewash smuggling with neighboring French territories. France permitted widespread free trade between its West Indian colonies and North America before 1782, and through designated free ports thereafter, and both Martinique and Guadeloupe experienced a boom in coffee exports. Indeed, like Dominica's mismatched trade statistics that began this chapter, the volume of exports exceeded what either colony's estates and plantations produced themselves, and Jamaican planters pointed the finger at British island governors' special concessions that allowed French vessels to enter British Antillean ports—or, like Vidal, to send British ships to French West Indian harbors—and resell Dominican and Grenadian coffee to U.S. traders as if the beans were of French West Indian origin. "Above twenty times the quantity of produce," one Jamaican petition decried, "has been exported from these islands [Martinique and Guadeloupe] since their conquest than ever grew upon them."[44]

Special concessions offered some relief to U.S. importers, but the amounts of coffee that changed hands through such measures was still only a fraction of what North Americans had brought in during the colonial period, and demand for the commodity continued to grow every year. To secure more stable sources of supply, especially where British island governors proved less flexible in their application of shipping legislation, some merchants took another tack. If North American ships were banned from certain colonial ports, then they would simply refashion their vessels to become non-American. Flying foreign flags and forging customs paperwork had both been common tools of smugglers before the American Revolution, as Captain Ash's venture described in Chapter 2 attests, but the practices became so pervasive during the 1780s that some British colonial governors thought "the Genius of all West Indians without distinction, seems turned to piracy and freebooting."[45] Often, as had been the case with special concessions, those willing to risk such maritime disguises were ably assisted in their endeavors by willing local partners, which attested to the durability of trade networks that reinforced the region's creole economy.

Henry Johnson, a commission merchant from New England, relied more than once on island customs officials' willingness to look the other way for the right price. Johnson, with his two half-brothers, headed the three-man Boston firm that traded as Johnson, Johonnot & Company.[46] When the brothers opened a branch office in Baltimore in 1783, Johnson, as the eldest, was chosen to oversee its early operations. Although surviving letters do not indicate why the firm elected to open a southern branch, it is likely that the brothers, like many other merchants, sought to capitalize on the Chesapeake city's rising fortunes. During the 1750s and 1760s, Baltimore had become one of the leading purveyors of mid-Atlantic grain to the Caribbean and southern Europe. Moreover, because Baltimore had neither been occupied by the British army during the Revolutionary War, as Philadelphia had been, nor blockaded by the British navy, it had become the principal port of entry for wartime trade with France. But this growth had developed quickly, straining local shipbuilding, which struggled to keep pace. The discrepancy between the volume of Baltimore's trade and the lack of local vessels to serve it presented Johnson with a commercial opportunity on which he hoped to capitalize. In a letter to a Portsmouth, Virginia, trader, Johnson noted that the docks of the Maryland port boasted "very few vessels of their own," adding that "chief of their trade is carried on by strangers."[47]

In Boston, Johnson, Johonnot & Company had principally operated as a commission firm that received cargoes and sold them for agreed-upon fees. The company also filled orders of all kinds with goods ranging from West Indian coffee, sugar, and rum to Portuguese wines, British porters, and teas. In Baltimore, the firm continued with these activities but also opened a store near "Hollingsworth's wharf" that catered to the needs of a diverse clientele. This retail enterprise stocked New England codfish, mackerel, and salmon, alongside locally produced wheat as well as coffee pots and tea kettles "for cash or country produce."[48] While the firm had already established ties with several North American trading houses, Johnson hoped to expand and further cement the company's commercial connections with Europe and the Caribbean. To that end, he wrote a series of introductory letters in 1784 to potential customers, outlining what he and his partners had to offer. He focused especially on French West Indian traders and encouraged their patronage with reassurances that he was "confident that Balti[more] will have its share of your trade as we are growing very fast here."[49] He went well beyond offering better rates or favorable commissions to drum up business, and his correspondence offers tantalizing glimpses into the creativity he and other traders demonstrated to stretch or circumvent established law.

Before 1776, Johnson, Johonnot & Company had imported most of its coffee from Jamaica and on occasion from elsewhere in the British Lesser Antilles. But after 1778 the firm shifted the base of its coffee operations to French Saint Domingue, and over the next five years turned a tidy profit through the import of beans as well as sugar and molasses produced in the colony. When Johnson moved to Baltimore at the end of the American Revolution, he had hoped to maintain these French lines of trade while reestablishing his British Caribbean commercial connections, so he was more than a little disappointed when France reclosed some of its Saint Domingue ports, including Port-au-Prince, L'Orient, and Cap François. These three cities had accounted for more than a third of the coffee shipped to the United States from the colony in 1781, but their combined shipments dropped to less than 7 percent after France's postwar reestablishment of mercantilist policies.[50] Johnson was even less pleased with Britain's 1783 exclusionary order in council, cutting off trade with that nation's West Indian colonies, a policy that he considered a consequence of "Parliamentary stubbornness."[51]

Instead of enjoying a peacetime boom, Johnson's commercial world looked to be collapsing around him as he faced the prospect of having to pay foreign coffee duties in both French and British ports that would have decimated his profits. He reacted swiftly to what he considered commercial betrayal and cast around for ways to cut costs. Johnson's willingness to move expeditiously between colonies, and even ports within colonies, to optimize his returns demonstrated his tolerance for risk as well as his disposition toward decisive entrepreneurial undertakings.

The letters he wrote in the months following French and British port closings, however, reveal that Johnson was willing to go much further to make his money. In November 1783, for example, he penned a series of nearly identical letters to different trading partners in which he suggested courses of action that came perilously close to out-and-out smuggling. To James Demie, a Saint Domingue merchant in Cap François, Johnson suggested that "should your port be shut against Americans," there could be "an opportunity of doing something clever here under the French flag." To the merchant firm of Marie & Company in Port-au-Prince, he admitted that prospects for North American vessels to "enter your port" were unfortunately "doubtful," but he advised that "should your trade be carried to the Mole of St. Nicholas," then "vessels under the French flag will bring the produce of your island to this Continent much easier than the Americans."[52] Johnson's brazen, even dangerous, ploy would be for merchants and their vessels to carry different sets of documents and colors that could quickly transform a ship's identity from "American" to "French" or vice versa, depending on which option best suited a given time or place.

It is impossible to know how much coffee Johnson imported through these clandestine manipulations of national identity, but such tactics had been sufficiently lucrative to entice him to broaden the range of nations his vessels could impersonate. In letters written to his brother Francis in 1784, he described efforts to branch out from French to British identities and paraphernalia. "You will not forget the proposition I made," he wrote, "respecting the vessel under British colours. I do believe there is an opening there." If a voyage "could be done this quarter," he continued, "I would soon have a set of British papers," but if conditions changed, he implied he could just as easily "put the vessel again under American colours."[53]

Johnson was not alone in his creative, if illicit, efforts to conduct business in the Caribbean. One Philadelphia newspaper openly reported on "a vessel just arrived from the West Indies" for which "English merchants are obtaining foreign papers in a clandestine manner in order to carry on a trade with us," while another article intimated that "the French and British West India islands refuse admittance to American vessels but in a very limited way" because, the author asked, to whom and where else "can her citizens look for some participation in the commerce of the world?"[54] The casualness of these descriptions, which seems to reflect a routine "way of doing business" attitude, reveals a broad-based and worldly wise acceptance by merchants and sea captains throughout the Atlantic region of how, if circumstances dictated, a supposedly fixed concept like national identity could become fluid and subject to manipulation. While technically illegal, these activities flourished because they drew on business partnerships that had previously been legitimate, sometimes only a few years before, where the imperatives of trade and the efficiencies of commerce—as well as regional loyalties and alliances—trumped the letter of laws imposed remotely whose provisions did not serve local business interests.

The ease with which Johnson could refashion his ships as North American, British, or French confirms Admiral Nelson's fears that U.S. merchants' collusion with British colonial insiders, who both had access to official forms or could replicate convincing counterfeits, had become a profitable reality. Thomas Shirley, who documented coffee smuggling in Saint Domingue's Bay of Monte Cristi before the American Revolution, became governor of Dominica by war's end, and he continued in his new post to search out commerce of dubious legality. Thousands of pounds of coffee and sugar, he contended, were being exchanged for North American produce in the British Leeward Islands. Lieutenant Governor James Edward Powell likewise reported on U.S. traders routinely smuggling Jamaican coffee out of the Bahamas and the Turks and Caicos. Meanwhile, Governor Parry of Barbados reported on a U.S. vessel that not only had failed to pay the export duties on foreign coffee when it left Bridgetown, but also had set sail with the city's customhouse officer aboard, a man whom Parry had no doubt could "provide the means and access to any British port in the West Indies" to the American ship.[55]

The consternation of high officials within British colonial administration, however, stood in contrast to the widespread acceptance of these tactics as being something other than deception or chicanery. Interimperial trading, which extended after 1783 to the United States, could only succeed because of the broad-based support and willing participation of those living in the Caribbean who saw such strategies as necessary economic tactics. In 1785, when Nelson seized four U.S. ships flying the British flag in Saint Kitts, he expected the resentment of the ships' crews, but he had not counted on the indignation of local port agents (functionaries within the metropolitan bureaucracy, after all), who promptly issued a writ for Nelson's arrest. Only by remaining on his vessel did Nelson manage to escape imprisonment, although he was charged with "arbitrary action" as well as for ignoring local court proceedings. "All the navy are very unpopular," he grumbled, "for hindering the American ships from trading with the islands."[56]

The ease with which North American merchants moved between empires in the first decade after American independence caused some European countries to reconsider their efforts to impose shipping restrictions, since they were clearly ineffective in practice if not as policy. Indeed, as early as 1785, Thomas Jefferson boasted in a letter to John Adams that "all the late advices from the West Indies are that they have now in their ports always three times as many vessels as there were before [the war] and that the increase is principally from our States."[57] Free ports, a handful of which had operated successfully in the West Indies before North American independence, proliferated during the 1780s and in some cases offered a satisfactory third-party alternative for vessels trading under the flags of various independent nations. They also provided U.S. merchants with a third vital avenue for building the nation's investment in Caribbean coffee.

The concept of free ports—trade cities where, as the name implied, normal customs and duties were not applied—was not new to the postrevolutionary Atlantic world. Holland had opened its first Dutch free port in Saint Eustatius in 1757 to encourage direct trade to North America, and Britain responded by opening five of its own within a year, all of them in Jamaica, at the ports of Kingston, Savannah la Mar, Montego Bay, Saint Lucea, and Port Antonio. France followed suit with Guadeloupe three years later but moved the policy one step further by allowing North Americans to purchase coffee, sugar, and rum while at the same time selling horses, lumber, and provisions. The French initiatives marked the first time that the concept of duty-free trade had been applied to exports as well as imports.[58]

Not surprisingly, free ports became popular very quickly, so much so that some European nations moved to circumscribe their growing economic reach by passing increasingly specific legislation about which goods could move between empires duty-free. Such thinking underlay Parliament's passage of the Revenue Act of 1764, whose express intention was to limit "the clandestine conveyance" of proscribed commodities—coffee, white and clayed sugars, indigo, wine, cloth, and several kinds of Persian, Chinese, and Indian silks—anywhere in British America. This Revenue Act more than doubled the tax on foreign coffee and sugar, but instead of ending North American's trade outside the British Empire, it served only to drive up the price of both commodities, a development that in turn encouraged Denmark to open Saint Thomas and Saint John as free ports a few months later.[59]

Dynamic and remunerative as it was, however, the prerevolutionary free port system paled in comparison to the extensive network that flourished by the late 1780s. Jamaica's free ports, temporarily closed during the Revolutionary War, reopened after 1787, as did those in Roseau, Saint George's, and Kingstown, the principal entrepôts of Dominica, Grenada, and Saint Vincent respectively. By 1790, Britain had established another seven free ports throughout the Caribbean, in the Bahamas (Nassau and Caicos), Tortola

(Road Harbour), Antigua (Saint John's), Trinidad (Saint Joseph), and Tobago (Scarborough), and farther out into the Atlantic, in Hamilton, Bermuda.[60]

In some respects, these ports were not necessarily as free as the name implied since the nations permitted to trade there, as well as the goods they could buy or sell, varied tremendously depending on which port they called on as well as the local conditions and particular needs of the island. Coffee, for example, and sugar, which were among the Caribbean's largest cash crops, were both conspicuously absent from most British free port legislation. Only Bermuda, Nassau in the Bahamas, and, after 1793, the Caicos and Tortola could legally trade in either commodity. These islands produced neither of these tropical staples but in the case of coffee had received an exemption so as to encourage importation of French beans from Saint Domingue and Spanish beans from Puerto Rico and Cuba, which would then be reexported to London.[61]

Nonetheless, places like Bermuda and the Bahamas were also close enough to North America to tempt some captains to look west for better markets. Stafford Dickinson, master and commander of the sloop *Necessity*, testified that those who wanted to do business with North America simply had to file the proper manifests for British ports with local customs authorities and then, "notwithstanding such clearances," would use bad weather, diminishing supplies, or some such excuse to justify emergency landings on the mainland. The practice was so common, according to Dickinson, that Bahamian captains rarely informed their crew of ships' itineraries. "All intended Voyages to America to trade," he stated, were kept "a profund Secret" lest they were "stopped on the Island" or by "British armed vessels at Sea."[62]

The Rise of Saint Domingue in U.S. Coffee Trading

Special concessions, colonial collusion, and outright smuggling each brought their share of coffee into the United States during the immediate postrevolutionary period, but still not in the volume that would satisfy either importers or consumers. Americans needed more. Increasingly, merchants turned to the French West Indies, which accounted for more than 60 percent of all the coffee that entered North America by 1789, a share that rose to 77 percent just two years later (Table 2). Philadelphia continued to dominate the coffee market, as it had during the colonial era, receiving up to one-third of all coffee imports into the nation, but other cities began making inroads of their

Table 2. U.S. Coffee Imports from the Caribbean, 1790–1791

Region of Production	Coffee (lbs.)	% of U.S. Coffee Imports
French West Indies	3,432,385	77
Dutch West Indies	559,613	13
British West Indies	346,875	7
Spanish West Indies	51,689	1
Danish West Indies	28,715	.7
East Indies	25,138	.6
Swedish West Indies	8,895	.1
Portuguese Brazil	1,108	<.01
West Indies (General)	8,472	.1
Other	15,783	.4
TOTAL	4,478,673	100

Source: *American State Papers, Commerce and Navigation*, 1:195.

own. Through the last decade of the eighteenth century, Baltimore brought in 20 percent of the nation's imported coffee, with New York and Boston receiving 11 and 13 percent respectively.[63]

Although some U.S. merchants still did business with the smaller French colonies of the Lesser Antilles, the greatest beneficiary of expansion in the U.S.-French Caribbean coffee trade was undoubtedly Saint Domingue. Although large by Caribbean standards, Saint Domingue was still a relatively small colony, occupying the western third of the island of Hispaniola and roughly the size of Massachusetts. By 1789, however, it was producing more than half of the world's sugar and over 60 percent of its coffee, garnering more money for France than all thirteen of the mainland colonies combined had previously earned for Britain.[64] Evidence of the tremendous wealth accruing to the colony appeared in the numerous published accounts that vividly described, for example, the "commodious and elegant houses" in Saint Domingue's port towns, and the lavish churches and theaters there that rivaled those of the cities of France itself. The residents of Cap François had by this time even established their own Academy of Agriculture to "improve the art of cultivation," recognizing that the success of this productive agronomy financed the colony's architectural and cultural glory. But this coffee and sugar economy, of course, relied on the brutal coerced labor of hundreds of thousands of enslaved workers, who toiled to produce the staples that enabled the colony's merchant firms to flourish and yet whose work is often absent from contemporary accounts.[65] Alexandre de Laujon, a young Frenchman who arrived in Saint Domingue in 1787, for example, succinctly described how "the riches of the land" were transported from the "mountains and plains, arriving in abundance, warehouses barely able to contain them," while tellingly, if not surprisingly, avoiding acknowledgment of the colony's dependence on slavery, instead using a range of phrases to dance around the colony's reliance on the practice.[66]

Saint Domingue's sugar economy boomed, with its production outstripping that of the leading colonies of Britain (Jamaica), Spain (Cuba), and Portugal (Brazil), but the rapid growth of its coffee economy during the third quarter of the eighteenth century was even more astonishing. The number of coffee trees in production rose from 22 million in the 1750s to over 100 million by the late 1760s, growing on more than three thousand coffee farms, or *caféières*, which comprised more than one-third of the agricultural properties in operation in the years leading up to the Haitian Revolution.[67] The coffee boom was also evident in the amount of beans exported, whose volume rose from 7 million pounds in 1750 to 40 million pounds in 1770, and reached 77 million pounds in 1790, as well as in the revenue such trade generated, which climbed from 12 million livres to 71.5 million livres between 1767 and 1787, by which time coffee nearly matched the colony's returns from refined sugar.[68]

A confluence of several factors accounted for this stunning rise in Saint Domingue's coffee production. First, after losing the Ceded Islands through the Treaty of Paris, all of which had been important coffee-producing sites, France sought through imperial reform to consolidate its control over what territories remained and to encourage expansion in agricultural production wherever possible, particularly in the already profitable colony of Saint Domingue. Sugar planting was well established in the low-lying plains near the coast, but the colony's mountainous, forested interior remained largely unpopulated and uncleared. At the same time, demographic changes that accompanied the rising number of Saint's Domingue's *gens de couleur*, or free people of color, and the arrival of migrants from France's former colonies in the Lesser Antilles swelled the colony's population. This, in turn, exacerbated competition for employment and increased land speculation in the colony's port cities and surrounding sugar plains. In particular, the aspirations of a free, non-white population bent on securing for themselves a place in colonial society intensified the strained relations that already prevailed between white and free non-white colonists. Evidence of this escalating racial tension appeared in the proliferation, and more rigorous enforcement, of discriminatory legislation against *gens de couleur* after the Seven Years' War, which, for example, prohibited them from entering certain professions, marrying whites, wearing European-style clothing, or carrying weapons in public. These laws were not, of course, only intended to limit the political and social power of the free colored people, but to also distinguish them for easier identification, since generations of racial mixing now meant skin hue no longer provided an accurate enough gauge.[69]

Partly in reaction to being relegated to what was essentially a second-class status of freedom, more and more of the colony's *gens de couleur* opted to move into what were then undeveloped highlands to the west and especially the south, where they invested in coffee farming, which as one contemporary commentator noted "was less lucrative than that of sugar, but subject to fewer vicissitudes and far less dear." Indeed, the writer contended, its profits were "more certain" since the initial capital outlay was lower, and prospective coffee farmers faced less competition from either the newly arrived contingents of white people of lower status (*petit blancs*) or the established plantocracy (*grand blancs*).[70] As a consequence, between 1763 and 1787, at least nine new parishes were founded in Saint Domingue, predominantly populated by *gens de couleur*, and all of them focused primarily on coffee production.[71]

If *gens de couleur* coffee planters hoped that increasing profits would lead to greater social and political acceptance, however, they would be sorely disappointed. Even as their economic standing grew, they were forced to witness the colony's white population working more assiduously to circumscribe other kinds of advancement. Consequently, with the outbreak of the French Revolution that extolled the principles of liberty and equality, *gens de couleur*, with the coffee planters in their ranks very much to the fore, launched appeals to the French National Assembly to end discriminatory practices based on race. Saint Domingue's white colonists, however, who had already been granted seats in the National Assembly, vehemently opposed any such concessions, arguing that the successful perpetuation of slavery, upon which the wealth of the colony depended, required that full citizenship exclude any people of African ancestry, regardless of whether their legal status was free or enslaved. Although the Assembly initially denied the appeal of the *gens de couleur*, they reconsidered it the following year and on May 15, 1791, granted full citizenship to those *gens de couleur* colonists whose parents had both been born free and been legally married. Such carefully defined legislation would only have affected a small proportion of Saint Domingue's population, but the real importance of the law was in what it symbolized—that freedom could trump race—and this, of course, exacerbated tensions in the West Indian colony between whites and the newly empowered *gens de couleur*.[72]

In their struggle for ascendency in Saint Domingue, both white and *gens de couleur* residents sought to co-opt the colony's enslaved peoples to their respective causes, and the consequences of the French Revolution, both ideologically and in terms of the internecine colonial conflict it had generated, would become clear in August 1791, when tens of thousands of enslaved men and women in Saint Domingue's northern plain went into open and violent revolt against their bondage and the systems responsible for it, burning cane fields and smashing the machinery of agricultural production. Within weeks, every parish near the port city of Cap François had been devastated and the rebels had laid waste to hundreds of plantations.[73]

Although the revolution created dark clouds that hovered both metaphorically and literally over the colony, astute North American coffee traders nevertheless found a silver lining in the fact that the cataclysm had not affected all parts of Saint Domingue at the same time or with the same intensity. Whereas the sugar plantations of the northern plains suffered major devastation as crops and works went up in flames, Saint Domingue's southern and western provinces, the heart of the colony's coffee production, experienced less damage, which ensured the continuing profitability of the trade for merchants willing to risk the hazards of navigating a battle zone.

U.S. politicians and merchants watched events unfolding in the Caribbean and France as avidly as the rest of Atlantic world but often with very different reactions. Politicians, with the notable exception of John Adams and his presidential administration, sought to distance themselves diplomatically from Saint Domingue and discouraged merchants from further investment in what they now perceived as an unstable and dangerous colony in the throes of a slave revolution. Slavery, of course, was driving much of the U.S. domestic economy, especially the plantation system of the southern states, where enslavers' persistent fears of rebellion by those they held in bondage were now heightened by the prospect of a revolutionary contagion traveling north from the Caribbean. Congress even passed a series of acts between September 1791 and June 1793 designed, if not to quell the revolution, then at least to offer Saint Domingue's white planters some financial relief.[74]

U.S. merchants, by contrast, saw opportunities in the fiscal turmoil that the rebellion had caused. Richard Stites, a Philadelphia-based ship captain, sailed the schooner *Industry* to Cap François no fewer than six times between June 1791 and August 1792, a time span that coincided with the height of the initial outbreak of violence. Over the next two years, as the revolution progressed, he continued to trade in the colony's southern, western, and northern provinces, docking variously in Port-au-Prince, Aux Cayes, and Saint-Nicolas, where he transacted business on behalf of at least four other Philadelphia-based merchants.[75] Far from curtailing trade, in other words, the revolution in Saint Domingue had undercut traditional lines of mercantilist power and opened up the colony, and especially its coffee economy, to North American shipping and enterprising merchants willing to take chances. Indeed, the level and profitability of trade between these two regions grew to an extent not enjoyed since the truncated experiments of the Treaty of Amity and Commerce with France in 1778. Over three hundred vessels sailed from Saint Domingue bound for Philadelphia's docks alone between 1789 and 1791, and another 430 did so in the three years that followed. Nor was this flourishing and expanding trade a one-way affair, since by 1790 the value of U.S. exports to Saint Domingue now exceeded the total to all other West Indian islands combined.[76]

Charting the Changing Coffee Networks of Dutilh & Wachsmuth

One company willing to gamble on this high risk-high reward strategy of doing business was the Philadelphia merchant firm of Étienne Dutilh and John Wachsmuth, who between 1790 and 1797, repeatedly sent their seven vessels to Port-au-Prince, Cap François, and Jeremie—and from there to any of a score of ports on the Atlantic's eastern and western shores. The firm's principals epitomized the mobile nature of Atlantic commerce in terms of both the goods they traded and their personal backgrounds. Dutilh had been born in France in 1732, and by the time he was age 39 was operating an import business in Rotterdam. By 1777, however, he had moved to London, and just after the American Revolution ended in 1783, he moved again, this time to Philadelphia, where he applied for U.S. citizenship. Within two years he had begun trading under his own name as Étienne Dutilh & Company at 212 South Water Street, where he focused his attentions on establishing connections with Saint Domingue, and particularly the port city of Cap François. By 1790 he had joined forces with John Godfrey Wachsmuth, changed the business name to Dutilh & Wachsmuth, and moved offices to 111 North Water Street, between Race and Vine Streets.[77]

Dutilh & Wachsmuth was not among Philadelphia's commercial leaders but not at its bottom rungs either. The location of its business reflected its mid-level status, situated at the upper edges of the mercantile district, just north of what was known as the "elite corridor" but only a few blocks south of "Helltown," a notoriously crime-ridden part of the city. While both partners had owned their own ships and had financed trading ventures before they joined forces in 1790, the merchant house initially advertised primarily as a commission business, dedicated to transporting the goods of others as well as facilitating commercial negotiations at home and abroad. Commission merchants such as Dutilh & Wachsmuth operated essentially as factors, or agents employed to buy or sell under their own name or the names of those who had engaged their services. Neither law nor custom required that Dutilh & Wachsmuth reveal, either to buyers or sellers, whether it was operating on its own behalf or that of others. Carefully detailed bills of lading, however, make clear how cargo ownership ultimately was distributed.[78]

The provisioning enterprise created by Dutilh & Wachsmuth stretched up and down the eastern seaboard states and reached far inland to the nation's interior. The two partners were as likely to ship tierces of rice from South Carolina, kegs of lard from New York, and hogsheads of tobacco from Virginia, as they were to consign Indian corn meal, pork, and flour from Pennsylvania and Delaware. Such goods often also appeared for sale in the merchants' retail store alongside imported sugar, molasses, spices, and teas, as well as several varieties of cloth and occasionally "beaver, raccoon, fox, cat, and bear skins." Coffee, however, was a staple of Dutilh & Wachsmuth's business dealings, appearing in various quantities on the cargo inventories of over three-quarters of its inbound and half of its outbound vessels, as well as in nearly every one of its store advertisements.[79]

Almost all of the coffee that Dutilh & Wachsmuth imported through its first few years in operation had come from Saint Domingue.[80] Indeed, as a mark of the colony's significance to his enterprises, and to ensure ready and consistent supplies, only a month after he and Wachsmuth had formed their partnership, Dutilh left Philadelphia for Cap François where, over the next several years, he managed the firm's affairs through three Saint Domingue subsidiaries: J. & E. Dutilh, which Étienne formed with his brother Jean; Judas Pilé & E. Dutilh; and Dutilh, Soullier & Company, a partnership with John Soullier. John Wachsmuth, meanwhile, oversaw the U.S. end of operations, planning and arranging incoming shipments, maintaining the accounts, and coordinating business correspondence, as well as selling coffee and other goods through the company's retail store on Water Street and through a network of North American wholesale and retail merchants, and via reexport partners in Europe.[81] Dutilh & Wachsmuth continued its ventures in Saint Domingue well after the outbreak of revolution in 1791, although with important organizational changes. When reports of unrest began to spread, Dutilh returned to Philadelphia, and the following month, in April 1791, left for Holland, where for two years he divided his time between Rotterdam and Amsterdam in coordinating the firm's European affairs. Dutilh & Wachsmuth also considered moving the base of its Saint Domingue operations out of Cap François after the house of their factor there, John Soullier, was burned to the ground. But while the number of ships the firm sent to Port-au-Prince and Jeremie certainly increased after 1791, a significant proportion of its trade still went to Saint Domingue's beleaguered chief port.

A series of letters just after violence escalated in Cap François indicated that both partners knew well the dangers posed to their trade during this period of conflict but nonetheless saw sufficient financial incentives to stay their course. Although they sent no ships to Saint Domingue between September 1791 and April 1792, they ended this hiatus when they advertised departure of the brigantine *Mary Sophie*, "for freight or passage" bound for "Cape-Francois" that May.[82] The *Mary Sophie* returned to Cap François in August, while the brigantine *Jason* sailed for Port-au-Prince and Saint Marc, as well as Cap François, a couple of months later, in November. The following March, the firm's vessel *American Hero* would set sail from Cap François bound for New York and then Philadelphia. Indeed, the dislocations and uncertainties wrought by the revolution were even opening up new commercial possibilities. Beginning in October 1793, Dutilh & Wachsmuth began running advertisements in Saint Domingue, in both English and French, that featured the schedules for its ships' departures to Philadelphia and targeted fleeing French émigrés from the devastated colony who were now flooding north to swell the port's Francophone population.[83]

Other signs of the revolution in Saint Domingue are scattered throughout the partners' business papers and struck a more ominous tone. In July 1792, Dutilh & Wachsmuth was hired by "a French family, who have had their property destroyed by fire" in Saint Domingue and had fled to Philadelphia. They were clearly a family of some means, as they had engaged the firm to help them pawn some of their possessions, such as snuffboxes, gold and diamond jewelry, and silver kitchenware, including a "small coffee pot, all of silver," presumably to provide them with liquid capital to finance their new circumstances as refugees.[84] And the following March, Dutilh & Wachsmuth agreed to act as a postal repository for a French colonial teacher who was leaving Saint Domingue posthaste with his family and students, and who needed an address to which his correspondence could be sent and then forwarded to him monthly once he had managed to relocate off the colony.[85]

Meanwhile, Saint Domingue merchants were using the power of the North American press to paint a rosier picture of conditions in the colony in hopes of continuing to attract the interest and business of their U.S. counterparts. "Times grow more quiet," reported one letter purportedly written by a trading firm based in Cap François, placed in Philadelphia's *Federal Gazette*. "Our market promises good prices for your produce," the author assured readers. A newspaper editorial published in the *Gazette of the United States* stressed Saint Domingue's need for U.S. imports and predicted rich returns. "There is very little provision in the place," this author contended, "so that there must necessarily be a demand."[86] Dutilh & Wachsmuth was willing to gamble on a favorable outcome on this risk versus return equation, and it sponsored seven voyages to Saint Domingue between May 1792 and the end of 1793, most of which offered passenger service south and carried tropical produce north, including more and more beans from the coffee-producing regions of the western and southern parishes less affected by the first wave of property destruction and bloodshed. These changes in trade patterns reflected larger trends. While shipping from Saint Domingue's sugar-rich northern provinces had made up 52 percent of the colony's total trade in 1789, their share had dropped to 33 percent by 1794 and dramatically to just 18 percent by the following year. Meanwhile the volume of shipping from the west and south had increased in comparable increments.[87]

The opportunities advertised by Saint Domingue boosters promoting U.S. investment in the French colony, however, were often more aspirational than achievable. Demand for North American imports was high, to be sure, since some cities were running low on even the most basic of resources, but these markets often lacked either the hard currency or the tropical staples to pay for what they needed.[88] And of course in these chaotic and rapidly changing circumstances, no captain would ever consider trading on credit. At times, desperate local officials in Saint Domingue discouraged U.S. ship captains from traveling from port to port in search of the best prices, and even imposed fines on those who visited the remote bays in search of buyers willing to pay more. A few local customs agents even tried to force U.S. ships to offload their cargoes by refusing them permission to leave port until they did so. Such actions, of course, undercut the openness and unencumbered freedom to trade that had made Saint Domingue's revolutionary-era markets so attractive in the first place. One American ship master, for example, complained that the harbor authorities in Port-au-Prince had delayed his departure for days because he had not transacted any local sales and, indeed, had threatened to deny him the appropriate clearing documentation until he transacted business there. A letter home from another captain, reprinted in the *Federal Gazette*, lamented that "I am still detained in this place, by the Assembly and Municipality." He would only be allowed to leave, he continued, after he had paid what was tantamount to an exorbitant bribe of ten thousand livres, in addition to the usual port charges and duties, as security for his oath that he would not land any of his cargo elsewhere on the island.[89] Even masters who did not face spurious levies conjured up by local officials in desperate need of cash or food, or both, nevertheless confronted the unpredictable fluctuations in prices that had become the cost of doing business in a climate of war. Charges for cargo weighing and portage soared, for example, while rates for maritime insurance nearly doubled between 1790 and 1793.[90]

Ironically, it was neither the insurrection of the enslaved nor the rising costs of doing business in Saint Domingue that caused Dutilh & Wachsmuth to reconsider its commercial dealings there. Instead, it was the actions of the British navy, and in particular its propensity to condemn and confiscate U.S. cargoes, and to seize and impress U.S. ships and crews into service, that ultimately changed the merchant partners' minds. British officials had been monitoring developments in the French West Indies as assiduously as had their North American counterparts since the onset of the French Revolution, and some saw the same prospects for commercial opportunity, albeit for their own nation. In 1789, Lord William Grenville, then secretary for the Home and Colonial Department, wrote to the commander in chief of the Leeward and Windward Islands that "the late transactions in France may be productive of effects in the West Indies."[91] As relations between France and its colonies deteriorated, and more and more colonists pushed to abolish the mercantilist policies that tied their incomes so tightly to those of their metropole, Britain hoped at the very least to gain a lucrative foothold in French West Indian commerce by expanding its own shipping at the expense of its rival European metropole. To facilitate this effort, the president of the British Board of Trade introduced legislation in 1791 that would allow foreign

sugar imported in British vessels to be reclassified as British, thus performing a creative end-run around the Navigation Acts. And despite significant
protest by the London Committee of West India Planters and Merchants,
whose members wanted to protect their own islands' produce, the bill became law in June 1792. This, however, was as far as Britain was initially
willing to go. So, when several Saint Domingue planters suggested that
Britain might take a larger role in managing the colony's affairs, the powers
that be in London politely but unequivocally turned them down.[92]

It was not that Britain was uninterested in the commercial potential of
Saint Domingue. Government ministers knew well the volumes of coffee
and sugar the colony had been exporting, as well as the revenues these
tropical staples had generated, and some officials quite openly speculated
about what would happen if the French colony fell into British hands. Throughout 1791 and 1792, however, British authorities remained content to watch and
wait. But rapidly changing circumstances, both in Europe and the Caribbean,
marked by a series of cataclysmic events provided sufficient inducement for
Britain to reconsider its hands-off policy toward Saint Domingue. First came
the ousting of the French monarchy and the declaration of a French Republic; then an alliance was struck between Toussaint Louverture and Spanish
Santo Domingo that aimed to push remaining French forces out of Saint
Domingue; and finally, the French National Assembly formalized the abolition of slavery, already in effect in some parts of the colony by late 1793, in an
effort to sway enslaved insurgents to rejoin the military effort and secure the
colony for France. Recognizing that France's hold on its colony was in jeop-
ardy, and that Spanish colonial officials were willing to form even specula-
tive political and economic alliances with formerly enslaved people, Britain
felt justified in entering the fray in February 1793, landing the first of what
would ultimately be nearly 20,000 British soldiers in a quest to take Saint
Domingue. Although cloaked in the language of imperial security and im-
pelled by a desire to quell both abolitionist sentiment and the possible spread
of revolutionary ideas to the hundreds of thousands of enslaved people in its
own colonies, Britain's interest in Saint Domingue sought to access lands and
trade networks that had, until very recently, been extraordinarily profitable.[93]

What Britain had not counted on was the impact that France's abolition
initiative would have on strengthening the French military effort, as well as
the devastating effects of yellow fever, which reduced British troops to a fraction of their former strength within months of their arrival.[94] To compensate, Britain turned to the well-worn strategy of impressment, beginning with

the North American vessels already docked in the ports of Saint Domingue, and this is what ultimately led to Dutilh & Wachsmuth recalibrating the company's business in the colony. In no small part, the decision to target U.S. boats was in reaction to Edmond Genêt's efforts earlier that year to license North American vessels as French privateers to prey on British shipping.[95] But the threat posed to American sailors had a devastating effect on U.S. trade to the colony, with the number of vessels leaving Saint Domingue for North America plummeting by nearly 40 percent in the space of just a year.[96]

As news that Britain was seizing U.S. ships and cargoes filtered back to Philadelphia, Dutilh & Wachsmuth reacted swiftly by recalling four of its vessels from Saint Domingue and thereafter redirecting the ships it did send to the colony's southern ports, where they would be less likely to encounter British forces.[97] Even so, not all of the firm's ships returned safely. In June 1793, Britain declared goods aboard its ship *Active* "non-neutral property" and confiscated the cargo, purportedly because of its connection to French trade. Although Dutilh & Wachsmuth immediately filed a claim for restitution, almost a year passed before the verdict was rendered, whereupon all charges were dropped and the ship's coffee, indigo, and cotton returned to the firm's possession.[98] Within months of that legal victory, however, British forces had also seized Dutilh & Wachsmuth's brig *Theodosia* and then its ship *Hannibal* on the same charge. And again, the courts ultimately ruled in favor of the Philadelphia traders, but the cases took nearly four years and a substantial outlay in legal fees to resolve.[99]

To avoid such depredations, other U.S. coffee merchants operated as they had in prerevolutionary times, by working through neutral intermediaries. Although North American traders could no longer safely do business within the French Empire, their counterparts from Holland could and did. Philadelphia buyers took advantage of this loophole, all the while complaining about the Dutch middlemen's inflated prices. "There are other things that attend this trade, that should not pass unnoticed," reported the *Pennsylvania Gazette*. "The Danes, or rather Dutch, under Danish colours," the report continued, "swarm here [Saint Domingue] from St. Thomas's," where their usual custom was to secure from Saint Domingue planters the best price for coffee, and then initiate a bidding war between U.S. and Danish exporters to drive up prices.[100]

Meanwhile Dutilh & Wachsmuth, despite the perils of impecunious colonists, unscrupulous local officials, and hostile British naval vessels, continued to do some business in Saint Domingue. Its outbound records include invoices for cheese, claret, and earthenware and glassware shipped from Amsterdam, Lisbon, London, and Rotterdam to Port-au-Prince and Jeremie, and as always, coffee was the dominant colonial commodity shipped back to Philadelphia on the several voyages that occurred between 1796 and 1797.[101] Two of Étienne Dutilh's brothers, Francois and Jean, oversaw most of these transactions, in their roles as the firm's principal agents in the West Indies after Étienne had left the region.[102] The firm also chose to redistribute some of its risk by reverting to its earlier strategy of conducting some of its ventures via the ships of others. Thus, while its cargoes might still be subject to confiscation by local authorities or on the high seas, the decision to transport its goods through a second party would at least not risk the firm's ships. In June 1796, for example, Dutilh & Wachsmuth shipped two hogsheads and sixty-six bags of coffee as well as fifty-eight bales of cotton from Jeremie to Philadelphia on the sloop *Antelope*, captained by William Dalzell, and owned by Anthony Morris Jr. Similarly, in May 1797, the firm engaged John Craig to carry goods on its behalf from Saint Thomas to Port-au-Prince and from there to Philadelphia.[103] Working through a commission firm would, of course, have incurred additional fees, but these might have seemed a bargain compared with the expenses the two partners had already paid lawyers to recover their ships and the goods aboard them that had been confiscated by British incursions.

Nevertheless, by 1797, and at least in part because of the cost of ongoing court cases, Dutilh and Wachsmuth moved to dissolve their partnership. They announced their decision in several Philadelphia newspapers that June and attached a brief notation to that effect on all of their business correspondence over the next several months.[104] Ironically, Britain, whose naval actions had caused so much of Dutilh & Wachsmuth's troubles with the coffee trade out of Saint Domingue, would evacuate its forces from the colony in strife the following year, but not before its navy seized the *Fair American,* one of Dutilh &Wachsmuth's last remaining ships doing business in the region.

The *Fair American* had arrived in Port-au-Prince just when a British commander stationed in the colony received orders to evacuate his troops to Jamaica and was looking for transport ships to use for that purpose. The *Fair American* caught his eye. And although he paid $600 to the vessel's captain and supercargo, converting the ship from cargo to passenger transport required "abandoning at the discretion of the French government" the ship's coffee cargo, valued at between $12,000 and $14,000, to make room for soldiers and military supplies. Following its usual modus operandi, Dutilh & Wachsmuth immediately filed suit for restitution, seeking financial damages not just for its coffee, but also for its vessel, which after its impressment by the British had been captured by the French, recaptured by the British, and ultimately sold as salvage in Martinique. It took four years of litigation before Dutilh & Wachsmuth finally received some relief from the British High Court of Appeals for Prizes, which held that the original British commander had unfairly confiscated the *Fair American* during the evacuation of Port-au-Prince. The judge awarded the merchant plaintiffs remuneration that amounted to 121,543 pounds of coffee valued at just over £3,000 as well as about £200 in cash, the latter made up of both local British West Indian currency and pounds sterling. It was a steep loss.[105]

Even the persistent threat of privateers and British naval harassment, however, did not deter all U.S. merchants from trying to trade with Saint Domingue, many of whom still sought access to the region's tropical staples in the early nineteenth century, when its agricultural production began to rebound. The sugar economy was harder to rebuild, as plantations had been razed and there simply was not enough capital to invest or labor available to bring them back to the production levels achieved under slavery. Coffee exports, however, had recovered to nearly two-thirds of their pre-1789 levels by as early as 1801.[106] At the same time the Adams administration, under mounting pressure from U.S. merchants, was considering how to reopen diplomatic relations with the revolutionary government that had replaced French colonial administration. Developments on the European front influenced Adams's decision. French and British commercial blockades and attacks enacted during the Napoleonic Wars had reduced North American trade east across the Atlantic to a trickle, a crisis that was exacerbated when Congress banned all trade to the French Empire after the onset of the Quasi-War between the United States and France in 1798. The ensuing difficulties for U.S. finances caused Federalists to begin actively encouraging Toussaint Louverture's aspirations for independence since they thought this would disentangle Saint Domingue trade from U.S. conflicts with France. Louverture, in return, proposed closing Saint Domingue ports to European privateers, whereupon Congress responded by passing a law authorizing the president to reopen trade with any French "island, port, or place" if it was considered to be in the best interests of the United States. This in turn allowed Adams to issue a formal proclamation reopening trade with Saint Domingue on August 1, 1799.[107]

The letters of Edward Hall, a Baltimore merchant who traded with the southern port of Aux Cayes, document the real possibility for profits from coffee during these volatile last years of the eighteenth century. In 1798, Hall wrote to one of his ship captains that Saint Domingue's economy had been reduced to a subsistence level. "Every person," he wrote, "waits the return of the Americans" since until then, he claimed, locals would be able to "only buy from hand to mouth."[108] But by June 1799, Hall appeared certain that change for the better was imminent, in terms of trade at least, and confided in another captain about the news from Baltimore that "communication would without doubt be soon opened between America and St. Domingo." He began assembling a cargo in Saint Domingue that included 120,000 pounds of coffee. Like Dutilh & Wachsmuth, however, Hall knew that the surrounding waters still teemed with privateers of all nations, so he distributed his risk by dividing his cargo between two vessels outbound from Aux Cayes. He shipped 848 bags of coffee (worth more than $15,000) on the schooner *Holstein*, a Danish ship that he hoped might prove less tempting to raiders than a U.S. vessel. The remainder of his coffee, as well as $1,500 in specie, was loaded onto the U.S. vessel *Penelope,* and both boats sailed for Saint Thomas. Hall's fears of interdiction were well founded since the *Penelope* was seized en route by a British frigate and subsequently condemned by a British Vice Admiralty Court, but the *Holstein* managed to reach the Danish colony safely. The subsequent legal battles over the *Penelope* would tie up Hall's profits from that shipment for several years, although he did ultimately realize over $12,000 from the venture.[109]

Coffee trading continued, albeit sporadically, even after the Jeffersonian Republicans took office in 1801 and moved to ban direct trade between the United States and Saint Domingue. The invasion of the colony by French forces in February 1802 upset coffee production further still, with exports dropping almost 25 percent, and later that year full-scale rebellion resumed in the western and southern parishes of Saint Domingue in response to Napoleon's reinstatement of slavery in Guadeloupe. New waves of violence brought the colony's foreign trade to a virtual standstill, and coffee imports recorded in Philadelphia's customs registers dropped from almost 26 million pounds to less than 9 million pounds between 1801 and 1803, with more and more U.S. merchants casting around for replacement suppliers.

A handful of more mercenary merchants were still willing to play a high-stakes game, however, as documented by the mariner Horace Lane, who sailed with the American privateer *Sampson,* and left an account of a voyage that carried arms and ammunition to Haitian revolutionaries during the summer of 1804. The *Sampson's* voyage was motivated not by revolutionary fervor or support for a fledgling "Black Republic," but by profit, since the ship would return from Port-au-Prince with thirty-two refugee white women and children as well as several tons of coffee—the latter illegal to import directly and so remade as "prize" goods that found their way to auction blocks in Philadelphia and New York.[110]

Étienne Dutilh and John Wachsmuth each also individually continued to invest in the coffee trade, and their business decisions mirrored the directions and choices of U.S. traders more generally during the first decade of the nineteenth century. Wachsmuth concentrated on the West Indian staples of coffee and sugar, even contracting with the U.S. federal government to provide both commodities to the offices of the U.S. Treasury located in Rotterdam and Amsterdam. He also partnered with John Soullier, Dutilh's former associate from Cap François, who had relocated to Philadelphia after Haitian independence, and the two did business together there until 1814. But by now instead of Saint Domingue, or later Haiti, Wachsmuth and Soullier were far more likely to seek out their beans directly from Spanish Cuba and French Guadeloupe or routed from these islands through the British Bahamas and Danish Saint Thomas.[111]

Dutilh also returned to Philadelphia in 1795 to develop his U.S.-based merchant business and anglicized his first name from Étienne to Stephen sometime around 1804. Coffee remained a principal commodity of his trade, although like Wachsmuth, he bought beans from a broad range of West Indian suppliers rather than focus on Saint Domingue/Haiti. An 1802 bill for weighing cargo of his eleven ships still lists one vessel sailing to Cap François, but the remaining ten went to French Guadeloupe and Spanish Puerto Rico, Santo Domingo, and Cuba, with six going to Havana alone.[112]

The two men's commercial practices did diverge, however, in terms of how much risk they were willing to assume. Wachsmuth's contracts with the U.S. government were clear-cut, reliable, and annually renegotiated affairs that supplied the steady market of a relatively large and predictable clientele with what was becoming their increasingly indispensable caffeinated beverage. Dutilh had more ambitious aspirations, however, which encouraged him to undertake higher risk ventures. The frequency with which his name appeared in the court system over the years suggests he had not yet lost his penchant for the more freebooting style of creole economics that skirted and flirted with trading legislation. This, of course, was the commercial world that he had come to know and trust—it had served him well, and he had faith that it would continue to do so.

The most striking example of Dutilh's "sailing close to the wind" strategy appears in several depositions that formed part of an 1804 suit brought before the Pennsylvania Circuit Court by the New York firm of Palmer & Higgins. The firm charged that Dutilh's crew had purchased coffee that had been illegally confiscated from their U.S.-registered ship off the coast of Cuba by a French privateer, then taken it to the Spanish colony and resold it as Cuban produce. Witnesses in Dutilh's defense argued that the purchase had been the confluence of accident and expediency rather than duplicity, but the details, which are murky at best, suggest instead that the incident bore all the hallmarks of the kind of official deceit that Lord Nelson had bitterly complained about over two decades earlier—dubious paperwork, international cooperation, complicit customs agents, and a willingness either to interpret laws creatively or simply ignore them in the interests of profit.

The saga began in December 1804, when Dutilh engaged Peter Dorey as supercargo of the schooner *Eliza*, a vessel bound for Kingston, Jamaica.[113] This role empowered Dorey to act on Dultih's behalf by negotiating the sale of his outbound cargo and purchasing goods for the return voyage. Poor weather, however, meant the trip south took fifty-five days before the vessel reached its destination and sold the flour, wood, and wheat it carried to the Jamaican merchants, Stephen Palot & Company, for just under $18,000. The next day the *Eliza* set sail for the port of Cayenne in French Guiana but was reportedly behaving "crank" by heeling abnormally and recovering slowly against headwinds. Dorey decided to put in at Santiago de Cuba on the island's southeastern coast, a large, natural harbor renowned for light winds and easy entry that could offer safe anchorage "where foreign vessels usually lie, in order to take on more ballast."[114]

When Dorey went ashore with some of the crew, however, he claimed they were "accosted and followed" by some local merchants "who shewed him samples of several Parcels of Coffee" that were available for sale. A deal was struck, and Dorey purchased more than 100,000 pounds of coffee, spending almost all of what the *Eliza's* outbound cargo had garnered in Jamaica. While Dorey swore that he thought the goods were the produce of the Spanish colony, he conceded that "it had come from the shore, and the night being exceedingly dark, had it been taken from on board vessels in the Road," and he continued, "this deponent could by no means distinguish from what vessels." Further compromising the veracity of Dorey's testimony was his admission that he knew the U.S. could not legally trade with Cuba at the time he was in port—that, he averred, "was the reason why, with the Connivance of the

Governor, the unloading as well as the shipping, was practiced by neutrals in the night."[115]

This kind of artifice was a time-tested tactic that indeed was virtually identical to that deployed in places like the Bay of Monte Cristi years before. The new wrinkle in the proceedings on this occasion, however, was that the coffee in question, whether it was of Spanish or French origin, was being claimed as the property of another U.S. merchant, whose star witness, Thomas Norton, master of Palmer & Higgins's brigantine *Ceres,* testified for the prosecution. Norton had personal and professional interests in the case's outcome since he was both the captain of the vessel and part owner of its cargo. The ship's master recounted in lengthy detail his December 1803 voyage from New York to Port-au-Prince, where he had loaded his cargo of coffee in clearly identifiable barrels. Norton took pains to emphasize that some of the hogsheads had been marked "BC" for the brig *Ceres* and other hogsheads "TN," the latter the personal property of Norton himself. The rest of the hogsheads were marked "PH," denoting that they were the property of Palmer & Higgins, the lead plaintiff in this particular suit.

Norton went on to describe what happened after the *Ceres* left Port-au-Prince. Five days into the voyage, on February 25, 1804, the master testified that the *Ceres* had been seized by the French privateer schooner *Regulator* and taken to Santiago de Cuba. Norton and his crew were then forced from the ship, after which the hatches were reputedly sealed, and French authorities "assured this deponent that nothing should be moved until there was a Trial." Just a few days later, on March 9, however, Norton learned that coffee cargo had been transferred in the middle of the night from the *Ceres* to Dutilh's vessel, the *Eliza,* with the latter then sailing from port early the next morning. Although Norton immediately reported the theft to French authorities, he claimed they did not seem overly concerned, telling him only that "if the hatches had been opened it was done without authority, and at the peril of those who did it."[116]

At first, Norton and his New York merchant associates hoped to sue the French privateers responsible for putting their cargo at risk, but eventually they opted instead to "pursue the property to America." No Admiralty Court had declared the *Ceres*'s coffee to be lawful prize, asserted Norton, so "the vessel and cargo would have been released" even if a prize hearing trial had occurred. Any subsequent resale of the coffee should thus be deemed a transaction in stolen goods. Norton claimed he was not able to investigate Dutilh's inventory closely, but he told the court that he did manage to glimpse one hogshead lying on its side "through broken places in the door," which he claimed was part "of the Brig *Ceres'* cargo." Meanwhile, he continued, the tops of several other barrels had been "turned inside out so that the deponent could not see whether his marks were on the same." Norton's testimony, however, was not without its flaws. He would not, for example, describe how and where he had marked the *Ceres's* casks, answering only that he had used a red pencil and was sure he would be able to identify his stamp if allowed to examine the cargo closely. He also mentioned that the casks aboard the *Ceres* had been constructed with "French hoops," and that those in Dutilh's inventory bore similar designs. The problem here was Dutilh had conducted business with the French West Indies for over a decade by the time of this lawsuit, so it would not have been unusual to find French-constructed barrels in his inventory.[117]

The case wound through the U.S. legal system for years before ending up before the U.S. Supreme Court in 1808, where the justices remained undecided about whether the *Ceres* had been legally confiscated by a French privateer or should have been considered safe within Spanish waters.[118] This Supreme Court finding closed the case without providing any clear resolution or clarifying its myriad ambiguities. But the final disposition of the *Ceres's* coffee, of course, was ultimately a less important story than the one told in the underlying machinations that enabled its cargo to move so expeditiously through French, Spanish, and American hands. That international partners were still willing to work together in the shadows, and to do so effectively, confirmed how a creole economy initially forged with British mainland colonies remained alive and well in the new United States.

*   *   *

The strength and increasing diversity of the young nation's coffee trade provides a powerful counterbalance to the traditional narrative of independence in the wake of the American Revolution. Far from separating themselves from the Atlantic economy, U.S. coffee merchants actively and enthusiastically embraced trade networks that provided them with a commodity cultivated beyond their borders and on which their prosperity depended. Throughout the 1780s, 1790s, and early 1800s, France and Britain had sought to influence U.S. political allegiance, first by supporting and then by attacking the new republic's trade routes. French ships stopped North American vessels suspected of trading with Britain and its colonies, condemning the ships or confiscating the cargoes. British vessels did the same to U.S. ships bound for France or the French West Indies, especially those trading with the politically troubled but still economically powerful Saint Domingue.

U.S. reactions to these pervasive depredations on the nation's shipping depended on the eye and motives of the beholder. The official political response for the most part was critical. In his 1805 letter to Congress, President Thomas Jefferson lambasted privateering as an omnipresent threat. "Our coasts have been infested and our harbours watched by private armed vessels," he declared, that "have captured, in the very entrance of our harbours, as well as on the high seas, not only the vessels of our friends coming to trade with us, but our own also."[119] U.S. traders, on the other hand, took a more ambivalent stance, finding ways to work with foreign privateers in mutually beneficial arrangements, just as Dutilh & Wachsmuth had managed so adeptly and for so long. Unlike politicians, merchants accepted some losses as an inherent risk of transatlantic shipping that they could possibly turn to their advantage, so long as incidents remained limited enough to ensure that the balance sheets ultimately tallied in the traders' favor. As one newspaper account about the state of trade with the Caribbean concluded:

> That many of our vessels had been condemned in the West Indies is certain; that others have been detained and ill treated, is equally certain; that some have been legally condemned for breach of revenue laws, cannot be denied; and that some have been falsely reported as condemned, when they were not, is now well known. At any rate our shipping is not all lost, as some would make us believe, for scarce a day passes, without some arrivals from the West Indies, and this day there were five reported on the coffee house books.[120]

Jefferson's image of "infested harbours" says more about his concerns over international acceptance of U.S. sovereignty than the realities of the Atlantic economy in the era of the early republic. The pragmatic attitudes of the merchant community, by contrast, reveal how business relationships had been recalibrated and reinforced after independence. European powers' decisions to open or close their ports, and to honor or disregard North American neutrality, shaped how U.S. merchants conducted their business abroad. But rather than limiting regional interaction, such legislation opened opportunities to

explore and compare suppliers, strike new alliances, and find the best bar-
gains. Occasional raids by European privateers were of less consequence
than the burgeoning trade in goods such as coffee, which was still being
conducted largely on U.S. ships despite the political machinations of the
governmental principals in Paris, Philadelphia, Washington, and London.

North America's political economy evolved over the first two decades of
its independence. In the early 1780s, U.S. foreign relations had used trade as
a tool of diplomacy—one of the few points of leverage the nation could at that
time employ to encourage broad-based acceptance of the expansive commercial principles through which it sought to secure its political autonomy.[121] By
the time Jefferson took office in 1800, he was decrying the "embarrassing commerce under piles of regulating laws, duties, and prohibitions" that encum-
bered trade both within and beyond the early republic's borders, and he
wondered whether the United States could "be relieved from all its shackles
in all parts of the world."[122] But free trade, as so envisioned, depended on
more than one willing participant. U.S. ambassadors found themselves stymied in their efforts to secure any such arrangement, which left them trying a variety of alternative options to promote the new nation's commercial
needs, such as courting limited trade treaties, suggesting circuitous routes
through European free ports, and fighting vigorously to protect U.S. maritime neutrality.

The nation's merchants were more creative than their political counterparts. They were adept and enterprising in the initiatives they pursued, en-
listing the assistance of intermediaries, customs officials, and colonial
revolutionaries to satisfy an international world of commerce that was growing beyond all recognition in size and scope. Interimperial trade in coffee
had existed before the American Revolution, but the multitude of ways that
such goods moved into and through North America between 1783 and 1804
signals an important shift in both the scale and pervasiveness of mercantile
commerce. Some enterprises flouted the law, and this smuggling was seen as
such by the courts. But ships sailing under flags of truce or putting into port
during times of distress were tacking so close to the winds of legality that it
made them harder to condemn outright, since although they often evaded
the spirit of the law, they might just be adhering precariously to the letters of
its strictures. What all of these coffee ventures shared, however, was the necessary and willing participation of a range of partners. This was not the work
of separate nations, in other words, but rather the collective efforts of the
producers and traders from many countries and colonies. Understanding

revolutionary and early republic business efforts within a regional context thus downplays the American Revolution as a pivotal event in shaping the Atlantic coffee economy, and runs counter to the historiographical tendency that has separated North America's colonial and early republic eras in the arenas of trade and commerce. Instead, by necessity, success in the coffee trade meant dependence on an international alliance of partners.

CHAPTER 6

The Americanization of Coffee

In January 1821, eighty-eight men and women from Pennsylvania and New Jersey filed a petition as the East Florida Coffee Land Association with the Public Lands Committee of the U.S. Congress to buy 24,000 acres of government land in Florida. They were interested in a parcel centered around Key Largo, where they proposed to grow cocoa, sugar, and indigo, although the focus of their agricultural activities, as their name implied, would be coffee production.[1] To convince legislators of the viability of such an undertaking, the petition included an extensive overview of coffee's growing conditions, as well as detailed examples of other tropical commodities that had been successfully transplanted to North America. Chief among these was sugar, which had been grown in southern Louisiana long before the United States bought the territory from France in 1803 and which had expanded appreciably in the years since, including into Florida.[2] The application also summarized years of customs data to demonstrate how much coffee U.S. citizens drank each year as well as how much coffee U.S. merchants reshipped overseas. These consumer and commercial trends, the applicants made sure to emphasize, depended entirely on imported produce.

The petitioners hoped their arguments would appeal to both sides of what was by then a decades-long debate over the relative importance of domestic production versus foreign investment for the future of U.S. economic growth. The association held out promise for both. Its venture would generate income at home for the nation's own prospective coffee farmers as well as profits for U.S. traders shipping coffee overseas. Set against this backdrop, the dream of a domestic source of coffee meant more than potential profit. It was a vision of economic independence and thus, its proponents argued, a matter of "national importance" undertaken to multiply "the resources of our country."[3]

Supplying the nation's growing numbers of coffee drinkers was no small undertaking by the time the proponents of the Key Largo experiment pled their case. Although coffee had been popular during the colonial era, its consumption had burgeoned by the nineteenth century. In 1783, U.S. citizens had drunk less than an ounce of coffee per person, but by 1840 they were consuming more coffee than almost any nation of the world—more than five pounds a year per capita. The volume of coffee that U.S. merchants shipped overseas grew almost as fast, accounting for nearly 10 percent of the country's export income in 1800 and over 15 percent by 1820.[4] But while more and more coffee both entered and left the United States through the years of the early republic, what remained constant was that it all had originated from beyond the fledgling nation's borders.

Key Largo's would-be coffee farmers recognized this dependence and deliberately positioned their project as the antidote, presenting themselves as "patriotic and enterprising citizens" in service to their country.[5] Nor were they alone in their efforts to remake coffee into a homegrown endeavor. State and federal agricultural competitions also promoted experiments in U.S. coffee cultivation (or the identification of local substitutes), and cookbook authors offered advice about how to buy, store, roast, grind, and brew coffee, while those writing etiquette manuals and "polite literature" introduced socially ambitious citizens to the range of occasions that could feature coffee drinking. The newly formed U.S. Patent Office also weighed in, processing a growing tide of applications for grinders, roasters, and brewing apparatuses by inventors who recognized coffee's potential profitability and hoped to cash in on its popularity. But while ever more writers from different sectors helped to solidify coffee's place in Americans' diets, fewer of these sources acknowledged the commodity's foreign pedigree as the nineteenth century progressed. Cookbooks and patent proposals targeted very different audiences, of course, but they shared the propensity to obscure coffee's imported origins. Instead, those promoting its sale, resale, and consumption quietly but increasingly associated the beverage instead with U.S. notions of domesticity and ingenuity—coffee was being Americanized.

Eating and Drinking Independently

The developing coffee culture of North America played out less dramatically than that of its rival beverage, tea, whose highly politicized story made

headlines at Boston Harbor in 1773. But the coffee trade too was shaped by
political decisions that tied Americans' daily lives and dietary habits to events
far beyond the nation's borders and control. This combination of coffee's production abroad and its popularity at home made it a frequent subject for
newspaper writers and pamphleteers debating the economic future of the new
United States. An anonymous contributor to the *Connecticut Courant*, for example, who wrote under the pen name "The Freeholder," understood the
"West India trade has ever been a force of wealth" that has supplied coffee as
well as "many other necessary articles." But intemperate consumption of such
luxuries, The Freeholder lamented, had created a nation in debt, and until
"the good sense of the people shall correct their habits of living," legislation
or taxation encouraging moderation or abstinence was, at least in this correspondent's opinion, the best course of action.[6] Given the steady rise in coffee's popularity for decades by the time the Freeholder's opinion appeared in
print, it was obviously disingenuous to think that people would readily ab-
stain from their habit, but the author was not alone in hoping to reduce the
nation's spending on foreign goods.

The pursuit of national self-sufficiency, or, even better, preeminence in
global markets, powerfully shaped the trajectories of agricultural production
in the early republic. As the prices of commodities fluctuated, farmers sought
crops that would garner them the highest revenues, at home and abroad. They
looked to botanists for help in testing wheat varieties for disease resistance,
for example, while considering the advantages and drawbacks of growing
peas or potatoes, or calculating the relative profitability of imported cane
sugar versus native maple sweeteners. Political observers, meanwhile, were
gauging North America's agricultural prosperity in terms of a national imperative. In *Arbustrum Americanum: The American Grove*, Humphrey Marshall, a well-known Philadelphia agriculturalist, argued that the federal
government needed to underwrite research in plant science. Experiments
with the cultivating of foreign plants, or, better still, locating native alternatives, Marshall contended, would relieve the United States of "foreign dependence." He posited, for example, that "the discovery of a plant as useful as
tobacco or the potato" that could serve as "a substitute for coffee would be of
inestimable advantage."[7]

Several learned societies launched competitions aimed at spurring agricultural innovations that encouraged local production of popular imports
or experimented with finding domestic alternatives for them. The Philadelphia Society for the Promotion of Agriculture and Agricultural Reform,

for example, offered cash awards "to promote the greater increase of the products of the land within the American States," and the fledgling Pennsylvania Horticultural Society's inaugural public flower show, which hosted hundreds of people at the elegant Masonic Hall on Chestnut Street, featured a class of useful plants "from whose prolific branches some of the greatest luxuries are derived," including an Arabian coffee tree and cuttings of West Indian sugarcane.[8]

Such efforts helped identify a few coffee substitutes, some more viable than others. As early as 1784, for example, General Lafayette wrote to George Washington asking about his interest in acquiring "seeds of the *Coffee Tree* which Resembles the Black oak" from Kentucky. Although it took him three years, Washington did finally plant some of these seeds at Mount Vernon, but apparently without much success since he provided no subsequent updates on the experiment.[9] The Kentucky coffee tree reappeared in 1793 when Thomas Jefferson wrote to James Madison and asked him to bring samples to Philadelphia so that William Bartram, the city's leading naturalist, could conduct a series of experiments. Madison assured his fellow Virginian that he would do so, but the resultant drink proved to be a poor replacement for the real brew.[10]

Coffee made from rye or barley enjoyed some popularity, particularly after the United States passed its embargo in 1807 banning U.S. exports and closing the nation's ports to British imports, thereby limiting coffee supplies. Proponents promoted homegrown concoctions, in language that was strikingly like the coffee endorsements in the early days of tea boycotts during the 1770s, as a substitute beverage for "respectable inhabitants." Recipes, particularly for rye coffee, became standard fare in period cookbooks but were most often touted as "domestic coffee" or "family coffee," the latter signaling that those authors thought it best for personal consumption rather than for guests.[11] Other options might have looked like coffee, but there the similarity ended. "Some use dry brown bread crusts, and roast them," one author suggested, while "others soak rye grain in rum" or roasted peas instead of coffee beans. But "none of these," she admitted, "were very good."[12]

Recipes for Nationalism

While botanists looked for alternatives to imports, cookbook and etiquette authors worked as assiduously to efface coffee's overseas origins, primarily through omission. Doing so allowed their readers to focus on aspects of coffee preparation and consumption that could be carried out in U.S. homes while sidestepping the implications of the commodity's foreign provenance. Cookbooks had become an increasingly popular genre of literature in the early republic, and these publications began offering much more than the basic instructions on how to prepare meals. They were now housekeeping guides intended to instruct their target audience of women about ways to supply their homes and feed their families. The provisions and preparations that authors chose to include in their texts speak volumes about shifting fashions in the cooking arts, etiquette styles, and popular health practices, and the increasing inclusion of coffee-based recipes in such publications confirms the evidence of trade statistics—that coffee was a burgeoning market attracting an ever-increasing consumer base. Some authors expressed qualms about the effect of too much caffeine in U.S. diets, but most acknowledged the inevitability of Americans' growing affection for the beverage and even touted its benefits. Their observations attest to coffee's ongoing popularity and broad acceptance.

Amelia Simmons's *American Cookery* is often credited as the first "American" cookbook.[13] Its publication was heralded as a gastronomic break with Britain because of its emphasis on specifically North American ingredients, such as corn-based recipes for Indian pudding, johnnycake, and slapjacks. Simmons did not include any recipes using coffee, since her volume included no instructions for preparing drinks, but evidence of the beverage's inroads into U.S. kitchens can still be found in the measurements she included in her recipes—her carrot pudding, for example, called for "a coffee cup full of boiled and strained carrots."[14] In phrasing her instructions in this way, Simmons made two assumptions: first, that coffee cups came in standard sizes, and, second, that such dishware would be readily available in her readers' kitchens. Richard Briggs's *The New Art of Cookery*, published four years earlier in London and reprinted in Philadelphia in 1792 and 1798, also used coffee cups for measuring amounts; he recommended, for example, "a coffee-cup full two or three times a day" of beef suet mixed with milk, water, and wheat flour as a medicine for "a disorder of the bowels."[15] Personal annotations in cookbook margins offer additional evidence that North American cooks used coffee cups as common kitchenware. For instance, Mrs. Thomas Chadwick of Philadelphia, whose copy of *The Universal Receipt Book* is now held by the Library Company of Philadelphia, handwrote a recipe for tea cake in the back of her book that required "1 coffee cup butter, 2 of sugar, 1 of milk."[16]

After 1800, more and more cookbooks provided recipes about coffee itself. Brewing may have seemed like a simple task but, as Maria Rundell noted when advertising her *New System of Domestic Cookery*, "Many receipts are given for things which, being in daily use, the mode of preparing them may be supposed too well known to require a place in a cookery book; yet, we rarely meet with butter properly melted, good toast-and-water, and well-made coffee."[17] While coffee cups appear to have been somewhat standardized, coffee brewing had not, and writers suggested a range of proportions. *The New Family Receipt-Book*, for example, recommended adding "one ounce of free ground coffee" per pint of boiling water and allowing the infusion to sit overnight before mixing it with one pint of milk, then "sweetened to every person's taste." This concoction, the authors assured, would provide "the most wholesome and agreeable breakfast, summer or winter, with toast, bread, and butter."[18] Rundell, on the other hand, recommended bringing "two ounces of freshly ground coffee" and "eight coffee cups of water" to a hard boil for six minutes, mixing in a bit of isinglass if cloudy, then boiling two to three minutes more and serving immediately.[19]

As the number of published cookbooks grew, the range of coffee recipes they offered expanded accordingly, adapted and modified to different kinds of drinkers and consumption schedules. Preparation instructions even addressed questions of health and status. Some authors recommended coffee "for literary and sedentary people" or as "especially suited to persons advanced in years," while others offered variations appropriate for children or the infirm.[20] The authors of *The New Family Receipt-Book*, which contained "eight hundred truly valuable receipts in various branches of domestic economy," especially favored coffee and promoted its use to combat a range of ills. The beverage, they asserted, cured everything from colic to flatulence and was "a powerful antidote to the temptation of spirituous liquors." Coffee could also promote productivity, they asserted, and as such was "a welcome beverage to the robust labourer, who would despise a lighter drink," a supposed attribute that no doubt would have appealed to boosters set on portraying the United States as an industrious nation.[21]

One of coffee's most frequently touted benefits was as an antidote for inebriation, a claim advanced by Robert Roberts in *The House Servant's Directory*. Published in 1827, the directory was the first such volume by an African American author released through a commercial publishing house in North America. It billed itself as an aid for servants and other domestic help, explicitly targeting audiences beyond a Black readership. The directory was sufficiently popular in its first year in print that a second edition was released in 1828. Different sections of the book offered various coffee-related instructions, which ranged from cleaning silver and silver-plated coffee urns and pots, to setting up breakfast and dessert tables, to explaining the appropriate protocols for serving after-dinner coffee and tea. Roberts provided largely functional information that accepted the popularity of coffee itself as an established fact: "You should have one cup of tea between every two of coffee," he suggested, "as they generally take more coffee than tea."[22] But it was Roberts's recommendation that "a cup of strong coffee without milk or sugar" helped in "recovering a person from intoxication" that would find its way into numerous early republic diaries.[23] John and Abigail Adams's grandson, Charles Francis Adams, for example, recounted dining with a Cambridge acquaintance, "Mr. Meredith," and as the night drew long and the two men reminisced, Adams recalled that they "drank some Sherry until I began to feel its weight." He believed that relief from his overindulgence was readily available, however, relating how he "Took a cup of Coffee to cure it and read part of Williston's *Eloquence of the United States*."[24]

Regardless of the reasons for drinking coffee—a cup at breakfast to start the day, a social engagement, relief from a previous night's immoderation, or whatever—advice writers rarely mentioned nor displayed any concern that this broadly popular commodity had to be imported. The beans seem to have just appeared on store shelves ready for North American customers to buy and consume, with no acknowledgment of either their origins as the product of the plantations of other nations, some of whom were friendlier to the United States than others, or the labor, overwhelmingly enslaved, involved in the beans' cultivation and processing. Indeed, one of the few non-U.S. references in any of these cookbooks is Maria Rundell's admission that Americans tended to drink their coffee weaker than people in other parts of the world. "If for foreigners," she added at the end of her entry for preparing coffee, "or those who like it extremely strong," she recommended upping the coffee to water ratio from two to three ounces.[25]

Even authors who were less enthusiastic about the amount of coffee consumed by U.S. citizens nevertheless recognized its increasing centrality at the nation's tables and counters over the years. Catharine Beecher, one of North America's foremost housekeeping authorities, understood that drinking coffee and tea had become deeply ingrained U.S. habits, but she implored housekeepers, whom she considered the principal guardians of domestic well-being, to minimize consumption of caffeinated beverages, at least among children.[26] That being said, despite her personal dietary reservations, Beecher still included coffee under her list of approved "temperance drinks" and offered advice about roasting, clarifying, brewing, storing, and serving, perhaps tacitly acknowledging that cookbooks had to include such basic information to appeal to a broad base of readers and purchasers. She even included a coffee grinder (Figure 13) in the volume's appendix of essential, basic kitchen furniture and utensils needed for a well-functioning U.S. household.[27]

Nor was evidence of coffee drinking's growing popularity limited to early republic kitchens. Two fortune-telling guides, both published in 1823, featured coffee—or more specifically, coffee grounds—in what were popular and lighthearted parlor room diversions for an afternoon with friends. Coffee residues that displayed the sign of a ring, for example, portended marriage, while an anchor shape promised hope and commercial success, and the outline of a mouse predicted theft and stealth. At first glance, the mystical prognostications in such publications seem to evoke coffee's imported origins through lingering associations with strange customs or foreign places. Indeed their titles, *New Norwood Gipsey; or, Complete art of Fortune-telling* and *The O.B., or West Indian Astrologer's Whole Secret Art and System of Prediction, by Planetary Influence, Laid Open,* written ostensibly by "Ignatius Lewis, the Jamaican seer of colour," self-consciously connected the art of reading coffee grounds with the exoticism of the West Indies, occult practices, and African-Caribbean fortune tellers within their marketing strategy.[28] But the texts themselves contain few references to the foreignness of either coffee or fortune-telling, and the interpretations offered for coffee ground divination were as conventional as they were humdrum. Symbols in the *New Norwood Gipsey* predicted the usual suspects of long life, good fortune, marriage and family, illness, and death, while those offered in *The O.B.* were briefer still and even more mundane, such as "small specks [for money]; a bird [for news] a cat [for an enemy]; and a dog [friendship]."[29] Neither booklet contained descriptions or visual images of either gypsies or West Indians. Indeed, the only image besides sample coffee-ground arrangements and their interpretations is a sketch depicting elite, young, white women enjoying themselves in the comfort of their home as they take turns telling each other's fortunes (Figure 14). No overseas places or magical influences are evoked in this scene of a domesticated afternoon, where the participants are well-dressed, apparently well-off, and presumably well-bred, as they savor their coffee and subsequently entertain themselves by

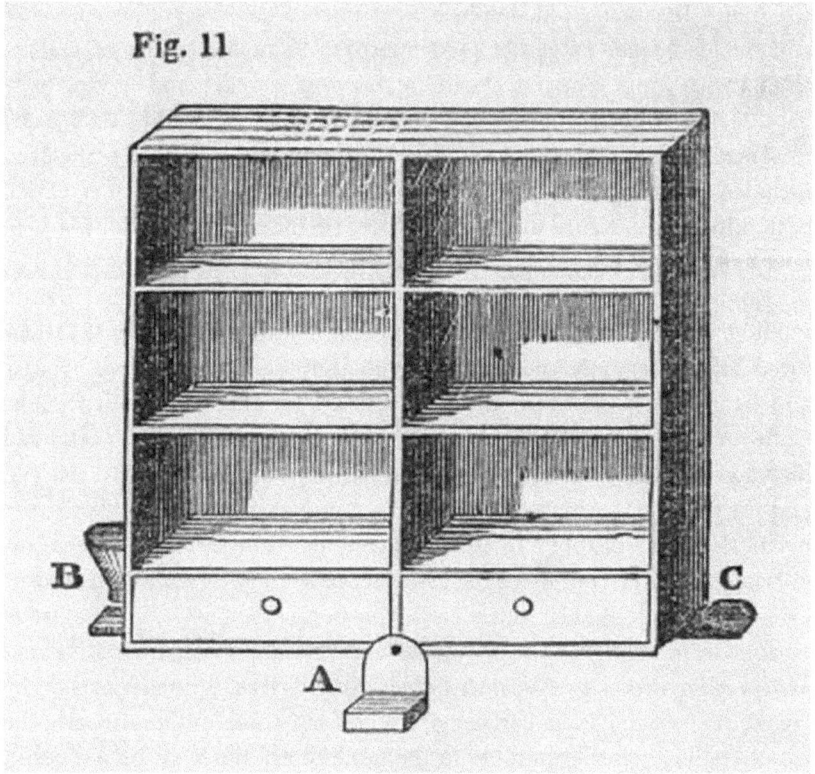

Figure 13. Catharine Beecher, *Miss Beecher's Domestic Receipt Book,* 3rd ed. (New York: Harper & Brothers, 1846), 256, Library Company of Philadelphia. The coffee grinder appears on the left side of the image marked as B; A is a salt box while C is a soap dish.

looking for the futures they hoped for in the bottoms of their matching cups and saucers.

Such popular publications recalibrated coffee to a place of comfort. Nothing about this commodity threatened either Americans' bodies or their body politics. Instead, the beverage had increasingly become pigeonholed as a pleasant everyday part of middle- and upper-class life, to be routinely enjoyed with friends and invariably part of special occasions. Even the Adamses, who had endeavored to forgo coffee during the American Revolution, resumed associating the beverage with notions of hearth and home after the founding of the republic. "I hope to be able to relieve you soon from

Figure 14. "Telling Fortunes by the Grounds of a Tea or Coffee Cup," *New Norwood Gipsey; or, Complete art of Fortune-telling* (New York: W. Borradaile, 1823), frontispiece, Library Company of Philadelphia.

domestick cares and anxieties," Abigail Adams wrote to her husband while he was traveling abroad, predicting that "I know you will want your own Bed and pillows and your Hot coffee.... How many of these little matters," she wondered, "make up a large portion of our happiness and content."[30]

But the expectation that coffee would be part of daily life soon went well beyond the middle and upper classes. By the end of the first quarter of the nineteenth century, New York City's Society for the Prevention of Pauperism was acknowledging the broad-based penchant for coffee drinking among the nation's populace regardless of class, race, or gender. In a promotional pamphlet intended to convince those of modest means to balance concerns of fitness and finance, authors urged readers to "Starve not the body to please the palate" in their weekly purchases, "but buy food that is cheap and nutritious." In this formulation, rye beat out wheat as the least expensive and healthiest grain, while peas and beans handily bested potatoes as the vegetables and starches of choice, but coffee and tea were considered in tandem rather than competition. Although the pamphlet authors acknowledged that there was "little or no nourishment in any of them," they also admitted that coffee and tea were "articles of general use, and doubtless will continue to be." And "as there are various kinds," they concluded, even "the poor ought to be economical in making their selection."[31] Coffee, in effect, had been reconceptualized by the early nineteenth century as the familiar, domesticated, and quintessentially everyday drink of the people, no matter their status.

Buy American, By Americans

The coffee featured in prescriptive literature became increasingly divorced from its countries or colonies of origin, but its foreign provenance could not be as easily excised from U.S. trade accounts. Concerned commentators continued to complain about the adverse financial consequences of the nation's burgeoning love affair with a commodity it could not provide for itself. Among the voices raised against U.S. coffee consumption, James Tilton was one of the most prominent and most strident. An American physician and soldier from Delaware, Tilton had served as a state delegate in the Continental Congress of 1783 and 1784 and would later become Surgeon General of the U.S. Army during the War of 1812. He was a fierce critic of coffee, which he considered injurious not just to the health and finances of individuals and families, but also to the nation. The latter concerns, which he publicly and repeatedly voiced, argued that the importation of coffee embroiled the United States in the disputes and conflicts of other nations and empires, a cost that he thought far too high a price to pay for what he dismissed as a trifling morning or evening repast. "Independence has been the theme from the days of 1776 from Georgia to Maine, and yet strange to tell, few or more of us think of eating and drinking independently," Tilton wrote in 1819. "Is it not a thousand times more ridiculous to send to the West Indies for breakfast or supper," he continued, that was in effect the result of North Americans' "obstinate adherence to tea, coffee, &c.?"[32]

        Other voices joined Tilton's in castigating Americans' embrace of the coffee cup. An anonymous article that appeared in the *National Recorder* under the heading "Rye Coffee" began with a lighthearted vignette in which a "re-spectable friend in the country" duped the author by serving a beverage of roasted rye in place of his traditional morning refreshment. "If it really can be made to answer as a substitute of coffee," the guest mused, "what an immense saving it would prove to the United States annually!"[33] But the tone quickly turned more serious when the author tried to estimate the potential ramifications of current trends in coffee drinking at the national level. While other goods such as "tobacco and ardent spirits" might be questionable as consumer choices, those goods themselves were "mostly the product of our own soil," so the impact of imprudent consumption was primarily limited, this author argued, "to the consumer and his own family." Coffee, on the other hand, posed a very different kind of problem. Its drinkers, "who prefer the gratification of their appetites to the good of the community," the author warned, indulged in a habit that could only be furnished by other nations and, consequently, drained millions of dollars out of the country annually.[34] Coffee critics such as these argued strenuously for the need of a domestic alternative.

Peter Stephen Chazotte, who led efforts to establish the East Florida Cof-fee Land Association, which opened this chapter, may at first glance seem like a strange spokesman for such nationalistic agricultural ambitions, as the United States was not his first, or even second, homeland. Formerly a Saint Dominguan coffee and cocoa farmer named Pierre Etienne Chazotte before he anglicized his name, Chazotte had fled to Charleston, South Carolina, in 1798 after British troops evacuated the French colony and the United States rescinded its treaties with France during the outbreak of the Quasi-War. Al-though Chazotte soon became a U.S. citizen, he nevertheless harbored hopes of eventually returning to Saint Domingue when there was "a tolerable state of peace." In 1800, he tried to resettle in the still war-torn French possession, but left it for Baltimore less than four years later when Haiti declared its independence.[35] On his return to North America, Chazotte's ship was blown off course and landed on the southernmost tip of Florida, where, although it was February, he encountered a "country, covered with green trees and flow-ers" that, based on his awestruck description, he thought captured perfectly "the image of an everlasting Spring."[36] The region's potential for agriculture likely impressed Chazotte from that moment on, although he would take years to formulate his vision for its development. In fact, a few months later, Chazotte sailed again, this time for France, where he spent a decade ex-perimenting with grape growing. Only when the Napoleonic empire collapsed did Chazotte return to the United States permanently, settling in Philadelphia. There he worked as a French teacher and occasional pamphleteer, publishing tracts on everything from banking regulation and foreign language education to the causes of the Haitian Revolution. He also returned to his prior interest in domestic coffee farming.[37]

Chazotte's transatlantic crossings mirrored those of hundreds of other people whose lives were disrupted in the late eighteenth- and early nineteenth-century Atlantic world. Revolutionary upheavals, as well as intra- and interimperial warfare from the Seven Years' War through the War of 1812 and the Age of Revolution transformed the circumstances of all classes, from impoverished enslaved laborers to wealthy planters. Colonies changed hands, political systems emerged and fell, and in the case of France's richest Caribbean colony, Saint Domingue, revolt ended a labor system based on chattel bondage. The United States was but one actor on this rapidly changing world stage, and its political independence was just the starting point in its physical, governmental, and economic transformations. Within three decades of its founding, the young republic had more than doubled in size, a geographic expansion that fueled a debate about U.S. diplomacy and economic strategy. The beginnings of this debate dated to the independence era and revolved around the questions of whether North America's future lay with internal investments and expanded domestic production or, as it had during the colonial era, in overseas trade forged through diplomatic relations and regional networks. Late in 1820, Chazotte, the quintessentially Atlantic world citizen and now Pennsylvania resident, published a pamphlet that endeavored to resolve this debate.

In *Facts and Observations of the Culture of Vines, Olives, Capers, Almonds &c. in the Southern States, and of Coffee, Cocoa, and Cochineal in East Florida*, Chazotte drew on his experience in Saint Domingue and France, as well as his brief unscheduled visit to Florida some sixteen years before that had so captured his imagination, to argue that coffee cultivation in the newly acquired southernmost peninsula of the United States could provide a model for developing an independent American agricultural economy free from reliance on foreign imports. As far-fetched as Floridian coffee farming may seem today, his plan attracted wide-ranging support at the time.[38] Marmaduke Burrough, a physician based in Camden, New Jersey, for example, was one of Chazotte's early allies, and the two men corresponded regularly about Florida's agricultural potential for two years before Burrough agreed to sign on to the effort.[39]

Chazotte also turned to some of the early republic's finest political minds for counsel and sponsorship. He sought advice from then ex-president Thomas Jefferson, as well as from his successor James Madison, and both prominent statesmen agreed to review and comment on drafts of the East Florida petition before it went to Congress. Madison, an avid farmer and proponent of domestic products considered it imperative that the United States remain on the cutting edge of agricultural innovation. "Experiments for introducing these valuable productions are strongly recommended," he wrote Chazotte, noting that rice and cotton, which were now cornerstones of early republic agricultural production, were "at one time as little understood as that of the article whose merits you discuss."[40]

Chazotte, Burrough, Madison, and Jefferson all recognized coffee's profit-making potential in 1821, and self-consciously associated the commodity with ideas of "Yankee ingenuity" and national identity. Jefferson and Madison thought the project might revitalize Florida, an area that many politicians considered an ecological wasteland. The Adams-Onis Treaty had formalized its transfer from Spain to the United States in 1819, but Congress had resisted immediate ratification for a territory that some, like Congressman John Randolph of Virginia, thought irredeemable. "It is," Randolph had argued before the House of Representatives, "a land of swamps, of quagmires, of frogs and alligators and mosquitoes! A man, sir, would not immigrate into Florida—no, not from Hell itself!"[41] But supporters of the East Florida Coffee Land Association project thought differently. Chazotte described Florida as a potential "grand national nursery" that could expand U.S. commercial and global significance by deploying "numerous consuls" to "procure the first qualities of plants and seeds." He also had no doubt that homegrown coffee would attract North American drinkers.[42] "Agriculture," he argued, "is alone capable of raising a nation to the highest degree of happiness and independence."[43]

By January 1821, the East Florida Coffee Land Association had renamed itself the even more patriotic-sounding American Coffee Land Association when Chazotte formally presented his proposal to the Speaker of the U.S. House of Representatives, John W. Taylor. He, in turn, forwarded the documents to the House Committee on Agriculture for review. Congress ratified the treaty ceding Florida during the committee's deliberations, which resulted in a preliminary report on Chazotte's coffee venture that declared it "laudable and praiseworthy," while commending its proposer for his "enterprising and patriotic" spirit. Rather than recommend immediate action, however, the committee resolved that the "matter be laid over to the next Congress." Florida, after all, had only been recently acquired, and due diligence necessitated careful consideration and study before land grants as large as that proposed by Chazotte could be fully assessed, much less awarded.[44]

Despite the delay, Chazotte remained optimistic and immediately set about raising funds for an exploratory expedition to have more details about Florida's agricultural potential at hand when Congress reconvened. He requested a passport from Secretary of State John Quincy Adams to travel into what was still a Spanish territory, and Adams obliged, requesting that "all persons in authority under the United States" provide delegates of the American Coffee Land Association with "such convenient aid as it may be in their power to render." Meanwhile, the energetic Chazotte had managed to recruit almost a hundred contributors to his enterprise by late spring of 1821.[45] Although some of the names appended to the petition suggest that early subscribers were either French or of French extraction, Chazotte strove to maintain as homegrown an image as possible for his coffee venture, hastening to reassure legislators that his backing came from "one hundred respectable families, not of foreigners, but of citizens of Pennsylvania, New-Jersey."[46] With both the requisite official sanction and financial support in place, Chazotte then engaged the services of the sloop *Hunter* for his voyage south. Burrough accompanied him, having volunteered to serve as the expedition's doctor, as well as its surveyor, along with four other members of the association and five men whom Chazotte had engaged as laborers.[47]

The American Coffee Land Association expedition set sail from Philadelphia on the portentous date of July 4, 1821, and arrived in Saint Augustine nine days later. Ceremonies commemorating the formal transfer of the former Spanish possession had ended just three days before the *Hunter* docked, and in what were no doubt unsettled times of transition, the contingent received an effusive welcome from the *Florida Gazette*. "This expedition," noted the *Gazette's* editor, "has created the most lively interest here because we are perfectly sensible of our impotence till agriculture furnishes us with those mines of wealth and abundance, which are inexhaustible riches, and can alone insure," he predicted, the territory's "prosperity and happiness."[48]

Chazotte and his party spent nearly three months exploring the eastern Florida coastline. After leaving Saint Augustine, they first visited Biscayne Bay, near modern-day Miami, where the group reported "a friendly reception and hospitality" from local U.S. residents, as well as terrain endowed with fertile soil, thick timber, and plentiful water, but they were not able to identify the locations that most suited the association's principal project. "We have been laying in the bay within the Cape of East Florida," Chazotte reported, "& have explored all the lands & rivers adjacent to it, a great deal of Sugar Cane land we have found—the coffee land, little." Hence, he continued, "this will not answer our views," and the expedition expanded its search.[49] The *Hunter* next set course for Key Largo and Florida's outlying coastal cays. Although these barrier islands were far from any established town or port, Chazotte nevertheless declared the territory "a situation suitable for the location of the intended settlement." It encompassed approximately the same acreage as stipulated in the petition still pending in Congress, and appeared "free from any prior claims, and so bounded as to make its limits easily described and defined."[50] He christened the new settlement-to-be Jeffersonville.

When the enterprising voyagers of the American Coffee Land Association returned north to Philadelphia they pronounced their expedition a success and proceeded to disseminate their findings to the association's membership at a general meeting held on December 26, 1821, at the Citizen's Hotel.[51] At this juncture, they also amended their earlier proposal to Congress by adding a third justification to their application for subsidized land that they hoped would appeal to the leaders of a young republic determined to raise their nation's profile on the world stage. The association's proposed settlement would not only provide individual investors with handsome returns while challenging the hegemony of British, French, Spanish, and Haitian coffee producers, but also purge the newly acquired territory of "the contraband traffic which existed under the late government."[52] The establishment of Floridian coffee plantations, in other words, could serve as the first line of defense against the smuggling of foreign-produced beans into North America from elsewhere in the Atlantic world, an illicit traffic that the association's promoters suggested would otherwise increase given the geographic proximity of Florida to the Gulf of Mexico and the various non-U.S. coffee producers of the Caribbean.

The only effort to establish coffee estates in continental North America was doomed before it began, of course. Chazotte and his followers had assembled a barrage of information that drew on scientific literature and trade data to consider the political, economic, and social impact of coffee growing in the United States. But while their report contained details down to the longitude and latitude of existing coffee-supplying colonies in the West Indies, it perplexingly failed to account for altitude. French and British West Indian prescriptive literature recommended that coffee trees be planted at least 2,000 feet about sea level for the best yields and most aromatic and high-quality produce; the crop fared even better if trees were planted higher still.[53] Consequently, even had Congress approved the plan, Key Largo was too close to sea level (indeed, it was below sea level in several places) for coffee to grow well and for the American Coffee Land Association to succeed. Congress did not deny their petition on grounds of practicality, however, but because public land grants were then limited to tracts valued at no more than $5,000, far less than the association's request for 24,000 acres at a total value of $30,000. Nonetheless, in its written decision, Congress acknowledged the benefits of a domestic coffee industry and applauded the petitioners for their "intelligence and ability." And while legislators could not lend their support to the endeavor, they concluded by acknowledging that these would-be coffee farmers had demonstrated "expanded and liberal views of national patriotism" in promoting these "experiments for introducing these valuable productions."[54]

Patenting Patriotism

If coffee itself could not be produced in the United States, the tools needed to prepare and serve it—unlike during the colonial era—increasingly could be. In 1790, Congress had passed the "Act for the Promotion of Useful Arts" intended to foster innovation and U.S competitiveness on the international stage, as well as to promote economic growth.[55] Eight years later, the U.S. Patent Office granted its first patent related to coffee, just the twenty-sixth invention overall to receive such protection. The applicant was Thomas Bruff, a dentist and inventor from Chestertown, Maryland, who had designed a wall-mounted coffee mill that an individual could operate using a hand crank (Figure 15). Roasted beans were poured into a hopper on the top of the machine and then ground as they passed through rotating three-inch, grooved iron plates. Bruff even penned a note to Thomas Jefferson, boasting that his coffee milling machine could grind "a pound [of coffee] in 4 & ½ minutes" and requesting the president's personal patronage, which he explicitly couched in terms of patriotism.[56] Indeed, the language he used to describe his invention was strikingly like Chazotte's justification for domestic coffee planting. "Nature has designed me for inventing," Bruff enthusiastically wrote his distinguished prospective investor, "such things are almost

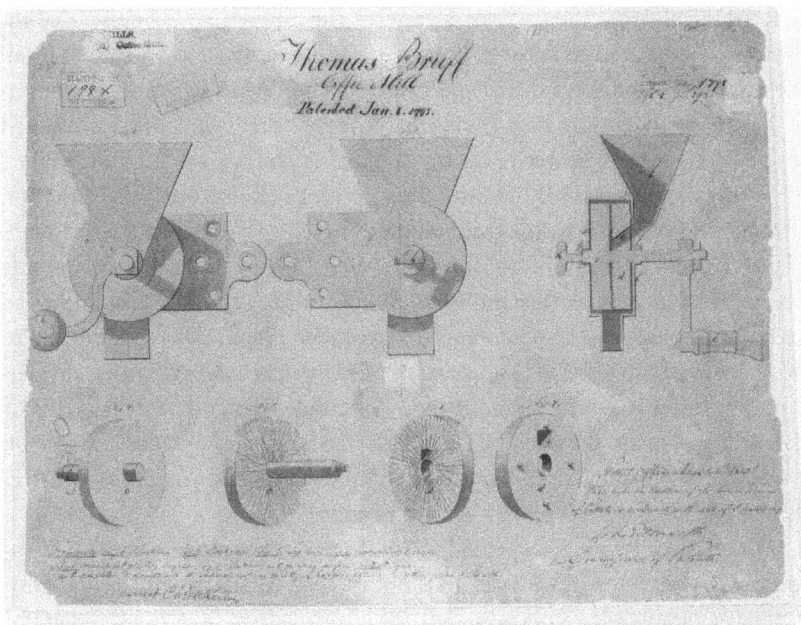

Figure 15. Thomas Bruff Coffee Mill, patented January 8, 1798. Record Group 241: Records of the Patent and Trademark Office, National Archives, Identifier 149285598, https://catalog.archives.gov/id/149285598.

as easy to me, as to eat or sleep; and if I could live by it . . . I would devote my life in that way, to the service of my country."[57]

Although there is no indication that Jefferson responded to Bruff's appeal, the U.S. president would have been an appropriate target as a backer. The Virginian once described coffee as "the favorite drink of the civilised world" and speculated that at least a pound of coffee a day was consumed at his Monticello home during the many years of his retirement. Estate inventories included unroasted beans in barrels stored in the estate cellars weighing as much as sixty pounds, and the records of more than one guest comment on Jefferson's propensity for offering coffee as well as tea at breakfast and after dinner.[58]

Bruff was in the vanguard of a wave of coffee-related innovators in the first half of the nineteenth century. As interest in the beverage grew, so too did the range of household devices necessary for its preparation and service. Although a fire in December 1836 destroyed most of the first four decades of

U.S. patent records, a legislative act passed the following year permitted inventors to submit either copies of their patent licenses or certified copies of the originals to reassert their legal title, so some drawings and descriptions of these early inventions have survived. Moreover, the Patent Office published re-created lists of registered patents, and although they are limited primarily to titles and basic outlines, and thus prevent detailed analysis of the science behind evolving coffee technologies, they do at least give a good sense of the range of innovators and innovations that emerged within this rapidly developing industry. Between 1790 and 1836, the U.S. Patent Office approved no fewer than seventeen patents related to coffee preparation. In addition to Bruff's mill, these included eight patents for coffee grinders or mills, another three for coffee roasters, and four more for coffee pots and other brewing or cleaning apparatus. Between 1837 and 1865, the numbers kept increasing, with eleven patents for coffee mills, thirty for coffee roasters, and at least thirty-three individual design patents for coffee pots.[59]

All of these inventions provided additional opportunities to link innovations in the coffee industry with ideas about U.S. progress and ingenuity, a strategy many innovators adopted. The Virginia firm of Waite & Sener, for example, which patented the Old Dominion coffee pot, consciously and repeatedly associated its product with notions of national pride. "Virginia, which has supplied us with several Presidents," claimed one notice for the coffee pot, "now steps forward and furnishes us with the very best kind of Coffee Pot that was ever invented." Another promotional announcement took a different tack but pursued the same goal by disparaging the "well-known French 'biggin,'" which the author noted "American travelers usually bring home with them," as "worthless beside the Old Dominion." Indeed, the author concluded, "We doubt that there can be such perfect coffee beverages, the world over, as this invention places on our breakfast table daily."[60] By mid-century, the nationalist appeal of Old Dominion coffee pot purveyors had reached full flower in this remarkable paean to nation, science, taste, and political economy that appeared in *Harper's Weekly*:

> There is a state well known to Fame,
> That ev'ry man admires,
> The noblest of the "Old Thirteen,"
> That State that "never tires."
> The mother, she, of Presidents;
> And it is our intention

To show that she has given birth
Through genius and invention,
To something more than one who rules
The people of a nation,
That is, a boon to bless mankind
Throughout the vast creation.

One of the Old Dominion's sons,
Fond of his coffee, very,
Conceived a plan by which to get
The flavor of the berry;
And as we live in days of steam,
He thought he'd not eschew it,
To bring about what he desired;
Steam was the thing to do it.
A coffee pot he then did make,
On which he placed reliance;
In its Construction based upon
The principles of science.

The appeal is clear: Purchasers of an Old Dominion coffee pot can be assured of its quality since it comes from the same state as many of the nation's first leaders and from a place lauded as a proving ground for national ingenuity and scientific principles. Buyers, in other words, were investing in much more than a kitchen implement when making their decision about a coffee pot. They were choosing to support a U.S.-based business with global aspirations. And just in case readers might think such technological advances beyond their means, the final stanza of what was, after all, an advertisement made sure to address any concerns about cost:

Don't think that, if you lay aside
The pot you have been using,
And buy an "Old Dominion" Pot,
Your purse you'll be abusing;
It is not so; what you invest
Is far from being lost,
The coffee savored within a year,
Will ten times pay the cost.

Everyone had a role to play, such advertising suggested, in advancing the nation's place in the coffee industry, and everyone could afford to do so.

Brazil, the U.S., and the Creation of a Global Market

The Americanization of coffee within the United States happened at the same time as equally significant changes in importation patterns that tied the fate and fortunes of the industry firmly to a different external supplier, the newly independent nation of Brazil. Necessity largely drove this move as production levels plummeted in the Caribbean following independence in Haiti (1804) and the passage of the Act for the Abolition of Slavery in the British West Indies (1834).[61] Haiti, Puerto Rico, and Cuba remained important sources of supply through the 1820s. Coffee from the British, French, Dutch, and Danish West Indies, however, became increasingly marginal to the American market. The United States also still brought in some coffee from both the Dutch and British East Indies that catered to specialized markets and high-end buyers, and even smaller amounts of coffee arrived from Africa, Asia, and Holland. But the clear change in coffee sourcing came from the rapid and sustained investment in Brazilian exports. Brazil had provided less than 0.33 percent of American's coffee in 1821. By 1832, that figure had leapt to 28 percent, and by 1844 it stood at more than 60 percent of total U.S. imports.[62]

Coffee had been a minor industry for the Portuguese colony of Brazil through the 1810s, providing less than 2 percent of its total export value, far less than the income generated by sugar and cotton, which stood at roughly one-third and one-quarter respectively.[63] But even during Brazil's late colonial period, patterns had emerged that set the stage for the subsequent engagement of the new Empire of Brazil (1822) with the United States to build what would become a spectacularly profitable and global industry for both nations.

Most existing studies about Brazil's early coffee economy focus on the factors that affected supply, such as abundant undeveloped land, cheap enslaved labor, and an extraordinary opportunity to capitalize on plummeting global production caused by revolution in the world's principal coffee producer, Saint Domingue. Such conditions, however, were not unique to coffee. Sugar, for example, could have benefited from the same circumstances, but that crop experienced no comparable production increase in Brazil. In fact, consumer demand as well as regulatory adjustments would put the two industries on quite different trajectories. Considering the timing of Brazil's rapid shift from sugar to coffee production alongside changes in U.S. legislation governing tariff rates reveals how codependent the Brazilian and American coffee markets had become by the mid-nineteenth century.

Despite a somewhat spotty documentary record, the remarkable increase in the amount of coffee passing through Rio de Janeiro, Brazil's principal port, is evident. In 1807, Rio exported 1,574 metric tons of coffee, much more than any other Brazilian city. By comparison, Bahia was the second largest exporter of coffee, but shipped an annual average of only 72 metric tons between 1796 and 1811. The disparity between these cities only grew through the nineteenth century. By 1817, Rio was shipping 13,447 metric tons of coffee overseas. The volume of this trade had grown to 52,582 metric tons by 1836 and reached 95,569 metric tons in 1848.[64] Indeed, as early as 1827, coffee had overtaken sugar as the nation's principal export, increasing at an average of 9 percent per annum over the next decade and a half.[65]

The destinations for this coffee also changed dramatically between the 1820s and 1830s. Years earlier, the first Brazilian coffee had come into the United States aboard the merchant ship *Marquis de Someriulas,* which arrived in Salem, Massachusetts, in 1809 with 1,522 bags of beans.[66] From these small beginnings, the influx of Brazilian coffee transformed the U.S. market in terms of both volume and source, and it did so quickly. In the 1820s, three nations—Germany, Belgium, and the United States—accounted for more than 60 percent of Brazil's coffee shipped abroad. By 1836, however, the United States had surpassed all other countries, doing so at a time when the amount of coffee Brazil sent overseas was growing exponentially. The number of American vessels arriving in Rio alone more than doubled from 62 to 159 between 1819 and 1824, and averaged 130 ships a year for the next decade and a half.[67] "Coffee is our gold," proclaimed U.S. merchants, "and in the place of its libations we are in the best and noblest society."[68]

These numbers tell only part of the story, however, for while Brazil's proportional share grew, the overall market for coffee itself was also skyrocketing. Total U.S. imports, which had amounted to just over 21 million pounds in 1821, reached nearly 100 million pounds by 1833, and stood at some 158 million pounds in 1842, an increase of more than 700 percent.[69] The value of the coffee trade likewise rose relative to the nation's balance of trade overall. In 1791, coffee imports were worth only $580,712, less than one-third of America's sugar imports. Three decades later, however, the amount of coffee brought into the United States was worth almost $4.5 million and in 1833 it had more than doubled to $10.5 million.[70] Not only did Brazilian sugar exports to the United States fail to keep pace, but they also shrank during the early 1830s. Although Brazil still produced sugar, it went to Portugal, Hamburg (Germany), and the Austrian Empire. While coffee had become very big business, one Brazilian historian tersely concluded that the country's sugar exports became "unimportant."[71]

Explanations for how and why the United States became both a prodigious consumer and a crucial partner in redistributing Brazilian coffee worldwide date back at least to the coffee tariffs first proposed in aid of national revenue just after U.S. independence. As early as 1791, Alexander Hamilton, then Secretary of the Treasury, had argued that domestic improvements flourished best under "the incitement and patronage of government." To encourage North American producers to enter competitive international markets, he recommended providing "premiums and other artificial encouragements," as well as the imposition of tariffs on specific popular imported commodities.[72] Hamilton's idea was deceptively simple. Taxes on foreign goods would not only reduce existing federal debt, but also finance the agricultural experimentation that might decrease foreign dependence on them in the future. While many of Hamilton's suggestions were not supported by Jeffersonians, who felt his ideas favored industry more than agriculture, his program of higher tariffs on specific imported commodities did garner bipartisan support. Among the goods targeted for such sanctions were coffee along with sugar, tea, and tobacco, all of which were criticized as habit-forming luxuries that symbolized the new republic's enduring and regrettable reliance on the production of foreign nations and colonies. But of course, these commodities were also extremely popular with North American buyers or else they would not have been eyed by the federal government as potential sources of revenue that the young republic so desperately needed.

Coffee quickly surpassed most other taxed imports, garnering over $600,000 in tax revenue or 15 percent of all import tariff income by the 1810s. Less than a decade later that amount had doubled, to $1.2 million per annum in duties, and by 1828 it approached $1.5 million. Still more notable was that these returns accrued even though the tax on tea was consistently two to three times higher than on coffee.[73] Hamilton and his successors had chosen their sources of tax revenue well.

Of the four goods singled out for import taxation, two—sugar and tobacco—were also grown in the United States, and protective tariffs undoubtedly supported the expansion of these domestic industries by limiting international competition. But of course, despite the best efforts of botanists and entrepreneurs, no homegrown option had been discovered for either coffee or tea, united again in public debate a half century after the Boston Tea Party and Boston coffee riots of the 1770s. And yet it was these caffeinated beverages that were increasingly in demand, not only by a growing number of U.S. drinkers, but also by temperance reformers who, seeking alternatives to distilled spirits, sought to reduce the price of coffee and tea enough to make them accessible to a broader range of consumers.[74] The anti-alcohol lobby certainly understood that coffee came from abroad, but it maintained that ongoing importation was essential and needed to be as unencumbered as possible to counter what reformers saw as Americans' much more dangerous dependence on liquor.

Weighing the benefits and costs of foreign imports against domestic social and economic consequences played out on the congressional floor during the debates about tariff reduction. John Reed, a representative of Massachusetts, acknowledged that neither coffee nor tea could "be produced in our country" but argued that they "are of universal use and essential to the comfort and happiness of the people of the United States." While some of his fellow delegates feared the loss of income should tariffs be repealed, Reed spoke passionately in favor of their elimination. "The great and glorious temperance reformation," he argued, "will greatly increase the use of tea and coffee, as a substitute for ardent spirits." He also pointed to the revenue generated by merchants who reshipped coffee overseas, as "we import tea and coffee, not only for ourselves, but for other nations." Indeed, of the roughly 79,000 pounds of coffee brought in during 1831, Reed estimated that more than half was sent back abroad "by the talent and enterprise of our merchants" who have made "our country . . . the great depository of the articles in question." He was not far off. Of the roughly 420 million pounds of coffee imported in the decade before these debates, 39 percent, or more than 162 million pounds, had been reshipped to other countries.[75] And Reed, like other coffee advocates of the early nineteenth century, also linked his arguments to notions of patriotism and progress, imploring Congress not to "check a reformation essential to national honor, character, and salvation."[76] The motion passed by a two-thirds vote and, in 1830, the tariff was cut in half. In July 1832 it was abolished altogether, making the United States the only nation at the time not to tax the importation of foreign coffee.[77]

The impact of this legislation was immediate and dramatic as America's share of global coffee imports rose from 7 percent in 1823 to 24 percent in 1835.[78] These soaring importation rates led in turn to increased consumption rates of the beverage domestically—more than doubling in the United States during the same period.[79] Indeed, so many Americans were enjoying their brew that one mid-nineteenth-century commentator reckoned "no article entirely of foreign production enters more largely into general consumption than coffee, and none has increased in such ratio."[80] Brazilians also celebrated the shift in trade patterns. An article appearing in one of the country's leading commercial newspapers of the time noted that "the imports of our coffee into the U.S. are now competing in terms of volume with those from Cuba and Saint Domingue. A traveler who visited the interior of Cuba said that in that island growers are abandoning the cultivation of coffee because, according to them, they cannot compete with Brazilians."[81]

Teetotalers pushed both caffeinated beverages, but a comparison of the relative value of coffee to tea imports in the United States from 1821 through 1865 (Table 3) demonstrates a decided preference for the former. These data also document a precipitous drop in the price of coffee. Grocers and retailers adjusted costs depending on city and state, of course, but the national average, based on quantity and value, suggests that coffee went from nineteen cents a pound in 1821 to eleven cents by 1833, and cost only seven cents by 1841. In other words, while coffee and tea sold at within a penny per pound of each other in 1821, tea had become three times more expensive by the 1830s. The elimination of import tariffs did not affect both caffeinated beverages equally. The end of taxes coupled with a reliable and ever-growing supply partner tilted the balance, and the United States thus became a predominantly coffee-drinking and coffee-trading nation.[82]

The nature of coffee shipping also changed as the trade grew in scale and profitability, and became concentrated in fewer and fewer hands. Before the development of railroads, coffee was transported to the Brazilian coast by mule, where it was warehoused, sacked, and then stored until purchased by an export firm for shipment overseas. Export firms, in this sense, acted as consignment brokers, intermediaries who provided the bridge between Brazil's coffee planters and foreign coffee importers.[83] Before 1828, British export firms had dominated this arena, the four largest firms managing up to a third of all coffee exports in a given year. But following the repeal of U.S. coffee

Table 3. Comparison of U.S. Coffee and Tea Imports by Volume and Value, 1821–1855

Year	Coffee Quantity (in lbs.)	Coffee Value	Tea Quantity (in lbs.)	Tea Value
1821	21,000,000	$4 million	5,000,000	$1 million
1822	26,000,000	$6 million	7,000,000	$2 million
1823	37,000,000	$7 million	8,000,000	$2 million
1824	39,000,000	$5 million	9,000,000	$3 million
1825	45,000,000	$5 million	10,000,000	$4 million
1826	37,000,000	$4 million	10,000,000	$4 million
1827	50,000,000	$4 million	6,000,000	$2 million
1828	55,000,000	$5 million	8,000,000	$2 million
1829	51,000,000	$5 million	7,000,000	$2 million
1830	29,000,000	$5 million	9,000,000	$2 million
1831	82,000,000	$6 million	5,000,000	$1 million
1832	92,000,000	$9 million	10,000,000	$3 million
1833	100,000,000	$11 million	14,000,000	$5 million
1834	80,000,000	$9 million	16,000,000	$6 million
1835	103,000,000	$11 million	14,000,000	$5 million
1836	94,000,000	$10 million	16,000,000	$5 million
1837	88,000,000	$9 million	17,000,000	$6 million
1838	88,000,000	$8 million	14,000,000	$3 million
1839	107,000,000	$10 million	9,000,000	$2 million
1840	96,000,000	$9 million	20,000,000	$5 million
1841	115,000,000	$10 million	12,000,000	$3 million
1842	118,000,000	$9 million	16,000,000	$5 million
1843	98,000,000	$6 million	14,000,000	$4 million
1844	161,000,000	$10 million	16,000,000	$4 million
1845	108,000,000	$6 million	20,000,000	$6 million
1846	138,000,000	$8 million	20,000,000	$5 million
1847	157,000,000	$9 million	17,000,000	$4 million
1848	151,000,000	$8 million	24,000,000	$6 million
1849	165,000,000	$9 million	16,000,000	$4 million
1850	145,000,000	$11 million	30,000,000	$5 million
1851	153,000,000	$13 million	17,000,000	$5 million
1852	195,000,000	$14 million	29,000,000	$7 million
1853	199,000,000	$16 million	28,000,000	$8 million
1854	162,000,000	$15 million	24,000,000	$7 million
1855	191,000,000	$17 million	25,000,000	$7 million

Source: Bureau of the Census, "Foreign Trade and Other International Transactions" (Series U-1-167), *Historical Statistics of the United States, Colonial Times to 1957* (Washington, DC: U.S. Census Bureau, 1960), 549.

tariffs, American shippers began commanding a far larger market share. By 1835, the five largest U.S. export firms controlled two-thirds of Brazil's coffee exports, with the top two export firms, Birckhead & Company and Maxwell, Wright & Company, holding fully half of that amount between them.[84]

Packed in bags and barrels, Brazil's coffee beans were consigned by these companies to U.S. ports already familiar with trading the commodity, including Philadelphia, New York, and Baltimore, as well as some new destinations, such as Charleston and especially New Orleans, where merchants were keen to cash in on its profitability.[85] What had not changed in this calculus, of course, was the ongoing U.S. reliance on foreign production. The number of ports shipping coffee may have declined as investors shifted from several West Indian islands to one dominant partner, and the number of American cities bringing coffee into the county may have grown, but the fact remained that this whole economy relied entirely on an imported commodity.[86]

The demand for more and more Brazilian coffee not only affected balance sheets in the United States, but also fueled the expanding and increasingly lucrative reexport trade that shipped coffee from the United States to Europe and elsewhere across the globe. Annual reports of the Secretary of the U.S. Treasury reveal not just how much coffee came into the country but how much was reconsigned abroad, as well as the revenues that this reexport trade accrued to the nation's economy.[87] Import statistics are available from 1791, but valuations are more consistent after 1821 and show sharp spikes in coffee reexports, especially after 1832, when overall volume of trade grew most dramatically.

One of the most important ramifications of this escalating demand was a pressure to increase Brazil's supply of beans, which was accomplished through the rapid development of predominantly small and middling coffee farms in the Brazilian southeast, accompanied by a simultaneous reinvestment and reentrenchment in slavery.[88] Prior to the 1820s, fewer than half of Brazil's coffee's producers relied predominantly on slavery. By 1836, however, almost all did.[89] One study estimated that over half a million people were imported into the country as coffee began its ascent, and up to 300,000 of these came after the official abolition of Brazil's slave trade in 1831. The vast majority of these enslaved men, women, and children ended up on coffee farms.[90] By 1843, Brazil led the world's coffee production (Table 4).

Not only did the United States turn a blind eye to Brazil's increasing reliance on coerced labor, but many traders also assisted in keeping the

Table 4. Comparison of Global Coffee Production, 1843

Producer	Lbs. of Coffee Produced	% of Global Trade
Brazil	170,000,000	37
Java and Sumatra	140,000,000	31
Cuba	45,000,000	10
St. Domingo	38,000,000	8.5
Puerto Rico and La Guayra	36,000,000	8
British West Indies	10,000,000	2
Ceylon	7,000,000	1.5
East Indies and Mocha	6,000,000	1.5

Source: "Commercial Statistics: Statistical View of the Coffee Trade," *Merchants' Magazine and Commercial Review* (September 1, 1845), 279.

transatlantic traffic in enslaved Africans alive. Secretary of State John Calhoun, writing to the U.S. minister in Brazil, Henry Wise, summed up his nation's political stance succinctly: "The avowed policy of Great Britain is to destroy that relation in both countries and throughout the world. If it should be consummated, it would destroy the peace and prosperity of both and transfer the production of tobacco, rice, cotton, sugar and coffee from the United States and Brazil to her possessions beyond the Cape of Good Hope."[91] Politicians, importers, and planters were united in their desire to prevent this from happening. Indeed, U.S. coffee importers not only tolerated but also facilitated slavery in the coffee-growing regions of Brazil. Both of the leading U.S. coffee importers, Birckhead & Company and Maxwell, Wright & Co., as well as the third-largest U.S. coffee importer, Forbes, Valentino & Co., either sold or chartered ships to slave traders after abolition of the legal slave trade.[92] This chapter in Brazilian history has been well charted by historians, who directly tie the country's reliance on enslaved labor, which persisted until near the end of the nineteenth century, to the soaring profitability of coffee cultivation. Less often is North America's role in the expansion and persistence of slavery in this part of the Americas considered. And yet, as Brazil's largest coffee importer, the United States was complicit in its trading partner's continuing reliance on chattel bondage through 1888, when Brazil became the last nation in the Americas to abolish a system of oppression that had held millions upon millions of its victims in thrall over the four centuries of post-Columbian history in the Western Hemisphere.

The ties that bound the United States to Brazil and coffee to slavery frequently featured in the financial newspaper *The Merchant*, published by New Orleans editor James Dunwoody Brownson De Bow, a prolific journalist and staunch proslavery advocate. In addition to *The Merchant*, De Bow published several volumes that provided detailed compendiums of trade statistics whose explicit goal was to showcase the continued profitability of slavery. Coffee was one of his preeminent examples.[93] After all, opportunities for U.S. merchants and shippers to reap huge profits had grown in tandem with their nation's burgeoning appetite for coffee, so when the demise of slavery in the Caribbean diminished that region's market share, a swift and adroit shift to Brazil's booming slavery-based production kept the beans coming, the consumption growing, and the wealth accumulating. As one Brazilian historian succinctly summarized the new arrangement: "In Rio, the vessels replaced the Africans with coffee for the U.S. market. Slaves were transmuted into coffee in this trans-Atlantic sleight of hand."[94]

Repackaging Provenance

If U.S. coffee importers recognized the increasing dependence of their industry on one dominant supplier, most U.S. coffee drinkers remained largely unaware of the impact their collective daily cup of coffee had on Brazil's economy and the expanding reliance on slavery. Advertising strategies, as they had since the 1790s, continued to homogenize and domesticate the beverage successfully. Coffee could be found everywhere, from Alexandria, Virginia, to Augusta, Georgia, and from Charleston, South Carolina, to Carlisle, Pennsylvania.[95] But in these newspaper and broadside notices it was always just coffee—sold by the pound, bag, or barrel, sometimes green, sometimes preroasted, but rarely with any controversy and almost never with any provenance. Instead of trading on the commodity's history or its origins in Latin America, the Caribbean, or the East Indies, coffee's promoters and purveyors very consciously aligned themselves with U.S. interests and images, as well as the nation's expansionist aspirations. A vision of the United States and what sellers thought their buyers wanted to believe the nation stood for, in other words, became the most common trope for American coffee companies, appearing again and again in their choice of marketing imagery and language.

John Arbuckle became one of the leading masters of this rebranding of coffee when he, along with his younger brother, Charles, founded Arbuckles

& Company in Pittsburgh in 1868. The brothers had worked together for nearly two decades in the wholesale grocery business, during which time the elder Arbuckle had perfected a glaze of egg white and confectioner's sugar to coat coffee beans after roasting, which ostensibly sealed in the flavor. He applied for a patent and immediately set about differentiating his product from those of his competitors. Although taste was a key ingredient in Arbuckle's enterprise, he also experimented with both product packaging and publicity strategies in trying to set his coffee apart. At a time when most vendors were still selling whole beans in paper bags, Arbuckles & Company sold its product not only already roasted, but also ground and packed into distinctive, reusable metal tins, with airtight paper packages added as a later innovation.[96]

By the late 1870s, the company's new distribution center in New York City had surpassed the production levels of its original western Pennsylvania base. At the same time, the company changed its name to Arbuckles Brothers, and divested itself of most of its other investments to concentrate on its coffee operation. What had begun as part of a wholesale merchant's offerings in the 1850s, and launched in 1865 as a stand-alone endeavor with just a single commercial roaster, had grown by 1881 to an 85-machine facility. By the decade's end Arbuckles Brothers was a national and then international enterprise, having expanded out of its Pittsburgh and New York offices to include bases in Kansas City and Chicago, as well as pilot branches abroad in Brazil and Mexico.[97]

The company's success was based on more than a consistent product and better and more resilient packaging. It invested in several innovative efforts—from building its own shipping fleet to bring beans directly from overseas suppliers to its factories, to sending out a veritable army of agents to establish the company's preeminence in local retail markets. Superior processing and parceling had enabled the Arbuckles to ship their coffee over long distances without any deterioration in quality. Their flagship brand, "Ariosa Coffee," was renowned nationwide, its reputation growing in tandem with expansion of the United States' boundaries.[98]

And it was precisely this moment of national expansion and flourishing patriotism that Arbuckles Brothers highlighted in its coffee marketing. Token giveaways and colorful keepsakes packaged with the goods it promoted date back as early as the 1820s. By mid-century, these gimmicks were a common commercial ploy, ranging from cheap rings and "silk" handkerchiefs to cut-rate prints, lithographs, and even outdated merchandize.[99] The Arbuckles' incentive of choice was serialized, collectible trade cards that sought to link the company and its (still all foreign grown) coffee to key events and places in U.S. history. Trade cards, of course, would go on to become one of the most ubiquitous forms of advertising during the second half of the nineteenth century. Often brightly colored, with eye-catching details and images on the front, and product information or instructions on the reverse, they were produced by the hundreds of thousands and included in the packaging of various domestic products, such as foodstuffs, cosmetics, cleaning supplies, soaps, and household appliances. Some cards sought to whet users' expectations by offering "before" and "after" scenes that displayed the supposed results and benefits of the product they were hawking. Other cards appealed to prospective customers by using popular but generic pictures of natural beauty, domestic harmony, or childhood innocence, which may not necessarily have had any direct connection to the products they were touting, but rather associated them subliminally with pleasing or affecting scenes that would, sellers hoped, entice buyers.[100]

Arbuckles Brothers experimented with several themes for its coffee trade cards. Some of its series adopted traditional pictorial motifs, such as cooking and food, or appealed to those with wanderlust and curiosity by showcasing images of countries from around the world. But the company's most popular series of trade cards disarticulated its product from any connection to the beans' origins on the highland estates in foreign lands, and instead linked it directly to the United States and its consumers there, by featuring maps of the states and territories of the nation. The original series included forty-seven cards, which remained so popular that it was reissued in 1915, but this time with the inclusion of Hawaii and Puerto Rico, which had become U.S. territories in 1898, and Alaska, a territory since 1912. On the back of each card, Arbuckle Brothers informed consumers that its series was "at once the most interesting, instructive and artistic. . . . Every card is a study in itself and affords an object lesson for both young and old."[101]

Arbuckles Brothers clearly thought that associating its coffee with patriotic sentiments would appeal to its domestic U.S. consumer base. The marketing ploy was, first and foremost, a story of economic growth. Colloquially known as the "map series," each card included both a map and a standard set of statistics, such as square mileage and population. These were accompanied by an image of a U.S. state or territory's principal economy or industry. Many of these sketches depicted agricultural products, such as tobacco for Virginia, grapes for California, and cotton (complete with African American laborers in the fields) for Alabama. But other cards showcased regionally specific natural resources or manufacturing enterprises. New Jersey's card, for example, featured pottery making, Alaska's depicted whaling and seal hunting, Colorado's was associated with silver mining, and Washington Territory, just recently carved out of the Oregon Territory in 1889, was linked to lumber.[102]

Coffee did not appear on any of the Arbuckles Brothers map series cards because, of course, it was not the principal commodity of any U.S. state or territory. Even the cards for Hawaii and the Sandwich Islands featured bananas, while that for Puerto Rico pictured sugar cultivation, although that territory's acquisition did mean that U.S. coffee grew on U.S. soil for the first time—albeit lands recently and rather controversially secured through warfare and invasion.

The idea of coffee as a national product nonetheless permeated the series. Graphic advertisements and details about how Arbuckles Brothers prepared and packaged its goods, as well as helpful hints for brewing the beverage, appeared on the reverse of every trade card in the set, and traveled with the commodity as it was distributed across the continent. In this sense, Arbuckles Brothers coffee shaped its consumers' understandings of the dimensions of their nation's growth—allowing the huge and ever-growing community of coffee drinkers across the length and breadth of the United States to learn details about the size and scope of their nation and celebrate the seemingly inexorable triumph of U.S. economic expansion, all the while sipping on what they now regarded as the nation's brew.

Arbuckles Brothers was not the only U.S.-based coffee company that consciously aligned itself with touchstone moments and symbols of the nation's history. Chase & Sanborn, founded in Boston in 1878, took a similar marketing tack when publishing a series of educational booklets to accompany its cans of ground coffee. These tracts included "The History of the American Flag," "North American Birds," and "The Story of the Pilgrim Fathers."[103] Another Arbuckles rival in the nation's coffee business, Schnull-Krag Coffee Company, promoted its "American" coffee by unfavorably comparing coffees from other places, such as "fine" but "expensive" beans from Java, while anointing its brew as "Washington's Coffee." Coffee purveyors Thomas Wood & Company took the Americanization of coffee further still, graphically demonstrating its support for U.S. expansionism and the simultaneous domestication and incorporation of Puerto Rico, Hawaii, and Manila, which its advertisements proclaimed had been brought into the national orbit of Uncle Sam as "his own possessions" and whose coffee crops could now be proudly counted as authentic products of the United States.[104]

Advertising was by far the most powerful tool in transforming coffee into a U.S. commodity in the nineteenth century. Courtesy of this fast-developing medium, what was clearly a tropical and (since the United States had no tropics) foreign staple was systemically refashioned in a marketing sleight of hand that defied historical reality. Instead of scenes of plantations and palm trees, or reaching even further back, images of Turkish or Middle Eastern purveyors, U.S. companies nationalized coffee by associating it with eagles, natural landmarks, the Star-Spangled Banner, and Uncle Sam. As the nineteenth century drew to a close, coffee's popularity and profitability were both firmly entrenched, and the beverage had been thoroughly Americanized.

Coffee Comes to the Fair

The 1876 Philadelphia Centennial Exposition, the first of its kind in the United States, opened to great fanfare to mark the one hundredth anniversary of the Declaration of Independence. Its organizers consciously drew on past European models but hoped to create an event that would not only commemorate the birth of U.S. independence, but also showcase the nation's emergence as a global industrial and economic power. The exposition cost more than $11 million to stage and took ten years to plan, but when it opened to the public that May, it was a resounding success. During its six-month run, over nine million people toured the exhibits showcasing the contributions of thirty-seven nations from around the world.[1]

The focal point of the Centennial Exposition was Machinery Hall, where visitors marveled at the engineering wonders of the age, including electric lights and elevators, locomotives, and fire trucks. Also making their manufacturing debut there were typewriters, Bell's telephone, and Edison's telegraph. But food and drink were well represented at the exposition too. These displays represented both the global reach of U.S. commerce and the sophisticated palates of its citizens, whose diets drew on culinary traditions from around the world. Agricultural Hall focused on domestic produce and farming equipment innovations, although coffee appeared in displays about both Hawaii and Brazil. Other sections of the fairgrounds had an even stronger international flair. Horticultural Hall, next door to Agricultural Hall, had been built to resemble a mosque or, as one reviewer described it, "a palace of Eastern romance, attractive and graceful."[2] Inside grew plants that promoters hoped might appeal to fairgoers' pocketbooks as well as their palates, including displays of coffee trees from Liberia, the brainchild of Edward S. Morris, a Philadelphia merchant who hoped to encourage U.S. investment in West African coffee plantations.[3] Interspersed between the buildings were German beer gardens, French bakeries, and local restaurants offering regional delicacies described as "southern" or "New England" fare. There were also three coffee vendors—a Tunisian coffeehouse, a Turkish coffeehouse, and a Viennese bakery and coffeehouse.[4]

In some respects, the regions and cultures represented by these coffee purveyors recalled the commodity's origins in North Africa and the Middle East, as well as early modern coffeehouses of western Europe, and detailed descriptions appeared in local newspapers to whet readers' appetites even before the exposition had opened. The *Philadelphia Inquirer* reported that the Turkish minister in Washington had requested 2,000 square feet to create his vision of the Ottoman Empire. There, visitors would be able to sample Turkish coffee and smoke Turkish tobacco in a bazaar-like setting staffed by wait staff wearing native garb. While they looked the part, these men were carefully selected for their English language fluency. The goal was not just to serve guests, of course, but also to encourage interest in, and hopefully commercial relations with, Middle Eastern and North African countries.[5]

Details about the Tunisian coffeehouse were even more tantalizing. Reporters described the cafe as octagonal in shape and draped in red, black, and blue fabric panels and "yellow stars, crescents, and open hands, with the palms outward." Here too, those doing the hiring ensured that employees could speak "English with sufficient fluency to make themselves more than partially understood" as they served their American customers while wearing white turbans and "bespangled gowns, and flowing trousers." The menu promised a "fragrant beverage" against the backdrop of "Arabian music, dancing, and feats of legerdemain."[6] An article that appeared in *Frank Leslie's Historical Register of the United States Centennial Exposition, 1876*, the event's official guidebook, included a sketch of the Turkish coffeehouse (Figure 16) featuring costumed and mustachioed men pouring traditional-style coffee from handled, copper serving vessels into porcelain bowls for their urbane and fashionable American clientele.[7]

On the surface, coffee appears to have come full circle, reconnected by the fair's organizers to ideas and images redolent of the regions that first brought the commodity to western Europe. But here is where the similarity ends. Turbans and coffee drinking in seventeenth-century England had evoked jingoism, fear of foreign invasion, and—at its most extreme—fears of westerners' "contamination" among those who opposed the beverage's consumption. The late nineteenth-century image of coffee drinking published in *Frank Leslie's Historical Register*, by contrast, could not have been more

THE GUESTS' COFFEE-ROOM.

Figure 16. "The Guests' Coffee-Room," *Frank Leslie's Historical Register of the United States Centennial Exposition, 1876* (New York: Frank Leslie's Publishing House, 1877), 96, American Philosophical Society.

harmless. Well-dressed ladies relax on upholstered divans, entirely at home in front of their exotically accoutered servers, presenting a quintessential picture of cosmopolitan consumption and sophisticated sensibilities. Such vignettes were harmless precisely because they were temporary, bounded by the circumscribed space of an event like the exposition and available only for the length of its run.

The coffee that most companies sold in the United States by the time the Centennial Exposition got under way was marketed very differently. It traded less on coffee's history in Africa or the Middle East, or even with the much closer—geographically and chronologically—coffee farmers of the Caribbean and Brazil, even though by 1876 the latter supplied four-fifths of U.S. imports. Instead, the coffee that most fair visitors stocked in their kitchens at home had been very consciously aligned with U.S. interests, images, and expansionist aspirations. Arbuckles Brothers, whose advertisements had been domesticating coffee for American purchasers and palates for decades, had become one of the largest U.S. coffee companies when the exposition began, and the firm celebrated the nation's hundredth birthday by patenting a new coffee brand in March 1876. Arbuckles christened it "Empire City Coffee" in honor of New York City, the location of its newest roasting and packaging plant.

*　*　*　*

The scale and profitability of today's coffee trade would no doubt astonish eighteenth-century traders and consumers. Coffee, in all its variations, is drunk around the world and consequently is one of the most profitable commodities traded globally. And yet the industry retains many of its early characteristics. Brazilian exports have risen and fallen over the last century but the country remains the world's largest coffee exporter, shipping nearly four times as many beans as the second-largest coffee producer, Indonesia, the site of the first Dutch coffee-growing experiments in the seventeenth century. Mexico, Colombia, and Venezuela, whose coffee economies grew alongside those of Brazil during the nineteenth century, continue to be valuable producers as well. But only two Caribbean nations appear on the list of today's top twenty coffee-exporting countries, the Dominican Republic and Haiti, who together contribute 0.5 percent of the world's coffee market.[8]

If Latin America, and particularly Brazil, retains significant control over coffee production, regions in Africa and Asia remain, or have become, important contributors. Coffee continues to be a significant part of both Ethiopia's and Uganda's economies, for example, and newer coffee economies in the Philippines, Vietnam, and Thailand are major players in the market for robusta coffee, a heartier, darker varietal than the arabica coffee that was the only option in the eighteenth and early nineteenth centuries.[9]

Today's coffee processing also looks remarkably like its colonial antecedents in many ways. Although agribusinesses dominate some coffee-growing regions, most farms are still small family or locally owned enterprises that are at best marginally profitable. More than 90 percent of all coffee is grown in poor nations, clustered largely in the Southern Hemisphere. Indeed, a map of coffee-growing regions in 1830 superimposed over one for today would be remarkably similar. Meanwhile, so many farmers in developing countries rely on coffee for their livelihoods that it has become the world's most widely traded tropical export. Their consumers, by contrast, overwhelmingly reside in first-world countries.[10] Consequently, there remain significant divisions between the circumstances under which coffee is produced and where it is enjoyed.

Coffee itself continues to appeal to people of all classes, races, and backgrounds although, as was the case in the colonial and early republic eras, how and where it is consumed continues to vary tremendously. It can be bought for a dollar or so at corner diners or fast-food restaurants or for much more in the niche coffee shops that have proliferated in the last few decades to sell varietals from around the world. The experiences of those frequenting high-end cafes, with their rows and rows of beans from across the globe, mirror in some ways the virtual tourism of the women who reclined on divans at the Centennial Exposition of 1876. Customers can have a taste of what it is like to visit the highland coffee farms of Brazil, Guatemala, or Jamaica without the bother of actually traveling there to do so.

Starbucks, the undisputed leader of coffee sales in the United States as well as a growing presence around the world, has perfected these vicarious vacations. Visitors to any of its corner stores, the opening of which has a well-documented impact on a neighborhood's property values, will encounter this armchair internationalization as soon as they enter the door. Each coffee-house interior is a carefully curated experience meant to transport customers to the hillsides and farms where their brew originated. Displays often include maps of different countries' coffee-growing regions, pictures of beans being harvested and processed, and "images of indigenous coffee farmers, and bulk coffee displays, often in archaic burlap bags."[11] The overall effect incorporates coffee's journey from farm to cup into the purchasing experience. For a few minutes out of their busy day, customers can peruse a menu of geographically far-flung options and feel connected, in some small way, to farmers in Kenya, Ethiopia, or Colombia.

Or do they? On the surface, such marketing seems to challenge the Americanization tactics of nineteenth-century coffee purveyors. Rather than hide coffee's foreign origins, its diversity is highlighted textually in the names of the carefully segmented bean varietals (not mixed as they might have been in an eighteenth-century colonial shopkeeper's barrel) as well as in the images and informative labels that accompany its display. And yet, these experiences are generated by, and mediated through, a decidedly U.S.-based corporation. Starbucks is not a passive partner in how this consumer behavior plays out; it is an active participant and a recognizable and trusted identity transforming imported commodities into an American experience for its customers—domestically and internationally—by ensuring that they each receive the homogenous, high-quality experience they have come to expect. If the coffee is diverse, the coffee-drinking experience in such venues is not. The brand succeeds because of its consistency and reliability, not just—or even primarily—because of the taste of its coffee.

Starbucks is not the only globally recognizable coffee company, of course. Alongside it are the market shares controlled by Dunkin', McCafe, Peet's Coffee, Folgers, Maxwell House, and Tim Horton's, all in North America, for example, as well as Nescafé (Switzerland), Costa Coffee (U.K.), Lavazza (Italy), and Gloria Jean's (Australia).[12] The amalgamation of coffee processing and shipping into the hands of these few companies, based predominantly in the United States and western Europe, is one of the most enduring legacies of the system whose origins can be traced back to the consolidation of distribution that was already under way in the United States by the mid-nineteenth century.

The United States also remains the largest coffee importer, as it had become by 1850, at least in terms of individual countries. It is no longer, however, the largest coffee-drinking nation per capita. That designation goes to Finland, followed by Sweden, Iceland, Norway, and Demark, which helps to explain why the United States consumed 31.7 million bags of coffee while the European Union bought 5.4 million bags in 2021–2022. Not all of Europe's coffee, however, arrives via European suppliers, and so even that continent's increasing demand continues to contribute to American coffee sellers' bottom line.[13]

It is understandably hard to cast Starbucks, or any western coffee company, in a position of dependence, particularly considering the obvious imbalance of power between coffee's growers and its sellers. And yet, in much the same way that Arbuckles or Maxwell, Wright & Company relied on the work of coffee's farmers and their enslaved laborers in Brazil in the nineteenth century, today's coffee purveyors are the pinnacle of a very broad-based pyramid of production. Statistics for how many people work in coffee are not exact, but the International Coffee Organization, established by the United Nations in 1963 because of the economic importance of coffee globally, estimates that nearly thirty million people work in coffee production.

Millions more contribute to its importation, roasting, packaging, and reselling. It is the toil of these workers in scores of countries across the world that makes possible today's spectacularly profitable coffee industry. But they are an aging cohort, which will have implications for global coffee production within a matter of years, and the inability to engage a new generation of workers in coffee farming has become a real concern. While fair trade and other social justice programs have not appreciably improved coffee growers' salaries, labor shortages just might.[14]

Depending on the time and place, coffee has been characterized as exotic, profitable, common, genteel, foreign, or patriotic. The coffee industry has been bound up with colonialism, enslavement, revolution, and nationalism, and has involved a huge cast of participants including entrepreneurial traders and planters, enslaved and coerced workers, ship captains and sailors, wholesale and retail merchants, storekeepers and vendue masters, newspaper advertisers, and a range of purveyors and consumers that run the entire social gamut. But coffee is not just a commodity—it drives an industry that tightly bound the United States to its Atlantic neighbors long after 1776. Its popularity with consumers dates from the colonial era and has grown exponentially ever since. Those involved in its trade went to great lengths to ensure access to regional producers, and to retain and defend these connections through diplomacy and even war. Indeed, coffee was a bellwether of U.S. imperialism and cultural hegemony as the nation expanded its financial investment in, and political control of, the Atlantic world.

Coffee drinking—the pleasant repast, the morning habit, the after-dinner ritual—involves simple acts whose worldwide popularity for over two centuries nevertheless has relied on intricate systems and international networks. The complicated commodity history of coffee from the era of the American Revolution through the century that followed affords the opportunity to rethink traditional notions about relationships between producers, traders, and consumers, commercial entanglements, and—in the case of the United States—national identity. By 1890, the die had been cast. Coffee was officially proclaimed the U.S. "national beverage."[15] America had become a coffee nation, and has been so ever since.

NOTES

Introduction

1. Letter from Abigail Adams to John Adams, April 20–21, 1777, and July 30–31, 1777 [electronic edition], *Adams Family Papers: An Electronic Archive* (Massachusetts Historical Society, https://www.masshist.org/digitaladams/archive/).

2. Scholars have used these events to show the privations of war as well as colonists' increasing willingness to use popular protest to solve social problems. For those studying consumer culture, these same activities also offer critical evidence about which goods British North American colonists had come to see as part of the daily fabric of their lives and how far they would go to acquire them. Barbara Clark Smith, "Food Rioters and the American Revolution," *William and Mary Quarterly* 51:1 (January 1994): 3–38; Gary B. Nash, *The Unknown American Revolution: The Unruly Birth of Democracy and the Struggle to Create America* (New York: Penguin Books, 2005), 232–235.

3. Kenneth Scott, "Price Control in New England During the Revolution," *New England Quarterly* 19:4 (December 1946): 453.

4. Scott, "Price Control in New England," 455. Tea, incidentally, did not make this list.

5. Prices set by the New England General Assembly appeared in Boston's *Independent Chronicle* on January 23, 1777, and continued to appear roughly every two weeks thereafter.

6. Samuel Cook, for example, appeared in the *Independent Chronicle* in the fall of 1777: "Found in Samuel Cook's Store at Watertown, by the Selectmen and Committee, a Cask of Coffee; this is to give notice to the Owner to come and sell it out to the inhabitants." (September 25, 1777).

7. Smith, "Food Rioters," 35–36; Fitch Edward Oliver, ed., *The Diary of William Pynchon of Salem: A Picture of Salem Life, Social and Political, a Century Ago* (Boston: Houghton, Mifflin and Company, 1890), 29.

8. Duties were reduced for British-produced coffee that was sold within the British Empire. R. C. Simmons and P. D. G. Thomas, eds., *Proceedings and Debates of the British Parliaments Respecting North America, 1754–1783*, vol. III (Millwood, NY: Kraus International, 1984), 206–208.

9. One of the most compelling studies about British North American's ongoing interest in tea is James Fichter's *Tea: Consumption, Politics and Revolution, 1773–1776* (Ithaca, NY: Cornell University Press, 2023). Fichter looks past the well-publicized protests to argue that tea remains a common commodity in colonial newspaper advertising and shopkeeper's ledger books, concluding that ongoing tea drinking says more about consumer habits than activism. See also Jane Merrit's chapter "Repatriating Tea" in *The Trouble with Tea: The Politics of Consumption in the Eighteenth-Century Global Economy* (Baltimore: Johns Hopkins University Press, 2017), 102–124.

10. Frank Shuffleton, ed., *The Letters of John and Abigail Adams* (New York: Penguin Books, 2003), 192–193. See also Nash, *Unknown American Revolution*, 232.

212 Notes to Pages 5–9

11. In addition to Nash's *Unknown American Revolution* cited above, representative examples include the following: David Waldstreicher, *Runaway America: Benjamin Franklin, Slavery, and the American Revolution* (New York: Hill and Wang, 2004); Carol Berkin, *Revolutionary Mothers: Women in the Struggle for America's Independence* (New York: Vintage Books, 2005); Woody Holton, *Unruly Americans and the Origins of the Constitution* (New York: Hill and Wang, 2008); Kathleen Duval, *Independence Lost: Lives on the Edge of the American Revolution* (New York: Random House, 2015); Alan Taylor, *American Revolutions: A Continental History, 1750–1804* (New York: W.W. Norton, 2017).

12. Ben McGrath, "The Movement: The Rise of Tea Party Activism," *New Yorker* (February 1, 2010).

13. There were a few islands without coffee plantations, notably the Bahamas, Barbados, Aruba, Bonaire, and Curacao, places so flat that they did not have the elevation that coffee plants need to thrive.

14. "An Act for Encouraging the Growth of Coffee in his Majesty's Plantations in America" *Anno Regni George II* (London: John Baskett, Printer to the King's Most Excellent Majesty, 1732). A sample of later petitions to Parliament in the immediate prerevolutionary period concerning excise duties or taxes on coffee include the following: NA/PRO T 1/453/136-319, "A Memorial concerning Coffee" (1766); NA/PRO T 1/453/89-92, "Account of the One Fourth Part of the Crops reaped from Estates of Which Temporary Possession were Granted in 1765, including an account of coffee and cocoa yields in Dominica and St. Vincent's" (1766); NA/PRO T 1/470/80-82, "The Memorial of Sir George Colebrooke, Sir James Stewart, and John Nelson, on behalf of themselves and the other proprietors of the Island of Dominica" (1769); NA/PRO T 1/509/72, "The Memorial of Merchants and Planters interested in Coffee Plantations in the British West India Islands" (1774); NA PRO T 1/511/16–24, 25–26, 265–268, 275–278, "Report upon the Memorial of the West India Merchants trading to the Sugar Colonies" (1774), "An Account of the Quantities of British Plantation and Foreign Coffee, and the Amount of the Excise Duty paid Annually" (1774), "Excise Report on the Memorial of Stephen Fuller, Esq., Agent for the Island of Jamaica" (1774), and "Petition of John Ellis, Esq., Agent for Dominica" (1774); NA/PRO T 1/515/174–184, "State of the Coffee Trade" (1775); NA/PRO T 1/523/294–297, "Memorial of the Coffee Planters in the West Indies" (1775).

15. Stanley J. Stein, *Vassouras: A Brazilian Coffee County, 1850–1900. The Roles of Planters and Slaves in a Plantation Society* (Princeton, NJ: Princeton University Press, 1985); William Roseberry, Lowell Gudmundson, and Mario Samper Kitschbach, eds., *Coffee, Society, and Power in Latin America* (Baltimore: Johns Hopkins University Press, 1995); Jeffrey M. Paige, *Coffee and Power: Revolution and the Rise of Democracy in Central America* (Cambridge, MA: Harvard University Press, 1997); Steven Topik and William Clarence-Smith, eds., *The Global Coffee Economy in Africa, Asia, and Latin America* (New York: Cambridge University Press, 2003).

16. "Their [Turkes'] best drinke is Coffaa of a graine they call Coava." *The True Travels, Adventures, and Observations of Captain John Smith* (1603–1630), 25, cited in the *Oxford English Dictionary* online; and William Harrison Ukers, *All About Coffee* (New York: The Tea and Coffee Trade Journal, 1922) 108.

17. Michelle Craig McDonald and Steven Topik, "Americanizing Coffee: Refashioning a Consumer Culture," in *Food and Globalisation: Consumption, Markets and Politics in the Modern World*, ed. Alexander Nützenadel and Frank Trentmann (Oxford: Berg Publishers, 2008), 111; and William Ukers, *All About Coffee* (New York: Tea and Coffee Trade Journal Company, 1922), 105.

18. Marquis de François Jean Chastellux, *Travels in North America, In the Years 1780, 1781, and 1782; translated from the French by an English gentleman . . . ; with notes by the translator*, 2nd ed., 2 vols. (London: Printed for G.G. J., and J. Robinson, 1787), 2:35.

19. Mifflin & Massey Ledgerbook, 1763–1766, vol. 2, Am. 9112—Business Accounts. Entries appear in 1763–1764 (Historical Society of Pennsylvania); Charles B. Dew, *Bond of Iron: Master*

and Slave at Buffalo Forge (New York: W.W. Norton, 1995), 116–117; Elizabeth Sandwich Drinker, *Extracts from the Journal of Elizabeth Drinker from 1759 to 1807 A.D.* (Philadelphia: J. Lippincott, 1889), 56, 64. "Mud Battery Fort" was Fort Mifflin, just outside Philadelphia on the Delaware River.

20. Donald Jackson and Dorothy Twohig, eds., *The Diaries of George Washington*, 6 vols. (Charlottesville: University Press of Virginia, 1976–1979), 3:261.

21. Benjamin Carp, *Defiance of the Patriots* (New Haven, CT: Yale University Press, 2010), 161–181.

22. James Madison to Edmund Pendleton, John Adams Diary, entry for October 6, 1774 (Massachusetts Historical Society).

23. David J. Mays, ed., *The Letters and Papers of Edmund Pendleton, 1734–1803*, 2 vols. (Charlottesville: University of Virginia Press, 1967), 1:129.

24. John Adams diary 22A, September—October 1774 [electronic edition], *Adams Family Papers: An Electronic Archive* (Massachusetts Historical Society), http://www.masshist.org/digitaladams/archives; Paul H. Smith et al., eds., *Letters to the Delegates of Congress, 1774–1779*, 25 vols. (Washington, D.C.: Library of Congress, 1976–2000), 1:149; J. Adams to A. Adams, July 6, 1775, and August 11, 1777, *Adams Family Papers* and *Adams Family Correspondence*, 2:295–296.

25. *South Carolina Gazette and General Advertiser*, May 4, 1784. After 1789, states could no longer levy import taxes individually, although the federal government continued to do so.

26. "Commerce with Great Britain and her Dependencies, and All Parts of the World," *American State Papers: Commerce and Navigation*, vol. 1 (Washington, D.C.: Gales and Seaton, 1832): 640–642. Combined coffee imports from all British West Indian islands were valued at $1,480,000; imports from all non-British sources were $8,373,000. This creates a total import value of $9,853,000. If the total reexport value for the same period was $7,302,000, then $2,551,000, or 25.9 percent, remained for U.S. consumption.

27. Ibid. This same report compared the volume of U.S. trade to Britain and the British colonies for several years with those to other parts of Eastern and Western Europe, the rest of the Caribbean, Africa, Asia, and the South Seas. Percentage derived by comparing total coffee reexport revenue of $7,302,000 to total reexport revenue of $28,533,000 for the years 1802 through 1804.

28. John J. McCusker and Russell R. Menard, eds., *The Economy of British America, 1607–1789* (Chapel Hill: University of North Carolina Press for the Institute for Early American History and Culture, 1985), 367.

29. While not an exhaustive list, examples of such scholarly trends in chronological order include the following: Carl Becker, *The Declaration of Independence: A Study of the History of Political Ideas* (New York: Harcourt Brace, 1922); Bernard Bailyn, *Ideological Origins of the American Revolution* (Cambridge, MA: Belknap Press of Harvard University, 1967); Gordon Wood, *The Creation of the American Republic, 1776–1787* (Chapel Hill: University of North Carolina Press for the Institute of Early American History and Culture, 1969); Pauline Maier, *From Resistance to Revolution: Colonial Radicals and the Development of American Opposition to Britain, 1765–1776* (New York: Knopf, 1972); Gary Nash, *The Urban Crucible: Social Change, Political Consciousness, and the Origins of the American Revolution* (Cambridge, MA: Harvard University Press, 1979); Linda Kerber, *Women of the Republic: Intellect and Ideology in Revolutionary America* (Chapel Hill: University of North Carolina Press for the Institute of Early American History and Culture, 1980); Mary Beth Norton, *Liberty's Daughters: The Revolutionary Experience of American Women, 1750–1800* (Boston: Little and Brown, 1980); Rosemarie Zaggari, *Revolutionary Backlash: Women and Politics in the Early American Republic* (Philadelphia: University of Pennsylvania Press, 1987); Michael Warner, *The Letters of the Republic: Publication and Public Sphere in Eighteenth-Century America* (Cambridge, MA: Harvard University Press, 1992); Woody Holton, *Forced Founders: Indians, Debtors, and Slaves and the Making of the American Revolution in Virginia* (Chapel Hill: University of North Carolina Press for the Omohundro Institute

for Early American History and Culture, 1999); Cassandra Pybus, *Epic Journeys of Freedom: Runaway Slaves of the American Revolution and Their Global Quest for Freedom* (Boston: Beacon Press, 2007); Jack Greene, *The Constitutional Origins of the American Revolution* (Cambridge: Cambridge University Press, 2010).

More recent work, particularly focusing on broad-based public participation and consumer behavior in the American Revolution and early national formation, includes Simon Newman, *Parades and Politics: Festive Culture in the Early American Republic* (Philadelphia: University of Philadelphia Press, 1997); David Waldstreicher, *In the Midst of Perpetual Fetes: The Making of American Nationalism, 1776–1820* (Chapel Hill: University of North Carolina Press, 1997); T.H. Breen, *Marketplace of Revolution: How Consumer Politics Shaped American Independence* (Oxford: Oxford University Press, 2004); Holton, *Unruly Americans*; Benjamin Irvin, *Clothed in Robes of Sovereignty: The Continental Congress and People Out of Doors* (Oxford: Oxford University Press, 2011); and David Jaffee, *A New Nation of Goods: The Material Culture of Early America* (Philadelphia: University of Pennsylvania Press, 2011). There is also a rich literature on connections between consumption and national identity in the later nineteenth and twentieth centuries, including the following: Lizabeth A. Cohen, *A Consumer's Republic: The Politics of Mass Consumption in Postwar America* (New York: Knopf, 2003); Kathleen G. Donohue, *Freedom from Want: American Liberalism and the Idea of the Consumer* (Baltimore: Johns Hopkins University Press, 2003); Meg Jacobs, *Pocketbook Politics: Economic Citizenship in Twentieth-Century America* (Princeton, NJ: Princeton University Press, 2005); Charles F. McGovern, *Sold American: Consumption and Citizenship, 1890–1945* (Chapel Hill: University of North Carolina Press, 2006); Kristin Hoganson, *Consumer's Imperium: The Global Production of American Domesticity, 1865–1920* (Chapel Hill: University of North Carolina Press, 2007); Lawrence Glickman, *Buying Power: A History of Consumer Activism in America* (Chicago: University of Chicago Press, 2009).

30. As examples, see Douglass C. North, *The Economic Growth of the United States, 1790–1860* (New York: W. W. Norton, 1966); Stephen Hornsby, *British Atlantic, American Frontier: Spaces of Power in Early Modern British America* (Lebanon, NH: University Press of New England, 2005). See also Cathy Matson, *Merchants and Empire: Trading in Colonial New York* (Baltimore: Johns Hopkins University Press, 1998); McCusker and Menard, *The Economy of British America*; Thomas Doerflinger, *A Vigorous Spirit of Enterprise: Merchants and Economic Development in Revolutionary Philadelphia* (Chapel Hill: University of North Carolina Press for the Omohundro Institute for Early American History and Culture, 1986). Matson as well as McCusker and Menard understand the importance of maritime commerce, but both studies also end within a generation after the American Revolution; however, Matson's epilogue gestures to the ongoing importance of such trade in the early republic. Some historians have argued for the centrality of the North American continent over the Atlantic even earlier still, most notably Paul Mapp, *The Elusive West and the Contest for Empire, 1713–1763* (Chapel Hill: University of North Carolina Press for the Omohundro Institute for Early American History and Culture, 2011).

31. Daniel Miller, *Material Cultures: Why Some Things Matter* (Chicago: University of Chicago Press, 1998), 17. Anthropologist Mary Douglas and economist Baron Isherwood similarly argued that economics alone could not explain commodities' appeal: "It is standard ethnographic practice to assume that all material possessions carry social meanings and to concentrate a main part of cultural analysis upon their use as communicators." Mary Douglas and Baron Isherwood, *The World of Goods: Toward an Anthropology of Consumption* (New York: Basic Books, 1979), 59. For examples of recent commodity histories, see David Hancock, *Oceans of Wine: Madeira and the Emergence of American Trade and Taste* (New Haven, CT: Yale University Press, 2009); Sven Beckert, *The Empire of Cotton: A Global History* (New York: Knopf, 2013); Judith A. Carney, *Black Rice: The African Origins of Rice Cultivation in the Americas* (Cambridge, MA: Harvard University Press, 2001); Marcy Norton, *Sacred Gifts, Profane Pleasures: A History of Tobacco and Chocolate*

in the Atlantic World (Ithaca, NY: Cornell University Press, 2008); Bennett Alan Weinberg and Bonnie K. Bealer, *The World of Caffeine: The Science and Culture of the World's Most Popular Drug* (New York: Routledge, 2002); Steve Striffler and Mark Moberg, *Banana Wars: Power, Production, and History in the Americas* (Durham, NC: Duke University Press, 2003); Mark Pendergrast, *Uncommon Grounds: The History of Coffee and How It Transformed Our World* (New York: Basic Books, 1999, republished in 2010); Jennifer L. Anderson, *Mahogany: The Costs of Luxury in Early America* (Cambridge, MA: Harvard University Press, 2012); and several popular histories on cod, salt, salmon, milk, and oysters by Mark Kurlansky.

32. This work has expanded prodigiously since Richard Bushman, *The Refinement of America: Persons, Houses, Cities* (New York: Vintage Books, 1992), and Cary Carson, Ronald Hoffman, and Peter J. Albert, eds., *Of Consuming Interests: The Style of Life in the Eighteenth Century* (Charlottesville: University of Virginia Press, 1994). See also Paul G. E. Clements, "The Consumer Culture of the Middle Atlantic, 1760–1820," *William and Mary Quarterly* 3rd ser., 62:4 (October 2005): 578–624; Ann Smart Martin, *Buying into the World of Goods: Early Consumers in Backcountry Virginia* (Baltimore: Johns Hopkins University Press, 2008); and Ellen Hartigan-O'Connor, *The Ties That Buy: Women and Commerce in Revolutionary America* (Philadelphia: University of Pennsylvania Press, 2009). Combined work by historians and economists that explicitly applies a commodity lifecycle model in other parts of the Atlantic world appeared in Steven Topik, Zephyr Frank, and Carlos Marichal, eds., *From Silver to Cocaine: Latin American Commodity Chains and the Building of the World Economy, 1500–2000* (Durham, NC: Duke University Press, 2006).

33. Charles Andrews first proposed in 1934 that North America's history could not be understood without including Canada and the West Indies, and his work influenced subsequent imperial studies, such as those by Frank Pitman and Lowell Ragatz, which also linked the British mainland and Caribbean colonies. See Charles Andrews, *The Colonial Period of American History*, 4 vols. (Reprint, New Haven, CT: Yale University Press, 1934–1938); Frank W. Pitman, *The Development of the British West Indies, 1700–1763* (New Haven, CT: Yale University Press, 1917); and Lowell J. Ragatz, *The Fall of the Planter Class in the British Caribbean, 1763–1833: A Study in Social and Economic History* (New York: Century Company, 1928). For a more expansive history of the emergence of Atlantic history as a field, see Alison Games, "Atlantic History: Definitions, Challenges, and Opportunities," *American Historical Review* 111:3 (June 2006): 741–757.

34. Alison Games was citing early Dutch Atlantic historian James Williams in "Atlantic History," 745. Such questions have special relevance in a time when the teaching of North American history has become increasingly politicized. In 2014, some Republicans criticized the new Advanced Placement (AP) U.S. history framework for allegedly downplaying positive elements of America's past. More specifically, they raised concerns that the framework was "closely tied to a movement of left-leaning historians that aims to 'internationalize' the teaching of American history," which would "end American history as we have known it" by substituting a more "'transnational narrative for the traditional account." The following spring, Oklahoma legislators even introduced a bill declaring the new AP curriculum an "emergency" threatening the "public peace, health and safety," to be defunded in the coming school year. Policymakers in Georgia, Texas, South Carolina, North Carolina, and Colorado have expressed similar concerns about the AP curriculum. At the heart of such initiatives is fear over a perceived undermining of national exceptionalism, an entrenched set of ideas that privilege notions of U.S. independence, democracy, and self-reliance. See Stanley Kurtz, "How the College Board Politicized U.S. History," *National Review* (August 25, 2014), http://www.nationalreview.com/corner/386202/how-college-board -politicized-us-history-stanley-kurtz; Colleen Flaherty, "Whose History?" *Inside Higher Education* (February 23, 2015), https://www.insidehighered.com/news/2015/02/23/oklahoma-legislature -targets-ap-us-history-framework-being-negative. Such debates over how U.S. history should be taught continue in the present day. The most notable example is the divided reception over Nikole

Hannah-Jones's *1619 Project*, which posits that the arrival of the first enslaved Africans in 1619 defined the character of what would become the United States even more powerfully than political independence in 1776. See Nikole Hannah-Jones, "Origins," *The 1619 Project* (New York: New York Times Company, 2021), xvii–xxxiii; Jake Silverstein, "The 1619 Project and the Long Battle Over U.S. History," *New York Times* (November 9, 2021); and Sean Wilentz, "A Matter of Facts," *The Atlantic* (January 20, 2022). More troubling, see Donald Trump's reaction to the broadening interpretation of early American history in "Remarks by President Trump at the White House Conference on American History" (November 17, 2020; https://trumpwhitehouse.archives.gov/briefings-statements/remarks-president-trump-white-house-conference-american-history/).

Chapter 1

1. Lawes married Elizabeth Coale (May 20, 1680), Frances Goodwin (May 23, 1685), Elizabeth Modyford (July 2, 1693), and Susannah Temple (June 11, 1696). Robert Mowbry Howard, *Records and Letters of the Family of the Longs of Longville, Jamaica and Hampton Lodge, Surrey*, vol. 1 (London: Simpkin, Marshall, Hamilton, Kent, and Co., 1925), 58–61; Frank Cundall, *The Governors of Jamaica in the First Half of the Eighteenth Century* (West India Committee, 1937), 75.

2. Lawes owned five estates, Snow Hill, Swallowfield, Temple Hall, Mount James, and Townwell. Vere Langford Oliver, *Caribbeana: Being Miscellaneous Papers Relating to the History, Genealogy, Topography, and Antiquities of the British West Indies*, 6 vols. (London: Mitchell, Hughes, and Clarke, 1910–1919), 5:55–58.

3. Lawes's speech to the assembly of Jamaica, August 1, 1718, *Journals of the Jamaican Assembly*, II, 256; NA/PRO CO 137/12/145, "Joseph Addison to British Board of Trade" (June 21, 1717).

4. British Board of Trade, *Journal for the Commission of Trade and Plantations from November 1718 to December 1722* (London: His Majesty's Stationery Office, 1925), 223–224. See also Casey S. Schmidt, "Virtue in Corruption: Privateers, Smugglers, and the Shape of Empire in the Eighteenth Century," *Early American Studies* 13:1 (Winter 2015): 89–99.

5. Maximillan E. Novak, "Colonel Jack's 'Thieving Roguing' Trade to Mexico and Defoe's Attack on Economic Individualism," *Huntington Library Quarterly* 24:4 (August 1961): 349–350.

6. "Extracts from the Journals of the House of Assembly, Jamaica, June 1720," in Augustus H. Oaees, Esq. ed., *British and Foreign State Papers, 1849–1850 (1); compiled by the Librarian and Keeper of the Papers, Foreign Office*, 170 vols. (London: Harrison and Sons, 1862), 38:703–705.

7. The record of Lawes's property sale to raise funds for Jamaican governance can be found in George Wilson Bridges, ed., *The Annals of Jamaica* (London: John Murray, 1828), 352. For descriptions of the impact of that 1722 hurricane, see Matthew Mulcahy, *Hurricanes and Society in the Greater British Caribbean, 1624–1783* (Baltimore: Johns Hopkins University Press, 2006), 29, 99.

8. For information about Lawes's role in the piracy trials of 1721, see *The Tryals of Captain Jack Rackham and Other Pirates* (Jamaica: Robert Baldwin, 1721) and Marcus Rediker, *Villains of All Nations: Atlantic Pirates in the Golden Age* (Boston: Beacon Press, 2004), 103–112. Rackham and four other accused pirates were quickly convicted and hanged; while both Read and Bonny were also convicted, they both pled pregnancy and so received a stay of execution.

9. Lawes died a wealthy man by contemporary standards. His probate inventory from 1731 included 564 enslaved people (279 men, 199 women, and 86 children) who made up more than half of his estate's total value (or £10,846 of £19,246.6 Jamaican currency). See Trevor Burnard, "Database of Jamaican Inventories, 1674–1784" (Centre for the Study of the Legacies of British Slavery, University College London), https://www.ucl.ac.uk/lbs/inventory/view/53943.

10. Benjamin Moseley, *A Treatise Concerning the Properties and Effects of Coffee*, 5th ed. (London: J. Sewell, 1792), xv. Moseley lists both the petitioners and their respective financial contributions supporting the treatise, including John Ascough, Esq. (£10.10), Thomas Beckford, Esq. (10.10), James Dawkins, Esq. (10.10), Henry Dawkins, Esq. (10.10), Messrs. Drake, Pennant,

and Long (21.0), Thomas Fish, Esq. (10.10), Mr. James Fitter (5.5), Cope Freeman (10.10), John Gibbon (10.10), Mr. John Gregory (5.5.), Capt. John Hiscox (10.10), Mr. Henry Lang & Co. (5.5), James Lawes, Esq. (10.10), John Lewis, Esq. (10.10), Mrs. Susannah Lowe (10.10), Samuel Long, Esq. (10.10), Charles Long, Esq. (10.10), Messrs. Mayleigh and Gale (10.10), Valen. Mumbee, Esq. (10.10), Favele Peeke, Esq. (10.10), and Capt. George Wane (5.5), for a total petition pledge of £220.10.

11. Simon D. Smith, "Sugar's Poor Relation: Coffee Planting in the British West Indies, 1720–1833," in *The Slavery Reader*, ed. Gad Heuman and James Walvin (London and New York: Routledge, 2003), 175–177.

12. *Journals of the House of Commons*, vol. 21 (London: Reprinted by the Order of the House of Commons, 1803), 845–846.

13. Smith, "Sugar's Poor Relation," 177–178; Edward Long, *The History of Jamaica, or Survey of the Antient and Modern State of the Island*, 3 vols. (London: T. Lowndes, 1774), 1:386.

14. Bryan Edwards, *The History, Civil and Commercial, of the British Colonies in the West Indies*, 3rd ed., 3 vols. (London: Printed for John Stockdale, 1801), 1:276–278. Edwards estimates that deficiency law revenue was £24,000 in 1788; slave imports generated £6,000, and rum sales another £14,000. Daniel Livesay provides an excellent summary of the impact of deficiency laws in Jamaican society in *Children of Uncertain Fortune: Mixed-Race Jamaicans in Britain and the Atlantic Family, 1733–1833* (Chapel Hill: University of North Carolina Press for the Omohundro Institute for Early American History and Culture, 2018), 26–35, 64–66.

15. Reduction of coffee duties would also provide an opportunity to challenge Dutch and French imperial investments in coffee. When a parliamentary member asked Laws if the Dutch did not already produce coffee in Suriname, he responded that indeed they did "and that 200,000 weight had been imported from thence to Holland," although he quickly assured the Commons that "it was not so good" while suggesting that Jamaica could rival the Dutch trade. *Journals of the House of Commons*, 845–846; "Petition of Several Planters of Jamaica, 2 March 1731," reprinted in *Sources of West Indian History*, ed. F. R. Augier and Shirley C. Gordon (London: Longman, 1962), 62.

16. *Journals of the House of Commons*, 21:846–847.

17. The act granting a rebate on coffee taxes first appeared as "An Act for Encouraging the Growth of Coffee in his Majesty's Plantations in America," 411–415. Earlier legislation had regulated coffee taxation, but this was the first time a law drew a distinction between coffee from the east and the west. This particular act reduced import taxes on British West Indian coffee to 1 shilling 6 pence per pound while taxing East Indian produce at 2 shillings and went into effect on March 25, 1735.

18. Zeila is known now as Saylac and is near the present-day border of Somalia and Djibouti. C. Schaeffer, "Coffee Unobserved: Consumption and Commoditization in Ethiopia before the Eighteenth Century," in *Le commerce du café avant l'ère des plantations coloniales: Espaces, réseaux, sociétés (XVᵉ-XIXᵉ siècle)*, ed. Michel Tuchscherer, Cahier des annals islamologiques, no. 20 (Cairo: Insitut Français D'Archáeologie Orientale, 2001), 23–34; Michel Tuchscherer, "Coffee in the Red Sea Area from the Sixteenth to the Nineteenth Century," in Topik and Clarence-Smith, *Global Coffee Economy*, 50–53. For reference to the first coffee traded, see Mustuo Kawatoko, "Coffee Trade in al-Tur Port, South Sinai," in Tuchscherer, *Le commerce du café*, 51–65.

19. Jürgen Schneider, "The Effects on European Markets of Imports of Overseas Agriculture: The Production, Trade and Consumption of Coffee (15th to late 18th Century)" in *Economic Effects of the European Expansion, 1492–1824*, ed. José Casas Pardo (Stuttgart: Steiner, 1992), 288–289.

20. Birsen Yilmaz, Nilüfer, Saniye Sözlü, "Turkish Cultural Heritage: A Cup of Coffee," *Journal of Ethnic Foods* 4:4 (December 1, 2017): 213–220.

21. Donald M. Lockhart, ed. and trans., *The Itinerário of Jerónimo Lobo* (London: Hakluyt Society, 1984), 88.

22. C. G. Brouwer, *Al-Mukha: Profile of a Yemeni Seaport as Sketched by Servants of the Dutch East India Company (VOC) 1614–1640* (Amsterdam: D'Fluyte Rarob, 1997), 21, 40.

23. Jean de La Roque, *A Voyage to Arabia Fœlix through the Eastern Ocean and the streights of the Red-Sea being the first made by the French in the years 1708, 1709 and, 1710; together with a particular account of a journey from Mocha to Muab or Mowahib, the court of the King of Yaman, in their second expedition in the years 1711, 1712 and 1713; also a narrative concerning the tree and fruit of coffee, and an historical treatise of the original progress of coffee [. . .]*(London: E Symon, 1732), 54–55, 207.

24. Jean de Thévenot, *Relation d'un voyage fait au Levant* (Paris: L. Billaine, 1665), translated as *Travels into the Levant* (London: Faithorne, 1687), 34.

25. John Ellis, *An Historical Account of Coffee: with an engraving, botanical description of the tree* (London: Edward and Charles Dilley, 1774), 11.

26. Simon Smith, "Accounting for Taste: British Coffee Consumption in Historical Perspective," *Journal of Interdisciplinary History* (Autumn 1996): 184–185.

27. William Foster, ed., *The Journal of John Jourdain, 1608–1616* (Nendlen/Liechtenstein: Reproduced by Permission of the Hakylut Society, 1925), 86.

28. Brian Cowan, *The Social Life of Coffee: The Emergence of the British Coffeehouse* (New Haven, CT: Yale University Press, 2011), 64.

29. The combined new and old English East India Companies became known as the United Company of Merchants of England Trading to the East Indies, commonly styled the "Honourable East India Company" (or HEIC) by some scholars, after 1708. As the intricacies of this arrangement are peripheral to this study, however, I have elected to maintain the EIC designation for simplicity throughout. See Sir George Birdwood, *Report on The Old Record of the India Office*, 2nd ed. (London and Calcutta: W. H. Allen & Co., 1891), 14. Figures were obtained from NA/PRO Customs 36, "Book of Customs: Statistics, Trade, and Shipping, 1699–1828"; Elizabeth Schumpeter, *English Overseas Trading Statistics, 1697–1808* (Oxford: Oxford University Press, 1960), 60; and Smith, "Accounting for Taste," 190–191. The price index fell from 46.7 to 43.6 between 1665 and 1675 but was up to 52.2 by 1685 and had more than doubled to 111.0 by 1702, based on a baseline of 100 and wholesale prices listed in NA/PRO Customs 3.

30. Cowan, *Social Life of Coffee*, 60–63.

31. J. W. Fortescue, ed., "America and West Indies: February 1698, 1–15," *Calendar of State Papers Colonial, America and West Indies: Volume 16, 1697–1998* (London: His Majesty's Stationery Office, 1905), 97–111. EIC ships, as well as those by the VOC, were frequent targets of piracy. Favorite bases included St. Mary's, a tiny island off the east coast of Madagascar; Perim, an island off Zanzibar; and Bab al-Mandab, a tiny island in the southern entrance to the Red Sea, also known as Bab's Key and most likely the "babs. Pirates" in Watson's account.

32. K. M. Chaudhuri, *The Trading World of Asia and the English East India Company, 1660–1760* (Cambridge: Cambridge University Press, 1978), 521.

33. M. R. Fernando, "Coffee Cultivation in Java, 1830–1917," in Topik and Clarence-Smith, *Global Coffee Economy*, 159; Anthony Farrington, *Trading Places: The East India Company and Asia 1600–1834* (London: British Library Publishing Division, 2002), 48–53.

34. Anne E. C. McCants, "Poor Consumers as Global Consumers: The Diffusion of Tea and Coffee Drinking in the Eighteenth Century," *Economic History Review* 61 (2008): 177.

35. Although the island was renamed Réunion in 1793 after the fall of the House of Bourbon in France, Bourbon remained the name by which the island's coffee exports were classified in price listings—except in France—well into the nineteenth century.

36. Harry Johnston, *Pioneers in India* (London, 1913, reprinted New Delhi: J. Jetley for Asian Educational Services, 1993), 248; James Douglas, *Arbor Yemensis Fructum Cofè Ferens: Or, a Description and History of the Coffee Tree* (London: Thomas Woodward, at the Half-Moon over-against St. Dunstan's Church, 1727), 16; François-Victor Mérat de Vaumartoise and Adrien Jacques de Lens, eds., *Dictionnaire Universel de Matiére Médicale et de Therapeutique Générale*, tome second C-D (Paris: J. B. Bailliére, Méquignon-Marvis, 1830), 353.

37. Gwyn Campbell, "The Origins and Development of Coffee Production in Réunion and Madagascar, 1711–1972," in Topik and Clarence-Smith, *Global Coffee Economy*, 68; Robert Montgomery Martin, *Statistics of the Colonies of the British Empire in the West Indies, South America, North America, Asia, Austral-Asia, Africa, and Europe* (London: Wm. Allen & Co., 1839), 497–498.

38. NA/PRO CO 5/1265, Nos. 30, 30 i, "Richard Beresford to the Council of Trade and Plantations" (June 23, 1716): "If the inhabitants of Carolina and the Bahama Islands were more numerous and protected severall other productions would thrive well in that climate, as sugar, fruit, coffee, olives, Spanish vines etc."; cited in Smith, "Sugar's Poor Relation," 65; and Douglas, *Arbor Yemensis*, 20, 22.

39. NA/PRO CO 116/19, Nos. 4, 4.i.-xii, "Samuel Beeckman to the Directors of the Dutch West India Company, Middelburgh" (August 9, 1700); Johannes Menne Postma, *The Dutch in the Atlantic Slave Trade, 1600–1815* (New York: Cambridge University Press, 1990), 189.

40. A shoot from this same Batavian plant, gifted to King Louis XIV and brought to the Jardin des Plantes in Paris in 1714, arrived in the French Caribbean colony of Martinique in 1720. See Richard Bradley, *New Improvements of Planting and Gardening, Both Philosophical and Practical*, 6th ed. (London: J. and J. Knapton, 1731), 607; and Francis Beatty Thurber, *Coffee: From Plantation to Cup. A Brief History of Coffee Production and Consumption*, 6th ed. (New York: American Grocer Publishing Association, 1884), 137. More detailed figures are available in Mario Samper and Radin Fernando, "Appendix: Historical Statistics of Coffee Production and Trade from 1700 to 1960," in Topik and Clarence-Smith, *Global Coffee Economy*, 412–415. In just under three decades, by the late 1740s, Suriname was growing more coffee than Java and exporting virtually its entire crop to Amsterdam. By 1761, Suriname exported more than three times what Java could produce.

41. Douglas, *Arbor Yemensis*, 20–21

42. Ellis, *Historical Account of Coffee*, 1–4.

43. John Lowndes, *The Coffee Planter, or an Essay on the Cultivation and Manufacturing of That Article of West India Produce* (London: C. Lowndes, 1807), 19–20.

44. Henry Bolingbroke, *A Voyage to the Demerary, containing a statistical account of the settlements there* (Philadelphia: M. Carey, 1816), 116–117.

45. Capt. John Gabriel Stedman, *Narrative, of a five years' expedition, against the revolted Negroes of Surinam, in Guiana, on the wild coast of South America; from the year 1772 to 1777*, 2 vols. (London: Printed for J. Johnson, St. Paul's Church Yard, & J. Edwards, Pall Mall, 1796), 2:354–360.

46. Ibid., 2:367.

47. Long, *History of Jamaica*, 1:407.

48. B. W. Higman, *Jamaica Surveyed: Plantation Maps and Plans of the Eighteenth and Nineteenth Centuries* (Kingston: Institute of Jamaica Publications, 1988), 164.

49. *Kingston Journal*, November 29, 1760.

50. Ibid.

51. Higman, *Jamaica Surveyed*, 164.

52. Maria Nugent and Frank Cundall, *Lady Maria Nugent's Journal: Jamaica One Hundred Years Ago* (London: Published for the Institute of Jamaica by Adam and Charles Black, 1907), 103.

53. NA/PRO T 1/515/174-184, West Indies Miscellaneous: Report of Excise Office London, and enclosed memorial and papers of West Indies coffee planters: duties, and their position threatened (November 28, 1775); Schumpeter, *English Overseas Trading Statistics*, 60. With the addition of the Ceded Islands, the British West Indies now produced almost 10 percent of the region's total coffee exports; see Lowell J. Ragatz, *Statistics for the Study of British Caribbean Economic History, 1763–1833* (London: Bryan Edwards Press, 1927), 14.

54. The Ceded Islands, defined by the 1763 Treaty of Paris, included Dominica, Grenada, Saint Vincent and the Grenadines, and Tobago. France also ceded parts of Canada and the eastern half of Louisiana to Britain by the same agreement.

55. R. G. Bruce to William Acanius Senior, Dominica, May 1, 1771, reproduced in Clare Tyler, "Aspects of Planter Society in the British West Indies before Emancipation," *National Library of Wales Journal* 20:4 (1978): 365–366.

56. Ibid.

57. R. G. Bruce to William Acanius Senior, Dominica, July 1, 1771, and R. G. Bruce to William Acanius Senior, February 27, 1772, in Tyler, "Aspects of Planter Society," 367–369.

58. NA/PRO Customs 36; Schumpeter, *English Overseas Trading Statistics*, 60.

59. Kathleen E. A. Monteith, "Planting and Processing Techniques on Jamaican Coffee Plantations During Slavery," in *Working Slavery, Pricing Freedom: Perspectives from the Caribbean, Africa, and African Diaspora*, ed. Verene A. Shepherd (Kingston: Ian Randle, 2002), 114; Higman, *Jamaica Surveyed*, 159; Pierre Joseph Laborie, *The Coffee Planter of Saint Domingo* (London: T. Caldwell and W. Davis, 1791), 7. Higman estimates that 92 percent of Jamaica's coffee plantations were over 1,000 feet above sea level, while 30 percent were above 3,000 feet.

60. Lowndes, *Coffee Planter*, 13.

61. Ibid., 13–15.

62. James Delle, Stephen A. Mrozowski, and Robert Paynter, eds., *Lines That Divide: Historical Archaeologies of Race, Class and Gender* (Knoxville: University of Tennessee Press, 2000), 192.

63. Laborie, *Coffee Planter*, 15.

64. Higman, *Jamaica Surveyed*, 164–166.

65. Paula Veronica Saunders, "Free and Enslaved African Communities in Buff's Bay, Jamaica: Daily Life, Resistance, and Kinship, 1750–1834" (PhD diss., University of Texas, 2004), 55–57.

66. Lowndes, *Coffee Planter*, 14; Laborie, *Coffee Planter*, 108, 115, 118. Lowndes estimated that lining would take four enslaved workers, two to stretch the line correctly and two to drive stakes, or what he termed "picquets," probably an alternate spelling of pickets, into the earth beneath each strip of colored cloth to mark the proposed planting site.

67. Laborie, *Coffee Planter*, 126, 130–149; Higman, *Jamaica Surveyed*, 171–172.

68. *Further Proceedings of the Honourable House of Assembly of Jamaica, relative to a bill introduced into the House of Commons for effectually preventing the unlawful importation of slaves, and holding free persons in slavery, in the British colonies [. . .]* (London: J. M. Richardson and J. Ridgeway, 1816), 99–100.

69. John Stewart, *A View of the Past and Present State of the Island of Jamaica: With Remarks on the Moral and Physical Condition of the Slaves, and the Abolition of Slavery in the Colonies* (Edinburgh: Oliver and Boyd, 1823), 114.

70. Radnor Coffee Plantation Journal, 1822–1826, MS 180 (National Library of Jamaica), estimates calculated from entries for January to June 1822; Kathleen E. A. Monteith, "The Labour Regimen on Jamaican Coffee Plantations During Slavery," in *Jamaica in Slavery and Freedom: History, Heritage and Culture*, ed. Kathleen E. A. Monteith and Glen L. Richards (Mona, Jamaica: University of the West Indies Press, 2002), 263–264.

71. Laborie, *Coffee Planter*, 151; John Wemyss, Hermitage Plantation Letterbook, 1819–1824, MS 250 (National Library of Jamaica), entry for December 7, 1819.

72. Higman, *Jamaica Surveyed*, 161–162.

73. Laborie, *Coffee Planter*, 45–49; Patrick Browne, *The Civil and Natural History of Jamaica, in Three Parts* (London: Printed for the Author, 1756), 161–163

74. Monteith, "Planting and Processing Techniques," 119–120. The practice of mill sharing is another trait distinguishing coffee from sugar. Sugar was much more time sensitive. Once cut, processing had to occur within hours to ensure that cane did not ferment. As a result, almost every sugar plantation had a separate wind- or animal-powered mill. The legacies of these

mills are still visible throughout the modern Caribbean. For a succinct description of the sugar milling process, see: Richard B. Sheridan, *Sugar and Slavery: The Economic History of the British West Indies, 1623–1775* (Kingston, Jamaica: University of the West Indies, 1974, reprinted 1994), 112–118.

75. Laborie, *Coffee Planter*, 58.

76. Michel-Rolph Trouillot, "Coffee Planters and Coffee Slaves in the Antilles: The Impact of a Secondary Crop," in *Cultivation and Culture: Labor and the Shaping of Slave Life in the Americas*, ed. Ira Berlin and Philip D. Morgan (Charlottesville: University of Virginia Press, 1993), 125; B. W. Higman, *Slave Populations of the British Caribbean 1807–1834* (Mona, Jamaica: University of the West Indies Press, 1995), 68–69; Kathleen Monteith, "Coffee Industry in Jamaica, 1790–1850" (MPhil diss, University of the West Indies, 1991), 15–23.

77. Trouillot, "Coffee Planters and Coffee Slaves," 131; Michel-Rolph Trouillot, "Motion in the System: Coffee, Color and Slavery in Eighteenth-Century Saint Domingue," *Review, A Journal of the Ferdinand Braudel Centre* 5 (1982): 346–348; David Geggus, "Sugar and Coffee Cultivation in Saint Domingue and the Shaping of the Slave Labor Force," in Berlin, *Cultivation and Culture*, 76–77; Christian Schnakenbourg, *Historie de l'industrie sucrière en Guadeloupe, XIXᵉ-XXᵉ siécles: La crise du système esclavagiste, 1835–1847* (Paris: L'Harmattan, 1980), 22; Higman, *Slave Populations of the British Caribbean*, 434, 699; Meredith A. John, *The Plantation Slaves of Trinidad, 1783–1816: A Mathematical and Demographic Enquiry* (Cambridge: Cambridge University Press, 1988), 117–119.

78. Laborie, *Coffee Planter*, 169.

79. Ibid., 161, 175.

80. R. G. Bruce to William Acanius Senior, Dominica, in Tyler, "Aspects of Planter Society," 367.

81. Laborie, *Coffee Planter*, 151; Geggus, "Sugar and Coffee Cultivation," 82.

82. Delle, *Lines That Divide*, 181; B. W. Higman, *Slave Population and Economy in Jamaica, 1807–1834* (Mona, Jamaica: University of the West Indies Press, 2000), 161; Marietta Morrissey, *Slave Women in the New World: Gender Stratification in the Caribbean* (Lawrence: University of Kansas Press, 1989), 35–42.

83. Laborie, *Coffee Planter*, 165.

84. R. G. Bruce to William Acanius Senior, Dominica, July 1, 1771, in Tyler, "Aspects of Planter Society," 367.

85. R. G. Bruce to A. M. Senior, Dominica, February 27, 1772, in Tyler, "Aspects of Planter Society," 368–369.

86. S. D. Smith, "Coffee and the 'Poorer Sort of People' in Jamaica During the Period of African Enslavement," in *Slavery Without Sugar: Diversity in Caribbean Economy and Society Since the 17th Century*, ed. Verene A. Shepherd (Gainesville: University of Florida, 2002), 113; Laborie, *Coffee Planter*, 166–168.

87. See David Geggus's and Michel-Rolph Troillot's chapters in Berlin, *Cultivating Culture*, 73–100, 124–137.

88. Ibid., 51–54.

89. NA/PRO T 1/484/323a-b and 324, "Memorial of Stephen Fuller, Esq., Agent of Jamaica" (1770); NA/PRO T 1/484/325a-b "Letter from Jno. Morse to Stephen Fuller Esq., Agent for Jamaica" (1770).

90. Thomas Ewbank, *Life in Brazil: Or, a Journal of a Visit to the Land of the Cocoa and the Palm* (New York: Harper and Brothers Publishers, 1856), 118. The degrading effect of this work also underlay the specific prohibition against using laborers to transport coffee to town or port in the Code Henry, a body of legislation implemented in Haiti in 1812 to govern the conditions of agricultural workers. Laurent Dubois, *Haiti: The Aftershocks of History* (New York: Metropolitan Books, 2012), 67.

91. Edgar Corrie, *Letters on the Subject of the Duties of Coffee* (London: T. Cadell and W. Davies, 1808), 8; James Knight, *The Natural, Moral, and Political History of Jamaica*, 2 vols. (Unpublished manuscript, London, 1746, Collections of the British Library), 1:19. Only slightly more manpower was needed to manage the plantation once established. "After the land is cleared, and planted, six or eight Negroes, who are capable of any laborious employment," Knight suggested, "are sufficient to manage 10 or 12 acres, and to raise provisions sufficient for their own existence."

92. Smith, "Coffee and the 'Poorer Sort of People,'" 116; *Saint Jago Intelligencer,* April 16, 1768.

93. *Gazette of Saint Jago de la Vega,* January 31, 1782.

94. Ibid., January 10, 1782.

95. *Dominica Mercury,* or *Free-Port Gazette,* September 3, 1768.

96. For advertisements of Bunel's and Jaison's estates, see *Dominica Chronicle,* May 6, 1775, and May 13, 1775.

97. Excerpted from the public sale notice for Ulysses Fitzmaurice's Bowood Estate, St. Andrew Parish, Dominica, *Dominica Chronicle,* May 6, 1775, and May 13, 1775.

98. Accounts Produce/Crop Accounts, 1B/11/4 (Jamaica Archives). The "Act for preventing frauds and breaches of trust by attorneys or agents of persons absent from this Island; and by trustees, guardians, executors, and administrators acting for and on behalf of minors and others" was first passed in 1740 (13 Geo. II c9, 1740); it lapsed in 1744 but was renewed in 1751 (24 Geo. II c19, s7). Accounts were maintained for estates overseen by agents on behalf of minors or persons deemed incompetent, or in probate.

99. Higman estimates that 176 of 204, or 85 percent, of coffee plantations were monocultural in 1832. In the earlier pre-1790 sample the figures are reversed: all but 2, or 77 percent, had important secondary economic activities. Higman, *Slave Population and Economy in Jamaica,* 13.

100. Monteith, "Coffee Industry," 86; Richard Sheridan, "From Chattel to Wage Slavery in Jamaica, 1740–1860," *Slavery and Abolition* 14:1 (1993): 13–24.

101. Since name duplication was common—at least fourteen William Smiths appear in the Accounts Produce between 1792 and 1813, for example—probate inventories had to include the same name, occupation, parish of residence, and approximate years of operation as a coffee plantation listed in one of two other documentary sources for inclusion in this sample set: (1) House of Assembly petitions for special privileges from free colored coffee planters or (2) contemporary printed sources, such as almanacs. The result is a sample of twenty-eight probate inventories between 1762 and 1800. Probate Inventories, #1B/11/3. libers 56, 61, 62, 63, 64, 65, 66, 68, 69, 70, 72, 73, 74, 75, 77, 78, 81, 82, 83, 84, 85, 86, 87, 89, 90, 91, 93, 95 (Jamaica Archives).

102. Stewart, *View of the Past and Present,* 112.

103. Based on an analysis of Jamaican Probate Inventories, #1B/11/3, vols. 56:135–137, 65:61–62, 70:154, 78:119–120, 81:165, 83:80, 83:152, 85:169–170, 86:23–24, 86:222, 86:167–168, 87:145, 89:40–43, 91:204–205, 93:148–149, 93:175–177, 94:112–113. The £3,564.15.0 listed as "other" in one probate inventory is the value of the land—planted, provision, and barren—as well as the value of living quarters, millworks, and drying barbecues; the £303.5.0 listed as "other" in another are coffee mills and pulping equipment. See also Higman, *Jamaica Surveyed,* 174; and Monteith, "Planting and Processing Techniques," 117.

104. Jamaican Probate Inventories, #1B/11/3, Inventory of Captain John Strachem, vol. 56:135–137 (September 28, 1775).

105. Ibid.

106. Probate Inventories vols. 132:189, 135:69, 149:20, 155:90, 159:158–159.

107. Smith, "Coffee and the 'Poorer Sort of People,'" 116–118.

108. Moseley, *Properties and Effects of Coffee,* xv; Fortescue, *Calendar of State Papers,* 580. For a more detailed discussion of female plantation owners, see chapter 3 of Christine Walker, *Jamaica Ladies: Female Slaveholders and the Creation of Britain's Atlantic Empire* (Oxford: Oxford University Press, 2020), 116–165.

109. Edward Brathwaite, *The Development of Creole Society in Jamaica, 1770–1820* (Oxford: Clarendon Press, 1971), 147.

110. Ibid.

111. Long, *History of Jamaica*, 2:283–286.

112. Like white women, people of color had been engaged in coffee production almost from its inception. A treaty between Jamaican authorities and Captain Cudjoe in 1738, for example, included coffee as one of the commodities that Trelawney Maroons could produce on the 1,500 acres granted to them, described in "Trelawney Town and the Cockpits: Articles of Pacification with the Maroons of Trelawney Town, Concluded March 1, 1738," reprinted in *The Proceedings of the Governor and the Assembly of Jamaica in Regard to the Maroon Negroes* (London: John Stockdale, 1796), xviii. The same legislation, however, also specified that selling their produce at market required both notification of the local customs official and a vending license.

113. "An act to prevent the inconveniences arising from exorbitant grants and devises, made by whites to negroes, and the issues of negroes," found in *The Laws of Jamaica*, 2nd ed., 2 vols. (St. Jago de la Vega, Jamaica: Alexander Aikman, 1802), 2: 23–26; see also Gad Heuman, *Between Black and White: Race, Politics and Coloreds in Jamaica, 1792–1865* (Westport, CT: Greenwood Press, 1981), 6.

114. Indeed, the origins of such "special privileges" petitions predated the 1761 inheritance limitations. John Golding, a planter in Vere, had his appeal granted in 1733, while Susanna Augier, a mulatto woman residing in Kingston, was accorded the same status in 1738, as were her two children, Mary and Francis. Even those who received "special privileges" were vulnerable in other ways, since they were still barred from holding seats in the Jamaican Council or Assembly, or from voting in elections. Heuman, *Between Black and White*, 6–7. See also Long, *History of Jamaica*, 2:320–322. Both Golding and Augier and their petitions for "the same Rights and Privileges as English subjects, born of white parents" appear in the "Table of the Acts" for volume 1 of *The Laws of Jamaica*; unfortunately, only the names of private acts, rather than the full text of the legislation, is printed.

115. Manning, whose father, Edward Manning, had been a wealthy merchant in Kingston and a member of both the Jamaican House and Council, was connected to some of Jamaica's leading families. Her mother, Elizabeth Pinnock, was a free woman of color with whom Manning had had a well-publicized, long-term relationship after suing his white wife, Elizabeth Manning, for divorce, accusing her of infidelity. Elizabeth Manning, in turn, was the sister of Sir Henry Moore, lieutenant governor of Jamaica from 1756 to 1761 and later governor of New York. See Trevor Burnard, "A Matron in Rank, a Prostitute in Manners," in Shepherd, *Working Slavery, Pricing Freedom*, 145–146. Dorothy Manning's birth appears in the Kingston Parish Registers, 1722–1825 (Jamaica Archives) as "Dorothy MANNING b. 6 Oct 1743 fa. Edward MANNING Esq$_{re}$ mo. Elizabeth PINNOCK mulatto."

116. "Inventory of John Rome the Elder" and "Inventory of Dorothy Manning," Probate Inventories vols. 86:23–24 and 116:162–163. See also Higman, *Jamaica Surveyed*, 31; and Betty Wood and Martin Lynn, eds., *Travel, Trade, and Power in the Atlantic, 1765–1884* (Cambridge: Press Syndicate of the University of Cambridge, 2002), 124. "An Act to entitle Dorothy Manning, Thomas Manning, and George Manning, of the Parish of Clarendon, free mulattos, the same rights and privileges with English subjects, under certain restrictions" appeared among the private acts passed in 1783; *The Laws of Jamaica, 1760–1792*, 2nd ed., 2 vols. (St. Jago de la Vega: Alexander Aikman, 1802).

117. "Johan Casper Weise, 03 Feb 1798 Christening," Jamaica Church of England Parish Register Transcripts, 1664–1880, FHL microfilm 1291763 (Registrar General's Department, Spanish Town).

118. The two inventories for Johan Casper Weise appear in Probate Inventories vols. 111:220–221 (sugar) and 113:153–154 (coffee).

119. Geo. II. C 24, 412–415. Confiscated coffee was divided between the state and the person who revealed the infraction; if discovered during or after shipping, the Crown took half and the remainder went to person who brought suit. If discovered in the colonies, a third went to the Crown, a third to the whistleblower, and a third to the colonial governor—presumably as incentive to discourage such behavior by other planters under his authority in the future.

Chapter 2

1. Several sources about the ship *Polly*, her owners, and distributors of her cargo have been used to construct this vignette, including shipping lists for 1765 located in NA/PRO CO 142/13-29, "Naval Office Shipping Lists for Jamaica, 1683–1818." The *Polly* reappears in these Naval Office Shipping Lists over the next several years; in addition to rum, sugar, and coffee, she carried molasses, tobacco, and cocoa (April 16, 1765, August 16, 1765, and August 8, 1767). One notable exception was the voyage of July 10, 1767, with ninety slaves on board, but this was uncharacteristic, and the *Polly* was temporarily consigned to another merchant, Peter Adams. Evidence of coffee reexports from Philadelphia appear in entries for April and May of 1765 in William West, West Family Business Records, 1769–1804 (Historical Society of Pennsylvania) and William Redmond, Journal, 1749–60 and Ledger, 1775–1809 (Historical Society of Pennsylvania).

2. For coffee's tax-free status, see, Great Britain, "An Act for Encouraging the Growth of Coffee in his Majesty's Plantations in America" (London, 1732).

3. List of goods summarized from NA/PRO CO 142/13-17, "Naval Office Shipping Lists for Jamaica, 1683–1818," for inbound vessels for 1762 and 1766. For coffee import rates, see NA/PRO Customs 16/1, "Ledger of Imports and Exports (American) January 5, 1768 to January 5, 1773," which lists eighteen cities regularly importing coffee. The next largest importers, James River in Virginia, Charleston, New York, and Boston, varied from year to year but averaged at most only 10 and 20 percent of the overall trade. Smaller cities such as Marblehead, MA, Piscataqua, ME, Providence, RI, New Castle, DE, and Savannah, GA rarely took in more than 1 or 2 percent, or 10,000 pounds of coffee a year, and often far less.

4. Jacob Price, "Summation: The American Panorama of American Port Cities," in *Atlantic Port Cities: Economy, Culture, and Society in the Atlantic World, 1650–1850,* ed. Franklin W. Knight and Peggy K. Liss (Knoxville: University of Tennessee Press, 1991), 262–278; Doerflinger, *Vigorous Spirit of Enterprise*, 78–79, 100. Doerflinger was the first to challenge the image of colonial merchants as "jacks of all trades." His analyses of tonnage records for 1765–1775 and 1785–1787 indicate that merchants began specializing much earlier than previously thought, with 86 percent of all Philadelphia firms focusing their efforts in one of four geographic areas by the 1760s: England and Ireland, southern Europe and Africa, the Caribbean, or the North American coast.

5. Mifflin & Massey Ledgerbook, folios 112, 125, and 131. A breakdown of all expenses—cargo, ship provisions, and wages and storage—for the first *Live Oak* voyage appears on folio 112. Coffee imports are recorded on folios 42, 60, 75, 109, 139, 146, 200, and 287. Profits this high were the exception rather than the rule but were not unknown. Doerflinger records proceeds of between £1,423 and £3,000 on single voyages in 1770 and 1773 respectively; Doerflinger, *Vigorous Spirit of Enterprise,* 120.

6. NA/PRO Customs 16/1. Customs records from 1768 to 1773 document Philadelphia sloops bearing coffee sailing most often to one of five locations: Massachusetts, Maryland, Virginia, North Carolina, and South Carolina.

7. J. A. Anderson, *Navigation of the Upper Delaware* (Trenton, NJ: McCrellish & Quigley, 2013), 16.

8. For information about Matthias Slough, see Samuel Rowland Fisher, "Trip through Pennsylvania, Maryland, and Virginia, 1787," entry for April 14, 1787, in Fisher Diaries and Accounts (Historical Society of Pennsylvania); Colleen Rafferty, "To Establish an Intercourse Between Our

Respective Houses: Economic Networks in the Mid-Atlantic, 1735–1815" (PhD diss., University of Delaware, 2012), 1–3.

9. Patrick Spero does an excellent job of outlining how, despite persistent military conflict, Pennsylvania's hinterlands and those of neighboring colonies continued to expand, in *Frontier Rebels: The Politics of War in Frontier Pennsylvania* (Philadelphia: University of Pennsylvania Press, 2016), especially 71–102.

10. Doerflinger, *Vigorous Spirit of Enterprise*, 110–111. Between 1768 and 1773, Doerflinger records 193 voyages to Jamaica compared with 34 voyages to Barbados, the second largest British West Indian port of call, and this figure may underrepresent the significance of this route as vessels listed as engaging in coastal commerce often originated farther south. William West Jr.'s venture on the brigantine *Polly*, for example, docked in Charleston to offload a portion of its sugar and coffee cargo before continuing to Philadelphia from Jamaica. Charleston was again the intermediate stop for the *Polly* four months later, this time for a shipment of tobacco, before heading down to the islands. Evidence of coffee re-exports from Philadelphia appear in April and May of 1765 in William West, West Family Business Records, 1769–1804. For details about the *Polly*, see William West, Letterbook, 91–101 (Historical Society of Pennsylvania).

Figures derived from a comparison of coffee imports in NA/PRO Customs 16/1. Imports are recorded in hogsheads. These figures were converted to pounds, one hogshead equivalent to between 12 and 14 cwt. (at 112 pounds per cwt.). Assuming an average of 13 cwt. per hogshead, the total is 1,456 pounds per hogshead for this Jamaican venture. Despite this impressive growth, those involved in this trade did not label themselves "coffee merchants" in the way that flour, lumber, and wine merchants appeared in tax lists and business directories of the mid-eighteenth century. Self-described flour merchants or wine merchants made a statement about the significance of that one commodity to their overall business, but coffee did not dominate any one person's account books in the same way until well into the nineteenth century. Instead, these early traders dealt in several tropical goods and juggled many important variables, including British and foreign sources, duties and tax rebates, merchandise quality, and, finally, fluctuations in consumer demand.

11. Henry Drinker to Abel James, October 29, 1756, James & Drinker Letterbook (Historical Society of Pennsylvania).

12. Benjamin Smith Barton, Papers, Series 2: Subject Files, c. 1789–1815, folder labeled "Botany: Potatoes, Coffee, Corn, etc." (American Philosophical Society).

13. For a comparison of East and West Indian coffee into Britain see NA/PRO Customs 36; Schumpeter, *English Overseas Trading Statistics*, 60; and NA/PRO T 1/511/20-21. For the impact of a proposed reduction on French coffee duties to the British Caribbean trade, see NA/PRO T/1/515-179-181.

14. The inaugural announcement of their business venture appeared in the *Pennsylvania Gazette*, April 11, 1754. Usher and Wharton dissolved their partnership in March 1767, although Abraham Usher continued to vend the same range of wares—including coffee—for some time thereafter. A notice appearing on March 3, 1757, announced both partnership dissolution and Usher's intention to carry on as a sole proprietor; see *Pennsylvania Gazette*, March 3, 1757.

15. Breen, *Marketplace of Revolution*, 133.

16. *Pennsylvania Gazette*, May 17, 1770, and July 12, 1770.

17. Similarly, coffee reached consumers already roasted unless designated as "green" coffee, which occasionally appeared for sale. For green coffee, see *Pennsylvania Gazette*, August 13, 1767. A few advertisements for "cocoa and coffee roasters," however, indicate that some drinkers may have chosen to do their roasting at home. *Daily Advertiser*, October 30, 1775. For ground coffee, see *Daily Advertiser*, November 6, 1775.

18. A handful of references to Java and Mocha coffee, from the East Indies and Port of Mocha respectively, appeared in Philadelphia newspapers between 1765 and 1780. More frequently,

Philadelphia stores advertised French coffee or "Port-au-Prince" coffee. The first could be coffee coming from any of the French West Indies, the latter specifically from Port-au-Prince, the principal port of Saint Domingue. Occasionally coffee arriving from the former French islands of Saint Vincent, Dominica, and Grenada still appeared as "French" coffee. Though these islands were technically under British control, in many respects these advertisements are correct. Most coffee plantations were still owned and operated by former French colonists who cultivated coffee in the same methods as before the islands were ceded. For Port-au-Prince coffee, see notice of Benjamin Harbeson, *Daily Advertiser,* July 8, 1780.

19. Philip Livingston, *New York Mercury,* March 26, 1764.

20. Samuel Hart, *New York Mercury,* October 1, 1764.

21. Isaac Adolphus, *New-York Gazette,* December 19, 1763. The last appearance of Adolphus's advertisement was in the *New-York Gazette* on March 12, 1764. The transition from seven to eight years in Livingston's coffee appeared in the *New-York Gazette* on August 20, 1764.

22. The *Snow* incident appeared in the *Pennsylvania Gazette,* September 23, 1756.

23. Henry Drinker to Robert Field, September 22, 1756, and Henry Drinker to Robert Field, October 29, 1756, James & Drinker Letterbook.

24. *Boston Evening-Post,* November 8, 1756. The *Snow* was one of over 400 privateer notices that included coffee during the Seven Years' War.

25. *Minutes of the Common Council of the City of Philadelphia, 1704–1776* (Philadelphia: Crissy and Markley, 1847), 293; William Patterson to William Wood, Secretary to the Honorable Board of Customs, July 5, 1751, included in a folder entitled "Transcripts of Documents relating to Colonial Policy" (Rhodes House Library, Oxford University).

26. *Pennsylvania Gazette,* August 23, 1774. Additional examples of vessel vendues can be found in the *Pennsylvania Gazette,* August 7, 1766, October 16, 1766, April 23, 1767, June 8, 1769, and March 15, 1770. Examples of Caribbean commodities: *Pennsylvania Gazette,* July 2, 1767, October 13, 1768, December 14, 1769, March 15, 1770, and January 18, 1775. British dry goods: *Pennsylvania Gazette,* June 26, 1766, December 24, 1767, November 3, 1768, June 7, 1770, and May 2, 1771. Wines: *Pennsylvania Gazette,* December 25, 1766, July 16, 1767, July 30, 1767, September 24, 1767, October 8, 1767, and September 1, 1768. Coastal commerce (for example, tobacco, rice, naval stores, wheat, or flour): *Pennsylvania Gazette,* February 20, 1766, March 26, 1767, March 10, 1768, April 23, 1772, July 21, 1778, July 23, 1778, and September 1, 1778. For the auction of the *Medusa* and *Seven Brothers,* see *Pennsylvania Ledger; or the Philadelphia Market-Day Advertiser,* January 7, 1778.

27. Samuel Howell's notice appeared in the *Pennsylvania Gazette* on December 26, 1765, and was republished almost verbatim eight times through January 22, 1767.

28. In May 1748, for example, cargoes of "sugar, coffee, cotton, and cocoa" were auctioned from three prize vessels alongside "some likely negroes." The notice appeared in the *Philadelphia Journal,* May 26, 1748.

29. *Pennsylvania Gazette,* January 23, 1772, and March 15, 1775.

30. *Daily Advertiser,* January 18 and 20, 1780.

31. William Patterson to William Wood, July 5, 1751, 43.

32. Other historians have described military personnel gawking at the variety of goods that entered New York without paying duties in the 1770s and estimate that as much as a quarter of the colony's coffee, sugar, and molasses arrived through less than legal means. See Matson, *Merchants and Empire,* 299.

33. NA/PRO T/1/401/14-15, "Extract of a Letter from William Shirley, Esq., Governor of the Bahama Island to the British Board of Trade, dated August 1st, 1760." While some Spanish colonists may have purchased English goods for their own consumption, Shirley argued that the volume of goods passing through this one port "so much exceeds the abilities of the settlers at

Monte Cristi to purchase any considerable quantities of those English and French cargoes, that the pretense seems not to deserve the least credit."

34. Letter written by a planter at Barbados, "The true Interest of Great Britain with respect to the Caribbe Islands; as well as the Old Settlements of the Neutral Islands and the Conquests. In which the Importance of Martinique is particularly consider'd," 1762, included in a folder entitled "Transcripts of Documents relating to Colonial Policy," folios 184–85; see also NA/PRO T 1/453/136-38, 308.

35. William Patterson to the Board of Customs, undated (although the letter's first sentence mentions 1751 correspondence as "seven years ago" and the end of the letter references Britain's current war with France, implying that it was written around 1758, or during the Seven Years' War), included in a folder entitled "Transcripts of Documents relating to Colonial Policy," 50.

36. NA/PRO T1/504, "Letter from Captain Ash to Messrs. Brown and Birch" (January 24, 1773). I would like to thank Amanda Moniz for bringing the case of Captain Ash to my attention.

A note about samples: if a ship captain arrived to trade without sufficient goods, money or credit to pay in full for what he wanted, as often happened, especially on unplanned voyages such as Ash's trip to Puerto Rico, it was common practice to provide "samples," or examples of wares or produce to be delivered after the next harvest as a down payment with a promissory note for the balance. If demand was sufficiently high, however, sellers might require immediate payment or a higher percentage of the total price rather than rely on the promise of future compensation. For a discussion of promissory notes in eighteenth-century West Indian trade, see Doerflinger, *Vigorous Spirit of Enterprise*, 97–126. Further evidence for this practice is found in the few coffee planters' accounts books that have survived. While admittedly later in the nineteenth century, examples of planters using future crops as leverage for current debts can be found in the letter books of Mrs. B. Boucher, Marlborough Plantation, Manchester Parish, Jamaica, 1827–1837, and John Wemyss, Letterbook, Hermitage Estate, St. Elizabeth Parish, Jamaica, 1819–1824, both in the National Library, Kingston, Jamaica.

37. NA/PRO T1/504, 2–3.

38. Ibid., 1–3.

39. For Garrigus, see *Pennsylvania Gazette*, August 16, 1770; for Wright, see *Pennsylvania Gazette*, August 9, 1775. Through March 1775, Patrick and James Wright, both from Edinburgh, jointly operated the confectionery. After August, Patrick appears as the sole proprietor; *Daily Advertiser*, February 13 and March 20, 1775. Anne Royall's description is cited in Lorena S. Walsh, "Provisioning Early American Towns: The Chesapeake, a Multi-Disciplinary Case Study, Final Performance Report," Colonial Williamsburg Foundation, National Endowment for the Humanities, RO-22643-93, September 30, 1997, 92. Breen documents the use of coffee as customer refreshment in *Marketplace of Revolution*, 128–129; Peter Anspach's letter appears in "Peter Anspach to John Mitchell, February 14, 1773," John Mitchell Sequestered Papers, box 2 (Pennsylvania Historical and Museum Commission); and the "Shirt Ordinary" advertisement including coffee was described in the *Boston Post-Boy*, May 31, 1773.

40. *The Ancient Museum, or Repository of Ancient and Modern Fugitive Pieces, Prose and Poetical* (Philadelphia: Printed by Mathew Carey, 1789), 235.

41. *Daily Advertiser*, May 2, 1780, and May 6, 1780.

42. This last development is one of the distinctions between wholesale/retail operators and strictly wholesale merchants, who relied principally on cash payments. For examples of wholesale and retail vendors, see Edward Role, *Pennsylvania Gazette*, August 23, 1770; John Jennings, *Pennsylvania Gazette*, September 6, 1770; and William Keaff, *Pennsylvania Gazette*, October 11, 1770.

43. See Brooke Hunter, "Rage for Grain: Flour Milling in the Mid-Atlantic, 1750–1815" (PhD diss., University of Delaware, 2001), especially chapter 3.

44. *Pennsylvania Gazette*, October 12, 1785.

45. Levi Hollingsworth, Account Book, 1768–1775 (Historical Society of Pennsylvania); Hollingsworth opened a retail store by 1780, where the percentage of coffee sales attributable to individual rather than wholesale buyers rose further still. Newspaper advertisements for this retail operation not only include coffee and other West Indian products, but also local investments in ironworks and flour mills outside the city; *Pennsylvania Packet or Daily Advertiser*, April 8, 1780.

46. Frederick Tolles, *Meeting House and Counting House: The Quaker Merchants of Colonial Philadelphia, 1682–1763* (Chapel Hill: University of North Carolina for the Institute of Early American History and Culture, 1948), 88–89.

47. John Baynton, Ledger B, 1754–1759, 15, 58, and 82, and Samuel Neave, Ledger, 1752–1756 (both Historical Society of Pennsylvania). See also Doerflinger, *Vigorous Spirit of Enterprise*, 125–126.

48. Mifflin & Massey Ledgerbook.

49. Ibid.; the use of coffee as payments to Miller, Oliver, and Ashmead appear on pages 23, 73, 180, 217, 334, and 343.

50. *Daily Advertiser*, July 22, 1780.

51. *Daily Advertiser*, August 22, 1780.

52. George Simpson Eddy, *Account Books Kept by Benjamin Franklin*, from Ledger D, 1739–1747 (New York: Columbia University Press, 1928), 85. The first almanac order was combined with a credit from Mifflin for another £3.14.9. The American Philosophical Society has digitized all of Franklin's ledger books and created a keyword-searchable, interactive database. See: https://diglib-legacy.amphilsoc.org/franklindata/.

53. *Pennsylvania Gazette*, May 10, 1770.

54. *Pennsylvania Gazette*, October 25, 1770, and November 29, 1770.

55. *Daily Advertiser*, April 10, 1775. See also advertisements on May 1, 1775, and May 8, 1775. In July 1775, Gray relocated his store further up Chestnut Street, between Second and Third Streets. His inventory remained largely the same. *Daily Advertiser*, July 17, 1775. See also Richard Bushman's description of retail grocers, "Shopping and Advertising in Colonial America," in Carson, Hoffman, and Albert, *Of Consuming Interests*, 240–242.

56. *Daily Advertiser*, September 25 and October 16, 1775. Rebecca Robinson also appeared as a grocer in "Constables Returns, 1775" (Philadelphia City Archives).

57. Cited in John W. Tyler, *Smugglers and Patriots: Boston Merchants and the Advent of the American Revolution* (Boston: Northeastern University Press, 1986), 113.

58. *Daily Advertiser*, April 18, 1780.

59. *Daily Advertiser*, January 2, 1775.

60. *Pennsylvania Gazette*, January 19, 1780, and March 29, 1780; *Daily Advertiser*, October 3, 1780; *Pennsylvania Gazette*, July 12, 1770.

61. After 1775, the *Packet* increased publication to three issues a week, appearing on Tuesdays and Thursdays as well as Saturdays.

62. Advertisers who did not list addresses were compared with city directories or tax lists to identify their location. Most stores ran notices once or twice a week, but as the goal of this analysis was to determine the location of sellers rather than the volume of their publicity, retailers were counted only once, regardless of how often they appeared in print each year, unless they changed location.

63. See James Daly and Allen Weinberg, *Genealogy of Philadelphia County Subdivisions*, 2nd ed. (Philadelphia: Athenaeum of Philadelphia, 1966), for an overview of Philadelphia's city ward system.

64. Dock Ward, with 751 households, and North Ward, with 468 households, were the most populous wards. These figures were derived from Sharon V. Salinger, "Spaces, Inside and Outside, in Eighteenth-Century Philadelphia," *Journal of Interdisciplinary History* 26:1 (Summer 1995): 1–31. Detailed descriptions of Philadelphia's neighborhoods, social and economic strata, and relative disposable incomes can also be found in Sharon V. Salinger and Charles Wetherell,

"Wealth and Renting in Prerevolutionary Philadelphia," *Journal of American History* 71:4 (March 1985): 826–840; Billy G. Smith, "The Material Lives of Laboring Philadelphians, 1750 to 1800," *William and Mary Quarterly* 38:2 (April 1981): 163–202; Sam Bass Warner Jr., "If All the World Were Philadelphia: A Scaffolding for Urban History, 1774–1930," *American Historical Review* 74:1 (Oct. 1968): 26–43, and *The Private City: Philadelphia in Three Periods of Its Growth* (Philadelphia: University of Pennsylvania Press, 1968); and Gary Nash, "Urban Wealth and Poverty in Pre-Revolutionary America," *Journal of Inter Disciplinary History* 6:4 (Spring 1976): 545–584, and "Poverty and Poor Relief in Pre-Revolutionary Philadelphia," *William and Mary Quarterly* 3rd ser., 33:1 (January 1976): 3–30.

Chapter 3

1. "Mary Shippen to Joseph Shippen, partially illegible date, 1772," Shippen Family Papers, 1701–1856 (Historical Society of Pennsylvania). A full service might include up to 12 teacups and saucers, 12 coffee cups, a teapot, cover and stand, a coffee pot with its own cover and stand, a basin and plate, a sugar dish with cover and plate, a milk pot and cover, a tea "jar" and cover, a slop dish and saucer, and a spoon tray. See Catherine Beth Lippert, *Eighteenth-Century English Porcelain in the Collection of the Indianapolis Museum of Art* (Bloomington: Indianapolis Museum of Art and the University of Indiana Press, 1987), 219.

2. Carson, "The Consumer Revolution in Colonial British America," *Of Consuming Interests,* 504–505.

3. Breen, *Marketplace of Revolution,* 281–289, 306–307. Breen goes so far as to argue that a common material culture helped fuel the boycott movements of the 1760s and 1770s because it could target goods familiar throughout the thirteen colonies—facilitating a shared means of protest.

4. Until recently, tropical goods have formed only a byline in studies of colonial material life even though, by 1772, money from groceries made up more than a third of the income of all goods imported into North America. See Carole Shammas, "The Revolutionary Impact of European Demand for Tropical Goods," in *The Early Modern Atlantic Economy,* ed. John McCusker and Kenneth Morgan (Cambridge: Cambridge University Press, 2000), 170; Carole Shammas, "How Self-Sufficient Was Early America?" *Journal of Interdisciplinary History* 13:2 (Autumn 1982): 247–272.

5. Landon Carter, *The Diary of Colonel Landon Carter of Sabine Hall, 1752–1778,* ed. Jack P. Greene, 2 vols. (Richmond: Virginia Historical Society, 1987).

6. Carter, *Diary of Colonel Landon Carter,* 1:241.

7. Ibid., 1:245.

8. Ibid., 1:245. For a description of spit roasters, see Ukers, *All About Coffee,* 616–618. Carter was especially careful to record "loss" or the difference in weight between coffee before and after roasting, as it became lighter when dried.

9. "Landon Carter Jr. to Landon Carter Sr., Pittsylvania, January 1, 1763[4]," in Walter Ray Wineman, ed., *The Landon Carter Papers in the University of Virginia Library: A Calendar and Biographical Sketch* (Charlottesville: University of Virginia Press, 1962), 16; Carter, *Diary of Colonel Landon Carter,* 1:249.

10. Carter, *Diary of Colonel Landon Carter,* 1:251, 344; 2:842.

11. Ibid., 1:350, 541, 545–546.

12. Ibid., 2:600.

13. *Pennsylvania Chronicle,* August 11 to 15, 1768.

14. Cited in Sarah Meacham, *Every Home a Distillery: Alcohol, Gender, and Technology in the Colonial Chesapeake* (Baltimore: Johns Hopkins University Press, 2009), 124–127.

15. Carter, *Diary of Colonel Landon Carter,* 2: 928, 944.

16. Thomas Balch, ed., *The Journal of Claude Blanchard: Commissary of the French Auxiliary Army sent to the United States during the American Revolution, 1780–1783* (Albany: Joel Munsell, 1876), 78.

17. Carter, *Diary of Colonel Landon Carter*, 1: 344.

18. Meacham, *Every Home a Distillery*, 127.

19. Nomini Hall was owned by Landon Carter's nephew Robert Carter.

20. Philip Vickers Fithian, *Journal and Letters of Philip Vickers Fithian*, ed. Hunter Dickinson Farish (Charlottesville: University of Virginia Press, 1968), 144.

21. Ibid., 156.

22. Ibid., 156.

23. Ibid., 195.

24. Ibid., 117, 123, 181.

25. Ibid., 199.

26. Ibid., 171.

27. John Hook Daybook, 1771 (Library of Virginia); Martin, *Buying into the World of Goods*, 83.

28. Meacham, *Every Home a Distillery*, 127; Roy Dickens, ed., *Archeology of Urban America: The Search for Pattern and Process* (New York: Academic Press, 1982), 378.

29. Catherine Cangany, *Frontier Seaport: Detroit's Transformation into an Atlantic Entrepôt* (Chicago: University of Chicago Press, 2014), 57–59.

30. Of the 65 percent that listed cups or saucers, 45 percent of these noted only coffee cups, which may reflect the common practice of using a single set of saucers for matching sets of coffee cups and teacups.

Gunston Hall's probate inventory study is available on the museum's website. This database was assembled from information contained in 319 Virginia and Maryland probate inventories dating from 1744 to 1810. See Susan Borchandt, Mickey Crowell, Ellen L. Donald, and Barbara A. Farner, "The Gunston Hall Plantation: Room Use Study," 2002, http://www.gunstonhall.org/mansion/room_use_study/methodology.html.

31. Martin, *Buying into the World of Goods*, 84–85.

32. Coffee pots and chocolate pots are more difficult to tell apart as both were tall and slender, with a spout high on the body to avoid pouring any sediment. Both could also have the handle fixed in line with the spout, or on the side of the pot. The easiest way to tell the difference was in the pot's lid. Chocolate pots could contain a hinged or detachable lid through which a stirrer might be inserted to remix chocolate that had settled on the bottom of the vessel. Steven Goss, *British Teapots and Coffee Pots* (Buckinghamshire, UK: Shire Publications, 2005), 4–6. The Folger Coffee Company silver collection, housed at the Cincinnati Museum of Art, includes several examples of English-manufactured, side-handled eighteenth-century pots. See J. A. Folger and Company, *Folger Coffee Company Collection of Antique English Silver Coffee Pots: Exhibition, September 26 to October 31, 1963* (Oshkosh, WI: Paine Art Center, 1963), 17–30.

33. John D. David, *Pewter at Colonial Williamsburg* (Lebanon, NH: University Press of New England for the Colonial Williamsburg Foundation, 2003), 257, 265. With an average serving size of three ounces, this meant that teapots held roughly twelve to eighteen ounces.

34. Goss, *British Teapots and Coffee Pots*, 5.

35. The number of silversmiths is based on city tax lists. Partial records of some city wards are available for 1762 and 1770; 1775 is the earliest complete set of all city wards. See "Constables Returns, 1762 (partial), 1770 (partial) and 1775," in the collection of the Philadelphia City Archives. By 1790 the first U.S. census listed eight silversmiths. An additional two operated in adjacent Southwark District, and several more were scattered throughout Philadelphia County, outside the city proper. A 1795 city business directory listed sixteen silversmiths, including two, Francis Poincignon and Bernard Georgeon, who specialized in French styles. See Edmund Hogan, *Prospect of Philadelphia, and Check on the Next Directory*, Part 1 (Philadelphia: Francis and Robert Bailey, 1795), 36, 78.

36. The exact date when Francis Richardson Sr. established his business is not known, but he wrote several letters to his mother from Boston in 1703 describing his acquisition of tools, and

the business already existed when he married Elizabeth Growden of Philadelphia in 1706. Correspondence outlining business preparations appear in letters dated in July 1703 in Richardson Family Papers, Box 2, folder 2, materials dating 1701–1703 (Winterthur Museum and Library). Joseph Richardson Sr. initially inherited his father Francis' business with his older brother, Francis Richardson Jr. Francis, had already established himself as a merchant, however, and while he created smaller silver wares through 1738, he left the smith business largely to Joseph, instead opening a clock making and repair shop alongside his import and export enterprises. Fales, *Joseph Richardson and Family*, 3–7, 22–30.

37. Morrison H. Heckscher and Leslie G. Bowman, *American Rococo, 1750–1775* (New Haven, CT: Yale University Press, 2013), 65; Fales, *Joseph Richardson and Family*, 79–82.

38. Fales, *Joseph Richardson and Family*, 78–81.

39. In chase work, a surface's underside is hammered to raise, depress, or push aside metal for decoration. "Joseph Richardson to Thomas How & John Masterman, 28th 9th mo. 1759," Joseph Richardson Letterbook, Downs Manuscript and Microfilm Collection (Winterthur Museum and Library).

40. Deborah Anne Federhen, "Paul Revere, Silversmith: A Study of His Shop Operations and Objects" (MA thesis, University of Delaware, 1988), 67–68.

41. Heckscher and Bowman, *American Rococo*, 83.

42. Paul Revere, "Wastebook and memoranda, Boston, 3 Jan. 1761–10 Oct. 1783," entry for September 2, 1773, Revere Family Papers, 1746–1964 (Massachusetts Historical Society); Heckscher and Bowman, *American Rococo*, 96; Fales, *Joseph Richardson and Family*, 244.

43. Fales, *Joseph Richardson and Family*, 78.

44. For more on Blunston, see Donna B. Munger, *Pennsylvania Land Records: A History and Guide for Research* (Wilmington, DE: Scholarly Resources, 1991), 68–70. Not all buyers wanted bigger, however, and Richardson still ordered a few smaller coffee pots to accommodate different preferences and budgets. In 1761, for example, he ordered one coffee pot of "one wine Quart about 25 oz.," another "to hold about half a Pint more than the Above," and yet a third to "hold 3 Pints About 32 oz." But the overall trend was toward grander vessels with more capacious holding capacities, a direct result of coffee's affordability. Fales, *Joseph Richardson and Family*, 78–79.

45. John Tabor Kempe, *New York Gazette*, January 14, 1760; Judah Hayes, *Newport Mercury*, August 24, 1762; Johnathan Evans, *Pennsylvania Gazette*, January 3, 1765. At least a dozen similar stories of theft span the 1760s and 1770s.

46. An additional method developed by Robert Ellis, called close plating, emerged in England in 1779. Fewer of these pieces were intended for export, however, and given his years of operation in Philadelphia, Richardson is more likely to have imported silver-plated vessels made according to the French or Sheffield method. For more information about the history of plating, see Eric Turner, "Silver Plating in the 18th Century," in *Metal Plating and Platination: Cultural, Technical and Historical Developments*, ed. Susan La-Neice (Oxford: Butterworth-Heinnemann, 1993), 211–222.

47. Fales, *Joseph Richardson and Family*, 225, 229, 231, 236, 255.

48. William White, *The History, Guide and Description of the Borough of Sheffield* (Sheffield: Printed for W. White, 1833), 41–43; Henry Newton Veitch, *Sheffield Plate: Its History, Manufacture and Art* (London: George Bell and Sons, 1908). While amounts varied somewhat, the industry standard was a silver sheet of roughly ten to twenty ounces for each eight pounds of copper. For other analyses of North American use of Sheffield silver plate, see Elizabeth Ingerman Wood, "Thomas Fletcher: A Philadelphia Entrepreneur in Presentation Silver," *Winterthur Portfolio* 3 (1967): 136–171; and Gerald W. R. Ward, "Jabez Baldwin: Silversmith-Entrepreneur of Salem, Massachusetts, 1802–1819," *Winterthur Portfolio* 23:1 (Spring 1988): 51–62.

49. Charles Dutens, *Pennsylvania Gazette*, May 23, 1754, and Benjamin Booth, *New York Journal*, August 26, 1768.

50. Of the twenty-four coffee pots Joseph Richardson ordered between 1758 and 1773, for example, twenty-one of them came with matching stands. Such stands served both decorative and
functional purposes. While they spoke to the status of their owners, adding one more piece to
service settings, many were also designed to be high enough to accommodate a small candle beneath them to ensure that the coffee in the pot remained warm longer. Heckscher and Bowman,
American Rococo, 98–99.

51. Fales, *Joseph Richardson and Family*, 78–79. Richardson's ledger includes an entry for this
reworked silver coffee pot, decorated with his engraved initials intertwined with those of his wife
Mary, that he gifted her in 1748. This same coffee pot appears in the probate inventory taken when
the silversmith died nearly four decades later, in 1784. The inventory listed objects room by
room, and the pot stood in a place of honor in the first-floor front room of his Front Street
home; a coffee mill, meanwhile was listed as part of the kitchen equipment. Both the pot and
the mill subsequently appeared in his wife's probate inventory when she died four years later.
See "An Inventory of the Goods and Chattels belonging to the Estate of Joseph Richardson deceased taken 10th mo. 18th, 1784," Box 8, folder 3, and "Inventory of the goods and chattels belonging to the estate of Mary Richardson taken this 7th day of the 1st mo. 1788," Box 2, folder 11,
Richardson Family Papers; Fales, *Joseph Richardson and Family*, 16, 40–42, 153–163.

52. Fales, *Joseph Richardson and Family*, 255.

53. Ibid., 233.

54. "JR to How & Masterman 9th 2nd mo., 1760," "JR to How & Masterman, 20th 10th mo.,
1760," and "JR to John Masterson, 11th 10th mo., 1770," Joseph Richardson Letterbook. Images of
Richardson's 1748 and 1754 coffee pots, the first in private hands and the second belonging to the
Historical Society of Pennsylvania, appear in Fales, *Joseph Richardson and Family*, 80, 82, and
Heckscher and Bowman, *American Rococo*, 104.

55. *Pennsylvania Gazette*, July 3, 1760. For prices of coffee pots, see John Drinker, Account
Books, 1776–1779, and Levi Hollingsworth, Receipt, April 16, 1789, Receipted Bills, 1768–1773 (both
Historical Society of Pennsylvania).

56. Wallace, Davidson & Johnson, Order Books, April 25, 1771—November 16, 1775.
MSA S 528-27/28 (Maryland State Archives), folios 9, 76, and 116. See also "William Lux to
Wallace, Davidson & Johnson, May 4, 1771," folio 29 (order on April 25, 1771, March 20, 1772,
and October 26, 1772); and Smith, Hue, and Alexander Daybook, 1791, Fredericksburg,
Virginia, 316, 446.

57. The Winterthur Museum and Library holds over 16,000 ceramic objects in its collections.
Among these are examples in each material type listed above, including redware (accession #:
1956.0038.035 A, B dating between 1740 and 1800 and 1957.0015.002 A, B, dating between 1750
and 1780, both of either British or North American manufacture); salt-glazed stoneware (also imported from Staffordshire, English, accession #: 1958.0937 A, B, dated between 1745 and 1770);
hard-paste porcelain (accession #: 2000.0061.056 A, B).

58. William Grant, *Pennsylvania Journal*, August 7, 1755, and Benjamin Harbeson, *Pennsylvania Journal*, November 14, 1771.

59. The first advertisement for the American China Factory appeared in the *Pennsylvania
Chronicle and Universal Advertiser*, December 25, 1769, several months before operations actually commenced.

60. It is not that there were no domestic ceramic manufacturers. Philadelphia was an important center for earthenware production in the eighteenth century, and some craftsmen even
tried their hand at stoneware and porcelain, most notably the American China Factory, which
opened in 1770. Most ceramics sold on the colonial market were imports through the end of
the eighteenth century. Indeed, whole industries developed within Britain to specifically
service the overseas market. See Susan H. Myers, "A Survey of Traditional Pottery Manufacture in the Mid-Atlantic and Northeastern United States," *Northeast Historical Archaeology* 6,

no. 1 (1977); and S. Robert Teitelman et al., *Creamware for the American Market* (Suffolk: Antique Collectors' Club, 2010).

61. Janine E. Skerry and Suzanne Findlen Hood, *Salt-Glazed Stoneware in Early America* (Williamsburg, VA: Colonial Williamsburg Foundation, 2009), 97–114; Ivor Noël Hume, *A Guide to Artifacts of Early America* (Philadelphia: University of Pennsylvania, 1969), 102–137.

62. Goss, *British Teapots and Coffee Pots,* 6–7.

63. Richard Clarke & Sons advertised "a few Hogsheads of Cream Colored Ware" for sale in the *Boston Evening-Post* on May 20, 1773, while Christopher Champlin offered "cream colored ware by the crate" in the *Newport Mercury,* September 20, 1773.

64. Raleigh Tavern Inventory, Anthony Hay, Tavern Keeper, Williamsburg 1771, York County Wills and Inventories, No. 22, 1771–1783 (Colonial Williamsburg Foundation), 19. See also Graham Hood, *Inventories of Four Eighteenth-Century Houses in the Historic District of Williamsburg,* (Williamsburg, VA: Colonial Williamsburg Foundation, 1974).

65. "An Inventory of the Estate of James Shields, deceased January 21, 1750," reprinted in J. Douglas Smith, "Wetherburn's Tavern Interpretation," Colonial Williamsburg Foundation Library Research Report Series—1638 (Williamsburg, VA: Colonial Williamsburg Foundation Library, 1968); reprinted as "Wetherburn Tavern's Historical Report, Block 9, Building 31" in 1994, 47–50.

66. John Stansbury, *Pennsylvania Packet or Daily Advertiser,* January 2, 1774.

67. Earthenware press-molded cauliflower coffee pot, 1762–1780, Staffordshire, England, accession #: 1993.0072 A, B (Winterthur Museum and Library); another example resembling a pineapple appears in the Williamsburg DeWitt Wallace Gallery, c. 1765, Staffordshire, England, accession #: 1958–286, A, B.

68. Lippert, *English Porcelain,* 46, and Jean Kane, ed., *Eighteenth-Century English Porcelain in the Collection of the Indianapolis Museum of Art* (Indianapolis: Indianapolis Museum of Art, 1987), 13–15. For example, see Porcelain Coffee Pot, 1730–1740, imported from Jingdezhen, China, Asia, accession #: 2000.0061.056 A, B. (Winterthur Library and Museum).

69. Ian M. G. Quimby, *Ceramics in America* (Wilmington, DE: Winterthur Museum, 1972), 17–35; Goss, *British Teapots and Coffee Pots,* 6–8.

70. *Baltimore Daily Intelligencer,* May 26, 1794

71. Balch, *Journal of Claude Blanchard,* 78–79.

72. Walsh, "Provisioning Early American Towns," 124.

73. *Pennsylvania Gazette,* May 14, 1767. Not that these objects appeared only in shops. "Coffee cups . . . to be sold by the box" were available at Footman and Jeye's vendue store, *Pennsylvania Gazette,* January 11, 1775, and several coffee pots were included in an estate auction arranged by Benjamin Taylor, *Pennsylvania Gazette,* December 6, 1775.

74. "Invoice from Richd. Farrer, April 1762," Series 5, George Washington Papers, Manuscripts Division (Library of Congress).

75. "Rawleigh Downman to Stephen Renaud, 16 December 1770," Rawleigh Downman Letter Book, 1760–1780, trans. Rockefeller Library (Colonial Williamsburg Foundation).

76. Will of Rawleigh Downman, September 3, 1782, Principal Probate Registry, Somerset House, London; photocopy, Rockefeller Library (Colonial Williamsburg Foundation).

77. Rawleigh Downman Letter Book, 1760–1780.

78. "Benjamin Franklin to Deborah Franklin. February 19, 1758," Benjamin Franklin Papers, 1706–1790 (American Philosophical Society).

79. Ibid.

80. Bushman, *Refinement of America,* 397; Grady McWhiney, *Cracker Culture: Celtic Ways in the Old South* (Tuscaloosa: University of Alabama Press, 1988), 342–344.

81. David Shields, *Civil Tongues and Polite Letters in British America* (Chapel Hill: University of North Carolina Press for the Omohundro Institute of Early American History and

Culture, 1997), 59, and James Walvin, *Fruits of Empire: Exotic Produce and British Tastes, 1660–1800* (New York: New York University Press, 1997), 40.

82. T. H. Breen, "Baubles of Britain," *Past & Present* 119:1 (May 1988): 456. Breen cites Esther Singleton, *Social New York Under the Georges, 1714–1776* (New York: D. Appleton & Co., 1902), 380–381. See also Breen, *Marketplace of Revolution*, 281, 288–289, 306–307.

83. *Pennsylvania Gazette,* April 26, 1775.

84. *Pennsylvania Gazette,* July 6, 1769.

85. *Pennsylvania Gazette,* June 23, 1773.

86. *Pennsylvania Gazette,* November 3, 1773.

87. *Daily Advertiser,* January 16, 1775.

88. Notice for Joseph Stansbury, April 27, 1785, and notice for John Bates, June 8, 1785, in the *Pennsylvania Gazette*; see also *Daily Advertiser,* April 10, 1775.

Chapter 4

1. *Pennsylvania Journal,* September 4, 1766, and NA/PRO T 1/144/1-6, "North America, Customs and Excise, Letters from Various Governors and Stamp Distributors on the Opposition of the Enforcement of the Stamp Act and the Difficulties of Distribution: John Hughes, Philadelphia" (1765). Hughes's letter was, ironically, written to two men inquiring about where to purchase stamped paper in Pennsylvania. That September evening, Hughes was lucky. "The Collection of Rabble begins to decrease visibly in the Streets," he later recalled, "and the Appearance of Danger seems a good deal less than it did." But when his commission as royal stamp collector arrived the following month, the crowds reassembled at the Old London Coffee House and set out for Hughes's home to a cadence rapped out by two "negro drummers" and accompanied by the muffled bells of the State House and Christ Church. The protestors threatened that unless Hughes resigned immediately, his "house would be pulled down" and his "substance destroyed." Faced by this real and immediate danger to his personal property, Hughes summarily quit his post.

An additional set of letters written from September 17, 1765, to March 21, 1766, between Hughes, John Penn, and Captain James Hawker, cover the same events. Hawker temporarily took custody of the stamped paper when Hughes refused to do so, warehousing the documents on his ship rather than distributing them himself. See Pennsylvania Stamp Act and Non-Importation Resolutions Collection, MSS 973.2.M31, vol. 1 (American Philosophical Society).

2. Additional goods enumerated in the Sugar Act included "indigo, and coffee of foreign produce or manufacture; for and upon wines (except French wine;) for and upon all wrought silks, bengals, and stuffs, mixed with silk or herbs of the manufacture of Persia, China, or East India, and all callico painted, dyed, printed, or stained there; and for and upon all foreign linen cloth called Cambrick and French Lawns." See "The Sugar Act" (1764), in the Avalon Project: Documents in Law, History and Diplomacy, electronic publication, Lillian Goldman Law Library, Yale Law School. William C. Fray and Lisa A. Spar, Co-Directors. The Avalon Project at the Yale Law School: Documents in Law, History and Diplomacy. New Haven, CT; Avalon Project (https://avalon.law.yale.edu/18th_century/sugar_act_1764.asp).

3. "John Adams to James Warren, October 7, 1775," Smith, *Letters to the Delegates of Congress,* 2:136–137.

4. See, for example, Rosalind Remer, *Printers and Men of Capital: Philadelphia Book Publishers in the New Republic* (Philadelphia: University of Pennsylvania Press, 1996), particularly chapter 1; and more recently, Joseph Adelman, *Revolutionary Networks: The Business and Politics of Printing the News, 1763–1789* (Baltimore: Johns Hopkins University Press, 2019).

5. Peter Thompson, *Rum Punch and Revolution: Taverngoing and Public Life in Eighteenth-Century Philadelphia* (Philadelphia: University of Pennsylvania Press, 1999), 92; Isaiah Thomas, *The History of Printing in America: With a Biography of Printers and an Account of Newspapers* (Albany: Joel Munsell Printer, 1874), 1:xxxvii–xl, 242–244, 312.

6. *Pennsylvania Journal*, March 6, 1776: "A list of the Letters now in the Coffee-house, which the owners are desired to call for, included the following:

A. –James Allan, house-carpenter. Charles Anderson of the brig. Unas.
B. –Johnson Briggs, on board Capt. Thomas Lee. James Blair, on Juniata River. John Blackhouse, merchant.
C. –John Cunningham, innkeeper. William Carr. John Cordue, taylor. William Clarke. John Cuthbertson, minister. William Church. John Carter. Margaret Corldran. Benjamin Crofts, painter and glazier.
D. –Capt. Ephraim Davis. Capt. Nathaniel Davis. John Dealing, shopkeeper. Benjamin Dunn. John Dunbar, nailor. Abraham Dehoff, Lancaster.
E. –Richard Ellenwood, of the brig. John. Timothy Eaton.
F. –John Ferguson, smith.
G. –John Gil. James Graham, house-carpenter.
H. –John Hewson, printer, Kensington. Christian Hewetson. Captain John Henderson.
J. –Israel Jacobs, Third Street.
K. –Charles Knight.
L. –Robert Little, at the Ship in Distress. Andrew Lisk, New Castle County. Benjamin Lawton.
M. –Owen McMarnis, to the care of William McCormick. John Margum, Falls Township, Bucks County. Saml. McKean, Jun. James Moore, Donegal Township, to the care of the Revd. Robert Cooper, Cumberland County. John Michael Heren. Joseph Montgomery. James Mouldsdale, Wilmington. Anthoy McQuesten.
P. —Margaret Pringle, Sugar Alley. James Perry. Shebeal Pratt.
S. –John Stanley, weaver. Fithian Stratton, Deerfield, Cumberland County. Joseph Smith. William Selly, near the New Market. Jonathan Smith, Morris River.
T. –John Taylor, West Notingham, to the care of John Glascow, Andrew Todd East Whiteland Township."

7. Thompson, *Rum Punch and Revolution*, 91–92.

8. James's fine was noted in Boggs and Boggs, "Inns and Taverns of Old Philadelphia" (Historical Society of Pennsylvania), 184–185. The diminution of this fine appears in the *Minutes of the Common Council of Philadelphia, 1704–1776* (Philadelphia: Crissy and Markley, Printers, 1847), 328. James was charged in 1733, but she had recently been widowed and so the Philadelphia Council, "taking her circumstances into consideration," reduced the amount by half in its next session.

9. John Shuebart, Receipt Book, 1734–1740, folios 5, 23, 25, 40, and 67 (Historical Society of Pennsylvania).

10. For discussion of the increasingly complex nature of tavern keeping, as well as the shift from local business to traveler needs, see David Hancock and Michelle McDonald, *Public Drinking in the Early Modern World: Voices from the Tavern, 1500–1800*, vol. 4 (London: Pickering and Chatto, 2011), 241–245, 313–322, 423–428. For taverns serving coffee, see Masons-Arms Tavern, *New York Mercury*, March 2, 1767; Sign of the Buck Tavern, *Pennsylvania Gazette*, July 6, 1769; and Vaux Hall Tavern, *Pennsylvania* Gazette, November 3, 1773.

11. "Letter of Edward Shippen of Lancaster, 1754," *Pennsylvania Magazine of History and Biography* 30 (1906): 89–90.

12. Seeking a servant, *Pennsylvania Gazette*, January 5, 1769; ship *Myrtilla*, *Pennsylvania Gazette*, August 4, 1775; James Bryon, *Pennsylvania Gazette*, July 6, 1749.

13. For examples of runaways, see *Pennsylvania Gazette*, November 17, 1768; *Boston Newsletter*, August 19–26, 1717; *New York Mercury*, December 12, 1763. For ship's cargo or passage, see *Pennsylvania Gazette*, February 1, 1759, and November 22, 1759. Trelawney's notice appeared in the *Pennsylvania Gazette*, June 23, 1748.

14. Boggs and Boggs, "Inns and Taverns of Old Philadelphia," 189–190; Thompson, *Rum Punch and Revolution*, 106. Bradford's coffeehouse was in part supported by money raised through sales of his newspaper, the *Pennsylvania Journal*, which at its height had over two hundred subscribers contributing an annual fee of between twenty and thirty shillings each. In addition to maritime auctions and vendues of personal goods and chattels, it also advertised the quarterly sheriff's auctions used to dispose of property seized for failure to pay taxes, debt, or other crimes.

15. In addition to newspapers and advertisements, the Stamp Act outlined fees for a variety of different court documents ("declaration, plea, replication, rejoinder, demurrer, or other pleading"), educational materials (including registrar's materials and certificates of degree), bills of lading, letters of marque, colonial council or assembly business, liquor licenses, bonds, and land deeds. For the full language, see Great Britain, *The statutes at large . . . [from 1225 to 1867]* by Danby Pickering (Cambridge: Printed by Benthem for C. Bathhurst, London, 1762–1869), accessed at the Avalon Project, Yale Law School.

16. *Pennsylvania Journal*, October 31, 1765.

17. *Pennsylvania Gazette*, December 26, 1765. Likewise, on March 20, 1766, the same paper reported that "two Blank Stamps, for the Clearance of a Vessel, and a stamped Bill of Lading, were burnt at the Coffee House in the Presence of a Full Company, who testified their approbation, by giving three Huzza's."

18. "Excerpts from the Diary of Jacob Hiltzheimer," *Pennsylvania Magazine of History and Biography* 16:1 (1892): 97.

19. *New York Mercury*, January 13, 1766.

20. "The Merchants of this City are earnestly requested to meet at the Coffee-House, on Monday, next, at Nine o'Clock, to consider a Matter of great Importance that will then be laid before them," 1774, Evans Collection (Library Company of Philadelphia).

21. Boggs and Boggs, "Inns and Taverns of Philadelphia," 190; Marc Egnal, *A Mighty Empire: The Origins of the American Revolution* (Ithaca: Cornell University Press, 2010), 209–211. Egnal provides a valuable and succinct history of the colonies' embargo movements but lists the number of Philadelphia's complying merchants as 208. A list of the embargo signers included in merchant Henry Drinkers's papers include 249 names; see: Henry Drinker, Business Papers, 1765–1769 "Alphabetical Listing of Subscribers to the Non-Importation Agreement entered into the 6th February to 10th March, 1769" (Historical Society of Pennsylvania).

22. "Continental Association, 20 October 1774," *Founders Online*, National Archives, https://founders.archives.gov/documents/Jefferson/01-01-02-0094. Original source Julian P. Boyd, ed., *The Papers of Thomas Jefferson, Volume I: 1760 to 1776* (Princeton, NJ: Princeton University Press, 1950), 149–154. The Coercive Acts, often called the Intolerable Acts in North America, ordered the blockade of Boston's harbor, a ban on all exports for foreign countries and territories, and a ban on imports except those needed by the British military. See David Ammerman, *In the Common Cause: American Response to the Coercive Acts of 1774* (Charlottesville: University of Virginia Press, 1974), 12–13.

23. Worthington C. Ford et al., eds., *Journals of the Continental Congress, 1774–1789* (Washington, DC: U.S. Government Printing Office, 1904–1937), I:75–80; the text was also reprinted in papers throughout the colonies, including the *Pennsylvania Gazette*, November 2, 1774.

24. Committee of Inspection and Observation, "Philadelphia Committee of Inspection and Observation Minutes," 1774, MSS# 3079 (Historical Society of Pennsylvania).

25. Richard Ryerson, *The Revolution Is Now Begun: The Radical Committees of Philadelphia, 1765–1776* (Philadelphia: University of Pennsylvania Press, 2012), 94–100.

26. Two months later, Fithian recorded the day the family heard the tax on tea had been repealed; they celebrated by drinking coffee. See Fithian, *Journal and Letters*, 110, 131.

27. *Essex Gazette*, November 30, 1773; *Boston Evening-Post*, February 7, 1774; John Adams to Abigail Adams, July 6, 1774, *Adams Family Papers*.

28. "John Adams to James Warren, October 20, 1775," in *Papers of John Adams*, 3:216.

29. "John Adams to Abigail Adams, October 11, 1777," in *Adams Family Correspondence*, 2:305.

30. "Abigail Adams to John Adams, July 16, 1775," ibid.

31. "Abigail Adams to John Adams, December 10, 1775," ibid.

32. *Pennsylvania Gazette*, July 17, 1775.

33. *Pennsylvania Gazette*, August 14, 1775.

34. *Pennsylvania Gazette*, January 31, 1776.

35. Jamaica exported 399,808 lbs. of coffee to North America in 1772, and 440,655 lbs. to England. Abigail Adams to John Adams, July 5, 1775, *Adams Family Papers*.

36. The data on privateers draws from a sample of nearly 200 privateering advertisements between 1777 and 1780 as reported in select U.S. newspapers. These specific examples come from *Connecticut Gazette*, June 14, 1776, and *Norwich Packet*, July 14, 1777.

37. Subsequent notices for the *True Blue* appeared in the *New York Gazette and Weekly Mercury*, July 17, 1776, the *American Gazette*, June 18, 1776, and the *Pennsylvania Ledger*, June 22, 1776, although Philadelphia's news was specifically reprinted from Newport, indicating that at least one additional city covered the news.

38. NA/PRO SP 78/306, "Letter from Captain Frazer to Lord Viscount Weymouth" (January 20, 1778). Britain also captured several French ships during the American Revolution. The number of coffee casks auctioned from such prizes was routinely equal to, if not higher than, those carrying sugar as listed in NA PRO CO 114/36, "Chancery Records, Sale of Cargoes of Prizes," (1779). For more information about Andrew Frazer, see Leslie Stephen and Sidney Lee, *Dictionary of National Biography*, vol. VII (New York: MacMillan Press, 1908), 669.

39. Abigail Adams to John Adams, April 7–11, 1776, *Adams Family Papers*.

40. The drop in coffee prices in Savannah was larger still, from a high of £2.15 per pound in May 1764 to £1.3 just a month later; it remained under £1.3 through the end of 1764. See current prices in the *Georgia Gazette* from April 7, 1763, through October 18, 1764. Representative examples of coffee price listings for the 1760s and 1770s from across the colonies come from *Pennsylvania Chronicle and Universal Daily Advertiser*, June 6, 1768; *New London Gazette*, May 29, 1767; *Providence Gazette*, October 19, 1771; and *Georgia Gazette*, August 2, 1764. The dropping price of coffee in the *Providence Gazette* specifically is based on current prices listings published from October 20, 1770, to September 26, 1772.

41. Anne Benzason, "Inflation and Controls, Pennsylvania, 1774–1779," *Journal of Economic History* vol. 8, Supplement: The Tasks of Economic History (1948): 4; Doerflinger, *Vigorous Spirit of Enterprise*, 197.

42. Benzason, "Inflation and Controls," 2–12.

43. *Pennsylvania Evening Post*, March 7, 1776.

44. Ibid.

45. *Connecticut Courant*, January 13, 1776.

46. *Pennsylvania Ledger*, March 6, 1776: "And if any person shall be so lost to virtue, honor, and the public good, as to demand greater prices. . . . or shall refuse to sell such articles under false pretenses of exportation, pre-engagement, or otherwise, in order to avail themselves of the scarcity of goods, and enhance the price, this Committee do declare that they will expose such persons by name as sordid vultures who are preying on the vitals of their country in times of sore distress." See also Breen, *Marketplace of Revolution*, 235–293.

47. *New York Gazette*, March 11, 1776.

48. Scott, "Price Control in New England," 453–454; quotations from the *Pennsylvania Ledger*, March 6, 1776. The full range of goods that the New England committee hoped to regulate, in addition to coffee, included wheat, rye, Indian corn, wool, pork, salt pork, beef, hides, cheese, butter, peas, beans, potatoes, salt, rum, sugar, molasses, stockings, shoes, cotton, oats, flax, tallow, tow cloth, and flannels.

49. See *New England Gazette*, March 14, 1776; *Connecticut Gazette*, March 22, 1776; and *New England Journal*, April 25, 1776. For higher prices, see *Independent Chronicle and the Universal Advertiser*, January 23, 1777, and January 30, 1777.

50. Abigail Adams to John Adams, March 23, 1777, April 17, 1777, and April 20, 1777, *Adams Family Papers*.

51. As examples, see William West, Ledger, 1770–1777, entry for John Nixon, April 20, 1771; John Drinker, Accounts Books, 1776–1779, entry for William Redmond, March 5, 1776; and William Redmond, Ledger, 1775–1809, multiple entries for 1776 and 1777 (all Historical Society of Pennsylvania). While coffee sales in Redmond's ledger appear by the pound and barrel, the latter was converted to a per pound price for comparison, and the average varied only from £1 and £1.3.

52. *Pennsylvania Evening Post*, April 6, 1776. The same notice also appeared the same day in the *Pennsylvania Ledger*.

53. Smith, "Food Rioters," 3–38. In addition to tea, coffee, and sugar, food protestors targeted salt, bread, and meat; in other cases, vendors were simply accused of generally high pricing rather than gouging for specific commodities.

54. Ibid., 6–7; Barbara Clark Smith, *After the Revolution: The Smithsonian History of Everyday Life in the Eighteenth Century* (New York: Pantheon Books, 1985), 3–42.

55. Abigail Adams to John Adams, July 31, 1777, *Adams Family Papers*.

56. Douglass Adair and John A. Schultz, eds., *Peter Oliver's Origin and Progress of the American Rebellion: A Tory View* (Stanford, CA: Stanford University Press, 1961), 73.

57. "Johannes Sleight to the Provincial Congress of New York, November 18, 1776," *Journals of the Provincial Council, Provincial Convention, Committee of Safety, and Council of Safety of the State of New York*, 2 vols. (Albany: Thurlow Weed, 1842): 1:714; Ronald Hoffman, "The 'Disaffected' in the Revolutionary South," in *American Revolution: Explorations in the History of American Radicalism*, ed. Alfred E. Young (Dekalb: Northern Illinois University Press, 1976), 273–316; William H. Whitmore et al., eds., *Reports of the Record Commissioners of the City of Boston*, 39 vols. (Boston: Rockwell and Churchhill, 1876–1908), XVIII, Boston Town Records, 260–261.

58. Oliver, *Diary of William Pynchon of Salem*, 15, 29, 34. Pynchon's quote is an inversion of Matt. 3:64 (King James Version): "Take therefore no thought for the morrow: for the morrow shall take thought for the things of itself. Sufficient unto the day is the evil thereof."

59. *Pennsylvania Packet*, June 24, 1776.

60. "An Act to Prevent Forestalling and Regrating, and to Encourage Fair Dealing" (1778), Broadside Collection, 1638-1980 (American Philosophical Society).

61. "Benjamin Rush, Diary," February 14, 1777, in *Letters of Members of the Continental Congress*, ed. Edmund C. Burnett, vol. 2 (Washington, DC: Carnegie Institute of Washington Publications, 1923), 251; Scott, "Price Control in New England," 458–459.

62. Ford, *Journals of the Continental Congress*, 9: 956–957: "Resolved, that it be earnestly recommended to the respective legislatures of the United States, without delay, by their separate authority, to adopt and effectually enforce a temporary regulation of the prices of provisions and other commodities for the supply of the army, in such manner as they shall judge reasonable; and to continue in force until the general regulation before proposed shall be adopted."

63. "George Washington to John A. Washington, November 26, 1778," George Washington Papers, 1741–1799: Series 4. General Correspondence, 1697–1799 (Library of Congress).

64. Smith, *Letters to the Delegates of Congress*, 15:105–107. Matthews and Peabody again requisitioned coffee on June 21 that same year, when they wrote to Ephraim Blaine, Commissary General of Purchases for the Northern Department of the Continental Army, who had overseen George Washington's troops during their bleak winter in Valley Forge; Smith, *Letters to the Delegates of Congress*, 15: 352, footnote 2. See also Simon Finger, *The Contagious City: The Politics of Public Health in Philadelphia* (Ithaca, NY: Cornell University Press, 2012), 67.

65. Benzason, "Inflation and Controls," 16–17.

66. "John Armstrong, Sr. to Rebecca Armstrong, June 21, 1779," in Smith, *Letters to the Delegates of Congress*, 13: 88–90.

67. Ford, *Journals of the Continental Congress*, 13:450

68. Drinker, *Journal of Elizabeth Drinker*, 57, 59.

69. The quotation is included in John Adams's notes, although he did not record the speaker. Cited in Staughton Lynd and David Waldstreicher, "Free Trade, Sovereignty, and Slavery: Towards an Economic Interpretation of the American Revolution," *William and Mary Quarterly*, 68:4 (October 2011): 628.

70. Robert Morris quoted in Doerflinger, *Vigorous Spirit of Enterprise*, 209. For trade statistics, see Alfred E. Eckes, *Opening America's Market: U.S. Foreign Trade Policy Since 1776* (Chapel Hill: University of North Carolina Press, 1995), 5–6; import and exports values taken from Edmond Buron, "Notes and Documents: Statistics on Franco-American Trade, 1778–1806," *Journal of Economic and Business History*, 4:1 (November 1931): 571–580. This balance shifted back in favor of the U.S. by the 1790s, but for the second half of the Revolutionary War, French imports played a key role in stabilizing prices for tropical produce. For more about the shift between the 1780s and 1790s, see Peter Hill, *French Perceptions of the Early American Republic, 1783–1793* (Philadelphia: American Philosophical Society, 1988).

71. Figures from Records of the Office of the Comptroller General, Port of Philadelphia Records, Registers of Duties Paid on Imported Goods (1781–1788); 6 vols., Record Group 4 (Pennsylvania State Archive).

72. Philadelphia coffee prices listed in the *Pennsylvania Gazette*, May 29 and June 26, 1779, and the same New York current prices ran in the *New York Gazette and Weekly Mercury*, January 17 through July 24, 1780. For South Carolina military provisions, see *Pennsylvania Gazette*, May 24, 1780.

73. Levi Hollingsworth's notices were published on July 30 and August 13, 1778, and January 9, 1779, in the *Pennsylvania Evening Post*, and January 5, March 20, and April 3 in the *Pennsylvania Packet*. For evidence of Baltimore imports, for Levi Hollingsworth as well as for Samuel and Thomas Hollingsworth, see the *Baltimore Weekly Times Current* from March 1806 through March 1809, which listed all goods that arrived in Baltimore's customhouse by type, weight, and consignee. For more information about familial relations between merchants in these two cities, see correspondence and joint bills of lading in Hollingsworth Family Papers, Series 2, Financial 1762–1849, subfolder h, "Shipping 1765-1828" (Historical Society of Pennsylvania).

74. The following year, Habacker partnered with Philip Wagner at the same address, a relationship that lasted for nearly a decade, dissolving shortly before Habacker's death in August 1793. His obituary was brief: "Died—on Saturday last, Mr. George Habacker of this city; a respectable merchant, and a worthy citizen." See *Pennsylvania Gazette*, April 12, 1780, and April 30, 1783; *Dunlap's American Daily Advertiser*, March 2, 1792 (for the dissolution of Wagner & Habacker); and the *Federal Gazette* and *Claypoole's Daily Advertiser*, August 13, 1792 (Habacker's obituary).

75. William West's obituary appeared in the *Pennsylvania Gazette*, November 13, 1782. For information about West & Haxall's connections to the West Indies trade, see Rafferty, "Intercourse Between Our Respectable Houses," 200–205, and Benjamin Fuller Letterbook, 1784–1787 (particularly correspondence to Robert Totten, at Cape Nicolas Mole on the northwest coast of Saint Domingue, throughout 1784).

Chapter 5

1. House of Assembly of Dominica, Minutes: September 27–29, 1787 (Dominica Archives).

2. While Dominica was technically ceded from France to Britain in 1763, it was invaded and occupied on several other occasions, so that it is more accurate to state that control of Dominica shifted between the British and French Empires no fewer than four times between 1757 and 1783. Lennox Honychurch, *The Dominica Story: A History of the Island* (Oxford: Macmillan Education, 1995), 40–71, and 93–90.

3. "Deposition of Pierre Rondeyon, overseer of Joseph Vidal against James Alms, Esq., Commander of His Majesty's Frigate *Prosperine*," Court of the Vice Admiralty, Miscellaneous Records, 1792 (Dominica Archives). For more about interimperial trading facilitated by the development of free ports, see David Watts, *The West Indies: Patterns of Development, Culture and Environmental Change since 1492* (Cambridge: Cambridge University Press, 1990), 277–283.

4. "Deposition of Pierre Rondeyon," folio 2–3.

5. Ibid., folio 3–5.

6. There are several gaps in Dominica's Court of the Vice Admiralty records and many documents are extremely fragile and unavailable for use, but similar cases of other vessels stopped with coffee were available in Court of the Vice Admiralty, Miscellaneous Records, 1793, "Public Notice of the Brigantine Les Sans Cutattes, dated February 1, 1794" and "Examination of Robert Walsh regarding the Brigantine *Thomas*, dated March 4, 1794"; Miscellaneous Records, 1796, "Claim of George Pilsbury late Master of the Vessel and Cargo, dated Oct. 28, 1796," "Dominica, Our Sovereign Lord the King against the Ship *Victoria*, dated July 29, 1796," and "Dominica, Our Sovereign Lord the King against the Schooner *Dolphin*, dated July 29, 1796."

7. Most coffee arrived from the Caribbean, although some came from the East Indies and other sources. *American State Papers: Documents, Legislative and Executive, of the Congress of the United States*, 38 vols. (Washington, D.C.: Gales and Seaton, 1832–1861), V: 203, 478, 512.

8. John Byres, *References to the Plan of the Island of Dominica; as surveyed from the year 1765 to 1773* (London: S. Hooper, 1778), 25. Joseph Vidal's thirty-acre farm appears in the list of freeholders for St. Paul's Parish.

9. Martinican scholar Aimé Césaire, for example, launched the 1930s literary movement "la negritude," which asserted that African rather than French colonial culture shaped West Indian society, while Melville J. Herskovits argued for the centrality of Africans in shaping North American religion, language, and the arts. See Aimé Césaire, *Cahier d'un retour au pays natal* (Paris: Présence Africaine, 1983); and Melville J. Herskovits, *The Myth of the Negro Past* (New York: Harper & Brothers, 1941).

10. Edward Kamau Brathwaite, *The Development of Creole Society in Jamaica, 1770–1820* (Oxford: Clarendon Press, 1972), xiv–xv. Brathwaite argues that the etymology of the word combines the Spanish *criar* (to create, to imagine, or to settle) and *colono* (a colonist or founder).

11. Long, *History of Jamaica*, 1:541; Brathwaite, *Development of Creole Society*, 81.

12. B. W. Higman, "Patterns of Exchange Within a Plantation Economy," in *West Indies Accounts: Essays on the History of the British Caribbean and the Atlantic Economy*, ed. Roderick A. McDonald (Mona, Jamaica: University of the West Indies, Press, 2002), 211–231. Higman first described livestock pens as "creole economies" in "The Internal Economy of Jamaican Pens," *Social and Economic Studies* 38:1 (1989): 61–86. More recently, Verene A. Shepherd suggested that a "creole economy" should be considered a fiscal mentality, one that pushed against colonial ideology, rather than merely a business system. See "Questioning Creole: Domestic Producers in Jamaica's Plantation Economy," *Caribbean Quarterly* 44:1–2 (March/June 1998): 93–107.

13. Roderick A. McDonald, "Independent Economic Production by Slaves on Antebellum Louisiana Sugar Plantations," in Heuman and Walvin, *Slavery Reader*, 486–506. See also Roderick A. McDonald, *The Economy and Material Lives of Slaves: Goods and Chattels on the Sugar*

Plantations of Jamaica and Louisiana (Baton Rouge: Louisiana State University Press, 1993). Anthropologist Katherine Browne shifted the study of creole economies to the non-Anglo-Caribbean, emphasizing motivation as much as action. Browne argues that slaves, ex-slaves, and free people of color practiced "entrepreneurialism" in Martinique when they worked outside formal economic networks and the law to create opportunities for themselves using cross-class strategies and activities. Such practices continued after abolition as the formerly enslaved continued to work "under the table" while maintaining a legal, wage-labor job. See Katherine Browne, "Creole Economics and the *Debrouillard*: From Slave-Based Adaptations to the Informal Economy in Martinique," *Ethnohistory* 49:2 (Spring 2002): 384. Browne first explored this subject in "Who Does and Who Doesn't Earn 'Off the Books'? The Logic of Informal Economic Activity in Martinique, FWI," *Anthropology of Work Review* 16: 1–2 (1995): 23–33. These ideas culminated in Katherine E. Browne, *Creole Economics: Caribbean Cunning under the French Flag* (Austin: University of Texas Press, 2004), 2.

14. Tessa Murphy, *The Creole Archipelago: Race and Borders in the Colonial Caribbean* (Philadelphia: University of Pennsylvania Press, 2021), 4–5.

15. Browne, "Creole Economics and the *Debrouillard*," 380, and *Creole Economies*, 11. Where I differ from Browne is her association of creole economics—and especially the term *debrouillard*—with illegality or at least questionability. The larger Atlantic creole economy I explore has actors who fit this profile, to be sure, but just as many saw nothing underhanded in their activity.

16. In some ways, my definition of creole economies mirrors what Kathleen Duval has argued about "advantageous interdependence" in *Independence Lost: Lives on the Edge of the American Revolution* (New York: Random House, 2015), xxi–xxii. While her model focuses primarily on relationships of power—political, colonial, familial, and legal—her conclusion is the same. Many in the United States not only did not fight for independence, but also recognized and sought to reify interdependent relationships that offered protection.

17. "John Adams to Livingston, July 30, 1783," in *The Revolutionary Diplomatic Correspondence of the United States,* ed. Francis Wharton, 6 vols. (Washington, D.C.: Government Printing Office, 1889), 6:618.

18. Adams noted, "By bringing our tobacco and fish to Italy we might unload at some of their ports, take in cargoes upon freight for other ports of Italy, and thus make coasting voyages, until we had made up our cargoes for return, or we might take in cargoes on freight for Germany or the Baltic." See "J. Adams to Livingston, July 31, 1783," in Wharton, *Revolutionary Diplomatic Correspondence*, 6:623.

19. Pauline Maier et al., eds., *Inventing America: A History of the United States*, 2 vols. (New York, 2002), 1:262.

20. "From Thomas Jefferson to James Madison, 8 May 1784," *Founders Online*, National Archives, http://founders.archives.gov/documents/Jefferson/01-07-02-0179 (updated 2015-06-29); see Boyd, *Papers of Thomas Jefferson*, 7:231–235. "From James Madison to Richard Henry Lee, 7 July 1785," *Founders Online*, National Archives http://founders.archives.gov/documents/Madison /01-08-02-0168 (updated 2015-06-29); see William T. Hutchinson and William M. E. Rachal, eds., *The Papers of James Madison, Volume 8: 10 March 1784–28 March 1786* (Chicago: University of Chicago Press, 1973), 314–316. See also Edwards, *History, Civil and Commercial*, 2:277–278.

21. These included France, the United Netherlands, and Sweden, with which the U.S. already had treaties of commerce, as well as England, Hamburg and Saxony, Prussia, Denmark, Russia, Austria, Venice, Rome, Naples, Tuscany, Sardinia, Genoa, Spain, Portugal, and the Barbary States of the Porte, Algiers, Tripoli, Tunis, and Morocco. Merrill D. Peterson, "Thomas Jefferson and Commercial Policy, 1783–1793," *William and Mary Quarterly* 3rd ser., 22:4 (October 1965): 590–591; Alice B. Keith, "Relaxations in the British Restrictions on the American Trade with

the British West Indies, 1783–1802," *Journal of Modern History* 20:1 (March 1948):1–2; and Selwyn H. H. Carrington, "The United States and the British West Indian Trade, 1783–1807," in *West Indies Accounts*, ed. Roderick A. McDonald (Kingston, Jamaica: University of the West Indies Press, 1996), 149–151.

22. An excellent recent history about widespread implications of the conflicts between European polities at the end of the eighteenth century and the beginning of the nineteenth century is Alexander Mikaberidze, *The Napoleonic Wars: A Global History* (Oxford: Oxford University Press, 2020).

23. In a letter to James Monroe, Jefferson argued that the states presented a stronger foreign relations front together than individually: "My primary object in the formation of treaties is to take the commerce of the states out of the hands of the states, and to place it under the superintendence of Congress." See "Thomas Jefferson to James Monroe, June 17, 1785," in *The Works of Thomas Jefferson,* ed. Paul Leicester Ford, 12 vols. (New York: G. P. Putnam's Sons, 1904–1905), 8:231.

24. In 1785, several states challenged congressional authority by asserting their own modified commercial systems. By October of that year, a frustrated Adams wrote to Jefferson that states should be coerced into complying with federal economic policy to ensure national interests: "It is impossible for any country to give to another more decided proof of preference than our thoughtless [individual] merchants have since the peace given to this in matters of commerce." See "John Adams to Thomas Jefferson, Oct. 3, 1785," *Thomas Jefferson Papers*, Series 1, General Correspondence, 1651–1827 (Library of Congress).

25. "John Adams to Robert Livingston, July 16, 1783," in Wharton, *Revolutionary Diplomatic Correspondence*, 6:552.

26. Andrew O'Shaughnessy, *An Empire Divided: The American Revolution and the British Caribbean* (Philadelphia: University of Pennsylvania Press, 2000), 214.

27. "John Adams to Robert Livingston, July 30, 1783," "Plan of a Treaty with Holland, Sept. 4, 1778," and "John Adams to Robert Livingston, July 23, 1783, and July 31, 1783," in Wharton, *Revolutionary Diplomatic Correspondence*, 6:619, 2:790–798, 2:623. The initial 1778 U.S. draft treaty with Holland did not include commodity-specific restrictions on imports and exports; these were added at Holland's insistence.

28. "John Adams to Robert Livingston, July 30, 1783," in Wharton, *Revolutionary Diplomatic Correspondence*, 6:619.

29. *Journals of the Continental Congress, 1774–1789,* 34 vols. (Washington, D.C.: Government Printing Office, 1904–1937), 27:721: "Wednesday, October 22, 1783; Rosencrone, Minister of Denmark, to Benjamin Franklin, July 8, 1783"; see also, Wharton, *Revolutionary Diplomatic Correspondence*, 6:519–527, including the "Counter Project of a Treaty with Denmark." For restrictions on U.S. shipping from the Danish West Indies to Europe, see Wharton, *Revolutionary Diplomatic Correspondence*, 6:527 which includes the "Explanation of the Counter Project of a Treaty of Amity and Commerce Received from Denmark," in which the Danish minister distinguished between U.S. ships intended for the United States, which were free of restrictions, and vessels bound for Europe, over which Denmark retained exclusive rights.

30. Adams acknowledged that a Danish alliance could never be military, only commercial. "Denmark remains," he noted, but "her islands in the West Indies, and her trade, are at mercy and she would not have force to defend her own." See "John Adams to Livingston, Sept. 17, 1782," in Wharton, *Revolutionary Diplomatic Correspondence*, 5:737.

31. "John Adams to Livingston, July 12, 1783," ibid., 6:539; Peterson, "Thomas Jefferson and Commercial Policy," 593.

32. "United States Treaties, 1786, Amity and Commerce Treaty between Portugal and the United States," *Thomas Jefferson Papers*.

33. "John Adams to Robert Livingston, Aug. 10, 1783," in Wharton, *Revolutionary Diplomatic Correspondence*, 6:628.

34. "Office of the Comptroller General, Pennsylvania, Registers of Duties Paid on Imported Goods, 1781–1788," 6 vols., Record Group RG-4.90 (Pennsylvania State Archive). Forty-four ships arrived from Havana in 1781 and 20 ships in 1782, but it dropped to just a handful thereafter (there were none, for instance, in 1783).

35. *Pennsylvania Gazette*, May 25, 1785.

36. For information about Russian reactions to the American Revolution see David M. Griffiths, "American Colonial Diplomacy in Russia, 1781–1783," *William and Mary Quarterly* 27:3 (July 1970): 379–410.

37. *Pennsylvania Gazette*, August 4, 1784.

38. "John Adams to Robert Livingston, July 30, 1783," in Wharton, *Revolutionary Diplomatic Correspondence*, 6:619. For Saint Martin's place in Lesser Antilles trade, see Robert L. Paquette and Stanley L. Engerman, eds., *The Lesser Antilles in the Age of European Expansion* (Gainesville: University of Florida Press, 1996).

39. Although Pennsylvania newspapers were optimistic, it is difficult to predict how a Russian Caribbean colony would have benefited American trade. In the early 1780s, Russia served as intermediary in the ongoing commercial and military disputes between Holland and Britain over the West Indian and Levant trades. Several U.S. congressmen, however, noted Russia's predisposition toward British interests. They questioned Russian impartiality and speculated that Russia's efforts to reduce animosity between the Dutch and British might have delayed Holland's recognition of U.S. sovereignty. See "Joseph Jones to James Hunter, March 26, 1782," in Smith, *Letters to Delegates of Congress*, 18:421.

40. "Society of West India Merchants, Resolutions of the West Indian Merchants and Planters in London, February 7, 1775" (Royal Commonwealth Society, London); Vincent Harlow and Frederick Madden, eds., "Resolutions of the Committee of West India Planters, February 6, 1784," *British Colonial Developments, 1774–1834: Selected Documents* (Oxford: Clarendon Press, 1953), 256; O'Shaughnessy, *Empire Divided*, 240.

41. NA/PRO T 64/72, "Lists of Imports in British Bottoms at Kingston, Jamaica, during the War." For discussions of the Jamaica House of Assembly's concerns about staple imports, see *Journals of the Assembly of Jamaica*, 14 vols. (St. Jago de la Vega, 1811–1829), 7:313, 314, 467, 577 (hereafter *Journals*). For the impact on British West Indian production, see NA/PRO T 38/269, "Imports into England from the West Indies, 1774–83." Figures based on annual reports by the island Naval Officer to the Jamaica House of Assembly reprinted in the *Votes of the Honourable Assembly of Jamaica*, 34 vols. (St. Jago de la Vega, 1795–1835) for each year (hereafter *Votes*).

42. NA PRO CO 152/64, "Horatio Nelson to Lord Sydney, Nevis, B.W.I." (November 17, 1785).

43. Edmund Burke and Robert Dodsley, *The Annual Register or a View of the History, Politics, and Literature for the Year 1806*, 80 vols. (London: J. Dodsley and F.C. & J. Rivington, 1791), 46:81–89.

44. *Journals*, 8: February 12, 1783. Thomas Atwood recorded in 1791 that "the principal and most productive of them [coffee plantations] belong to the French proprietors, who raise great quantities of coffee, which they dispose of to English merchants." Though ceded to the British in 1763, Dominica was recaptured by the French in 1778 and held until 1782. Britain reclaimed Dominica in 1782 and it was officially returned to Britain by the Treaty of Versailles in 1783. See Thomas Atwood, *The History of the Island of Dominica: Containing a Description of its Situation, Extent, Climate, Mountains, Rivers, and Natural Productions* (London: Printed for J. Johnson, 1791), 81.

45. For a detailed account of St. Eustatius's role in supplying military equipage, see O'Shaughnessy, *Empire Divided*, 213–237. For naval orders, see NA/PRO CO 101/21, "Macartney

to Germaine" (October 22, 1777), and Naval History Division, *Naval Documents of the American Revolution*, 7 vols. (Washington, D.C.: Department of the Navy, 1964): 1:949, 3:254, 4:604.

46. Rhoda Dorsey, "The Conduct of Business in Baltimore, 1783–1785: As Seen in the 'Letterbook of Johnson, Johonnot & Co.,'" *Maryland Historical Magazine* 5:3 (1960): 230–242.

47. "Henry Johnson to Hewes and Anthony, April 24, 1784," Johnson, Johonnot & Co. Letterbook, 1783–1785 (Maryland Historical Society).

48. Johnson and Johonnot's commission rates remained fairly standard over these years, 5 percent for receiving and 2.5 percent for discharging cargoes; Dorsey, "Conduct of Business in Baltimore," 233. For a list of goods vended in Baltimore, see *Maryland Journal*, December 23, 1783.

49. "Henry Johnson to James Demie, November 8, 1783," Johnson, Johonnot & Co. Letterbook.

50. French ports made up 38 of 199 Caribbean ports that sent ships to North America in 1781, and only 11 of 163 ships arriving in 1782. Records of the Office of the Comptroller General, Port of Philadelphia Records, Registers of Duties Paid on Imported Goods (1781–1788), 6 vols. (Pennsylvania State Archive).

51. For information about Henry Johnson's prerevolutionary trade, see Anne Rowe Cunningham, ed., *Letters and Diary of John Rowe, Boston Merchant, 1759–1762 and 1764–1779* (Boston: W. B. Clarke and Co., 1903), 312. See also Richard S. Chew, "Unforeseen Troubles: Baltimore's Atlantic Trade and the Commercial Frustrations of the Confederation Period," *Maryland Historical Magazine* 98 (Winter 2003): 410–441. Chew argues that while Franco-American commerce thrived in the Caribbean, trade to continental Europe failed to materialize, and that French metropolitan merchants saw little use in perpetuating a free trade system that allowed North American goods to enter French markets and North American ships to profit from carrying French colonial produce abroad, resulting in the closure of some French West Indian ports—including some of those Johnson frequented.

52. "Henry Johnson to James Demie, November 8, 1783," "Henry Johnson to Marie & Company, November 8, 1783," and "Johnson, Johonnot & Co. to Francis Johonnot, February 21, 1784," Johnson, Johonnot & Co. Letterbook.

53. "Henry Johnson to Francis Johnson, March 6, 1784," Johnson, Johonnot & Co. Letterbook.

54. *Pennsylvania Gazette*, January 7, 1784, and April 19, 1786.

55. Herbert C. Bell and David W. Parker et al., eds., *Guide to British West Indian Archive Materials in London and in the Islands for the History of the United States* (Washington, D.C.: Carnegie Institute of Washington, 1926), 33 and 265.

56. NA/PRO CO 28/110, "Letters received from Various Government Offices," 345–346.

57. Thomas Jefferson to John Adams, August 10, 1785, in *The Adams-Jefferson Letters: The Complete Correspondence Between Thomas Jefferson and Abigail and John Adams*, ed. Lester Cappon (Chapel Hill: University of North Carolina Press, 1959), 1:52.

58. NA/PRO CO 318/1, "Colonial Office and Predecessors, West Indies Original Correspondence: Freeport Laws," 69. For a good overview of the British free port operation, see Frances Armytage, *The Free Port System in the British West Indies, A Study in Commercial Policy, 1766–1822* (London: Longmans, Green & Co., 1953).

59. Figures derived from Danby Pickering, *Great Britain: The statutes at large . . . [from 1225 to 1867]*, 46 vols. (Cambridge: Printed by Benthem for C. Bathhurst, London, 1762–1869). See also Watt, *West Indies*, 278.

60. Parliament voted in February 1783 to "permit the produce of such British islands as have been captured by the enemy during the present war to import in neutral bottoms . . . for a limited time." *Journals*, 8: February 12, 1783; see also NA/PRO CO 318/1, "Colonial Office and Predecessors: West Indies Original Correspondence, A Statement, shewing the names, and

positions of the several West India Free Ports, the Free Port Articles of Trade, and the Policy," 80–81. In the listing, Caicos came under the heading of "the Bahamas" because in 1766, after being controlled by the Spanish, French, and British, Turks and Caicos became, for a time, part of the Bahamas colony and was placed under the Bahamian government.

61. Other cities, including Exuma in the Bahamas and Saint George and Pembroke in Bermuda, petitioned to trade coffee; Parliament's Council on Foreign Trade even seconded their proposals so long as prices remained relatively stable. There is no evidence, however, that either the cities' petitions or the Privy Council's suggestions were carried out. NA/PRO CO 318/1, 81, and NA/PRO PC 1/63/24, Records of the Privy Council, "Representation of the Lords of the Committee of Council for Trade and Foreign Plantations with the Draught of an Order in Council declaring His Majesty's Approbation of certain Ports in the Bahama and Bermuda Islands therein named, to be ports for the importation of sugar & coffee the produce of any foreign country or plantation pursuant to an act passed in this session of Parliament entitled 'An Act for Regulating the Allowances of the Drawback and Payment of the Bounty on the Exportation of Sugar and for Permitting the Importation of Sugar and Coffee into the Bahama and Bermuda Islands in Foreign Ships'" (June 13, 1793).

62. Language of maritime subterfuge appears in the records more than once. The quotation above appears in Case No. 33, Taylor v. Sloop *Polly*, Court of Admiralty for the Port of Philadelphia, October 20, 1787. David Library of the American Revolution, Film 5, Reel 4; Revolutionary War Prize Cases: Records of the Court of Appeals, in Cases of Capture, 1776–1787 (American Philosophical Society).

63. For a breakdown of coffee imports into all states, see *American State Papers: Commerce and Navigation*, 1:64, 68, 73, 74, 76, 81, 83, 88, 89, 92, 97, 99, 101, 634, 676, 682, 706, 712, 757.

64. Geggus, "Sugar and Coffee Cultivation," 73–74; Dubois, *Haiti: The Aftershocks*, 19.

65. Bryan Edwards, *An Historical Survey of the French Colony in the Island of Santo Domingo* (London: Printed for John Stockdale, 1797), 17; Francis Alexander Stanislaus, *A Voyage to Santo Domingo in the Years 1788, 1789, and 1780* (London: T. Cadell Jr. and W. Davies, 1797), 170.

66. Alexandre Paul Marie de Laujon, *Precis Historique De La Derniere Expedition De Saint-Domingue* (Paris: Chez Delafolie, 1805), 6–7. See also Philippe Girard, "What's in a Name: Slave Trading During the French and Haitian Revolutions," *William and Mary Quarterly* 76:4 (October 2019): 763–796.

67. The number of coffee farmers grew with each passing year; while only 21 new sugar plantations were recorded in 1789, over 300 new coffee farms went into operation the same year. Laborie, *Coffee Planter*, 249; Stanislaus, *Voyage to Santo Domingo*, 145; Bryan Edwards, *A History of the Island of Santo Domingo* (Edinburgh: J. Pillans & Sons, 1802), 19.

68. Dubois, *Haiti: The Aftershocks*, 19; Trouillot, "Motion in the System," 331, 336–337.

69. Laurent Dubois, *Avengers of the New World: The Story of the Haitian Revolution* (Cambridge, MA: Harvard University Press, 2004), 62–66.

70. Stanislaus, *Voyage to Santo Domingo*, 68.

71. Trouillot, "Motion in the System," 349–364.

72. Jeremy D. Popkin, "The French Revolution's Royal Governor: General Blanchelande and Saint Domingue, 1790–92," *William and Mary Quarterly* 3rd ser. 71:2 (April 2014): 208.

73. Carolyn Fick, *The Making of Haiti: The Saint Domingue Revolution from Below* (Knoxville: University of Tennessee Press, 1990), 97–105.

74. Donald R. Hickey, "America's Response to the Slave Revolt in Haiti: 1791–1806," *Journal of the Early Republic* 2:4 (1982): 362–364. The amount of $726,000 in loans was drawn against America's existing Revolutionary War debt to France. For an analysis of John Adams's negotiations with Toussaint Louverture, and the intriguing, if unfulfilled, possibility of alliance between Saint Domingue and the United States, see Ronald Johnson, *Diplomacy in Black and White: John*

246 Notes to Pages 153–157

Adams, Toussaint Louverture, and Their Atlantic World Alliance (Athens: University of Georgia Press, 2014).

75. James Alexander Dun, "'What Avenues of Commerce, Will You, Americans, Not Explore!': Commercial Philadelphia's Vantage onto the Early Haitian Revolution," *William and Mary Quarterly* 3rd ser., 62:3 (July 2005): 480.

76. Ibid., 480–482.

77. Little is known about Wachsmuth other than that he originated from Hamburg. John C. Wills, "The Politics of Taste in the New Republic: The Decorative Elaboration of the Philadelphia Household, 1780–1820" (PhD diss., University of Michigan, 1994), 102–105.

78. For examples, see Bill of Lading Commerce, December 1, 1791, Box 2, Folder 1, Miscellaneous 1789–1782; Bill of Lading for the *Amiable Creole*, November 5, 1796, Box 2, Folder 3, Miscellaneous 1796–1800; and Bill of Lading for the *American Hero*, March 23, 1793, Box 2, Folder 23, Bills, Receipts, and Invoices, 1793, all from Dutilh & Wachsmuth Papers (Historical Society of Pennsylvania). See also Bill of Lading for the *Antelope*, June 6, 1796, author's private collection.

79. For goods imported from other states, see entries in Box 1, Folder 3, Bills and Invoices, 1791–1794; Box 2, Folder 18, Receipts 1790–1792; Box 2, Folder 20, Bills, Receipts, and Invoices, 1791; and Box 2, Folder 22, Bills, Receipts, and Invoices, 1792, all in the Dutilh & Wachsmuth Papers. Representative examples of store advertisements include *Pennsylvania Packet and Daily Advertiser*, June 12, 1790, and *Dunlap's American Daily Advertiser*, March 2, 1791 (rice); *Federal Gazette, and Philadelphia Daily Advertiser*, November 28, 1793 (flour); *Pennsylvania Packet and Daily Advertiser*, January 26, 1790 (animal skins).

80. Dun, "What Avenues of Commerce," 479. Dun traces the movement of several Dutilh & Wachsmuth vessels through the "Inward and Outward and Coastwise Manifests, 1789–1918" [entry Io59B], Boxes 2–12, Record Group 36 (National Archives and Records Administration).

81. The business partnership of Dutilh and Soullier was announced in the Saint Domingue newspaper *Moniteur General de la Partie Francaise de Saint-Domingue* on February 4, 1793. See also Michelle Mormul, "Revolutions, Merchants, and Goods in the Atlantic World and the Partnership of Dutilh and Wachsmuth," paper delivered at the Pennsylvania Historical Association, February 2003, 2–5, 9; "Articles de Société entre Jacques Dutilh et Étienne Dutilh, 1 January 1790," Dutilh & Wachsmuth Papers 1772–1846 (Hagley Museum and Library); Ernest F. Schell, "Stephen Dutilh and the Challenge of Neutrality: The French Trade of A Philadelphia Merchant, 1793–1807," paper delivered at the Conference on Franco-American Commercial Relations, 1765–1815 (Eleutherian Mills Historical Society, 1977), 54.

82. *Dunlap's American Daily Advertiser*, May 29, 1792.

83. *Claypoole's Daily Advertiser*, August 25, 1792 (*Mary Sophie*), and November 12, 1792 (*Jason*); *Moniteur General de la Partie Francaise de Saint-Domingue*, March 1, 1793 (*American Hero*); *Dunlap's Daily Advertiser*, May 10, 1793 (*Theodosia*); *Federal Gazette*, October 7, 1793 (*Lydia*); *Federal Gazette*, November 4, 1793 (*Isabella*). The French notices for the *Lydia* began appearing in the *Federal Gazette* on October 9, 1793.

84. *Dunlap's American Daily Advertiser*, July 24, 1792.

85. *Moniteur General*, March 8, 1793.

86. *Federal Gazette*, January 7, 1792, and *Gazette of the United States*, January 11, 1792.

87. Dun, "What Avenues of Commerce," 493, 502.

88. Coffee and sugar were the two goods that captains would readily accept in barter exchange. See Jeremy Popkin, *You Are All Free: The Haitian Revolution and the Abolition of Slavery* (Cambridge: Cambridge University Press, 2010), 57, 168–9, 267, 319.

89. Dun, "What Avenues of Commerce," 496.

90. Charges for weighing, March to July 1791, Box 1, Folder 3, Bills and Invoices, 1791–1794; Account of Freight to Joseph Walker, November 1791, Box 2, Folder 20, Bills, Receipts, and Invoices, 1791; Account of Portage Fees, July 1793, Box 1, Folder 11, Bills & Receipts, 1793–1808; and

Insurance Account in Wharton & Lewis's Office, September-December 1792, Box 1, Folders 1 and 2, Account Statements, 1762–1799, all in Dutilh & Wachsmuth Papers (Historical Society of Pennsylvania); Schell, "Stephen Dutilh and the Challenge of Neutrality," 8–9.

91. NA/PRO CO 102/16, "Lord Grenville to Lieutenant-General Mathew" (December 2, 1789).

92. David Geggus, "The British Government and the Saint Domingue Slave Revolt, 1791–1793," *English Historical Review* 96 (1981): 290–291.

93. Michael Duffy, "The French Revolution and British Attitudes to the French West Indian Colonies," in *A Turbulent Time: The French Revolution and the Greater Caribbean*, ed. David Barry Gaspar and David Patrick Geggus (Bloomington: Indiana University Press, 2003), 80–85.

94. David Patrick Geggus, "Yellow Fever in the 1790s: The British Army in Occupied Saint Domingue," *Medical History* 23 (1979): 38–58.

95. Douglas Bradburn, *The Citizenship Reunion: Politics and the Creation of the American Union, 1774–1804* (Charlottesville: University of Virginia Press, 2009), 107–111.

96. Dun, "What Avenues of Commerce," 478. For more about the critical role Edmond Genêt played in relations between France, Saint Domingue, and the U.S., see Popkin, *You Are All Free*, especially 289–326.

97. Dutilh & Wachsmuth Papers, Box 2, Folder 2, Miscellaneous 1793, Notary Public Statement, July 7, 1793.

98. Schell, "Stephen Dutilh and the Challenge of Neutrality," 58 note 71.

99. "Invoice of Sundries shipped by E. Dutilh and Wachsmuth on board the ship *Hannibal*, August 1, 1794," Dutilh & Wachsmuth Papers, Box 1, Folder 3, Bills and Invoices, 1791–1794 (Historical Society of Pennsylvania). In addition to the *Active, Theodosia*, and *Hannibal*, Dutilh & Wachsmuth's London lawyer, Honorius Combauld, reviewed cases for the capture of the *Eliza, Mary, Kitty, Lydia*, and *Fair Lady*, all seized during the French wars. Legal brief on the seizure of the *Theodosia*, 1794, Dutilh & Wachsmuth Miscellaneous no. 184 (Historical Society of Pennsylvania); correspondence on the *Hannibal*, Claude Unger Collection, Box 9, Dutilh & Wachsmuth Business and Correspondence, 1780–1800 (Historical Society of Pennsylvania).

100. *Pennsylvania Gazette*, April 1, 1795.

101. Examples of goods exported from Europe to the Caribbean, as well as from the Caribbean to Philadelphia, appear in "Foreign invoice book E. Dutilh and Wachsmuth, 1796–1797," and "Foreign sales book E. Dutilh and Wachsmuth, 1796–1797" (Hagley Museum and Library). See also "Coffee and sugar shipped via Bill of Lading, November 5, 1796," Box 2, Folder 3, Miscellaneous 1796–1800, Dutilh & Wachsmuth Papers (Historical Society of Pennsylvania).

102. Neither trader, however, had a terribly long career. Francois died in 1799 following a long illness, while Jean died at sea in November 1804 en route to Guadeloupe. Invoices dated December 15, 1801, and July 1, 1803, Dutilh & Wachsmuth Papers, Folder 1, Box 10, 1801–1810 Ships, Claude Unger Collection (Historical Society of Pennsylvania). A bill for Francois Dutilh's funeral expenses totaling $86.00 is in the Thomas E. Richardson Collection (South Caroliniana Library, University of South Carolina).

103. "Bill of Lading for the sloop *Antelope*, Wm. Dalzell, Master, June 6, 1796," private collection of the author; "Memorandum of Insurance for the ship Catherine from St. Thomas to Port au Prince and Philadelphia, May 1797," Box 2, Folder 3, Miscellaneous 1796–1800, Dutilh & Wachsmuth Papers (Historical Society of Pennsylvania). See also Schell, "Stephen Dutilh and the Challenge of Neutrality," 7, appendix I.

104. The end of the partnership was advertised in local papers; see *Aurora General Advertiser*, July 1, 1797, and *Claypoole's American Daily Advertiser*, July 10, 1797. The partners had also begun including news in business correspondence as early as November of that year; see "Dutilh & Wachsmuth to Messrs. Bouillon, Haller & Co., Marseilles, Notice of the sale of the rotten ship Deux Jacques, November 30, 1797," Dutilh & Wachsmuth Papers, Box 2, Folder 3, Miscellaneous 1796–1800 (Historical Society of Pennsylvania).

105. See "J. Wagner, Department of State, to Messrs. Dutilh and Wachsmuth. Concerns possible claim against the British for a captured ship, May 11, 1797," in Papers Relating to the British Seizure of American Ships, 1793–1801, Box 1, FF 4, MS 82–04 (Wichita State University Special Collections); "The Memorial of Stephen Dutilh, A Citizen of the United States and Merchant of Philadelphia," Dutilh & Wachsmuth Papers, Box 1, Folder 13, *Fair American* Vessel Papers (Historical Society of Pennsylvania).

For record of salvage sale, see "Statement of Sale, Gustavus Hughbothum, August 11, 1801," Dutilh & Wachsmuth Papers, Box 1, Folder 13, *Fair American* Vessel Papers (Historical Society of Pennsylvania). Notification of the award of damages included 121,543 pounds of coffee worth £3,038.11.6, cash worth £199.18.2, trinkets worth £234.14.10, and commission of charge worth £223.0.1. The total in Bermuda currency was £3,461.9.9 or £2,307.13.2 in sterling currency. See "Extract from the Registry of his Majesty's High Court of Appeals for Prizes, June 18, 1798," Dutilh & Wachmuth Papers, Box 2, Folder 4, Miscellaneous 1796–1800 (Historical Society of Pennsylvania).

106. Dubois, *Avengers of the New World*, 249.

107. Hickey, "America's Response," 365–367.

108. Cited in Richard S. Chew, "Certain Victims of an International Contagion: The Panic of 1797 and the Hard Times of the Late 1790s in Baltimore," *Journal of the Early Republic* 25:4 (Winter 2005): 593–595.

109. "Edward Hall to Captain John Johnson, June 30, 1799," and "Edward Hall to David Stewart & Sons, July 26, 1799," in Edward Hall Papers (Maryland Historical Society).

110. Horace Lane included his account of the *Sampson* in his autobiography *The Wandering Boy, Careless Sailor, and Result of Inconsideration* (Published for the author by L.A. Pratt, 1839). See also Myra C. Glenn, "Troubled Manhood in the Early Republic: The Life and Autobiography of Sailor Horace Lane," *Journal of the Early Republic* 26:1 (Spring 2006): 74–76.

111. "Memorandum of Agreement between John G. Wachsmuth and the U.S. Treasury, April 5, 1797," Dutilh & Wachsmuth Papers, Box 3, Folder 3, Miscellaneous 1796–1800 (Historical Society of Pennsylvania).

112. "Account Sales of 690 Bales Java Coffee, recd. by Sundry Vessels from Hon. Combauld & Co., London, August 20, 1796," Box 2, Folder 17, Bills, Receipts, and Invoices, 1790; "Account of Freight and Charges on Thirty One Bags of Coffee per the American Ship *Hannibal*, April 21, 1796," Box 3, Folder 4, Bills, Receipts, Invoices, and Misc., 1796; and "Bill of John Graff to Stephen Dutilh for Weighing Fees," Box 3, Folder 15, Bills, Receipts and Invoices, 1802, all in Dutilh & Wachsmuth Papers (Historical Society of Pennsylvania). Voyages predominantly carried sugar and coffee, and ship names and destinations included *Sloop Cicero*, Havana; *Schooner Nancy*, Puerto Rico; *Schooner Favorite*, Guadeloupe; *Brig. Two Sisters*, Cap François; *Schooner Sally*, Havana; *Ship Little Martha*, Havana; *Brig. Jane*, Havana; *Schooner Almira*, Port Republic; *Brig. Jane and Eliza*, Havana; *Brig. Ruth and Mary*, Havana; and *Brig. Eliza and Sarah*, Havana.

113. The *Eliza* was loaded with 554 barrels of superfine flour, 200 half barrels of superfine flour, 200 barrels of pork, 50 barrels of beef, 20 barrels of potatoes, 1,000 staves, and 300 heading.

114. "Deposition of Adam Drewis, master of the schooner *Eliza*," Dutilh & Wachsmuth Papers, Box 1, Folder 18, Palmer & Higgins v. Dutilh (litigation), Depositions, 1804 (Historical Society of Pennsylvania).

115. Ibid.

116. "Deposition of Thomas Norton," Dutilh & Wachsmuth Papers, Box 1, Folder 18, Palmer & Higgins v. Dutilh (litigation), Depositions, 1804 (Historical Society of Pennsylvania).

117. Ibid. Subsequent questions by the court led Norton to note that the door through which he had spied into Dutilh's storehouse had "since been repaired."

118. *Reports of Cases Argued and Adjudged in the Supreme Court of the United States, Vol. 4: In the Years 1807 and 1808*, 2nd ed. (New York: C. Wiley, 1812), 298. Palmer & Higgins v. Dutilh

was used as a precedent in the case of Rose v. Himley, in which a French privateer had been captured; ibid., 240–291.

119. "Letter from President Jefferson to the House and Senate, Dec. 3, 1805," *American State Papers: Foreign Relations*, 1:66.

120. *Pennsylvania Gazette*, May 21, 1794.

121. See especially Jefferson's *Report on the Privileges and Restrictions on the Commerce of the United States in Foreign Countries*, begun in February 1791, in which he argued that U.S. foreign and economic policies should be synonymous, in Ford, *Works of Thomas Jefferson*, 6:470–484.

122. Ibid., 6:479.

Chapter 6

1. No. 353, "Application of the 'Coffee Land Association' for a Grant of 24,000 Acres in Florida, at the Minimum Price," *American State Papers: Documents Legislative and Executive of the Congress of the United States in Relation to Public Lands, March 4-1789 to June 15, 1834* (Washington, DC: Printed by Duff Green, 1834), 457–466.

2. McDonald, *Economy and Material Culture of Slaves*, 3–4.

3. "Application of the 'Coffee Land Association,'" 459.

4. Francis Beatty Thurber, *Coffee: From Plantation to Cup: A Brief History of Coffee Production and Consumption* (New York: American Grocer Publishing Association, 1881), 204–209; John Crawford, "History of Coffee," *Journal of the Statistical Society of London* 15:1 (April 1852): 55–56.

5. "Application of the 'Coffee Land Association,'" 459.

6. "The Freeholder," *Connecticut Courant*, September 21, 1789.

7. Humphrey Marshall, *Arbustrum Americanum: The American Grove, or, An Alphabetical Catalogue of Forest Trees and Shrubs, Natives of the American United States [. . .]* (Philadelphia: Joseph Crukshank, 1785), preface.

8. Lucius F. Ellsworth, "The Philadelphia Society for the Promotion of Agriculture and Agricultural Reform, 1785–1793," *Agricultural History* 42:3 (July 1968): 189; "Pennsylvania Horticultural Society" in *The Register of Pennsylvania*, vol. IV, ed. Samuel Hazard (Philadelphia: William F. Geddes, 1829), 46.

9. "To George Washington from Lafayette, 17 December 1784," *Founders Online*, National Archives, https://founders.archives.gov/documents/Washington/04-02-02-0155. [Original source: *The Papers of George Washington*, Confederation Series, vol. 2, *18 July 1784–18 May 1785*, ed. W. W. Abbot (Charlottesville: University Press of Virginia, 1992), 194.]

Washington's Kentucky coffee seeds came courtesy of Thomas Marshall: "To George Washington from Thomas Marshall, 27 October 1787," *Founders Online*, National Archives, https://founders.archives.gov/documents/Washington/04-05-02-0362. [Original source: *The Papers of George Washington*, Confederation Series, vol. 5, *1 February 1787–31 December 1787*, ed. W. W. Abbot (Charlottesville: University Press of Virginia, 1997), 389–390.]

10. "To James Madison from Thomas Jefferson, 2 June 1793," *Founders Online*, National Archives, https://founders.archives.gov/documents/Madison/01-15-02-0026. [Original source: *The Papers of James Madison*, vol. 15, *24 March 1793–20 April 1795*, ed. Thomas A. Mason, Robert A. Rutland, and Jeanne K. Sisson (Charlottesville: University Press of Virginia, 1985), 24–25.] Barton's specimen of Kentucky coffee, or *Gymnocladus dioica*, is now in the museum collections of the American Philosophical Society (call number 01086551).

11. "Domestic Coffee," *Poulson's Daily Advertiser*, April 7, 1815; William Woys Weaver, *35 Receipts from "the Larder Invaded"* (Philadelphia: Library Company of Philadelphia, 1986), 30–31.

12. Lydia Maria Child, *The American Frugal Housewife: Dedicated to Those Who are Not Afraid of Economy*, 12th ed. (Boston: Carter, Hendee & Co., 1833), 82.

13. Amelia Simmons, *American Cookery [. . .] adapted to this country, and all grades of life.* (Hartford: Printed by Hudson and Goodwin for the author, 1796). See also Mary Tolford Wilson, "Amelia Simmons Fills a Need: American Cookery, 1796," *William and Mary Quarterly* 3rd ser., 14:1 (January 1957): 16–30.

14. Simmons, *American Cookery,* 38; Susannah Carter, *The Frugal Housewife: Or, Complete Woman Cook [. . .]* (Originally printed London, 1772; reprinted Philadelphia: Mathew Carey, 1802).

15. Richard Briggs, *The New Art of Cookery, According to the Present Practice: Being a Complete Guide to all Housekeepers, on a Plan Entirely New* (Philadelphia: Printed for W. Spotswood, R. Campbell, 1792), 326.

16. *The Universal receipt book, or, Complete family directory; being a repository of useful knowledge in the several branches of domestic economy; containing scarce, curious, and valuable receipts, and choice secrets. By a society of gentlemen in New-York* (New York: I. Riley, Van Winkle & Wiley, 1814). This volume is in the Library Company of Philadelphia and is inscribed "Mrs. Thomas Chadwick from her mother." Additional recipes using coffee cups and teacups, as well as teaspoons, tablespoons, and wine glasses, as measuring implements appear in several manuscript cookbooks at Wyck House in Germantown, Pennsylvania, including Jane Bowne Haines, Receipt Book (undated, early nineteenth century, accession # 1993.6.1); Hannah Bowne Haines, Receipt Book, 1811–1813 (accession #92.1668); and Hannah Haines Bacon, Receipt Book, 1822–1908 (accession #1994.4).

17. Maria Eliza Ketelby Rundell, *A New System of Domestic Cookery, formed upon Principles of Economy, and Adapted to the use of Private Families* (Boston: Published by Andrews & Cummings and L. Blake, 1807), iii.

18. *The New Family Receipt-Book: containing eight hundred truly valuable receipts in various branches of domestic economy, selected from the works of British and foreign writers, of unquestionable experience and authority, and from the attested communications of scientific friends* (Philadelphia: Collins & Croft, 1818; New Haven, CT: Howe & Spalding and Samuel Wadsworth, 1819), 172.

19. Rundell, *New System of Domestic Cookery,* 259. Isinglass is a semitransparent, very pure gelatin prepared from the air bladders of fish (such as sturgeons) and used as a clarifying agent, as well as a congealer in jellies and glue, prior to the development of bone-based gelatins. See Alan Davidson, "Isinglass," *Oxford Companion to Food* (Oxford: Oxford University Press, 1999), 407.

20. *New Family Receipt-Book,* 169–173.

21. Ibid., 170.

22. Robert Roberts, *The House Servant's Directory, or A monitor for private families: comprising hints on the arrangement and performance of servants' work* (Boston: Munroe and Francis, 1827), 48.

23. Ibid., 102.

24. Charles Francis Adams, entry for September 5, 1828, in *Founding Families: Digital Editions of the Papers of the Winthrops and the Adamses,* ed. C. James Taylor (Boston: Massachusetts Historical Society, 2007), http://www.masshist.org/ff/.

25. Rundell, *New System of Domestic Cookery,* 259–260.

26. Catherine Esther Beecher, *Miss Beecher's Domestic Receipt Book: Designed as a Supplement to her Treatise on Domestic Economy* (New York: Harper & Brothers, 1846), 18, 23–24, 187–189, 221.

27. Ibid., 187.

28. *New Norwood gipsy; or, Complete art of fortune telling: by cards, moles, the wheel of fortune, lines in the hands, features of the face, colour of the hair, and by the grounds of tea or coffee-cups, together with the evil and perilous days throughout the year [. . .]* (New York: W. Borradaile, 1823). Ignatius Lewis, *The O.B., or West Indian astrologer's whole secret art and system of prediction, by planetary influence, laid open [. . .]* (London: Printed & sold by J. & H. W. Bailey, 1823).

29. Lewis, *The O.B.*, 12.

30. Letter from Abigail Adams to John Adams, May 31, 1789 [electronic edition], *Adams Family Papers*.

31. Society for the Prevention of Pauperism, *Plain Directions on Domestic Economy: Showing Particularly what are the Cheapest, and most Nourishing Articles of Food and Drink, and the Best Modes of Preparation* (New York: Samuel Wood & Sons, 1821), 9. Seth Rockman also notes that coffee had become part of working-class life in Baltimore by the 1820s, although he frames this as a part of a nutritionally deficient diet: "The urban poor received the vast majority of their sustenance from carbohydrates and stimulants, chiefly bread, tea, coffee, and sugar as well as alcohol." See Seth Rockman, *Scraping By: Wage Labor, Slavery, and Survival in Early Baltimore* (Baltimore: Johns Hopkins University Press, 2009), 179.

32. James Tilton, "Variety and Observations," *American Journal*, October 16, 1819.

33. "Rye Coffee," *National Recorder*, July 3, 1819, 5.

34. Ibid., 6.

35. Peter Stephen Chazotte, *Historical Sketches of the Revolutions, and Foreign and Civil Wars in the Island of St. Domingo with a Narrative of the Entire Massacre of the White Population of the Island* (New York: Wm. Applegate, 1840), 16.

36. Peter Stephen Chazotte, *Facts and Observations on the Culture of Vines, Olives, Capers, Almonds &c. in the Southern States, and of Coffee, Cocoa, and Cochineal in East Florida* (Philadelphia: J. Maxwell, 1821), 13.

37. Chazotte, *Historical Sketches*, 27–36. Chazotte appears as a French language instructor in both John Adams Paxton's *The Philadelphia Directory and Register for 1818* (Philadelphia: E & R Parker, 1818) and Edward Whitely's *The Philadelphia Directory and Register* (Philadelphia: M. Carey & Davis, 1820). See also Peter Stephen Chazotte, *A New System of Banking, Developed and Exemplified in a New Scheme to Establish a Merchants Bank of General Deposits* (Philadelphia: Peter Stephen Chazotte, 1815) and *An Essay on the Best Method of Teaching Foreign Languages as Applied With Extraordinary Success to the French Language* (Philadelphia: E. Earle, 1817).

38. "East Florida Coffee Land Association: Preliminary Articles" (Printed by P.M. Lafourcade, June 7, 1821), in the collection of the Marmaduke Burrough Papers, 1814–1832 (Historical Society of Pennsylvania).

39. "Letter from Stephen Chazotte to Marmaduke Burrough, Sept. 11, 1821," Marmaduke Burrough Papers. For more regarding Burrough's animal import business, see "Letter from Jonathan W. Rolan to Marmaduke Burrough, Jan. 18, 1830" and "Letter from Marmaduke Burrough to James Amory, Dec. 30, 1830," as well as a contract detailing division of profits or losses—in the event an animal died—in the same collection. While Key Largo coffee never came to fruition, Burrough continued searching for a reliable American coffee supplier, a topic that reentered his correspondence when he applied for and received a diplomatic post to Vera Cruz in 1834. "John Pemberton to Andrew Jackson, March 4, 1834," Pemberton Papers ALS 1800–1910 (Historical Society of Pennsylvania).

40. "Peter Stephen Chazotte to James Madison, January 15, 1821," and "James Madison to Peter Stephen Chazotte, Jan. 30, 1821," James Madison Papers, General Correspondence, Series 1: Microfilm Reel 19 (Library of Congress); "Peter Stephen Chazotte to Thomas Jefferson, January 15, 1821," with Thomas Jefferson's return note dated January 29, 1821, *Thomas Jefferson Papers* Series 1, General Correspondence, 1651–1827 (Library of Congress).

41. Cited in George E. Buker, "The Americanization of St. Augustine, 1821–1865," in *The Oldest City: St. Augustine, Saga of Survival*, ed. Jean Parker Waterbury (St. Augustine, FL: St. Augustine Historical Society, 1983), 151.

42. Chazotte, *Facts and Observations*, 20–21.

43. "Application of the 'Coffee Land Association,'" 460.

44. *Annals of the Congress of the United States,* 16th Cong, 2nd sess., 901; "Report of the Committee on the Public Lands on the Petition of Peter S. Chazotte and others, on behalf of the American Coffee Land Association," House Report no. 7, 17th Cong., 1st sess., 31; and *Annals of the Congress of the United States,* 16th Cong., 2nd. sess., 1270–1271.

45. "Report of the Committee on the Public Lands," 1, 31–32.

46. A listing of the association's subscribers can be found in ibid., 32–35.

47. Ibid., 35.

48. *Florida Gazette,* July 28, 1821.

49. "Pierre Chazotte to John R. Bell, August 18, 1821," Letters Received by the Secretary of War, Registered Series, 1801–1860, Record Group 107, Microcopy M-221, Roll 92 (National Archives, Washington, DC).

50. "Report of the Committee on the Public Lands," 4.

51. *Reif's Philadelphia Gazette and Daily Advertiser,* December 24, 1821.

52. "Report of the Committee on the Public Lands," 3–5.

53. Kathleen E. A. Monteith, *Plantation Coffee in Jamaica, 1790–1848* (Kingston, Jamaica: University of the West Indies Press, 2019), 13.

54. "Application of the 'Coffee Land Association,'" 457 and "James Madison to Peter Stephen Chazotte, Jan. 30, 1821," James Madison Papers, General Correspondence, Series 1: Microfilm Reel 19 (Library of Congress).

55. U.S. Patent Office, *The Story of the U.S. Patent System, 1790–1840* (Washington, DC: U.S. Patent Office, 1940), 1–2.

56. Ukers, *All About Coffee,* 621.

57. U.S. Patent Office, *A List of Patents Granted by the United States from April 10, 1790 to December 31, 1836* (Washington, DC: Commissioner of the Patents, 1872), 16; "To Thomas Jefferson from Thomas Bruff, 16 December 1801," *Founders Online,* National Archives, http://founders .archives.gov/documents/Jefferson/01-36-02-0076 (last update: 2014-10-23). Source: Barbara Oberg, ed., *The Papers of Thomas Jefferson, Volume 36: 1 December 1801 to 3 March 1802* (Princeton, NJ: Princeton University Press, 2009), 123–125. Bruff and Jefferson maintained an ongoing correspondence for over a decade—primarily about the nature of Bruff's inventions, five of which were ultimately patented.

58. Margaret Baynard Smith, for example, noted "we had tea, coffee, excellent muffins, hot wheat and corn bread, cold ham and butter" during her stay at Jefferson's home, while Secretary of the Treasury Albert Gallatin's 19-year-old niece Frances Few observed that, following dinner at the White House, "the ladies left the table and were soon followed by the gentlemen," whereupon "tea & coffee were then handed us" before the company took their leave. See Gaillard S. Hunt, ed., *The First Forty Years of Washington Society: Portrayed by the Family Letters of Mrs. Samuel Harrison Smith (Margaret Baynard) from the Collection of Her Grandson, J. Henley Smith* (New York: Scribner, 1906), 69; Noble E. Cunningham Jr., ed., "The Diary of Frances Few, 1808–1809," *Journal of Southern History* 29:3 (August 1963): 350.

59. For figures before 1836, see *List of Patents Granted by the United States,* 190, 193, 214, 242, 283, 291, 295, 377, 386, 559, 563, 626, 627, 647, 777. For figures from 1837 to 1850, see *Index of Patents Issued by the United States Patent Office from 1790 to 1873* (Washington, DC: Commissioner of the Patents, 1874), 345–349. Another 229 patents were filed between 1865 and 1880 for not only coffee mills, roasters, and pots, but also cleaners, polishers, hullers, percolators, boilers, and strainers.

60. Newspaper advertisements were collected from several papers and excerpted and republished in an extended notice that appeared in *Harper's Weekly,* August 15, 1858. The poem "The 'Old Dominion'" appeared on the facing page.

61. Stuart McCook, "Environmental History of Coffee in Latin America," *Oxford Research Encyclopedia: Latin American History* (July 27, 2017), https://oxfordre.com/latinamericanhistory

/view/10.1093/acrefore/9780199366439.001.0001/acrefore-9780199366439-e-440?rskey
=UQMFC3&result=2).

62. "Commercial Statistics: Statistical View of the Coffee Trade," *Merchants' Magazine and Commercial Review,* September 1, 1845, 276–277. Ada Ferrar, *Cuba: An American History* (New York: Scribner, 2021), 86.

63. Christopher David Absell, "The Rise of Coffee in the Brazilian South-East: Tariffs and Foreign Market Potential, 1827–40," *Economic History Review* 73:4 (2020): 965–968. Absell calculates the relative value of sugar and cotton as 35 and 24 percent of Brazil's total export value by the 1810s.

64. Ibid., 967–968. A metric ton is roughly equivalent to 2,204 pounds of coffee. While not identical, Absell's figures track relatively closely with those offered by James Birckhead, owner of one of the leading U.S. coffee exporters operating in Rio de Janeiro, who tabulated exports in pounds. See James Birckhead, *Pro-forma Sales and Invoices of Imports and Exports at Rio de Janeiro* (Salem, MA: Printed by W. Ives & Co., 1838), 38.

65. Robert Walsh, *Notices of Brazil in 1828 and 1829,* 2 vols. (London: Frederick Westley and A.H. Davis, 1830), 2: 535–536; "Notes from Brazil—The Coffee Trade," *New York Times,* August 1, 1859; Absell, "Rise of Coffee," 970.

66. Robert Hewitt, Jr., *Coffee: Its History, Cultivation, and Uses* (New York: D. Appleton and Company, 1872), 63.

67. Absell, "Rise of Coffee," 969–970, and William Aldrus Alcott, *Tea and Coffee: Their Physical, Intellectual, and Moral Effects on the Human System,* 5th ed. (New York: Fowlers and Wells, 1836), 64. For a more complete analysis of the scope and value of imports as well as exports between the U.S. and Brazil, see Christopher David Absell and Antonio Tena-Junguito, "The Reconstruction of Brazil's Foreign Trade Series, 1821–1913," *Revista de Historia Economica* 36:1 (2017): 87–115. The number of American ships docking in Rio de Janeiro comes from Maxwell Wright & Co., *Commercial Formalities of Rio de Janeiro* (Baltimore: Sherwood & Co., originally printed 1828, reprinted 1841), 4.

68. "Virtue of Coffee," *North American Archives of Medical and Surgical Science* (Baltimore: Carey and Hart, 1835), 353; "Commercial Statistics," 279.

69. "Commercial Statistics," 276–277.

70. Samuel Hazard, ed., *Hazard's United States Commercial and Statistical Register* (Philadelphia: William F. Geddes, 1840), 90.

71. Absell, "Rise of Coffee," 970.

72. Alexander Hamilton, *Report on Manufactures, Communication to the House of Representatives, December 5, 1791* (Philadelphia: Childs and Swaine, 1791), 3.

73. No. 457, "Receipts from Customs, Sales of Land, and from Internal Duties and Direct Tax, with the Expenses of Collection," *American State Papers: Finance,* Senate, 14th Cong., 1st sess., vol. 3, 35–38; No. 693, "Duties and Drawbacks Communicated to the House of Representatives February 4, 1824," *American States Papers: Finance,* House of Representatives, 18th Cong., 1st Sess., vol. 4, 460–462; No. 719, "Duties on Importations for these Three Quarters to June 30, 1824," *American State Papers: Finance,* 18th Cong., 2nd sess., vol. 5, 174–178.

74. W. J. Rorabaugh, *The Alcoholic Republic* (Oxford: Oxford University Press, 1981), 100, and Sarah Meecham, *Every Home a Distillery: Alcohol, Gender, and Technology in the Colonial Chesapeake* (Baltimore: Johns Hopkins University Press, 2009), 120. See also "Commercial Statistics," 274.

75. "Commercial Statistics," 275.

76. John Reed, *Speech of Mr. Reed of Massachusetts on the Tariff Bill* (Washington, DC: Gales and Seaton, 1833), 14–15.

77. Augustine Sedgewick, "What Is Imperial About Coffee: Rethinking 'Informal Empire,'" in *Making the Empire Work: Labor and United States Imperialism,* ed. Daniel E. Bender and Jana K. Lipman (New York: New York University Press, 2015), 313.

78. Absell, "Rise of Coffee," 972.

79. J. D. B. De Bow, ed., *De Bow's Review of the Southern and Western States. Devoted to Commerce, Agriculture, Manufactures*, XIII: 2 (New Orleans: Office, Merchant Exchange, 1852), 185; "Commercial Statistics," 273.

80. "Coffee and the Coffee Trade," *The Merchants' Magazine and Commercial Review* vol. 42 (1859): 165.

81. The quotation comes from *O Jornal do commercio*, June 11, 1831, translated by Christian Robles-Baez in "Setting Up the Coffee Empire: The United States and Brazil in the Early Nineteenth Century," presented at the Stanford University U.S. History Workshop (March 2, 2022), 11.

82. The national averages for the value of tea in those same years would have been 20 cents (1821), 36 cents (1833), and 25 cents (1844) per pound.

83. Birckhead, *Pro-forma Sales and Invoices*, 29–30.

84. Absell, "Rise of Coffee," 984.

85. "Commercial Statistics," 273–277. See also "Our Commerce with Brazil," which sought to summarize import and export trends from 1820 to 1850, *New York Times*, October 6, 1851. For a breakdown of coffee shipments from Rio to specific U.S. ports, see Wright & Co., *Commercial Formalities*, 85–86.

86. V. D. Wickizer, *Coffee, Teas, and Cocoa* (Stanford, CA: Stanford University Press, 1951), 36.

87. "Commercial Statistics," 274–275.

88. Luiz Aranha Corrêa do Lago, *Da Escravidão ao Trabalho Livre. Brasil, 1550–1900* (São Paulo: Companhia das Letras, 2014), 459–460.

89. Herbert S. Klein and Francisco Vidal Luna, *Slavery and the Economy of São Paulo, 1750–1850* (Stanford, CA: Stanford University Press, 2003), 58. Escalating reliance on slavery was also reflected in the relative cost of purchase. David Eltis calculates that the price of a male slave more than doubled in southeast Brazil between 1821 and 1841. See David Eltis, *Economic Growth and the Ending of the Transatlantic Slave Trade* (Oxford: Oxford University Press, 1987), 263.

90. Eltis, *Ending of the Transatlantic Slave Trade*, 243–244; Absell, "Rise of Coffee," 980.

91. "John C. Calhoun, Secretary of State of the United States, to Henry A. Wise, United States Minister to Brazil, May 25, 1844," reprinted in *Diplomatic Correspondence of the United States, InterAmerican Affairs, Volume 2, 1831–1860,* ed. William Manning (Washington, DC: Carnegie Endowment for International Peace, 1932), 127–128.

92. Leonardo Marques, "The Contraband Slave Trade to Brazil and the Dynamics of U.S. Participation, 1831–1856," *Journal of Latin American Studies* 47 (2015): 669–675.

93. Matthew Karp, *This Vast Southern Empire: Slaveholders at the Helm of American Foreign Policy* (Cambridge, MA: Harvard University Press, 2016), 147–148.

94. Robert W. Thurston, Jonathan Morris, and Shawn Steiman, eds., *Coffee: A Comprehensive Guide to the Bean, the Beverage, and the Industry* (Lanham, MD: Rowman & Littlefield, 2013), 242.

95. The Early American Newspapers Database includes more than 265,000 advertisements for coffee between 1800 and 1815 alone, in 18 states and territories and 56 cities. The following examples all come from December 1815: *American Beacon and Commercial Diary*, December 30, 1815 (Norfolk, VA); *Augusta Herald*, December 28, 1815 (Augusta, GA); *City Gazette and Daily Advertiser*, December 30, 1815 (Charleston, SC); *Kline's Weekly Carlisle Gazette*, December 6, 1815 (Carlisle, PA).

96. Arbuckle included a lengthy description of the glazing process in his patent application letter: "I take any good article of green coffee, and roast it by any of the known means. I then cool it as quickly as possible. I then prepare a mixture of the following ingredients, in about the following proportions: One ounce of Irish moss; half an ounce of isinglass; half an ounce of gelatine; one ounce of white sugar; and twenty-four eggs. I boil the Irish moss in a quart of water, and then strain it. I then boil the isinglass and gelatine in a pint of water. I then mix the sugar and eggs well together, and when the mixture of Irish moss, isinglass, gelatine, and water

has become cold, I mix the whole of the ingredients into one homogeneous compound. I then pour the whole over about one hundred pounds of the roasted coffee, and stir and so manipulate the coffee that each grain will be entirely coated, after the coffee is coated, and the coating has become dry and hard, which is accomplished by forcing currents of air through it while stirring it, for the purpose of coating it with the glutinous or gelatinous matter described." John Arbuckle Jr., Allegheny, PA, Letters Patent No. 73,486, dated January 21, 1868, U.S. Trade and Patent Office, available in digital form through Google Patents.

97. Ukers, *All About Coffee*, 522. Arbuckles Bros. aggressively entered the sugar industry in 1896, but between 1871 and 1895 it focused almost exclusively on coffee production and sales.

98. Francis Fugate, *Arbuckles: The Coffee That Won the West* (El Paso, TX: Texas Western Press, 1994), 25–50.

99. Wendy A. Woloson, *Crap: A History of Cheap Stuff in America* (Chicago: University of Chicago Press, 2020), 115–116.

100. Margaret E. Hale, "The Nineteenth-Century American Trade Card," *Business History Review* 74:4 (Winter 2000): 683–688.

101. This quotation appeared on the reverse of each trade card in the original and reprinted series. Eighteen Arbuckles Bros. trading cards are in the Joseph Downs Collection of Manuscripts and Printed Ephemera, Winterthur Museum and Library.

102. Examples are all drawn from the Joseph Downs Collection. There were a few outliers. The card for Utah, for example, did not include an economic activity, instead featuring the Mormon Temple, while those for Arizona and Texas depicted a Native American settlement and cowboys roping steers respectively, but did not actually list the state's principal source of income.

103. Pendergrast, *Uncommon Grounds*, 51.

104. Schnull-Krag Coffee Co., "It Is the Best Coffee Ever Sold," cited in *Coffee: A Comprehensive Guide to the Bean, the Beverage, and the Industry*, ed. Robert. W. Thurston, Jonathan Morris, and Shawn Steiman (Lanham, MD: Rowman & Littlefield, 2013), 240; "Washington's Coffee," *New York Tribune*, June 22, 1919; Thomas Wood & Co., "Uncle Sam's High Grade Roast Coffee" (1880), Serial and Government Publications Division (Library of Congress).

Epilogue

1. These exhibits, along with thousands of others that were collected and preserved, became the foundation for the new Arts and Industry Building of the Smithsonian Institution. Robert W. Rydell, *All the World's a Fair: Visions of Empire at American International Expositions, 1876–1916* (Chicago: University of Chicago Press, 1984), 9–38.

2. Thompson Westcott, *Centennial Portfolio: A Souvenir of the International Exhibition at Philadelphia* (Philadelphia: Thomas Hunter, 1876), vi, 3.

3. Morris also tried to encourage coffee cultivation in California. The undertaking was as ill-fated an endeavor as Chazotte's Floridian scheme, but the fact that it garnered interest and sponsorship indicates the enduring hope of some North Americans to find a domestic source of coffee production. See Luther N. Steward Jr., "California Coffee: A Promising Failure," *Southern California Quarterly* 46:3 (September 1964): 259–264.

4. *Frank Leslie's Historical Register of the United States Centennial Exposition, 1876* (New York: Frank Leslie's Publishing House, 1877), 67, 119, 213, 312.

5. "The Turkish Display," *Philadelphia Inquirer,* August 28, 1876.

6. "The Tunisians," *Philadelphia Inquirer,* June 9, 1876.

7. "The Guests' Coffee-Room," *Frank Leslie's Historical Register,* 96.

8. "World Coffee Consumption, 2017–2021," International Coffee Organization, https://www.ico.org/prices/new-consumption-table.pdf.

9. Ibid. Robusta, as its name implies, thrives well in conditions in which other varietals do not, such as lower elevations, and it forms the bulk of instant, mixed, and ground coffees sold worldwide.

10. John M. Talbot, *Grounds for Agreement: The Political Economy of the Coffee Commodity Chain* (Washington, DC: Rowman & Littlefield, 2004), 50; El-Mamoun Amrouk, "Depressed International Coffee Prices: Insights into the Nature of the Price Decline," *Food Outlook: Biannual Report on Global Food Markets* (Food and Agricultural Organization of the United Nations, November 2018), 25.

11. Craig J. Thompson and Zeynep Arsel, "The Starbucks' Brandscape and Consumers' (Anti-corporate) Experiences of Glocalization," *Journal of Consumer Research* 13:3 (December 2004): 634.

12. "Top 10 Popular Coffee Brands Worldwide," *Business Standard* (October 16, 2020).

13. "Coffee Report and Outlook, CRO," International Coffee Organization (April 2023), 28–29.

14. "The Future of Coffee: Investing in Youth for a Resilient and Sustainable Coffee Sector," International Coffee Organization (2021), 1–78.

15. "The American Grocer" cited in *The Spice Mill* (July 1891): 172.

INDEX

Ducheman, Daniel, 103
Dunkin' company, 208
Dunmore, Lord, 114
Dutch colonies, 14, 134; coffee economy in, 35; smuggling and, 64–66; U.S. trade treaty with Holland and, 138. *See also* Suriname; West Indies, Dutch
Dutens, Charles, 93
Dutilh, Étienne (Stephen), 153–55, 160, 163–64, 246n77
Dutilh, François, 160, 247n102
Dutilh, Jean, 154, 160, 247n102
Dutilh, Soullier & Company, 154
Dutilh & Wachsmuth, 153–67, 246n81, 247n104
Duval, Kathleen, 241n16

East Florida Coffee Land Association, 170, 181, 183. *See also* American Coffee Land Association
East India Company, Dutch (VOC), 24, 25, 28, 218n31
East India Company, English (EIC), 21, 25–27, 218n29, 218n31
East India Company, French (FEIC), 27
East Indies, *149*, 190, *197*, 198
Easton, Phill, 9
Edwards, Bryan, 22, 217n14
Eliot, Robert, 70
Eliza (schooner), 164, 165, 248n113
Elliot, Charles, 47
Ellis, John, 24
Ellis, Robert, 231n46
English Coffee House (York County, Virginia), 97
Essequibo, colony of, 28
Ethiopia, 28, 206
Étienne Dutilh & Company, 153
etiquette, 16, 79, 101–2; effacement of coffee's overseas origins and, 173–74; manuals of, 171
European Union, coffee consumption in, 208
Evans, Jonathan, 92
Ewbank, Thomas, 45–46
export firms, as intermediaries, 194

Facts and Observations (Chazotte), 182
Fair American (ship), 160–61
fair trade programs, 209
farmers, small-scale, 6, 206

Federal Gazette (Philadelphia newspaper), 156, 157
Few, Frances, 252n58
Fichter, James, 211n9
Finland, coffee consumption in, 208
Fithian, Philip, 84, 104, 115, 237n26
Fitzmaurice, Ulysses, 47
Fleming, Sol, 9
Flood, Nicolas, 97–98
Folgers company, 208
Footman, Richard, 63–64, 72–73
Forbes, William, 70
Forbes, Valentino & Company, 197
fortune-telling, coffee grounds and, 177–78, *179*
Franklin, Benjamin, 73, 101, 137, 139
Franklin, Deborah, 101
Frazer, Andrew, 117
free people of color (*gens de couleur*), 50–51, 132, 150–52, 223nn114–116
free ports, 10, 139, 142, 147
French colonies, 14, 41, 134; coffee economy in, 35; coffee taken by British privateers, 61–62; smuggling and, 64–65, 68, 142. *See also* West Indies, French
French Revolution, 151–52, 157

Gallatin, Albert, 252n58
Galvez, Count, 140
Games, Alison, 14, 215n34
Garrigues, Samuel, 69
Genêt, Edmond, 159
Georgia, 125, 180, 198
Gloria Jean's company, 208
Golding, John, 223n114
gossip, in coffeehouses, 11, 16
Grant, Daniel, 103
Grant, William, 95
Gray, Isaac, 74, 228n55
"green" coffee, 225n17
Grenada, 35, 61, 128, 147, 220n54. *See also* Ceded Islands
Grenville, Lord William, 157
Griffin, Samuel, 108
grocers, 74, 76, 77
ground coffee, 56, 60, 104, 175, 201, 256n9
Guadeloupe, 41, 65–66, 128, 132, 163; boom in coffee exports, 142; Dominican coffee shipped to United States through, 132, 133; free ports in, 147; slavery reinstated in, 162

Guatemala, 207
Gunston Hall, probate inventory of, 86, 230n30

Habacker, George, 75, 129, 239n74
Haiti, 14, 181, 190, 206, 221n90. *See also* Saint Domingue
Haitian Revolution, 17, 150, 182
Hale, Jonathan and Hezekiah, 122
Hall, Edward, 161–62
Hamilton, Alexander, 13, 192
Hannibal (ship), 159
Harbeson, Benjamin, 95
Harper, David, 88
Harper, Thomas, 116
Harrower, John, 83–84
Hart, Samuel, 60
Hawaii, 3, 200, 201, 203
Hawker, Captain James, 234n1
Hay, Anthony, 97
Hayes, Judah, 92
Hermitage Plantation (Jamaica), 40
Herskovits, Melville J., 240n9
Higman, B. W., 33, 35, 43, 135, 220n59, 240n12
Hill, Jacob, 47
Hispaniola, 65, 139, 149
Historical Account of Coffee, An (Ellis, 1774), 24, *30*
hoarding, 2, 4, 17, 119; Boston merchants accused of, 121; price-fixing as measure against, 120
Holland, 15, 17, 66, 131, 140, 155, 243n39; dominance in Indian Ocean, 28; trade relations with United States in postrevolutionary era, 131, 138, 139, 159, 190; U.S. trade treaty with, 138, 242n27. *See also* Dutch colonies; West Indies, Dutch
Hollingsworth, Levi, 70–71, 74, 78, 129, 228n45, 239n73
Hollingsworth, Samuel, 129, 239n73
Hollingsworth, Thomas, 129, 239n73
Holstein (Danish schooner), 162
Hook, John, 85–87
House Servant's Directory, The (Roberts, 1827), 175–76
Howell, Samuel, 62, 226n27
Hughes, John, 105, 234n1
Hunter (sloop), 184, 185
Hutchinson, Thomas, 111
Hutton, John, 90
Hyatt, John, 108
Hyne, Elizabeth, 51

Iceland, coffee consumption in, 208
"in cherries" method, 40–41
indigenous peoples, 5
Indonesia, 206
industrialization, in North America, 13
Industry (schooner), 152
inns, 106, 108
International Coffee Organization, 208
Isherwood, Baron, 214n31
Islam, coffee drinking and, 23

J. & E. Dutilh, 154
Jaison, Sorhaindo, 47
Jamaica, 19–20, 33, 66, 133, 207; British customs officials in, 68; coffee and white settlement in, 135; coffee export dominated by port of Kingston, 52; coffee exported to Philadelphia, 58; competition with Lesser Antillean British colonies, 142; "deficiency law" in, 21, 49, 50, 217n14; enslaved African labor in, 22–23, 41, 45, 46; free ports in, 147; small coffee planters, 46–47, 222n91; sugar cultivation in, 150; U.S. ships excluded from, 141; white population of, 21
Jamaican Accounts Produce inventories, 48, 49, 222n101
James, Abel, 61
James, Sarah, 108, 235n8
James & Drinker, 61
James's Coffee House, 108
Jason (brigantine), 155
Java, 15, 27, 59, *197*, 201, 219n40
Jay, John, 137
Jefferson, Thomas, 13, 146–47, 167, 242nn23–24; Bruff's coffee mill and, 186–87, 252n57; Florida coffee-growing scheme and, 183; Kentucky coffee tree and, 173; vision of free trade, 168
Jeremy, King of the Mosquito Indians, 20
"jobbing" system, 40
Johnson, Henry, 143–46, 244n51
Johnson, Johonnot & Company, 143–44, 244n48
Jourdain, John, 25
Judas Pilé & E. Dutilh, 154

Kempe, Jack Tabor, 92
Kentucky coffee tree, 173, 249nn9–10
Kenya, 207

ACKNOWLEDGMENTS

Many individuals and institutions contributed to this book. If you have read this far, you know that I like to count, so acknowledging all of them is a welcome if daunting task. First and foremost, I thank David Hancock, who read more chapter drafts than I (or he) probably care to remember, and with a keen eye and high standards that pushed me harder than I would have pushed myself. He never lost faith in me or the value of the argument I sought to make, and I am lucky to count him among my friends and as my advisor. John Carson, Sue Juster, and Carol Karlsen, as well as the late Michael MacDonald and the late Julius S. Scott, were also valuable mentors from this project's beginning at the University of Michigan. They brought their own disciplinary perspectives and challenged me to think more broadly and critically.

As the manuscript evolved, I benefited from the insights of many colleagues. For their time and their input, my thanks go out to Linzy Brekke-Aloise, Christopher Bilodeau, Cary Carson and the late Barbara Carson, Audre Diptee, Alec Dun, Kathleen Duval, Paul Erickson, Ellen Hartigan-O'Connor, the late Ron Hoffman, Brooke Hunter, Ben Irvin, Dan Livesay, Brian Luskey, Robin McNichol, Jane Merritt, Stephen Mihm, Amanda Moniz, Carla Pestana, Rosalind Remer, Daniel Richter, Liam Riordan, Jess Roney, Colleen Vasconcellos, Stevie Wolf, and Michael Zuckerman. I am grateful as well to my former colleagues at Stockton University for their support, and to my new colleagues at the American Philosophical Society, whose generous encouragement helped this project cross the finish line.

I learned from many conversations with scholars of the history of slavery, the Atlantic world, and business history, including Richard Blackett, the late Trevor Burnard, Marissa Fuentes, Virginia Gould, Gad Heuman, Barry Higman, Howard Johnson, Philip Morgan, and Andrew O'Shaughnessy. And a few people deserve special mention for supporting me—personally and professionally—including Zara Anishanslin, the late Richard and Mary

Dunn, Alison Games, Richard Kagan and Shreve Simpson, Patrick and Laura Spero, Jim Williams, Wendy Woloson, and David Miller.

Several institutions contributed to the research found within these pages, and I am indebted to the librarians, archivists, and reference staffs of the American Philosophical Society, the Historical Society of Pennsylvania, the Library Company of Philadelphia, the Pennsylvania State Archives, and the Philadelphia City Archives. In Jamaica, I worked with the Jamaica Archives and Record Department, the National Library of Jamaica, and the West Indies and Special Collections at Mona Library, University of the West Indies. This project expanded well beyond the original confines of my dissertation, and later research required work at the National Archives in London, the Bodleian Library in Oxford, and the National Archives of the Commonwealth of Dominica (with special thanks to its archivist Renita Charles).

I am also grateful to several organizations whose support made my far-flung research agenda possible. The McNeil Center for Early American Studies at the University of Pennsylvania, under the directorship of Dan Richter, funded my first year in Philadelphia, and he and my fellow cohort helped make the city my home. The Fulbright Foundation underwrote my research in Jamaica, and I particularly thank Kathleen Monteith and Swithin Wilmot for their hospitality and support. The Program in Early American Economy and Society at the Library Company of Philadelphia funded a year of archival work and provided additional important mentors in John C. Van Horne, Jim Green, and Cathy Matson. Postdoctoral fellowships at the Harvard Business School and the Winterthur Museum and Library introduced me to the rich worlds of business history and material culture respectively.

I have presented portions of this project at several academic venues and benefited from the thoughtful comments and questions of their attendees. I am thus indebted to the Omohundro Institute for Early American History and Culture, the Society for Historians of the Early American Republic, and the Business History Conference. I especially want to thank the generous community of the Association of Caribbean Historians for its ongoing support. I presented my research at the ACH more than at any other conference and appreciate the important insights afforded there by historians based in the West Indies and beyond.

Aspects of this research appeared in the *Pennsylvania Magazine of History and Biography, Commonplace: The Journal of Early American Life*, and the *William and Mary Quarterly*, as well as in two chapters coauthored with

Steven Topik and published in Trentmann and Nützenadel (eds.), *Food and Globalisation: Consumption, Markets and Politics in the Modern World* (Oxford: Berg Publishers, 2008) and in Thurston, Morris, and Steiman (eds.), *Coffee: A Comprehensive Guide to the Bean, the Beverage, and the Industry* (Lanham, MD: Rowman & Littlefield, 2013).

At the University of Pennsylvania Press, Dan Richter and Bob Lockhart, as well as the press's generous readers, offered valuable suggestions for how to refine my arguments. Their recommendations shaped three versions of this manuscript over the years, and I hope the result justifies their investment.

I want to acknowledge my parents (William Craig and the late Susan Bierly Craig), as well as my sister and her family (Melissa, Tim, Meg, Ethan, and Loie Kemmer) who inspired and supported me in so many ways—and continue to do so. Finally, I owe a debt to my husband, Roderick—my inspiration, my nudge, my cheerleader, my editor—that I look forward to taking a lifetime to repay.

*9 7 8 1 5 1 2 8 2 7 5 5 2 *